The Crimean War

Alan Palmer

Dorset Press
New York

Originally published as *The Banner of Battle*

Copyright © 1987 by Alan Palmer
All rights reserved.

This edition published by Dorset Press,
a division of Marboro Books Corp.,
by arrangement with Campbell Thomson & McLaughlin Ltd.

1992 Dorset Press

ISBN 0-88029-776-X

Printed and bound in the United States of America

M 9 8 7 6 5 4 3 2 1

Contents

Maps

. . . . So I wake to the higher aims
Of a land that has lost for a little her lust of gold,
And love of a peace that was full of wrongs and shames,
Horrible, hateful, monstrous, not to be told;
And hail once more to the banner of battle unroll'd!
Tho' many a light shall darken, and many shall weep
For those that are crush'd in the clashing of jarring claims,
Yet God's just wrath shall be wreak'd on a giant liar;
And many a darkness into the light shall leap,
And shine in the sudden making of splendid names,
And noble thought be freer under the sun,
And the heart of a people beat with one desire:
For the peace, that I deem'd no peace, is over and done,
And now by the side of the Black and the Baltic deep,
And deathful-grinning mouths of the fortress, flames
The blood-red blossom of war with a heart of fire.

from Alfred Tennyson, *Maud*
(written in the spring of 1854)

Preface

During the hundred years which separate the first abdication of Napoleon from the battles of Tannenberg and the Marne there were, in all, fifteen wars between the nations of Europe, great or small. Their average length, however, was no more than eight months. One contest alone dragged on so long that its memorials record dates from four calendar years: this was the struggle which began when Turkish troops attacked Russian outposts in October 1853 and continued until the Great Powers signed a general treaty of peace at Paris in March 1856, twenty-nine months later. As most of the fighting took place on the western littoral of a peninsula remote from familiar battle zones, the conflict soon became known in Britain, France and Italy as the Crimean War. So, too, it has been remembered in the Soviet Union since Stalin's day. But in Tsarist times Russian writers, conscious always of the risk of invasion from the West, called it the 'Eastern War' (*Vostochnaia Voina*). This difference of nomenclature throws an interesting light on strategic geographical thought both in St Petersburg and in the Western European capitals at the height of the nineteenth century.

The Crimean War has a general interest today on three counts. It remains the only occasion in history when British troops fought against the regular organized army of a Russian state, Tsarist or Soviet. It was the first war fully covered by the Press, with graphic reporting and illustrated magazines bringing to the public at home a horrible awareness of active campaigning and exposing the ineptitudes of an archaic military system. And, while participants on both sides were drawing on muddled recollections from a Napoleonic past, it became a war that anticipated the future: warships were damaged by a minefield; battle orders settled at great distance before being flashed thousands of miles by electric telegraph; and there were plans for threatening Russia's capital city with chemical warfare, for aerial reconnaissance by balloon, for a submarine, even for a 'locomotive land battery', a proto-tank. Historically, the Crimean War poses questions of wider interest still. Old friendships between veteran diplomats made a conflict seem improbable when, at Christmas in 1852, Lord Aberdeen became prime minister: why, then, did war follow within fifteen months? Once the fighting began it was assumed, both in London and in Paris, that Russia would be threatened on a northern front as well as around the Black Sea: why, then, was the clash of armies contained within so small an arena of battle?

The key to both answers lies in the inner politics and diplomacy of the Great Powers of Europe at mid-century. It might indeed be argued that the Crimean War has its greatest significance as a turning point in international relations. *The Banner of Battle* therefore seeks to place the conflict of 1853–6 in the general context of nineteenth-century history. The war is seen, not simply as a dramatic moment in the Eastern Question, but as a decisive campaign which lowered the stature of both defeated Russia and non-belligerent Austria as Great Powers, thereby changing the European balance between nations in the second half of the century. The title, chosen from some of the best-known stanzas of Tennyson's *Maud*, has a double purpose. It recalls the last occasion upon which British troops marched into battle against a Great Power with colours flying and regimental bands playing; but it also emphasizes the strange mood of imperceptive patriotic pride with which the Poet Laureate, like so many of his countrymen, welcomed the passing of forty years of peace. It is perhaps as an essay in the dangers of a fickle public opinion that this book has its principal contemporary relevance.

My debt to earlier authors will be clear to anyone glancing at the bibliography. I have found some different sources from the ones cited in those two invaluable books, Cecil Woodham-Smith's *The Reason Why* and Christopher Hibbert's *The Destruction of Lord Raglan*, but there must inevitably be some overlapping of material. Among papers deposited in the British Library I found the diary of Sir Hamilton Seymour informative on his 'sick man of Europe' conversations with Tsar Nicholas I, while the journals and letters of Sir Hugh Rose (Lord Strathnairn) threw an interesting light both on British diplomacy in the spring of 1853 and on the Crimean campaign itself, for, after serving in the embassy at Constantinople, General Rose became Britain's commissioner attached to the French army at Varna and in front of Sebastopol. Brief extracts from the letters sent by Colonel Alexander Gordon to his father have been quoted in biographies of Lord Aberdeen by Lucille Iremonger and Meriel Chamberlain but, so far as I am aware, they have not appeared in any narrative of the Crimean War; I have made rather more use of them, for it is clear that they were the most important direct link between the Prime Minister and a serving officer during the critical months of the Crimean campaign. The publication of Mrs Duberly's edited journal before Christmas in 1855 was welcomed as an opportunity for readers to 'canter' through the campaign while the war was still in progress and, more than twenty years ago, Mr E. E. P. Tisdall made use of her letters in his *Mrs Duberly's Campaigns* before they were catalogued by what was then the British Museum Library. I was pleased, however, to find additional material in the letters of both Fanny Duberly and her husband. Professor John Curtiss's *Russia's Crimean War* and Colonel Seaton's *The Crimean War: A Russian Chronicle* have been valuable, not only in themselves, but as guides to printed Russian sources, all of which I was able to locate either in the Bodleian or British Libraries; and I would especially like to acknowledge that Dr Brison Gooch's *The New Bonapartist Generals in the Crimean War* suggested French printed material which I had not hitherto encountered.

The Earl of Clarendon kindly gave me permission to quote from the papers of his ancestor, the fourth Earl. I am grateful to him and, for their help, to the staffs of the British Library, the Public Record Office at Kew, the London Library and the Bodleian. I also acknowledge Griselda Fox Mason for permission to quote from *Sleigh Ride to Russia* (published by Sessions of York in 1985) and John Murray Ltd. for permission to quote from *The Fields of War* by R. Temple Godman which they published in 1977. I would like also to thank Miss Candida Brazil for her patience in preparing the book for publication and in finding the illustrations. My wife, Veronica who once again assisted me at every stage and completed the index; I deeply appreciate her encouragement and consistent support.

Woodstock,   *Alan Palmer*
Oxford

Map 1: Russia's frontiers, 1854

Norwegian Sea

Barents Sea

NORWAY & SWEDEN

White Sea • Archangel

URALS

Pechora

Ob

FINLAND

Gulf of Bothnia

Aaland Is. • Abo Sveaborg
• Kronstadt
Reval • **St. Petersburg**
Gulf of Finland

RUSSIAN

Skaggerak

Kattegat

DENMARK

Baltic Sea

• Riga

EMPIRE

• **Moscow**

Kiel

Berlin

Vistula

• Königsberg

PRUSSIA

• Warsaw

POLAND

• Kiev

Don

Dnieper

Volga

Danube • Olmütz

Vienna

AUSTRIAN
EMPIRE

Dniester

Bug

MOLDAVIA

• Odessa

Adriatic Sea

WALLACHIA

Danube • Bucharest

Sebastopol

Silistria

• Varna

Black Sea

Caspian Sea

ITALY

TURKEY

• Sinope

Kars

Constantinople

• Scutatri

Besika Bay

Erzerum •

Gallipoli

TURKEY

GREECE

Athens •

Aegean Sea

Vourla Bay

Mediterranean Sea

OTTOMAN

EMPIRE

Tigris

Euphrates

Cairo ▪

Nile

Red Sea

0 Miles 50

Dnieper

• Kherson

Kinburn

Sea of Azov

Cape Tarkhankut

CRIMEA

• Kerch

Eupatoria • Bakchisarai

Theodosia

Sebastopol •

• Balaclava

Black Sea

0 Miles 500

CHAPTER ONE

'This Greatest of All Earthly Potentates'

On the last evening of May in 1844 Baron Philip Brunnow, the Tsar's envoy in London, set out by carriage from the Russian Legation at Ashburnham House and travelled down to Woolwich to await the arrival of the packet-boat from the Scheldt. Brunnow, a much respected diplomat in his late forties, was worried on that Friday night. He knew that aboard the steamer *Cyclops* was an important dignitary, who had left St Petersburg eight days before and who was coming to London to talk high politics with the Prime Minister, Sir Robert Peel, and his Foreign Secretary, the Earl of Aberdeen. He could not, however, be sure of the traveller's identity. It was perhaps his old colleague, Count Orlov, whom Brunnow had accompanied to London in 1837 when the Count brought their Emperor's congratulations to Queen Victoria on her accession. But it might even be Tsar Nicholas I himself. Ten years before, Nicholas had arrived in Berlin unexpectedly and unannounced; and Brunnow was taking no chances. His carriages were at Woolwich before dusk on Friday, even though the steamer was not expected to come up-river until after daybreak on Saturday.[1]

There had been casual talk of an imperial visit to London on several occasions over the last five months. Twice in conversation with Brunnow the Prime Minister had indicated that the Tsar would be a welcome guest; and, at a court ball in St Petersburg shortly before Christmas, Nicholas was heard to say that he would like to go to England again, as he had enjoyed the four months which he spent there when he was a twenty-year-old bachelor grand duke. The Prince Regent, who offered Nicholas the choice of a hundred dishes for his nine-course dinner at the Royal Pavilion in that January of 1817, was long since dead; but the British host who had most impressed the young grand duke was still at Apsley House, serving both as Commander-in-Chief of the Army and as a member of Peel's cabinet. Tsar Nicholas, an autocrat who felt diminished in sovereignty when out of uniform, held the Duke of Wellington in great respect. He had welcomed the victor of Waterloo to St Petersburg in 1826 and he would be glad to meet him again. But there was more behind Nicholas's projected visit than an agreeable renewal of old acquaintance. The Tsar believed in the efficacy of personal diplomacy, ruler to ruler. If he came to London, he might charm the young Queen by his social grace and persuade her husband of the need for continuous Anglo-Russian co-operation to ease the tensions of the Eastern Question. To win the backing of so shrewd a judge of Europe's politics as Prince Albert was in itself almost worth the long journey from St Petersburg.

The Queen, however, hoped that she would not have to entertain Tsar Nicholas: early in August she was expecting her fourth child, and Albert had already induced her to invite 'the dear good King of Saxony' for June. Moreover, the court was about to move to Windsor for Ascot races, a week in which the Queen's burden of official duties was habitually lightened. But the uncertainty remained. 'His Majesty travels with such rapidity and maintains so much mystery about his movements that one can never be prepared for him', reported Lord Bloomfield, the British minister in St Petersburg, on 18 May; the Tsar's 'journey really appears no longer feasible', he added. As a precaution, a suite was hustled into readiness for a Russian visitor at Buckingham Palace, but on Wednesday, 29 May, the Queen told her Foreign Secretary she was convinced that Nicholas would not come this summer. Next day two messages from St Petersburg suggested that the Tsar might already be on his way.[2]

Throughout Saturday Baron Brunnow's carriages waited at Woolwich. The summer evening was darkening into a moonlit night before the *Cyclops* was sighted steaming slowly up the Thames, and it was nearly ten o'clock when the passengers disembarked. Among them, according to the ship's papers, was 'Count Orlov'; but when the distinguished Russian traveller appeared on deck, with a light grey travelling cloak protecting his shoulders from the breeze, Brunnow at once recognized the stiff parade-ground silhouette of his imperial master. Only the commandant of the Woolwich dockyard and the superintendent of the Royal Arsenal were present to greet the first ruler of Russia to land in Britain for thirty years.

Nicholas did not reach the Legation until nearly midnight. By then it was too late to travel on to Buckingham Palace, and he spent the rest of the night at Ashburnham House, sleeping on the military camp-bed which he insisted on taking with him on his travels. Next morning, having in the small hours notified Prince Albert of his arrival, Nicholas was conducted in state to the Palace. *The Times* records a surprise encounter in the Mall, as the Tsar's carriage and escort passed the King of Saxony's carriage and escort, travelling in the opposite direction, and 'the two rulers recognized each other'.[3]

The Tsar's arrival in London ran true to form; for his reign was a mock-heroic tragedy sweetened by farce. In part, the characteristic confusion sprang from concern with personal security, a double conviction that his Polish subjects were out to kill him and that any military commander of courage and stature should thwart the knavery of an assassin. But it was caused, too, by a muddled autocratic possessiveness which left Nicholas reluctant to devolve authority. Even the Tsar's most trusted advisers, Nesselrode, his Foreign Minister, and Paskevich, the commander of the army in the field, could never be certain that their imperial master was not improvising policies of his own. In particular, on more than one occasion Nesselrode found the complexities of the Eastern Question intensified, rather than diminished, by Nicholas's initiatives of personal diplomacy.

The 'Eastern Question' was the name given to the problems caused by the weakness of the Ottoman Empire and the rivalry between its potential successors. At its zenith in the early seventeenth century, the Sultan's Empire included not only modern Turkey, but the whole of the Balkan peninsula, the central Hungarian plain, the Ukraine, the shores of the Black Sea (ruled either directly or through subject princes), the Arab lands of the Middle East – called collectively 'the Levant' – and most of the African shore of the Mediterranean. In the eighteenth century Ottoman power receded: Austria freed Hungary from Turkish rule; and the Russians swept southwards around both sides of the Black Sea, reaching the Danube delta in the west and penetrating the mountains of the Caucasus in the east. Although the Levant remained under Turkish administration, successive Sultans had little control over outlying provinces in the Balkans and North Africa. Serbia and Egypt enjoyed effective autonomy; and an embryonic Greek state was recognized by the Sultan in 1829, four years after Nicholas I's accession.

In Britain and France a romantic philhellenism won sympathy for Greek independence among a governing class educated in the classics, but effective support for the Greeks was always curbed by suspicion of Russian territorial ambitions in south-eastern Europe. By the middle of the nineteenth century there were more than thirteen million Orthodox believers (Greek Christians') within the Ottoman Empire, spiritually led by the Patriarch of Constantinople, a dignitary elected by a church synod but ceremonially enthroned by officials of the Sultan's Government. The Patriarch possessed some secular authority throughout the Empire, provided he retained the Sultan's confidence. More significantly, he could count on the backing of the Tsar, whose role as Protector of the Orthodox Church ensured Russia a privileged position at the 'Sublime Porte', as the Sultan's court and administration was called. In order to enforce his protective rights Nicholas I was at war with Turkey in 1828–9, glorying in the victories of an army which penetrated the Balkan mountains and threatened Constantinople itself, the capital of the Sultans for four centuries. Nesselrode, however, consistently maintained that Russia could best maintain influence at the Porte by sympathetic support for the Sultan, not by intimidation. This policy was triumphant in July 1833 when the treaty of Unkiar Skelessi established a Russo-Turkish military alliance and, for the eight years of its duration, ensured Russia political primacy at Constantinople.

When Unkiar Skelessi expired, Nesselrode gave yet another twist to Russian policy. There was already a tradition of Anglo-Russian hostility over the Eastern Question, caused partly by fear that Britain's trade would suffer if 'the Black Sea became a Russian lake' and partly by a conviction that the Tsar's Empire could become an overbearing weight in Europe's affairs. Nevertheless Anglo-French rivalry predated Anglo-Russian, and in 1840 Nesselrode, with Brunnow's active support, completed a minor diplomatic revolution. The Russians worked in partnership with the Whig Foreign Secretary, Lord Palmerston, against French attempts to turn the Levant into a commercial satrapy. This Palmerston–Nesselrode combination produced the Straits Convention of July 1841 which closed the Dardanelles and the Bosphorus to all foreign warships so long as Turkey was at peace. When, two months later, the Tories returned to office, Nesselrode and Brunnow found it even easier to collaborate with Peel and Aberdeen. The two countries worked together over problems in Persia and in 1843 concluded a trade treaty. British radicals, on the other hand, were implacably hostile: in 1831 Nicholas's troops had suppressed the revolutionary movement for an independent Poland and, until 1852, the House of Commons continued to vote Poland's exiles a grant of £10,000 a year. But the noisy Russophobia of the 1830s was muted by now. Nesselrode and the leading executants of his policy were satisfied with the embryonic Anglo-Russian entente.

Only Tsar Nicholas remained uneasy. A private visit by Queen

Victoria to King Louis-Philippe in 1843 alarmed him, for he always attached great importance to dynastic diplomacy and he feared a reconciliation between Britain and France. He resolved to go to England and breath new life into Nesselrode's entente by a vigorous display of his masterful personality. Already he had tried to interest Prussia and Austria in the Eastern Question, for he was concerned over what would happen if the Sultan's weak empire began to fall apart. But Berlin and Vienna had no liking for contingency planning. Nicholas counted on a better response from London.[4]

Despite their lack of warning, the British improvised a state visit. Nicholas accompanied the court to Windsor and dutifully escorted Victoria to Ascot races. On 5 June a military review was held in his honour in Windsor Great Park. 'A great event and a great compliment his visit certainly is,' Victoria wrote to her uncle, King Leopold of the Belgians; 'Really it seems like a dream when I think that we breakfast and walk out with this greatest of all earthly Potentates.' She thought Nicholas 'still very handsome' and 'quite alarmingly civil', but the 'formidable' expression of his eyes disturbed her. She was worried at Windsor that some exiled Polish revolutionary might attempt to shoot him. Behind surface charm, she saw an empty character. 'Politics and military concerns are the only things he takes great interest in', she remarked.[5] But it was to talk 'politics and military concerns' that her guest had made this thirteen-hundred-mile journey to her capital.

Nicholas explained Russian policy to his hostess and her husband and to the leading politicians of both parties. With Peel and Aberdeen he could talk at Windsor, the Prime Minister on one occasion leading him away from an open window when he was expressing himself frankly but indiscreetly. 'I highly prize England; but for what the French say about me, I care not at all – I spit upon it', people remembered his saying.[6] His message was clear and concise: 'Turkey is a dying man', he insisted; but the Sultan's Empire should be kept intact as long as possible, with Russia and Britain encouraging the Powers to enter into discussions if the fall of the Empire seemed imminent. He told the Foreign Secretary that he did not want to see any foreign Power dominant at Constantinople, not even Russia; and he agreed with Lord Aberdeen that it was desirable to keep Egypt from falling under a hostile government which might close 'the commercial road' from Alexandria to Suez and on to India and the Orient. To Nicholas, these words were a reassuring sign of British mistrust of France, for throughout successive crises it had always been the French who had favoured a strong and independent Egypt.

On Sunday evening, 9 June, Prince Albert accompanied Nicholas back to Woolwich, where the steamer *Black Eagle* was ready for the crossing to Rotterdam. A Marine Guard of Honour lined the quayside, which was flagged out of all recognition. The Tsar embraced the Prince warmly and set out for the Continent well satisfied. *The Times* might report that twelve hundred protesters meeting in Holborn had denounced the Queen's guest as the arch-oppressor of Polish liberty, but two nights later he had been warmly received at the opera house when the Queen thrust him forward to take the applause.[7] At Kissingen, where Nesselrode met his imperial master a few days later, Nicholas was still talking of his personal triumph among the English.

To the sceptical Nesselrode, reality fell short of the Tsar's make-believe; and he was right. The British attitude to foreigners, be they Russian, French or Austrian, was fickle; and it would not be difficult for the newspapers to rouse old enmities, now lying dormant. British ministers listened to Nicholas's observations on the Eastern Question with interest, but thought them vague: no estimate of how long he believed Turkey would survive; no discussion on the eventual disposal of the Sultan's territories. Little more than a month after the Tsar's departure from Woowich, Nesselrode himself travelled to England for 'some weeks at Brighton for the benefit of sea bathing'.[8] But the real purpose of his journey was to convert the verbal agreements of Windsor into a written understanding.

The Foreign Secretary looked 'forward with the utmost pleasure to the opportunity' of meeting Nesselrode again.[9] The two men were old friends, who had collaborated closely in the autumn of 1813, when Lord Aberdeen – then not quite thirty – was a diplomat attached to Allied headquarters in Germany and Nesselrode, four years his senior, was minister in attendance on Tsar Alexander I. Together Aberdeen and Nesselrode had witnessed the aftermath of the battle of Leipzig and followed the retreating French army to the Main and beyond, seeing for themselves the burning homes and the stripped bodies of stragglers murdered along the route. From such an experience Aberdeen retained a deep horror of war; and he did not doubt that this sense of revulsion was shared by his Russian colleague.

Nesselrode's visit consummated the Tsar's more flamboyant personal diplomacy. Aberdeen encouraged him to draw up a memorandum which affirmed the desire of both Britain and Russia to preserve the Turkish Empire as long as possible; if Turkey threatened to fall apart, the two governments would collaborate in discussing 'the establishment of a new order of things to replace that which exists today'. The first draft of the memorandum was presented to Peel and Aberdeen by Nesselrode in the third week of September 1844. It was never discussed in cabinet and was kept among Aberdeen's private papers rather than in the Foreign Office archives. Correspondence was exchanged between Aberdeen, Nesselrode and Brunnow over the next four months before the Foreign Secretary felt able to assure the Russians that Peel and himself accepted the memorandum as an accurate summary of their views. He emphasized that the agreement could bind only the present government, but he did not question Nicholas's assumption that the Turkish Empire was close to disintegration.[10]

Thereafter official London forgot the Nesselrode Memorandum for almost a decade. There was nothing to recall Nicholas I's surprise visit, apart from engravings in *The Illustrated London News* and a horse race at Ascot, for which the Tsar offered each year of his life a plate worth £500, with the Imperial Arms upon it.[11]

CHAPTER TWO

From Friendship to War

Four years after Nicholas's visit to London the foundations of the old conservative system imposed on the Continent in 1815 began to crack. Palmerston, who became Foreign Secretary again when Lord John Russell formed a Whig government in July 1846, called the revolutions of 1848 a 'political earthquake rolling Europe from side to side'. Louis-Philippe's monarchy gave way to a republic in Paris; Metternich resigned after nearly forty years as Austria's foreign minister; the Hungarians sought independence from Habsburg rule; and throughout Italy and Germany there were movements for representative government and unified nation states. Russia survived without serious upheaval, but news of revolution in Paris made Nicholas fear that 1792 had come again. At first, his ministers could barely curb the Tsar's impetuosity. Nicholas, however, possessed a maturity of character rare among Russia's imperial sovereigns: occasionally he pursued, somewhat furtively, hidden policies of his own devising; but reasoned argument often cooled a choleric temper and induced second thoughts; and, unlike other members of his family, he did not then indulge in third or fourth thoughts, changing his policy to accommodate the views of whoever had spoken to him last. Hence, in the spring of 1848, an imperial manifesto called for the defence of Holy Russia and the army was put on a war footing, but the Tsar was persuaded not to gratify the Russophobes of western Europe by ordering his Cossacks across Germany to hold the line of the Rhine.

On 3 April, Nicholas sent to Windsor one of the strangest congratulatory letters preserved in royal correspondence: while rejoicing in the birth of the Queen's sixth child (Princess Louise), the Tsar turned a message of greeting into an appeal for joint action against the Revolution. Since the Windsor conversations, he wrote, 'hardly four years are passed, and what remains standing in Europe? Great Britain and Russia! Is it not natural to think that our close union may be called upon to save the world?' But at Windsor such speculation was not 'natural'; Nicholas's appeal evoked no response.[1]

Although Britain made no move, Russia was not able long to remain on the sidelines. Liberal unrest in the nominally Turkish 'Danubian Principalities' of Moldavia and Wallachia led to Russian occupation in the last week of July 1848. None of the Powers protested. As Palmerston told Parliament, the Russians were entitled to be in the Principalities, for the treaty of Kuchuk Kainardji of 1774 accorded them rights to protect the Christian population of Moldavia and Wallachia, and their presence had been tolerated by the Roumanian inhabitants of the Principalities from 1829 to 1834. But Russia's action had greater significance than Palmerston appreciated, for by advancing into the Danubian plains the Tsar's armies were poised like a crescent around eastern Hungary, ready for a show of conservative solidarity should the Habsburgs need aid against their rebellious Magyar subjects. And in the spring of 1849 the young Emperor Francis Joseph did indeed ask for Russian assistance in stamping out the independent Hungary of Lajos Kossuth's creation.[2] There followed a summer campaign of some eight weeks, in which the Hungarians found it impossible to defy the imperial armies of both Russia and Austria. Four thousand Hungarians sought sanctuary across the frontier of the Turkish Empire, and with them were eight hundred Poles, veteran revolutionary enemies of the Tsarist system. When the Tsar put pressure on the Turks to hand over four leading Polish generals, British and French naval squadrons sailed for the Dardanelles to give the Sultan protection against what was seen in London and Paris as Russian intimidation. Nicholas did not persist with his demands.[3]

The Tsar's armed intervention in Hungary and the much-publicized storm in a samovar glass over the Polish generals conjured up the old Russian bogey in Britain. In the mind of every liberal progressive, St Petersburg became the centre of international reaction, and the Tsarist state machine was denounced as a cumbersome despotism which menaced western civilization. Tories and Whig businessmen deplored the incursion of Russian traders in the Far East and along the borders of Central Asia as well as in the eastern Mediterranean. Almost every political group in Britain had a grievance, genuine or feigned, against Russia. At the same time, a restless national pride gripped large sections of the country. In the spring of 1850 Palmerston ordered Admiral Parker's Mediterranean squadron to sail to Phaleron Bay and impose a blockade of the harbours serving Athens in order to enforce the pecuniary claims against the Greek Government of a number of

British subjects, the most famous being the Gibraltar-born money-lender, David Pacifico. This high-handed action, which left Britain diplomatically isolated in Europe, was attacked in the Commons by a formidable array of gifted parliamentarians including Peel, Cobden, Gladstone and Disraeli; but it was defended by the Foreign Secretary in a speech which made Palmerston the darling hero of Britain's patriotic Radicals. At a dinner in his honour in the Reform Club, the members greeted their guest with a vigorous rendering of 'Rule Britannia!'

This blustering national belligerence ran counter to the ideal with which, in 1851, Prince Albert promoted his 'Great Exhibition of the Works of Industry of all Nations'. When, barely ten months after the Pacifico debate, the Queen opened the Great Exhibition she emphasized that it was, above all, a 'peace festival' and she continued to hope throughout the summer that the Exhibition's success would encourage friendly competition between the nations. But Victoria and Albert were out of touch with the public mood, for the thousands who flocked to the Crystal Palace delighted in specifically British achievements and were content to cast curious glances of patronizing approval on what had come from overseas. With some satisfaction they noted, in this first week of May 1851, that only one country had failed to ship its exhibits to London in time for the opening ceremony; as the Queen and her consort, the Prince and Princess of Prussia, a bevy of younger royalty and the indomitable Duke of Wellington inspected the six-hundred-yard glass and iron conservatory there was not a single exhibit from Russia to catch their eye. The Great Exhibition did nothing to allay Russophobia. Within a fortnight of its closure in October, cheering crowds were greeting Kossuth in London and the provinces, thrilled by the masterly rhetoric of his fluent English as he denounced the twin tyrannies of Vienna and St Petersburg. It was Russian intervention which rankled most of all. 'Do not give a charter to the Tsar to dispose of the World', was Kossuth's message to 'the English people' at a monster open-air meeting in Islington's Copenhagen Fields.[4]

The froth and bubble of this newest wave of English hostility did not unduly disturb Nicholas I. He was more concerned with the pretensions of France's Prince President; for Louis Napoleon, nephew of the Emperor whose army had entered Moscow in 1812, had been elected head of the Second French Republic in December 1848. Resurgent Bonapartism threatened to destroy the peace settlement of 1814–15, seeking to draw a new map of Europe based upon respect for the continent's submerged nationalities. Most immediately, Louis

Napoleon challenged Russian primacy in the Levant, for in May 1850 he took up the defence of Roman Catholic rights in the Palestinian Holy Places of the Turkish Empire. Britain and Austria recognized that Louis Napoleon was only reviving claims traditionally exercised by France's Bourbon rulers and asserted by King Louis-Philippe as recently as 1842; and they assumed that his initiative was intended primarily for domestic consumption, a move to ensure clericalist support for his general policies. But Nicholas, for whom even the judiciously circumspect Louis-Philippe had seemed a dangerous interloper, saw in Louis Napoleon's championship of 'the Latins' a direct threat to Russian influence on the Straits. The Prince President was in a hurry to win prestige for the French Republic; and the Tsar could not understand why Britain, the only Great Power other than Russia to remain unscathed by the revolutions of 1848, should not share his apprehensions. It was, he felt, one of the failings of that 'perfidious pig', Lord Palmerston, not to perceive that the nephew was potentially as grave a menace to the peace of Europe as his uncle, the First Consul, fifty years before.[5]

On 2 December 1851 a military *coup d'état* in Paris destroyed the parliamentary trappings of the French Republic and made Louis Napoleon a virtual dictator. But it was with some satisfaction that Tsar Nicholas learnt that, on this occasion, two of his personal enemies had tripped over each other. For Palmerston failed, for once, to cast his spell on the British public; private congratulations to Paris on the Prince President's coup offended his sovereign, his colleagues and his supporters. Palmerston left office, but the Whigs could not survive without him and by the end of February 1852 Britain had a Conservative government again. In April a scare that the French would march into Belgium led to amicable conversations between Brunnow and the new Foreign Secretary, Viscount Malmesbury; perhaps a Russian expeditionary force of 60,000 men might help the British defend the Low Countries once again from a Napoleonic army. But the French threat to Belgium's independence soon receded and nothing more was heard of any Anglo-Russian military alliance. Nevertheless Nicholas was well satisfied. With Palmerston gone, relations with Britain seemed as friendly as in the year of his visit to Windsor.[6]

By contrast, Russo-French relations remained strained. Early in February 1852 the Sultan made concessions to the French over the vexed question of access to the Holy Places; but at the same time he tried to reassure the Orthodox believers that there would be no change in 'the existing state of things'. The dispute was therefore resumed, with the French taking an even stronger line in their negotiations with the Sultan's ministers. At midsummer France's ambassador, the Marquis de Lavalette, returned to Turkey from Paris in great state, sailing through the Dardanelles in the heavily-armed and steam-powered warship *Charlemagne*, a breach of the Straits Convention. The Turks were much impressed: here was a floating fortress able to challenge 'the most rapid currents of the Bosphorus by the sole power of the screw'.[7] Thereafter they assumed that Louis Napoleon's warships could outspeed and outgun any Russian or Turkish vessels. To the Tsar's chagrin, Sultan Abdul Medjid was inclined more and more to listen to the French. In October he appointed a Grand Vizier, Mehemet Ali, who found the bribes offered by the French gratifyingly generous; and on 6 December instructions were sent to Jerusalem requiring 'the Greeks' to surrender certain keys to the Holy Places in Bethlehem to the French-backed 'Latins'.

Nicholas looked upon this decision as a personal affront. Here, he felt, was confirmation of all that he had preached over the years to the other Great Powers: Turkey was feeble and corrupt, incapable of resisting external pressure or internal unheaval. As news reached Vienna and St Petersburg of vicious clan warfare along Turkey's north-west frontier, it seemed self evident to him that the Sultan's emissaries could no longer hold together an empire which stretched from the Balkan ranges to the Caucasus and down to the Persian Gulf and the Red Sea. The alternative was partition.

In retrospect these winter months of 1852–3 stand out as the moment when an Anglo-Russian entente drifted finally beyond reach. But at Epiphany it still seemed attainable to Nicholas, remote in his dark red palace flanking the frozen Neva. The ambassadorial reports from western Europe, delayed as ever by the frost and snow, made interesting reading. Two days before the Sultan settled the Holy Places dispute in France's favour, Louis Napoleon was proclaimed 'Emperor of the French' in Paris. A fortnight later, across the Channel, Lord Derby's Conservative administration was defeated over the budget, and before Christmas the British people had their first avowed coalition government for nearly half a century.

The coalition of Whigs and Peelites was headed by the Earl of Aberdeen and seemed full of ministerial talent. Gladstone early made his mark as Chancellor of the Exchequer, and another Peelite, Sir James

Graham, returned to the Admiralty, where he had been an energetic reformer twenty years before. Lord John Russell was leader of the Commons and became Foreign Secretary, but held that office for only eight weeks before making way for the more orthodox ex-ambassador, the Earl of Clarendon. Palmerston entered the cabinet as Home Secretary. It was thought, wrongly, that this appointment would keep him muzzled over issues of war and peace; his thoughts ran more naturally to war risks on the lower Danube than to the case for and against a sixty-hour week for factory workers under eighteen. Exclusion from the Foreign Office freed the incorrigible old intriguer from all inhibitions of executive responsibility in international affairs; and in the following summer his speeches in and out of Parliament and his influence over the *Morning Post*, the *Globe*, and the *Morning Chronicle* encouraged a Russophobia which would have hindered his conduct of diplomacy had he been Foreign Secretary.

But, for the moment, Palmerston seemed no threat to the Russians. Nicholas was convinced that the new British Government would be alive to the menace from Napoleon III's ambitions and that Aberdeen and Clarendon would welcome any chance to improve Anglo-Russian relations.[8] The Tsar was already resolved on a direct approach to Britain over the Eastern Question. In the week that Aberdeen was busy forming his coalition, Nicholas suggested to Nesselrode that the time had come to draw up partition plans for the Ottoman Empire. But, after a long conversation with the British ambassador, Nesselrode decided that his imperial master's approach to London was misguided: 'plans for an uncertain future' would be 'both dangerous and utterly useless', he told the Tsar and warned him that talk of partition might swing the British into lasting hostility. Nicholas, who respected his minister's long experience of British diplomacy, decided to wait upon events.[9]

Five days later – on Thursday 6 January 1853 – news that Aberdeen was now prime minister reached St Petersburg. The following Sunday was the forty-sixth birthday of the Tsar's widowed sister-in-law, the Grand Duchess Elena Pavlovna; and she celebrated the occasion with a private concert at the Mikhailovsky Palace. Among her guests were the British minister, Sir Hamilton Seymour, and his wife. A few weeks before, Seymour had complained in a letter home that, in fifteen months at St Petersburg, he had talked high politics with the Tsar only once.[10] Now was his opportunity, and he made the most of it.

Seymour's journal (recently acquired by the British Library) gives a more vivid impression of the conversation than the well-known official despatch, with its 'sick man' metaphor. 'The great event of the day was our going to a concert at the Grand Duchess Elena's', Seymour wrote in his diary that evening.

We were made much of – taking tea at the Empress's teatable. I had a long talk with the Emperor, who was very civil. H.M. spoke of the close alliance which ought always to exist between us, saying that if England and He, He and England were on good terms in W. Europe, what anyone else thought mattered little . . . He would send for me soon. As H.M. shook hands by way of parting, I said I should like some assurances as to Turkey to send to England. A curious answer was elicited: the country was falling to pieces – who can say when? *L'homme est très malade: ce serait un grand malheur si un de ces jours le malade nous échappes.*

In his despatch to the Foreign Office, written two days later, Seymour gave a fuller version of this famous exit line: 'We have a sick man on our hands, a man who is seriously ill; it will be . . . a great misfortune if he escapes us one of these days, especially before all the necessary arrangements are made.' After repeating his wish soon to receive Sir Hamilton in audience, Nicholas left for his carriage. As for the Grand Duchess's concert, Seymour's diary notes, 'The music was capital – there at least there was plenty of harmony.'[11]

On 14 January the journal records that 'the Emperor sent for me' and that there followed a '50 minute conversation about Turkey', but there was then a gap in these talks, for the Tsar himself became 'a sick man'. It was, his wife wrote to her sister-in-law in Holland, 'an exhausting . . . salutary crisis'; Nicholas was in a high fever for almost a week, 'sweating violently', and, although he was said to have 'gout in the foot', the symptoms seem similar to the fatal influenza attack which he suffered two years later.[12] Eventually, on 21 January, Nicholas received Seymour, with three further audiences over the following twelve weeks, as well as several meetings of Seymour and Nesselrode.

They were a strange series of conversations, and Seymour's perplexity shows through the cautious gradations of officialese in his despatches to London. The Tsar repeatedly returned to his main theme: 'The Bear [Turkey] is dying; you may give him musk, but even musk will not keep him alive'. Nicholas did not, he insisted, wish to discuss immediate issues or seek any formal agreement: 'A general understanding . . . between gentlemen is sufficient,' he told Seymour in the third week of February.[13] Sometimes Seymour could not remember the precise terms in which the Tsar outlined his views on the future of south-eastern Europe, notably 'the commercial policy' to be followed at the Straits after Turkey had collapsed. But the sweep of Nicholas's vision was startling enough: a hint that Serbia, Bulgaria and the Danubian Principalities should become 'independent' states 'under my protection'; a suggestion that Britain might find compensation in Egypt, while the island of 'Candia' (Crete) 'might suit you and I do not know why it should not become an English possession'; an inference that what St Petersburg decided would be acceptable to Vienna – and all without reference to the parvenu emperor in Paris. Such talk came close to the partition proposals against which his foreign minister had warned Nicholas at the start of the year; and Nesselrode barely concealed his disquiet from Seymour. In April he admitted that he thought there was 'inconvenience in the prolonged discussion of a matter of so much delicacy as that upon which the Emperor has spoken.'[14]

This was a diplomatic understatement. The response in London to Nicholas's initial remarks was cautious, but not hostile. Aberdeen told the Queen that Tsar Nicholas anticipated 'an early dissolution of the Turkish Empire' but was prepared, in such a case, to work in harmony with Great Britain.[15] Yet, as the conversations continued, the mood in London hardened: no one in the cabinet liked the hypothetical discussion of remote problems, least of all the suggestion that anarchy at Constantinople might lead Russia 'temporarily' to occupy the Turkish capital; and the British made it clear that they wanted no territorial aggrandizement at the expense of Turkey.[16] Had the Seymour conversations taken place in a diplomatic void, with no Russian pressure exerted on the Sultan's government and no reports of troops massing north of Turkey's Danubian frontier, Nicholas might, perhaps, have dispelled the suspicion which habitually vitiated every move towards an Anglo-Russian understanding. But the three months of amicable exchanges in St Petersburg coincided with the most overt Russian coercion of Turkey for twenty years. The Tsar who spoke so sincerely to Seymour in February of his need to concert arrangements with Lord Aberdeen had already decided, at the beginning of the month, to send Prince Menshikov on a special mission to Constantinople. The Prince arrived in the Bosphorus in great state three weeks later aboard the *Gromovnik* (Thunderer). The vessel – an armed paddle-steamer, unimpressive compared with France's ninety-gun *Charlemagne* – was, for Menshikov's purpose, aptly named.

Alexander Menshikov, sixty-six in that spring of 1853, was descended from a disgraced favourite of Peter the Great. While so many other counsellors in St Petersburg were as German in ancestry as the dynasty itself, Menshikov prided himself on being a Russian, through and through. He had first fought against the Turks as a cavalry officer in his early twenties and by 1817 had become a full general, basking in Tsar Alexander I's favour until 1821 when he made the mistake of quarrelling with the influential General Arakcheev. Nicholas I welcomed him back to court and in 1827 appointed him Chief of Naval Staff. These new responsibilities did not prevent Menshikov from seeing active service again against Turkey in the following year; but on this occasion he was seriously wounded by Turkish roundshot. He became a member of the Council of State in 1830 and a full admiral in 1833; he was Governor-General of Finland for several uneventful years and thereafter attained some celebrity in St Petersburg society for an ostentatious show of wealth, a mordant wit, and an open mistrust of almost every other public figure whether in the army or navy, the diplomatic service or the civil administration. He was particularly envious of the honey-tongued Count Orlov, whose tactful charm made him Nicholas's ablest negotiator. In 1833 Orlov had achieved remark-able success at Constantinople in persuading Sultan Mahmud II to accept the treaty of Unkiar Skelessi. Twenty years later, to Menshikov's satisfaction, Russia's church leaders persuaded their Tsar to send him rather than the more westernized Orlov on this latest special mission to the Straits. By now Menshikov's health was poor and he no longer thought his long years of service would end with victory in war; but the opportunity of carrying off a diplomatic triumph at Byzantium was attractive. 'I have high hopes that this will provide me with the last official undertaking of my . . . life, which now requires repose,' he wrote to a friend on the eve of his departure for Sebastopol, where he reviewed the Black Sea Fleet before embarking for Con-stantinople. [17]

Nesselrode had wished the Tsar to send Orlov, and his disquiet is clear from the confused instructions which, as Foreign Minister, he gave Menshikov. The Prince was warned that 'the Ottoman Empire would dissolve at the first clash of arms' and that Tsar Nicholas 'did not wish to precipitate this catastrophe'; but he was authorized to use 'threatening or friendly language' to secure a convention recognizing Russia's right to protect Turkey's Orthodox Christians. Sultan Abdul Medjid would be offered a secret defensive alliance so that he might safely rescind every concession to the French. Should Abdul Medjid prove obdurate, Menshikov was to leave for Sebastopol within three days.[18]

Menshikov began sensationally. He summoned the Grand Vizier to come outside the walls and escort him in state through the gates of the city and he refused to negotiate with the Foreign Minister, holding that he had shown 'bad faith and duplicity' in his dealings with Russia. No *elchi* (ambassador) was ever received in such state as the Prince demanded and the Grand Vizier would not sanction so great a variation in protocol. But Menshikov had his way over the Foreign Minister: Rifaat Sadyk, who was allegedly pro-Russian, was given the post. The Sultan was duly assured that Menshikov had not intended to insult his authority and talks began on the old question of Orthodox rights at the Holy Places. Menshikov thereupon dropped his peremptory manner – and with good reason, for although in St Petersburg he was renowned for his excellent memory and attention to detail, someone on his staff had blundered: the Tsar's personal envoy had arrived in Constantinople without the collection of maps essential for any discussion of Turkish affairs. Several weeks went by before Menshikov could be sure that he had the necessary geographical information at his fingertips.[19]

The delay enabled the British and French governments to reshape their policies in the light of Menshikov's mission. Curiously enough, neither country had an ambassador in Constantinople at that time. Lord Stratford de Redcliffe, who had spent nineteen years safeguarding British interests in the Ottoman Empire, left the Bosphorus in June 1852 on leave; and it was assumed that the 'Great Elchi' – as the Turks called Stratford – would not return for a sixth term of residence at Constantinople. In the absence of an ambassador, Great Britain was represented by a chargé d'affaires, Colonel Hugh Rose, who had served as consul-general at Beirut for ten years before becoming secretary of Stratford's embassy in 1851. The fiery French ambassador, the Marquis de Lavalette, was recalled to Paris a few weeks before Menshikov arrived, and France, too, was represented by a chargé d'affaires, Vincente Benedetti, a professional diplomat who was to win his moment of fame seventeen years later in an encounter with the King of Prussia on the promenade at the spa town of Ems.

Both Rose and Benedetti witnessed Menshikov's dramatic entry into Constantinople and were alarmed by such an arrogant display of Russian strength. Rose was an astute soldier who, in later years, distinguished himself as commander-in-chief in India and Ireland, gaining a peerage (Lord Strathnairn) and a field marshal's baton. Persistent reports of Russian troop movements north of the Danube troubled his military mind. Without waiting for his government's approval, he therefore sent an urgent appeal to Admiral Dundas, at Malta, to bring his fleet 'to Vourla Bay', an anchorage near the modern town of Izmir and over a hundred miles south of the approaches to the Dardanelles.[20] At the same time Benedetti appealed to Paris for the despatch of French warships to Turkish waters. Napoleon III was glad of an excuse to counter the Menshikov mission with a show of force. Although the British made it clear in Paris that they were opposed to a build-up of naval forces, a French squadron left Toulon for the Aegean on 25 March. It did not return to the western Mediterranean until the Crimean War had been fought and won.[21]

Rose's message to Malta had a different fate. Dundas refused to sail without orders from London, and the First Lord of the Admiralty was astounded that Rose should think he could 'treat Admirals with their fleets' in such a way 'with impunity'.[22] The British Government did not wish to see the Mediterranean Fleet so closely involved in Turkish affairs. Only a few weeks before, Aberdeen had discussed with Lord John Russell and with Lord Clarendon the merits and risks of employing naval power as an auxiliary to diplomacy. Russell wished Stratford de Redcliffe to set out once more for Constantinople, partly because he was the one ambassador whom the Turks held in high respect, but also because if Stratford chose to remain in London and speak on foreign affairs in the Lords, he could be an infernal nuisance to the Government. Aberdeen, however, was uneasy. Stratford wanted permission to summon British warships to enter the Straits and bolster the Sultan's authority in times of crisis; 'We ought not to trust the disposal of the Mediterranean fleet (which is peace or war) to the decision of any man', Aberdeen told Russell.[23] Stratford was duly informed that, although as ambassador at Constantinople he might 'in case of imminent danger to the existence of the Turkish government' ask the commanding admiral at Malta to hold his fleet in readiness, no British warship should enter the Dardanelles without direct orders from London. It is not surprising that Colonel Rose received a curt rejoinder from the Foreign Office: 'Admiral Dundas has been ordered to remain at Malta', Rose was told. [24]

The British cabinet, still interested that April in Seymour's exchanges with the Tsar at St Petersburg, had no wish to precipitate a crisis on the Straits. Seymour reported that Nesselrode was pleased to learn that Aberdeen and Clarendon had refused to send the fleet eastwards from Malta; their decision seemed to him proof that the government in London was much too sensible to believe exaggerated rumours put about by the French and the Turks. When Lord Stratford arrived back in Constantinople on 5 April he sent reassuring messages to London. With Stratford's assistance the original dispute over Orthodox and Christian rights of guardianship at the Holy Places was settled by the end of the month.[25] 'We did quite right in showing confidence in the pledged word of the Emperor of Russia', Clarendon wrote contentedly to Stratford in mid-April. [26]

Nicholas, however, wanted a clear-cut political victory. Briefly he considered a military expedition, with the Black Sea fleet covering the landing of several divisions between Lake Derkos and the entrance to the Bosphorus, some twenty miles north of Constantinople. His military advisers insisted that neither the army nor the navy was ready for so ambitious a project. Nevertheless, at the very time that Clarendon in London was commending the Tsar's good faith, Nicholas was emphasizing to Nesselrode the need for 'a show of strength' at Constantinople in order that his embassy might 'recover the degree of influence which it had earlier exercised' at the Porte. [27] On 5 May Menshikov accordingly gave Rifaat a draft convention which, although couched in vague language, was assumed by the Turks, the British and the French to assure Russia a protectorate over all the Orthodox subjects of the Sultan, both in Europe and in Asia. It was this demand which brought a long-simmering Eastern crisis to the boil.

Abdul Medjid did not turn down the Russian proposals out of hand; he even changed the Grand Vizier and the Foreign Minister, yet again, at Menshikov's request. But his new counsellors listened more and more to Stratford, who urged them to reject Russia's draft convention. Menshikov, who was naturally impatient, had had enough. On 21 May he left for Odessa, furious with the Sultan and the British ambassador. Stratford, he reported to St Petersburg, had 'betwitched' Abdul Medjid's advisers by his 'frantic activity'.[28]

Stratford rejoiced that the Turks had stood up to Menshikov. 'All now depends upon our cabinet at home,' he wrote to his wife. '*Shilly-shally* will spoil all.' But shilly-shallying was by now part of Aberdeen's nature. When the cabinet met on 28 May the Prime Minister, still confident that the Tsar did not want war, persuaded his colleagues that

Britain should, for the moment, take no action whatsoever. It was, they agreed on that Saturday morning, far better to wait until more information reached them from the Turkish and Russian capitals. Brunnow, who on the following Tuesday was travelling back to St Petersburg for consultations, encouraged Aberdeen to believe that the diplomats would find a solution to the crisis; and the Prime Minister hoped that Nesselrode and Orlov might persuade their imperial master to disavow Menshikov. But a weekend of rumour and reflection dented cabinet unity.[29] Pressure mounted for the fleet to be sent once again to Turkish waters.

The movement of warships seemed to Aberdeen needlessly provocative at such a time. But he was constitutionally punctilious. Before the next meeting of the cabinet, on 4 June, he let his colleagues know that he would accept the verdict of a vote to settle the issue. Most of the cabinet favoured the move; and on 5 June Admiral Dundas was ordered to leave Malta for the anchorage of Besika Bay, off Turkey's Asiatic coast, ten miles south of the entrance to the Dardanelles. At the same time the Prime Minister reluctantly acknowledged that Lord Stratford should be given authority to summon the vessels up to the Bosphorus so as to protect Constantinople from a Russian attack. 'We are drifting fast towards War', the Prime Minister told Clarendon two days later; did the cabinet realize 'where they are going', he asked plaintively?[30]

Lord Aberdeen mistrusted all manifestations of public opinion, especially any which reflected popular concern with foreign affairs. After a particularly noisy outburst of patriotic feeling that summer he wrote tellingly to Palmerston, recalling that Alcibiades, on finding himself applauded by the crowd, asked whether he had said anything unusually foolish.[31] But the Whig members of the Coalition could not affect such aristocratic detachment. The English newspapers were demanding action; some of them contrasted Napoleon III's apparent firmness with the 'senile hesitation' of the British Prime Minister. A new daily newspaper, founded by Benjamin Disraeli, was particularly tiresome: *The Press*, published for the first time on 7 May, offered a challenge to both the Palmerstonian newspapers and *The Times*, which consistently supported the Government throughout the first five months of the year. The newcomer sought to exorcize the traditional bogey of Bonapartism and urged Anglo-French collaboration against Russia. 'England and France are the two policemen of Europe, and they can always keep the peace', *The Press* declared in its nineteenth issue.[32]

This sudden intensive rivalry between London's newspapers perplexed Lord Aberdeen. For a prime minister to find himself abused at the breakfast table morning after morning in so many unsigned articles was a new and disagreeable experience. A leader writer in *The Press* described how his 'naturally morose' temper 'has become peevish. Crossed in his Cabinet, he insults the House of Lords, and plagues the most eminent of his colleagues with the crabbed malice of a maundering witch'.[33] This mischievous character sketch came, anonymously, from Disraeli's incisive pen; and it was too near the truth to be laughed off as journalistic licence. For in cabinet Aberdeen was intensely irritated by Palmerston and Russell, both of whom assumed that they possessed a detailed understanding of Europe's affairs. The Prime Minister claimed one advantage over his colleagues; he knew the terrain. Aberdeen had indeed visited Constantinople, exploring the city and the surrounding countryside for eight weeks and seeing for himself the problems of a warship seeking to sail up the Bosphorus against winds sweeping down from the north. By now this experience was half a century in the past, but everything about the Turkish Empire and the curious conventions of Ottoman government remained vivid in Aberdeen's memory: 'I know the spot well', he told the First Lord of the Admiralty when problems arose over naval passage of the Straits. [34] Such magisterial finality made for tetchiness in a cabinet which contained, as well as the incumbent Foreign Secretary, four of his predecessors, among them the Prime Minister himself.

But, to Aberdeen's satisfaction, once the fleet sailed for Besika Bay, his colleagues became less belligerent. Even when, at the beginning of July, Tsar Nicholas ordered his armies to re-occupy the Danubian Principalities as a means of putting pressure on Turkey, the cabinet did not succumb to the war fever of the rival newspapers. Russia's action infuriated Austria, whose trade would suffer if the lower Danube became a war zone. The British and French encouraged the Austrians to mediate. Hurriedly the Austrian Foreign Minister, Count Buol, convened a conference in Vienna, attended by British, French and Russian diplomats, but no envoy from the Sultan. Compromise seemed easy. The 'Vienna Note' of 1 August, 1853 sought to establish what was virtually a joint Franco-Russian protectorate over the Sultan's Christian subjects. Lord Aberdeen was optimistic; and so was his Russian friend, Brunnow. When news reached London, late on 5 August, that Russia accepted the 'Vienna Note', the Prime Minister was convinced that 'everything was settled'. Political commentators praised his courage 'in defying public clamour, abuse and taunts'. The news from Russia was 'decidedly favourable to the cause of peace', the Prime Minister told the Queen next day. [35]

But what of the Turks? For more than a fortnight no hard news came from Constantinople, only rumour. Gradually Aberdeen's inner circle of ministers became suspicious of Stratford's activity. Lady Clarendon was only echoing her husband's doubts when, in mid-August, she explained to her sister-in-law that the Eastern Crisis 'might soon be settled, yet there are hitches and bothers at every turn and I am afraid Lord Stratford will be an *empêchement*, he is so evidently bent upon getting a triumph over Russia'.[36] Legend insists that the Great Elchi was, in Lady Clarendon's words, 'a dreadfully unsafe man', who encouraged the warlike mood of the Sultan's chief counsellors. But, although Stratford considered the Vienna Note impolitic because it imposed Great-Power surveillance on Turkey, he tried to make it acceptable to the Sultan. When at last the Turks rejected the existing form of the Note and sought amendments, Stratford was blamed by Aberdeen and his colleagues for the failure of a policy never thought out carefully in London. Already the Peelite members of the cabinet had talked among themselves about the possibility of recalling Stratford; but, with the newspapers building him up as a popular idol, they knew that any move against the ambassador would topple the Coalition Government and bring Russell, Palmerston and the fire-and-thunder patriots into office. 'Lord Aberdeen believes that there is a strong party at Constantinople desirous of war and that this party has been greatly encouraged by the hope of English and French assistance', the Prime Minister told the Queen in the first week of September.[37] A few days later anti-Russian riots, instigated by the Turkish Minister of War, threatened European life and property in the Sultan's capital.

Yet by the middle of September Aberdeen and Clarendon were ready to believe that Stratford was right in stiffening the Sultan's resistance, for comments by Nesselrode, leaked to a newspaper in Berlin, showed that he interpreted the Vienna Note as a means of perpetuating Russian dominance at Constantinople. This 'violent interpretation' (to use a phrase coined by Clarendon) brought Britain close to war that autumn. For the first time, Aberdeen's belief that Nicholas sought a reasonable settlement of the Eastern Question was undermined. The newspapers resumed their demand for action. Once again, there were public meetings to denounce Russian tyranny. On 23 September Clarendon ordered Stratford to summon Admiral Dundas's squadron up from Besika Bay. It was to sail through the Dardanelles and anchor in the Golden Horn, off the Sultan's palace. There it could defend Constantinople from any invader and help keep order in a city where the riots were undermining the Sultan's authority.[38]

'I see little chance of averting war, which even in the most sacred cause is a horrible calamity; but for such a cause as two sets of Barbarians quarrelling over a form of words, is not only shocking but incredible', wrote Clarendon to a friend early in October.[39] But the war which everyone by now anticipated was astonishingly slow to come. Stratford delayed summoning the fleet to Constantinople for fear that the arrival of British warships, followed by a French squadron, would stampede the Turks into a rash declaration of war on Russia. Momentarily indeed, it seemed as if the Austrians might successfully mediate, after all: Nicholas met Francis Joseph at Olmütz and approved a revised version of the Vienna Note, circulated to the British and French ambassadors in Vienna in Buol's name. But bungling diplomacy left this 'Buol Project' stillborn. Napoleon III was prepared to accept it and join Britain in putting pressure on the Sultan, but for the sake of prestige he would not initiate a diplomatic retreat; and since, to the British, Buol was an untrustworthy Russian puppet, Aberdeen denied the Project the backing which he had given to the original Vienna Note five weeks before. Between 1815 and 1848 fear of general upheaval on the Continent ensured that Europe's statesmen kept the braking system of diplomacy well greased. In the decade which followed the Year of Revolutions mutual suspicion prevented effective maintenance of the old safeguards.

It was, perhaps, already too late. Turkey formally declared war on Russia on 5 October, complaining that the Tsar had refused to withdraw his armies from Moldavia and Wallachia. There was still a faint hope of a rapid settlement, and over a fortnight passed without any sign of military operations. Tsar Nicholas spent much of September and early October emphasizing the solidarity of the three eastern autocrats. He visited Berlin before going to Olmütz, entertained the Austrian and Prussian rulers at Warsaw for five days, and travelled to Potsdam for further conversations. 'The reunion of the three of us had the aim of showing to the world that we need none other and that in a moment of danger they will find us together,' Nicholas explained in a private letter to his sister Anna, the Queen Mother of the Netherlands. 'The blind hate of the English knows no limits,' he added. 'It seems Louis Napoleon has condemned himself to march at their bidding. These follies take us straight to war. I do not look for it but I shall not flee from it.'[40]

Four days after Nicholas wrote this letter from Tsarskoe Selo, Turkish troops were ferried silently across the Danube at dawn and surprised Russian outposts facing Tutrakan, the nearest point to Bucharest along the great river. As yet, Great Britain and France stood aside. Russia and Turkey had fought against each other in four long campaigns during the previous ninety years and on no occasion had the Turks received active military support from any ally in the West. But Nicholas was under no illusions: Russia, he knew, was about to face a harder struggle than ever before in defence of her Black Sea steppe lands. When news of the Turkish crossing of the Danube reached St Petersburg, Nicholas urged his loyal subjects to show unity with their sovereign in protecting the Orthodox faith by taking up arms for a just and sacred cause. Like his brother, Alexander I, in 1812, the Tsar turned to the scriptures and found inspiration for his peoples in the Psalms. To wage war against the Turk was, he told his sister Anna, 'a holy vocation to which Russia is once more called'.[41]

CHAPTER THREE

Sinope

'Things get worser and worser,' Lord Clarendon wrote to his wife from the Foreign Office on the first Monday in October. 'The beastly Turks have actually declared war.'[1] Such spluttering indignation did not correspond with the general response of the British public to news of Turkey's decision to challenge the might of Russia. Mass meetings in London, Glasgow and several northern towns denounced the barbarism of the Tsar, with frequent references to the suppressed liberties of Poland and Hungary, and there were calls for immediate help to the Sultan. One cabinet minister went even further. On 4 October Lord John Russell sent the Prime Minister and the Foreign Secretary a memorandum in which he argued that, if Russia would not now accept a 'fair' settlement, British troops should be prepared to serve 'as auxiliaries of Turkey'. He raised, too, the question whether 'England and France' ought then to become major participants in the conflict. If so, he argued, they should 'not confine themselves to operations in the Bosphorus and the Black Sea, but employ their mighty resources in the Baltic and at every point where Russia can be resisted or attacked'. These proposals – the first suggestion by a responsible member of the Government that Britain might embark on a major war against the Russian Empire – received scant attention from Lord Aberdeen, who seems to have treated them as a move in Russell's bid for the premiership. At Russell's request, however, Aberdeen sent a copy of the memorandum to Prince Albert later in the month; but the Prime Minister added the damning comment that he thought these proposals 'not very practical or very consistent'.[2] In Aberdeen's opinion, Palmerston had more cogent recommendations to lay before the cabinet, for they relied primarily on the traditional use of sea power: an immediate pledge of support to the Sultan, with naval patrols protecting the Black Sea approaches to the Bosphorus and a formal convention authorizing the Queen's subjects to serve in Turkey's army or navy in return for an undertaking that London would be consulted over the eventual Russo-Turkish peace treaty. Aberdeen did not agree with Palmerston, but he recognized the force of his argument.[3]

No other cabinet minister looked so far ahead as Russell and Palmerston, and none contemplated with such equanimity the prospect of general war. Each successive report from Constantinople confirmed the Foreign Secretary's contempt for everything Turkish. Gladstone, the Chancellor of the Exchequer, loathed the thought of military or naval operations but feared that it might be difficult to stay out of the conflict. Sidney Herbert, who as Secretary-at-War was the executive minister responsible for army administration, hoped the conflict could remain localized and be speedily ended, but he was as pessimistic as the Chancellor.[4] The cabinet had not met at all during September, and when ministers came together at the end of the first week in October one of its least belligerent members – Sir James Graham, the First Lord of the Admiralty – was at Balmoral in attendance on the Queen; but, even so, Lord Aberdeen was satisfied with the mood of his colleagues. 'The aspect of the Cabinet was, on the whole, very good,' he wrote to Graham. 'Gladstone, active and energetic for Peace . . . . Lord John warlike enough, but subdued in tone; Palmerston urged his views perseveringly, but not disagreeably.'[5] The cabinet, following Clarendon's lead, 'came at last to a sort of compromise': the fleet would remain off Constantinople and only enter the Black Sea if the Russians attacked the Turkish coast or crossed the Danube and began to penetrate the Balkans. Graham thought even this proposal fraught with danger, and in a letter from Balmoral he echoed the doubts of the Queen and Prince Albert. Suppose that British sympathy encouraged the Turks to rash behaviour which culminated in disaster, he asked: 'Are we bound in that case to be dragged into hostilities by a Barbarian whom we are unable to control?'[6]

Aberdeen was alive to the danger. For two months there was a flurry of diplomatic activity in London, Paris, Vienna and Constantinople as peace proposals followed each other in quick succession, 'the Thousand and One Notes' as Stratford de Redcliffe's secretary quipped at the time.[7] By the end of November the Russians were willing to accept mediation by the other four Great Powers. Soon, Aberdeen hoped, the Turks, too, would welcome peace talks. Amicable messages were exchanged between Nicholas at Tsarskoe Selo and his former hostess at Windsor; and Nesselrode authorized the Russian field commander in the Danubian Principalities to negotiate with any Turkish pleni-potentiary who might come, under a flag of truce, to his headquarters.

But no peace envoy crossed the Danube.[8]

In Paris Napoleon III was edging away from the brink of a war he had at first seemed to welcome. The prestige of successful arbitration – ideally a congress in his own capital – would establish the Second Empire's status in Europe as effectively as a string of victories from little-known shores around the Black Sea. Privately Napoleon was heard to wish that the Turks would suffer a defeat and come to the conference table chastened and realistic in mind.[9] He sensed that the prospect of new Russian campaigns, conjured up in the French press earlier that year, aroused no response from his strongest supporters in France, the commercial classes and the peasantry. Anxiously, in Paris and in London, responsible ministers awaited news from the Danubian Principalities and from that even more remote theatre of war across the Black Sea, where Russian outposts kept watch over the valleys of the Caucasus.

In St Petersburg, too, they awaited news of battles or peace parleys from the south, where the war zones were as distant from the Russian capital as the Channel coast of France. First reports were gloomy. Prince Michael Gorchakov, the Tsar's commander-in-chief on the Danube, had strictly observed the orders issued when his troops occupied the Principalities in July: he remained on the defensive, concentrating on the defence of Bucharest, but he authorized his subordinate commanders to counter-attack individual Turkish units which were digging in north of the Danube. But the Russians were beaten off at Kalafat on 28 October; a week later they were forced to fall back on Bucharest when they mounted a determined assault on Turkish positions at Oltenitza, 250 miles downstream from Kalafat and close to the point where the invaders had first crossed the great river. Russian veterans successfully fought off a surprise Turkish incursion in the southern Caucasus; but on that front the commander-in-chief, Prince Vorontsov, warned St Petersburg that his armies were below strength. It would be difficult, he said, to hold the Georgian coast and the southern foothills of the mountain chain next spring if, during the winter, a Turkish fleet brought men and munitions across the Black Sea.[10]

Nicholas I prided himself on being a soldier. He was ill-at-ease out of uniform, and he thought no military detail too insignificant to merit his attention. Successive ministers of war had been, not formulators of policy, but mere executive adjutants of their sovereign's will. The most impressive architectural achievement of his reign, the General Staff Building in St Petersburg, was a vast neo-classical crescent, fittingly planned so that most of the seven hundred windows looked out towards the Winter Palace; for the building housed a military secretariat as dependent on the whim of the autocrat across the square as Tsar Paul's terrified garrison commanders had been sixty years before, when Nicholas's paranoiac father had set out on his provincial tours of inspection.

The Tsar listened to the advice of all his generals. He recognized that many possessed a campaigning experience denied him because of his princely and imperial status. But among these generals there was only one whom Nicholas considered a great soldier, in the tradition of Suvorov. When Nicholas, too young to serve in the field against Napoleon, had joined the army of occupation in Paris in June 1814 he had admired a 32-year-old veteran of bayonet charges against the Turks and of the terrible battles of Austerlitz and Borodino, Lieutenant-General Ivan Paskevich.[11] Now, more than forty years after these campaigns, Field Marshal Paskevich, Prince of Warsaw and Commander-in-Chief of the Active Army, was still serving his sovereign, his reputation as a general inflated by victories over the rebellious Poles and Magyars. The million-strong army which owed its allegiance that autumn to the Tsar of Russia owed its training and operational assignments to the Prince of Warsaw. But it was not a debt for which Paskevich deserved to feel any pride in achievement.

On the parade ground the Russian Army looked impressive. Sleekly groomed cavalry horses wheeled with the geometric exactitude demanded of equine choreography. The Guard Regiments were precise in their goose-step and alert in their arms drill; they took care to ensure that the foot was held at the correct angle as their colours were lowered before the saluting-base on those ceremonial occasions which filled Russia's military calendar month by month. But field training was neglected, many of the infantrymen were too old for effective service, and they were weighed down by the half-remembered lessons of old campaigns. In the 1790s Suvorov had taught his men to despise the bullet in favour of the bayonet and his officers to rely on 'Intuition, Rapidity and Impact'; and these maxims still held good. Paskevich's army prepared for battle in tight formation, with bayonets at the ready; there were few battalions with rifled weapons. Nor was it only the soldiery who were ill-prepared for a new war. In 1810 a British general reckoned the artillery brigades of the Tsar's army to be as well equipped as any in Europe and two years later Russian guns matched the firepower of Napoleon's *Grande Armée* at Borodino; but since 1814 nothing had been done to modernize the Tula Arms Works or the foundries at Bryansk, Ekaterinburg and other centres. Thus, although the artillery regiments were up to strength in the winter of 1853–4, doubts remained over the supply of munitions to the battle front in any protracted campaign.[12]

One great problem was still unresolved from Napoleonic days: the rapid movement of men and supplies over the vast expanse of the Tsar's Empire. Paskevich had his headquarters in Warsaw, astride the vital artery to the heart of old Muscovy. The General Staff was in attendance on the Tsar in the capital which Peter the Great had created between Lake Ladoga and the headwaters of the Baltic Sea. A major war against the Ottoman Empire would require the transfer of troops and material at short notice from Poland and the shores of the Gulf of Finland to the Black Sea and the Caucasus. Troops could by now be moved speedily between St Petersburg and Moscow along 404 miles of railway track as straight as any Roman road, and when this 'Nicholas Railway' was opened in 1851 it excited interest as the longest line in the world. But south of Moscow there were no railways at all, and by 1853 only 250 miles of track existed anywhere else in the Tsar's Empire, almost all of it along the railway from St Petersburg to Warsaw, which reached no further from the capital than Pskov. By contrast the German Confederation had almost seven times as much railway track as Russia; and in France troops could be moved from the Channel coast to the Mediterranean ports with only two gaps in the railway system, both at points where it was possible to transfer to barges on the river Saône. Marshal Paskevich – who had been born in the Ukraine, close to Tsar Peter's triumphant battlefield of Poltava – accepted, as part of the natural order, his army's logistical problems south of Moscow: long and slow marches down terrible roads; supplies brought in convoys of wagons drawn, at times, not by horses but by oxen.

But familiarity with the hard facts of geography left Paskevich uneasy at the thought of denuding the exposed Polish salient, a region which was without natural geographical boundaries and therefore open to attack from Prussia or Austria should they side with the Tsar's enemies. He therefore proposed to retain his crack regiments in the north, concentrated along the traditional invasion route through Poland and on either shore of the Gulf of Finland. To advance southwards to Constantinople, he urged Nicholas to raise a volunteer army from 'the Turkish Christians' – Roumanians, Bulgars, Serbs and Greeks. By Paskevich's reckoning, thirty or forty thousand bitter enemies of the Sultan were ready to win their own independence, with Russian officers and Russian muskets.[13] The plan interested Nicholas; but he was not yet ready to use it. He had no wish to offend the Austrians by encouraging national sentiment among the Southern Slavs and the Roumanians, who formed minority groups within the Habsburg Empire as well as the Ottoman Empire. Nesselrode confirmed the Tsar's intention of keeping his armies on the defensive if there remained a prospect of peace talks.

Paskevich also recommended the evacuation of all the outlying forts in the Caucasus, for he thought that they could not be supplied unless Russia was sure of naval mastery within the Black Sea. Nicholas rejected this proposal, which was resented by his Chief of Naval Staff, the ubiquitous Prince Menshikov. The admirals were divided among themselves. They knew that it would be difficult to keep the forts supplied from Sebastopol, but they were less inclined to wait upon events than the army along the Danube. The senior sea-going commander at Sebastopol in the autumn of 1853 was Vice-Admiral Paul Nakhimov, a somewhat outspoken officer and a good seaman, much respected by his men. In October 1827 the 25-year-old Nakhimov had been a junior officer in the Russian Adriatic squadron which, in collaboration with British and French warships and under the joint command of Admiral Codrington, had sunk the combined Turko-Egyptian fleet in Navarino Bay, at a crucial moment in the struggle for independence. Now, twenty-six years later, Nakhimov resolved to take a leaf out of Codrington's book: he would carry the war to the enemy's coast.

In the third week of November Nakhimov's flagship, the newly commissioned *Imperatritsa Mariia*, accompanied by two other sail of the line, reconnoitred the Anatolian coast, searching for a Turkish flotilla which had sailed eastwards from the Bosphorus earlier in the month and was believed to be escorting men and munitions to the southern Caucasus. Nakhimov found the flotilla on 24 November in the small harbour of Sinope, together with other ships which he assumed were troop transports. The vessels were protected by a line of forts along a spit of land which commanded the anchorage. There was near-panic in Sinope, but the Russians sailed away without a shot being fired, and the Turkish commander, Osman Pasha, sent an urgent message to Constantinople for reinforcements. Sinope was only a hundred miles south of the great Russian base at Sebastopol, but it was three hundred miles from the Bosphorus, where the French and British fleet kept watch on the Sultan's palace. Not a single warship sailed east from Constantinople. There was, however, great activity at Sebastopol, and Vice-Admiral Novosilskiï sailed across the Black Sea with four more large vessels and two frigates to reinforce Nakhimov's squadron.

Six days after his reconnaissance cruise, Nakhimov returned to Sinope, bringing his vessels close inshore soon after midday. The Turks opened fire first. But with 720 guns, 76 firing shells rather than the traditional cannon shot, the Russians were much stronger than the Turks, even with support from their shore batteries. After little more than an hour's bombardment, with several Turkish vessels in flames and Osman Pasha's flagship aground and sinking, Rear-Admiral Kornilov arrived with three steam-powered warships from Sebastopol to ram home Russia's superior naval strength. By four in the afternoon on that last day of November, the Turkish flotilla was no longer a fighting force. Seven frigates, two corvettes, two transports and two paddle steamers had been destroyed. A small British merchant vessel had also been sunk, and it was alleged that the Russians had fired on Turkish seamen in the water as they sought to escape from the inferno. Some three thousand Turks perished either in the fires or in the sea; and several hundred were taken prisoner, including the wretched Osman Pasha. Fire, fanned by a stiff inshore wind, spread from the ships to the waterfront and soon enveloped the whole of the straggling town. The Russians suffered no more than light casualties, for smoke from the burning wooden vessels effectively screened Nakhimov's squadron from the Turkish coastal batteries. A single Turkish steamer, with an English commander, escaped destruction and put to sea, hotly pursued along the coast by Kornilov's vessels. Some forty-eight hours later this one surviving warship brought news of the disaster to the Sultan and to the Anglo-French fleet riding at anchor off the Golden Horn.[14]

Odessa, the southernmost port of the Ukraine, learnt of the battle earlier than Constantinople and, indeed, before Nakhimov's fleet sailed triumphantly up the Bay of Sebastopol. From Odessa the news sped to St Petersburg (where a great victory was duly celebrated) and to Vienna, whence it was telegraphed to Paris and London. *The Times* carried the first reports in its later editions on Monday, 12 December, although reserving leader comment for Tuesday and Wednesday. An enterprising and legitimate act of war by the Black Sea Fleet was represented as a 'massacre' and no one accepted St Petersburg's argument that Sinope was an attempt to forestall an invasion of the Caucasus. 'The English people are resolved that Russia shall not dictate conditions to Europe, or convert the Black Sea, with all the various interests encompassing its shores, into a Russian lake,' declared *The Times*. 'To stop the unprofitable contest by striking down the aggressor with a blow is as plain a duty towards humanity as it was to send succour to Sinope' reflected the *Morning Chronicle* a week later.[15] A Turkish defeat on land, with Russia's armies heading south towards the Balkan Passes, would have stirred excitement at Westminster – and then passed rapidly into the margin of history as peace talks followed, in Vienna or Paris. But for the Russians to claim a naval victory against an empire whose capital was under the protection of British warships was another matter. To the general public it seemed a humiliation, the Nelson touch brushed aside or – even worse – appropriated. When, on that Wednesday after the news broke, Palmerston told the Foreign Secretary that 'something must be done to wipe away the Stain', he spoke – as so often – with the authentic, unreasoning voice of John Bull.[16]

A few months later the Poet Laureate could rejoice, no less patriotically, that 'the peace, that I deem'd no peace, is over and done', as he waited for 'the sudden making of splendid names . . . by the side of the Black and the Baltic deep'. Without Nakhimov's victory at a remote roadstead in Asia Minor there would have been no such mood among the British people. Sinope, the last occasion upon which wooden vessels were in combat, was no more a great naval engagement than Navarino had been. Yet it was, none the less, an historic event. The idea of a general crusade against Tsarist tyranny, popular that winter with radicals in Britain and in France, was conceived long before Nakhimov's gunfire echoed along the Anatolian shore; but it was to avenge Sinope and prevent similar naval sorties that the principal expedition of the war set its sights on the destruction of Sebastopol.

Throughout most of the previous two months the Eastern Question had seemed less pressing in London than in the late summer. Rumours of war shook the stock market from time to time: 'Rothschild called on me last night in great alarm,' Graham wrote to Clarendon on 22 November. 'He had heard that Brunnow was about to be recalled and would leave London in 3 days.' There was still deep mistrust of Russia: the arrival at Portsmouth of the Tsar's warship *Aurora* in such urgent need of repairs that the captain maintained he could not risk sailing his vessel as far as the Scheldt strained the limits of naval hospitality, and Brunnow's protest to Lord Aberdeen when *The Times* suggested that the *Aurora*'s officers were spies lacked conviction.[17] But, for the most part, the Lords and Commons gave their attention once more to domestic problems. Chief among them was Russell's insistence on committing the Coalition to parliamentary reform, a measure to which several leading Whigs remained hostile.

Over this issue Palmerston and Russell could never agree. It continued to separate these two belligerent interventionists in the cabinet when, in December, the news became graver and graver. Even before the first reports from Sinope, Palmerston was warning the Prime Minister that he felt bound to leave the Government and lead the anti-reformers in the Commons. Aberdeen doubted Palmerston's sincerity and thought he was making a bid for popularity: 'P. has stolen a march by combining the Eastern question with reform', he told Graham two days before London heard of Sinope.[18] The Queen and Prince Albert, who had long mistrusted Palmerston's robust geniality, urged Aberdeen 'to let him go at once'; and suspicion of palace intrigue heightened Palmerston's desire to quit the cabinet and speak his mind on the burning topics of the moment. A curt letter of resignation duly reached the Prime Minister on 14 December, Wednesday in the week in which Sinope held the headlines. Thursday's *Morning Post* printed the letter, adding the gratuitous information that, even if reform was the ostensible reason for the Home Secretary's resignation, Palmerston was really going because of his shame at the Government's mis-handling of the Eastern Question.[19]

There followed, not so much a 'day of dupes', as a month of mugs. For no tale seemed too improbable to merit credence that December. The noisiest sections of the press not only backed Palmerston but turned against the court, with muddle-headed patriots blaming the Home Secretary's decision to leave the Government on 'Coburg intrigue' and suggesting that Prince Albert was 'a subservient tool of Russian ambition'. This extraordinary wave of public hysteria con-tinued well into January 1854 and, as Lord Derby complained, on one occasion 'led thousands to attend at the Tower to see His Royal Highness go in' when it was rumoured that he had been arrested for high treason. Palmerston never in fact surrendered his seals of office. After basking for a week in popular idolization, he decided on 23 December that he had misunderstood the reform proposals. On Christmas Eve he was back at the Home Office, his political standing in the cabinet strengthened by what was, in this pre-Gallup era, clear evidence of a high rating in public opinion. Another month went by before an inspired announcement in the *Morning Post* emphasized that Lord Palmerston's offer to resign 'had not the remotest connection with anything on the part of the Court'.[20] The 'escapade' did nothing to enhance his reputation at Windsor.

This strange affair meant that, although Palmerston attended every cabinet in the three months preceding Britain's declaration of war, he took no part in the meetings of ministers which discussed how the Government should react to Sinope. Among the Peelite members of the Coalition there was still a strong movement in favour of negotiation. During the first week of December Buol had presided, with some success, over a conference of envoys from Austria, Britain, France and Prussia; and it was hoped that the Tsar would send a high-ranking diplomat to Vienna, with authority to accept Four-Power mediation in the Russo-Turkish conflict. Even at Constantinople, more than a week after news of Sinope reached the city, Stratford de Redcliffe was seeking Turkish backing for an immediate armistice, direct Russo-Turkish talks, and a Great-Power guarantee of a settlement based on renewal of existing treaties. [21] All this uncertainty helped make the cabinets of 17 and 20 December indecisive. It was agreed at the first meeting that Clarendon could inform Stratford that he might allow British warships to enter the Black Sea, something which the cabinet suspected (wrongly) that the ambassador would already have ordered. Three days later Clarendon went a little further and obtained cabinet approval for telling Stratford that the Anglo-French fleet must enjoy 'complete command of the Black Sea'. But both Graham, as First Lord of the Admiralty, and Granville, the ex-Foreign Secretary who served as Lord President of the Council, had by now come to believe it was time for decisive action; and so, too, did Lord John Russell who was already threatening to out-Palmerston Palmerston by resigning specifically over this issue. To show that he was in earnest, Russell even stayed away from the third cabinet of the week, which met in the afternoon of Thursday, 22 December, and dragged on well into the evening.

Thus the leading 'hawks' left the decisions at this vital meeting to their twelve colleagues. Traditionally the cabinet is said to have been most influenced by pressure from Paris, by Napoleon III's threat 'to act alone' and order the French squadron 'to sweep the [Black] Sea of the Russian flag'. But Palmerston and Russell were eloquent by their absence. The Coalition was as near foundering as Osman Pasha's breached flagship at Sinope. Clarendon was prepared to send orders to the fleet which had, in effect, been drafted by Russell. This was too much for Aberdeen: he still hoped for peace; he believed it just possible that war could yet be avoided, but only through collaboration with the French. Accordingly the instructions sent to Stratford on Christmas Eve specifically adopted the 'mode of action proposed by the Emperor', Napoleon III: 'All Russian vessels, other than merchant-men, met in the Black Sea, should be required to return to Sebastopol', the ambassador was told. Seymour in St Petersburg was instructed to inform Nesselrode of these orders; and he did so on 12 January.[22] The sands of peace were fast running out.

CHAPTER FOUR

Unrolling the Banner

The new orders for the navy reached Constantinople on Tuesday, 3 January 1854, and by Friday all the British and French vessels had passed through the Bosphorus and into the Black Sea. There were ten ships of the line from the Royal Navy and nine from France. To the fury of the commander-in-chief, Admiral Dundas, Lord Stratford believed that his instructions gave him authority over the British squadron. The ambassador at once ordered the main force to sail for Sinope, with Dundas's deputy, Rear-Admiral Sir Edmund Lyons, flying his flag in the newly built *Agamemnon*, which, with her ninety-one guns, was the first steam-screw ship of the line in the Royal Navy. In these weeks of non-belligerent watchfulness there was no better qualified naval officer for so difficult an assignment. Lyons, who was five years younger than Dundas and expected soon to succeed him, had returned to the Royal Navy only ten weeks before, after eighteen years in diplomacy, first as Britain's envoy to Athens, and later in Berne and Stockholm. Both the First Lord of the Admiralty and the Prime Minister wanted him back at sea: 'Lyons is the best man to be employed for the service required, whatever it may be', Aberdeen told Clarendon with characteristic imprecision when, in the previous September, he sought Lyons's release from the diplomatic service.[1] Lyons knew the waters of the eastern Mediterranean well and as a naval captain in 1829 had paid courtesy calls to Sebastopol, Odessa and Varna. Only the mysteries of steam-power were new to him.

News that Stratford had ordered the squadron to Sinope caused consternation at Westminster. Soon, Graham was to become highly critical of Dundas's hesitancy; but in January he sided with the commander-in-chief in his dispute with an ambassador whom the Government lacked the courage to recall. For Graham there was one consoling thought: 'If a misfortune happens the blame is Stratford's and not ours; and by all means let it rest upon him', the First Lord told the Foreign Secretary.[2] But there was no cause for alarm. The British squadron remained at Sinope, undisturbed by the Russians, for some ten days, with Lyons's flagship and three other vessels convoying Turkish troopships as far as Trebizond to keep the Sultan's army along his Caucasian frontier up to strength. One of the smaller steamships, HMS *Retribution*, crossed the Black Sea on 6 January and approached Sebastopol. Her commander, Captain Drummond, fired a courtesy salute which was returned by a corvette; a ship's boat was then lowered and an officer handed over a message for Prince Menshikov informing him that any vessel of the Black Sea Fleet outside Russian waters was liable to be challenged by British or French warships. *Retribution* was ordered out of the roadstead when she approached the inner harbour, but her officers were able to report that there were 'upwards of three hundred guns commanding the harbour' and 'three lines of battleships with springs on their cables, and probably with guns shotted.'[3] It is remarkable that so daring an act of impudence did not provoke retaliation.

There is no doubt that Captain Drummond was primarily engaged on a spy mission. Graham had already written to Admiral Dundas emphasizing the importance of Russia's main naval base: 'Should any such opportunity present itself,' the First Lord declared, 'I conclude that you will have your eye on Sebastopol. That is a place where a blow might be struck which will be memorable in Europe, and which would settle the affairs of the East for some time to come.'[4] By now members of the cabinet were beginning to focus their minds on these unfamiliar problems of grand strategy. *The Times* of 23 December reported that the British and French Governments were considering other possible theatres of war than the Black Sea, but the report mentioned only 'an expedition to the Baltic in the early spring'. On Christmas Day Earl Granville, who as Lord President of the Council held a non-departmental post in Aberdeen's cabinet, questioned the nation's preparedness for war with Russia in a letter to the Foreign Secretary. Was the destruction of Sebastopol 'the only or the best thing to be done?' he asked.[5] In the summer months the Baltic and the Gulf of Finland seemed more accessible, and closer to the political heart of Russia.

This debate on the rival merits of a 'northern' or 'southern' approach continued throughout much of the following year, but not in the narrowly partisan spirit of the contest between 'easterners' and 'westerners' in later wars. In 1854 there was deep uncertainty over how and where to fight Russia, and ministers frequently changed their opinions. What would the two central European autocracies, Prussia and Austria, do? If they entered the war against Russia, a thousand-mile front would be opened up in the East. If they entered the war alongside Russia, Napoleon III would need his armies for a campaign along the Rhine. And, even if the war did not spread, was France a reliable ally? The Queen – or her husband – had doubts: 'Who can say it is impossible that our own shores may be threatened by Powers now in alliance with us?' a worried note from Buckingham Palace asked Lord Aberdeen in the last week of February; the army should at once be augmented by 30,000 men. The Prime Minister told the Queen that he was seeking 25,000 recruits for the army, with double that number if the country went to war; and it was hoped to find another 10,000 seamen, and 3,000 marines for service with the fleet.[6] Effectively the British Army in January 1854 comprised some 60,000 men in the United Kingdom, with 40,000 troops in the colonial Empire and another 30,000 serving in India. This total of 130,000 men – considerably smaller than the army maintained by post-imperial Britain in the 1970s and 1980s – was almost as large as the real strength of the French and Turkish standing armies but less than a sixth the size of the active Russian army.

In London and in Paris the coming land campaign was seen at first as a colonial expedition rather than a contribution to a major continental war. Napoleon III looked, in the first instance, to his armies in North Africa, and the British ambassador received the impression that he was not anticipating a French contribution of more than 10,000 men. By mid-Janury 1854 the War Office in London was making preparations to transport troops to Malta and eventually to Turkey, probably in defence of Constantinople. But neither of the ministers responsible for army affairs, the Duke of Newcastle and Sidney Herbert, had any real understanding of the problems involved in raising an army for service overseas. As every regiment in the United Kingdom was below strength, Newcastle told his cabinet colleagues that he hoped 5,000 trained troops would be sufficient for the expeditionary force.[7] This totally inadequate estimate was challenged by the one minister who faced the coming of war with competent realism, the First Lord of the Admiralty, Sir James Graham, one of Aberdeen's least warlike colleagues in the weeks before Sinope. It was Graham who pressed for 20,000 men to be sent at once to the Straits in order to guard this vital artery of the fleet from a Russian offensive once the snows melted in the Balkans. And it was Graham who induced the cabinet to send five engineer officers to Malta, where they were to pick up a detachment of sappers to help the Sultan re-fortify Sinope and strengthen the defences of the Dardanelles and the Bosphorus.[8]

Graham was in close touch with the two most senior and respected officers in the army, Raglan and Burgoyne. The 75-year-old Lord Raglan, Master-General of the Ordnance for the past fifteen months, had been Wellington's right-hand man in the Peninsula, at Waterloo, and on his diplomatic missions to Paris, Verona and, in 1826, to St Petersburg. Sir John Fox Burgoyne, the Inspector-General of Fortifications, a gnarled 72-year-old, had entered the army as a boy soon after the death of his soldier father, 'Gentleman Johnny' Burgoyne, who, in his last years, won acclaim as a dramatist to compensate for the reputation lost in 1777 on surrendering to General Gates at Saratoga. Sir John too fought the Americans – in 1815 – but most of his knowledge came from serving Moore and Wellington in the Peninsula. No one remembered the 108 forts in the lines of Torres Vedras so vividly as General Burgoyne. On 19 January 1854 he left London for Calais and ultimately for Constantinople to give the Sultan the benefit of his military experience.

Napoleon III found Sir John's conversation 'enchanting' when he spent forty-eight hours in Paris. This is hardly surprising, for Burgoyne talked not simply of ways in which the Turks could defend Constantinople, but of the means by which an Anglo-French expedition could aid the Sultan should the Russians sweep down through the Balkan Mountains. Not surprisingly, Burgoyne favoured the establishment of a military base, easily supplied from the sea. Unfortunately the promontories around Turkey's capital were, in this respect, less obliging for the fleets of western Europe than the familiar indentations of Portugal. Burgoyne therefore decided to recommend, not a line of forts covering Constantinople through Chatalja, but a base on the Gallipoli peninsula, easily defended by positions across the isthmus south of Bulair. An allied army encamped on this narrow neck of land would possess a springboard from which to strike at the flank of any Russian force investing the Sultan's capital.[9] Not for the last time, the place-name Gallipoli loomed large in Anglo-French strategic planning.

Momentarily, after threatening to act alone in the fourth week of December, Napoleon III seemed to waver in his resolution to stand up to the Russians. The British ambassador in Paris reported that the Emperor and Empress had been especially gracious to his Russian colleague at a New Year's Eve Ball; and on the very day that Burgoyne crossed the Channel, Napoleon sent to the Tsar a last appeal for peace.[10] Clarendon, who had read the letter in advance, thought the appeal weak: Napoleon asked for a Russo-Turkish armistice, a withdrawal of forces from the Danubian Principalities and direct Russo-Turkish peace talks. But Clarendon failed to see the rapier covered by the velvet glove, for Napoleon listed all the old Anglo-French grievances against Russia, raising again Nesselrode's violent interpretation of the Vienna Note and the treacherous 'massacre' of Sinope. This was a document more likely to goad Nicholas than appease him; and a fortnight later the Tsar sent a ringing reply: should France decide on war, he said, 'Russia will be the same in 1854 as in 1812'.[11]

While these exchanges were passing between Paris and St Petersburg, the cabinet in London seemed resigned to the inevitability of war. Only Lord Aberdeen still held out, hoping to check 'rash or hasty determination'. Before he left for Turkey Burgoyne had sent Graham two memoranda which were circulated among ministers. Both emphasized that Sebastopol 'was not open to attack by sea': the first memorandum considered the possibility that the base might be destroyed 'if the land defences be taken by an army equal to cope with the Russian garrison'; but the second document said roundly that 'the thing is impossible'. 'To enter the port with shipping would be madness', Burgoyne declared; thirty or forty thousand of even the best British troops could do nothing against the thirty or forty thousand Russians who were reported to be holding Sebastopol, for 'the finest feat of landing in any enemy's country' – by Abercromby's army in Egypt – had shown the need for a military superiority of three to one. Burgoyne spoke with authority; in March 1801 he had been there.[12]

Burgoyne's memoranda stimulated comments from all the leading ministers, except Gladstone and Aberdeen himself. Palmerston, who was Secretary-at-War continuously from 1809 to 1828, agreed that 'an attack on Sebastopol is an enterprise not to be undertaken without full deliberation. A naval attack ought certainly not to be attempted without the co-operation of a land force.' He thought, however, that Burgoyne overlooked the value of Turkish troops: personally he was inclined to use the British and French squadrons to ferry Turkish troops to the Crimea, and leave them to crack the nut of Sebastopol. Palmerston looked to the Asian shores of the Black Sea: a British expedition might concentrate on 'the sweeping away of all the Russian forts and establishments on the coast of Circassia'; and, as an afterthought, he added: 'Something, too, might be done in the Sea of

Azov.'[13] Russell, too, thought Sebastopol so strongly defended that it would be unwise to mount any assault on the city. He was content to see ten thousand men, half of them French, encamped on the Bosphorus, either to defend the Sultan or to undertake offensive operations 'in the Black Sea'. The Duke of Newcastle did not look so far ahead, but, like Burgoyne, he favoured an encampment on the Dardanelles.[14]

Graham wanted a base at Gallipoli. He was 'anxious to abate any extravagant expectation' that the Royal Navy could 'humble the pride of Russia or strike any decisive blow . . . to the heart of Russia' either in the Black Sea or the Baltic. 'Prussia and Austria must co-operate to compel the evacuation of the Principalities and prevent . . . the march on Constantinople', he added.[15] And while, in the following weeks, he concentrated on fitting out a powerful Baltic fleet, he was constantly pressing on the Foreign Secretary the need to build up a grand coalition, 'my darling project of a northern maritime confederacy against Russia', as he called it in one note to Clarendon.[16]

After a cabinet meeting on Wednesday, 8 February, the Prime Minister told the Queen that 'active preparations, both naval and military' had been authorized, although he added that 'Lord Aberdeen cannot abandon the hope that they may still turn out to be un-necessary'. This was a curious piece of optimism. At noon on the previous Friday Aberdeen had received Brunnow, his personal friend for the last fifteen years, and both men acknowledged that diplomatic relations were about to be severed.[17] The formal break came on the Monday before the cabinet meeting. No one else rated the prospects for peace highly. On 9 February Newcastle, as Secretary for War and Colonies, gave orders for the first 10,000 men to be transported by steamship to Malta, as a staging-post for the eastern Mediterranean.[18] In the following week *The Times* began a daily column of military intelligence headed 'Preparations for War', which was of course available for study in St Petersburg within a fortnight. There was speculation about the military commanders. It was anticipated that the Queen's cousin, the Duke of Cambridge, would be entrusted with one division and that the other senior posts would be held for the most part by trusted – and elderly – officers who had served 'the Duke' in Portugal and Spain. On the Saturday following the severance of diplomatic relations, the editor of *The Illustrated London News*, a weekly paper with a circulation of some 100,000 copies, predicted a three months' campaign against the Tsar's armies, with the conquest of the Crimea, gains in the Caucasus and Bessarabia and victories in the

Baltic. 'Nothing that can warrant the name of disaster is to be apprehended for a moment.'[19]

Small wonder if other issues of the day received scant attention. When, on 13 February, Lord John Russell introduced into the Commons the Reform Bill which he had first promised the House twelve months before, it aroused little interest in the country as a whole. His speech was remarkably short; and a Conservative backbencher at once sought to have debate on the measure postponed 'in the present state of our foreign affairs'. So long as the nation was technically still at peace, Russell stuck to his principles and once more threatened to leave the Government if the Bill were dropped. But by April even Lord John had given way; and the Second Parliamentary Reform Bill became the first British casualty of the Crimean War.[20]

On the day following Russell's introduction of his short-lived brain-child to the Commons, the people of the capital saw, for the first time, these 'preparations for war'. Shortly after twelve noon the First Battalion of the Coldstream Guards swung out of St George's Barracks, Trafalgar Square. The regimental band, 'cheerfully' playing 'the familiar air of *The Girl I Left Behind Me*' (for was it not St Valentine's Day?) turned eastwards down the Strand. Ahead of the column lay one and a quarter miles of roaring Londoners, for when it was said that the Guards were leaving for the Mediterranean a fever of excitement brought cheering crowds out into the streets. It was, *The Times* explained next day, 'a spectacle to which for many years they had been strangers, and which it is impossible they could see without emotion'. For the moment, the nation remained at peace and the Coldstreams were travelling no further than Chichester, where they would be closer to the troopships of Portsmouth and Southampton than in barracks off Trafalgar Square. But few people doubted that war with Russia was imminent and, at the sight of the Guards, London exulted in anticipatory triumph.

'Even the occupants of the omnibuses and cabs joined in these manifestations,' *The Times* recorded, 'and ... for some time the thoroughfare was entirely suspended.' The turnstile gates on Waterloo Bridge could not stem 'the torrent of people' eager to say farewell to the troops; the tollkeepers were swept aside, and a proud mob escorted the Guards to the railway terminus named after the greatest of recent victories. Two hours later, the Third Battalion of the Grenadier Guards, marching westwards from the Tower to replace the Coldstreams in St George's Barracks, was also cheered along the Strand. On that Tuesday the people of London, who had treated the rank-and-file as social outcasts not so long ago, thrilled easily to the tread of soldiery in the streets.[21]

The mood continued for the remainder of the month. On Thursday in that same week the Fusilier Guards, quartered in the Tower, held a farewell banquet in the London Tavern, at which their band played 'inspiriting airs' and the Duke of Cambridge was cheered. So, on the following Monday, was the much-wronged Prince Albert when he inspected 'our beautiful Guards', as the Queen called them in a letter to her uncle in Brussels. *The Times* of the following morning sounded a gloomier note: 'It may perhaps serve as a salutary check upon that impulsive enthusiasm with which people are too apt to regard the commencement of war ... if ... note is taken of the movement of medical stores from Apothecaries Hall and from Savory and Son of New Bond Street to the Tower'; and it listed what it regarded as 'the needs for a campaign on the Danube' – 1,000 yards of adhesive plaster, 1,000 lb of lint, 12 large medicine chests and 30 panniers for carriage on mules or donkeys, all of which were conveyed through the City in four wagons.[22] But the 'impulsive enthusiasm' was back next day as the cheers rang out at Southampton when the Grenadier Guards went aboard the P. & O. steamer *Ripon*, with the Coldstreams boarding the *Orinoco* and most of the Fusiliers the *Manilla*. Some twenty hours later – it was the morning of Thursday, 23 February, and only a fortnight since the War Office had given the first orders for troops to be ready for service in Malta – the three steamers sailed out into the Solent, leaving the Needles to port at a quarter past eight as they turned into a strong south-westerly; ahead lay a stormy five-day passage before they reached the Straits of Gibraltar. No ultimatum was yet on its way to St Petersburg.[23]

While the troopships headed down-Channel on their first evening out from Southampton, an unusual trio of peace emissaries were travelling up from Dover to London at the end of a 3,000-mile journey to the Tsar's capital and back. Shortly before Christmas, when the newspaper columns were breathing fire and thunder after Sinope, a sixty-year-old Birmingham corn merchant and philanthropist, Joseph Sturge, proposed to a group of his fellow Quakers that a deputation from the Society of Friends should travel to St Petersburg with an Address to the Tsar imploring him 'to put a stop to the effusion of blood and human misery' in the war with Turkey. Tsar Nicholas's brother, Alexander I, had shown great interest in the Society of Friends during his visit to England in 1814 and gave his patronage to individual Quakers who visited Russia; and there was thus a better prospect of receiving a sympathetic hearing from the ruler of Russia than from other crowned heads in Europe. Sturge, who had actively supported conferences of the Friends of Peace at Frankfurt and Manchester, was backed by the principal executive committee of the English Quakers. It was decided that he should be accompanied by Robert Charleton, from Bristol, and Henry Pease, a successful railway promoter from Durham, whose elder brother had been, in 1832, the first Quaker Member of Parliament.[24]

The three men left London on 20 January and reached St Petersburg at seven at night on 2 February, a thirteen-day journey which, on their way back, they cut to an astonishingly rapid nine days. Trains took them from Calais to Berlin and on to Königsberg (now Kaliningrad); and they then continued by carriage to Riga, where the frost was so severe that the vehicle was placed on a sledge for the last four hundred miles of the outward journey.

To their surprise, Joseph Sturge and his companions were treated as distinguished emissaries by the Russians, although they emphasized that they had come on a religious mission rather than with any political purpose. Nesselrode received them on Monday, 6 February, with much civility and on the following Friday afternoon they were allowed to present their petition to the Tsar. Henry Pease wrote to his nephew while his impressions of the Winter Palace were still fresh in his mind:

Upstairs, upstairs, along galleries through rooms, here soldiers of one province, there attendants of another sort, arrived at the top. Enter the ante-room a little before time, chat with Baron N. at the window looking down upon the Neva, talk about sledge races and the burning of the Palace a few years since, try to appear at ease when in reality it was not just so ... Enter the Emperor, coldly inclines towards us, a fine powerful tall frame with an unmistakable countenance which one thinks quite capable of saying 'Siberia' although by no means incapable of genuine kindly relaxation.[25]

Nicholas listened graciously while the petition was read to him. He then explained his views, in a reply which was later handed to the deputation as a statement countersigned by Nesselrode. Once more Nicholas emphasized his regard for Queen Victoria and his original intention of seeking a settlement in the East in anticipation of a later crisis: 'What on my part was prudent foresight, has been unfairly construed in your country into a designing policy, and an ambitious desire of conquest,' he complained. Joseph Sturge explained that, as they were not on a political mission, the Quakers could not discuss details of the dispute: they held, however, that although the followers of Mahomet might believe in an appeal to arms, a Christian should seek peace: and they therefore hoped that international disputes could be settled by arbitration. The Tsar 'shook hands with us all very cordially', said 'my wife also wishes to see you' and 'with eyes moistened with emotion, turned hastily away'. The Quakers then spent ten minutes with the Tsarina and, they assumed, one of her daughters, both of whom spoke good English. Four days later, on the eve of their departure, they were received by Nicholas's eldest daughter, the widowed Duchess of Leuchtenberg, who treated them with no more than formal politeness, probably because by then diplomatic relations had been severed between Russia and Britain.[26]

The British press gave the peace mission considerable attention. The Quakers were gently satirized in *Punch* as 'The Doves of St Petersburg', but their efforts so caught the imagination of *The Illustrated London News* that on 11 March it produced an engraving which showed the Tsar listening to Sturge as he read the petition to him. Some provincial newspapers grudgingly conceded that their intentions were 'benevolent', even though they might be 'misguided' and 'deluded individuals', incapable of resisting Russian blandishment. *The Times* was more outspoken: 'Nothing could be more ludicrous than an attempt upon the part of 3 Quaker gentlemen to stop the aggressive career of a half-mad Emperor by cool speeches and ethical points', Sturge and his companions could read in a leading article on the day they landed at Dover. But five days later the paper printed the text of their Address to the Tsar and of his reply; and on 19 March it gave considerable space to reporting an account of the deputation's experiences which was given by Henry Pease to an audience of some two thousand men and women at the Central Hall in Darlington and at which 'Mr Pease was heartily cheered'. Not everyone looked on the approach of war with 'impulsive enthusiasm'.[27]

Official London treated the deputation with a similar courtesy to official St Petersburg; but the three peacemakers left no mark on policy. The Prime Minister received them on Saturday, 25 February, and made clear to them his detestation of any resort to arms. Yet Lord Aberdeen seems by now to have become an inert slave of events. He held out little hope for Buol's protracted conference in Vienna. Instinct inclined him to retire into private life: a sense of service to the Queen made him cling to office so as to keep out Palmerston, Russell and 'the War Party'. On the Monday after Aberdeen's conversation with the Quakers, the Foreign Secretary sent a demand to the Russians for the evacuation of the Danubian Principalities before the end of April. A similar message was by then on its way from Paris to St Petersburg, and the Russians were left in no doubt that the joint demands constituted an Anglo-French ultimatum.[28] There was, perhaps, one concession to the Quaker pleas for quiet diplomacy. Rather than risk humiliating a proud autocrat, these latest Anglo-French demands were not made public. Aberdeen hoped that, with stalemate on the Danubian front, the Tsar might even now pull his armies back. But, to the Prime Minister's fury, the demands were leaked to the press and carried in full in Tuesday's *Times*. It seemed likely that Russian newspapers would print details of the ultimatum before the British consul in St Petersburg could deliver Clarendon's message in person. There was thus no longer any chance of reaching a private, face-saving compromise which could reduce tension in the East. The diplomats in Vienna had certainly read their *Times* before Buol reconvened the conference on 5 March; their meeting achieved nothing.[29]

Already there had been one other traditional leave-taking in London. In 1793 King George III had ridden down the Mall one February morning at seven o'clock and taken the salute on the Horse Guards as the Duke of York's expeditionary force marched off to the Low Countries at the start of the longest war in the history of a unified Britain. Now, on the last day of the month sixty-one years later, the Scots Guards, with York's nephew, the Duke of Cambridge, as their divisional commander, were about to set out from their barracks in Birdcage Walk for a war as yet undeclared. Thousands of onlookers waited expectantly through two hours of a cold, dark morning, before 'precisely at seven o'clock the barrack gates were thrown open' and George III's granddaughter and her husband came out on the balcony of Buckingham Palace. 'We stood on the balcony to see them – the morning fine, the sun rising over the tower of old Westminster Abbey – and an immense crowd collected to see these fine men,' Victoria wrote to her uncle in Brussels later in the day. 'They formed line, presented arms, and then cheered us *very heartily* and went off cheering. It was a *touching and beautiful* sight.'[30] Earlier that month, when first she heard that the Guards would be sent to the East, the Queen had confessed that 'my heart is not in this unsatisfactory war'.[31] But the sound of regimental bands, the deafening cheers as her Guardsmen tossed their bearskin caps 'high into the air' in a salute no drill manual recognized, left her exultant, like so many of her subjects that February. As in 1914 – and even in the spring of 1982 – a generation of Britons whose imagination remained insensitive to war's reality welcomed its approach as an escape from the boredom of a protracted peace. 'Hail once more to the banner of battle unroll'd', wrote Tennyson, down on the Isle of Wight, as ships of the line, frigates and black-hulled, buff-uppered troopships passed across his horizon at Farringford bound for Malta and the East.[32]

But there were dissentient voices, too. At Westminster John Bright, meeting Lord Granville in the street, reproached him for holding office in a government which was making ready to fight for the despotism of the Turk over European Christians. And in Cheyne Row Thomas Carlyle heard of 'soldiers marching off' to the 'Russian War' and thought he had hardly known 'a madder business'. 'Never such enthusiasm seen among the population. Cold I am as a very stone to all that,' he noted in his journal; and he added, 'It is the idle population of editors &c., that have done all this in England.'[33]

CHAPTER FIVE

Strange Allies

No conflict in modern times gestated for so long as the Crimean War. A clash of arms with Russia had seemed inevitable as early as the middle of December 1853; but the ultimatums were not despatched from London and Paris until the last days of February 1854 and war was not declared until 31 March. Even then four more weeks elapsed before Lord Aberdeen read the Queen's Message announcing the outbreak of hostilities to the House of Lords. The first British shots were fired on 22 April, by warships bombarding the port of Odessa; and British soldiers were not engaged in serious fighting for another five months, when an expeditionary force at last landed on the shores of the Crimea.

There were four main reasons for these successive delays. Chief among them were the folly of embarking on a war with Russia before a spring thaw opened up the Baltic and the slowness with which notes between governments crossed the Continent at a time when the electric telegraph still reached no farther east than Berlin and Vienna. Thirdly, a war between the fringe empires of Europe posed unfamiliar logistical problems. It was relatively easy to order infantry regiments or battalions intended for service in Malta or India or Algeria to sail instead to the Dardanelles; but it was far harder for the military administration to improvise a service of troopships, convey field guns and munitions 3,000 miles from British shores, and find, not only cavalry horses, but suitable vessels in which the animals might be transported so great a distance.

A diplomatic problem also delayed the opening of hostilities. Lord Aberdeen (and his sovereign) believed that the war would be shortened – perhaps, even at this late hour, avoided – if Austria joined Britain and France in putting pressure on the Tsar. This was a matter of deep concern to the Prime Minister. He was convinced that, in a cabinet of specialists on foreign affairs, he alone possessed the experience to handle the vacillations of Vienna; for had he not been ambassador to Austria in those crucial months of the great coalition against Napoleon?

But here, as in his belief that he 'knew' Constantinople and the Turks, Lord Aberdeen was mistaken. He was right to emphasize the key importance of Austria's role, but wrong in thinking that he could make sense of what was happening in Vienna. Uncertainty over Austrian policy continued to hamper military decisions in London and Paris throughout the first six months of the year.

On 10 April Great Britain and France concluded a military alliance, the Convention of London, which pledged the two governments 'to do all that shall depend upon them for the purpose of bringing about the re-establishment of peace between Russia and the Sublime Porte on solid and durable bases'. Article Five of the Convention invited 'the other Powers of Europe' to join the allied 'naval and military forces' in imposing a settlement. Primarily this Article was intended to coax Austria into the war; and in the third week of March the Austrian Foreign Minister, Count Buol, had indeed recommended intervention to Emperor Francis Joseph.[1] But there was a difference between the war aims of the allies and of the Austrians. 'We enter upon the war for a definite object. It is to check and repel the unjust aggression of Russia,' the Foreign Secretary told the House of Lords on 31 March; but in the same speech he made it clear that Britain sought security against Russia's 'mighty armaments' in the Baltic and the Mediterranean and, above all, to deny the Tsar possession of Constantinople. And Napoleon III had already told his Senate and Legislative Assembly that Russian 'sovereignty over Constantinople means sovereignty over the Mediterranean', a concept which would have denied France her 'rightful influence'.[2] The Mediterranean bogey did not worry the Austrians. They had narrower objectives: Buol wanted the Russians out of Moldavia and Wallachia, ideally with Austrian troops standing guard along the lower Danube and creating a neutral buffer between the armies of the Tsar and the Sultan. In Vienna it was suspected that, however conservative Aberdeen's outlook on European affairs might be, the Whigs in his cabinet wished for radical changes in the map of the Continent which no Austrian or Prussian could accept. Emperor Francis Joseph was not prepared to collaborate with governments who offered sanctuary to Kossuth or showed sympathy with Poland's exiles. Nor, indeed, was King Frederick William IV in Berlin.

Austria's eldest statesman saw clearly what should be done. From retirement in his suburban villa, Metternich recommended Buol to follow in 1854 the policy he had pursued in 1813: to stay out of the war and avoid entanglement in any coalition until Austrian intervention could be decisive. For the moment, Austria stood aside; but Francis Joseph reinforced his armies along the border with Wallachia, and, within ten days of the Convention of London, signed a treaty of alliance with Prussia. The German Powers would work together to make Russia evacuate the Danubian Principalities. Buol did not, however, cut off his contacts with London and Paris. He was willing to keep peace talks going in Vienna while the allies decided where and how the war should be fought.[3]

The Convention of London posed more problems than it solved: 'the description, number and destination' of the forces required to wage war against Russia would, it stipulated, 'be determined by subsequent arrangements'. But the new allies were suspicious of each other. It was almost two centuries since French and British soldiers had fought side by side, back in the days of Mazarin and Cromwell; and old enmities were slow to die. Only fifteen months previously Lord Aberdeen and Lord Palmerston had exchanged letters on the probability of going to war against the French yet again, for they feared French designs on the independence of Belgium.[4] Both men had been active in political life during the campaigns which defeated the great Napoleon; they could not easily accept his nephew as 'our great friend and ally'. Lord Raglan, the commander-in-chief of the British expedition to Turkey, had spent over forty years in the shadow of Wellington, whose niece he married. He was a courteous man, more patient and less caustic than the great Duke, delighting in good food and affable society, pleased by the attention lavished on him and on the Duke of Cambridge as they passed through Paris at Easter on their way to Turkey. But he could not shake off his doubts about the French: had they not, after all, been 'the enemy' for the seven most formative years of his army career?

Others, too, found adjustment difficult. Lord Cowley, who was Wellington's nephew and who served as Britain's ambassador to France from 1852 to 1867, remained suspicious of Napoleon III. He failed to realize that, for the Emperor, the 'English Alliance' was as prestigious as a military victory; and he listened too readily to Orleanist critics of neo-Bonapartism who belittled Napoleon III and his military commanders. No one doubted that there was a need for genuine collaboration between such strange allies as the British and the French, although there was a more marked inclination for partnership in Paris than in London. Napoleon told Cowley, at the end of February 1854, that he thought the expedition to Turkey should be under the command of a French soldier, while the joint naval squadrons should be entrusted to a British admiral.[5] But the British insisted on separate national commanders who would, it was hoped, work amicably together through liaison officers. Vice-Admiral Dundas was already at Constantinople and collaborating closely with the senior French naval officer, Vice-Admiral Hamelin. It remained to be seen whether the soldiers, too, would work together.

On 11 March Napoleon chose as commander-in-chief the 55-year-old Marshal Le Roy de Saint-Arnaud, Minister of War for the past three years. As a young mercenary Saint-Arnaud fought for the Greeks against their Turkish overlords, until he was outwitted by the sharp practice of patriot pirates and returned home in disgust. But, like most of his contemporaries in the French army, Saint-Arnaud's military reputation was made in Algeria, originally as a colonel in the early 1840s and more recently for stamping out the first serious native revolt against the Second French Republic. He became known to the people of Paris as stage-manager of Louis Napoleon's *coup d'état* in December 1851, an episode which led foreign observers to over-emphasize Saint-Arnaud's political opportunism and to discount his courage, his initiative in the field, and his skill as an organizer. It was this 'Marshal of December' who restored imperial panache to an army so recently republican at heart. In Saint-Arnaud's favour was his energy and his ability to speak fluent English. Against Saint-Arnaud were murky tales of a rakish youth and of privileged information used to speculate on the Paris Bourse. Prince Albert, whose brother Ernest reported back to him on a visit made to Paris that spring, feared that the Marshal's moral standards were so low that he might accept money from the Russians; and Parisian gossip invented a duel in which Saint-Arnaud was said to have shot a senior officer of the Army of Paris who accused him of peculation. More serious than these slanders were doubts about the Marshal's health. He suffered from intestinal troubles which were so grave that for five weeks in the spring of 1853 he was unable to carry out the deskbound duties of a minister of war, let alone sit in the saddle on the parade ground.[6]

During Wellington's premiership, in 1828–9, Saint-Arnaud lived in poverty among the pimps and trollops east of Drury Lane and gave lessons in fencing and dancing to earn a few shillings. These months of London low-life made him welcome France's new ally with a worldly cynicism. The Emperor hoped that he would learn to trust the British and that they would come to trust him. But, on this score, Napoleon was uneasy. Although he had found Burgoyne excellent company, his generals questioned the strategic thinking of Raglan and Cambridge after meeting them in conference in Paris on the eve of Easter. 'I beg you not to let yourself be influenced by first impressions, for that might be fatal,' Napoleon wrote to Saint-Arnaud, who was about to set out from Marseilles. 'Today the English government is cooperating fully with us; it shows complete confidence in me; I shall do the same . . . Leave me with the responsibility of safeguarding the country's interests; we will be nobody's dupes.'[7] Saint-Arnaud duly met Raglan at Marseilles, found him full of goodwill and was impressed by the fittings of HMS *Caradoc*, the steam frigate which was to serve Raglan as a headquarters ship. 'I went aboard his *Caradoc*; that is certainly not a typical English set-up [*installation anglaise*]', the Marshal wrote to his brother.[8] He watched Raglan's steamer sail out into a heavy swell on 22 April. By then three senior French generals – Canrobert, Bosquet and Martimprey – had already been at Gallipoli for three weeks intimidating local pashas so that they would provide huts and firewood for the French expeditionary force; and the Emperor's cousin, Prince Napoleon, was due at Constantinople on 1 May, to take command of France's 3rd Division. But Saint-Arnaud was in no hurry. He was unwell again in that fourth week of April: there were strong gales along the French coast; and vessels arriving at Toulon brought news of snow-storms in the Dardanelles. Better to remain in the Hôtel d'Orient until he could leave Marseilles in grand style.

Saint-Arnaud embarked at last on 29 April with a fitting show of panache: 'a fine looking-man of about 50', noted a British traveller hurrying home from the fighting in the Balkans to train with the Surrey militia.[9] From Marseilles the *Berthollet* carried the Marshal, his wife and his staff through heavy seas to Malta, the island seized by General Bonaparte in the summer of Saint-Arnaud's birth and occupied by the British two years later. At Malta the Marshal's command of spoken English and his genial cordiality impressed his hosts. But, being a good Bonapartist, Saint-Arnaud could not resist writing home, 'What a jewel lost to France!'[10] The *Berthollet* entered the Dardanelles on the night of 6–7 May, allowing Saint-Arnaud to land briefly at Gallipoli before anchoring off the Golden Horn two days later. Raglan had arrived a week earlier.

By now a powerful allied army was concentrated around Constantinople: 14,000 British troops, with another 11,000 on the way eastwards; and more than 30,000 Frenchmen, including Zouave regiments of veteran colonial infantry from Algeria, with the promise of more to come. For the first time in history, steamships plied regularly across the eastern Mediterranean, building up the expeditionary forces of the two nations week by week. The Guards regiments who sailed from Southampton at the end of February spent a month in Malta before embarking for Turkey, but the first troopship had entered the Dardanelles on 5 April, just nine days after the declaration of war.

For the *Golden Fleece* – an ominous name for a vanguard sailing up the Hellespont – it was not the most propitious of landfalls. 'The blast of English light infantry trumpets broke the silence of those antique shores' for 'the first time', wrote a passenger aboard the troopship; and 'no one took the slightest notice of us'.[11] At Gallipoli, the base Burgoyne had pinpointed on the map for the French generals a few weeks before, nothing was ready for the British. The French advance guard was already ashore: tricolour flags fluttered over a neat line of tents, while the Turkish governor of the region had assigned the more salubrious houses in the gimcrack town to French officers. There was even an *Auberge de l'Armée Expeditionnaire*. The first thousand British troops landed on 8 April and at once set out for Bulair, eight miles to the north. 'Our encampment is very wretched, and hardly anything except the men's rations to be got to eat . . . The French have everything – horses, provisions, good tents and every kind of protection against contingencies', wrote an officer in the 50th regiment in the first of many letters to find their way into the English press.[12] It was galling to see French steamers disgorge their human and animal cargoes 'with ease and celerity'. Years of experience in Algeria gave French administration a professionalism which the British might envy and admire, but which they could not emulate so long as the minutiae of transport and supply – once the daily study of the great Duke – were left to chance and a civilian Commissary-General.

George Evelyn, the Surrey militia colonel who travelled out to study the early stages of the war, first heard of Burgoyne's 'Torres Vedras' plan while he was observing Russians and Turks firing at each other across the Danube: 'An absurd arrangement, our troops might as well be at Malta as at Gallipoli', he at once wrote in his diary.[13] It was a point of view with which both Raglan and Saint-Arnaud came to agree as soon as they set foot in Turkey. Most of the British advance party, and all later contingents, were accordingly settled in or around the old Turkish barracks at Scutari, on the Asiatic shore, facing the Golden Horn. There, between a line of cypress trees and a beach 'which somewhat resembled that at Folkestone at high water', Lord Raglan established his headquarters in a modest wooden hut. Saint-Arnaud preferred a villa at Yenikoy, some twelve miles up the Straits and on the European side of the Bosphorus.[14] But Scutari and Yenikoy were still more than three hundred miles away from northern Bulgaria, where the Turkish commander, Omar Pasha, was faced with Russia's long-awaited spring offensive. On 18 May Saint-Arnaud and Raglan sailed up through the Bosphorus for Varna and an urgent first meeting with Omar.

Once the first signs of a thaw came to St Petersburg, the Tsar turned his attention to ways of winning a dramatic success before the allies could come to Turkey's assistance. To Nicholas's dismay, however, his trusted Paskevich was unco-operative. Years of living in Warsaw had narrowed the Field Marshal's strategic horizon. He had urged Nicholas not to denude Poland and the Baltic coasts as soon as the first shots were exchanged along the Danube and in the Caucasus. Now constantly his eyes focused on the long curving line of the Vistula as it ran northwards from Austrian-held Cracow, to wind through the vulnerable Polish plains and into East Prussia, that land of woods and lakes and marshes where Paskevich had fought against the great Napoleon nearly half a century before. Every rumour of troop movements in Austria or Prussia put Paskevich on the alert. To mount an offensive on the lower Danube, while leaving Russia's Polish salient exposed to Austrian or Prussian invaders, seemed to the old Marshal the height of folly. Nicholas's generals seemed unable or unwilling to implement the Paskevich Design of fomenting a grand anti-Turkish insurrection in the Balkans; and every subsequent plan proposed by the Tsar to carry the war into Turkey's Bulgarian provinces was met by the Marshal's gloomy warning to think of Poland. 'Common sense demands that we should leave the Danube and the Principalities', Paskevich wrote in a memorandum two days before Saint-Arnaud embarked at Marseilles. To this bald proposal Nicholas's response was a line of three exclamation marks in the margin'.[15]

With Paskevich dragging his feet so obstinately, the 'Eastern War', as the campaign against the Turks was called in St Petersburg, offered the Russian people neither victory nor defeat. The Tsar, ignoring Paskevich, at last ordered Prince Michael Gorchakov, his field commander on the Danube, to take the offensive, cross the river, mop up the outlying Turkish defences and attack the two key fortresses, first

Silistria and then Ruschuk (Ruse).

So successful were Gorchakov's troops that they forced Paskevich to give his support to the offensive. But it was only a qualified support. The Field Marshal moved cautiously. The siege artillery was slow to reach Silistria, and Paskevich vetoed plans for an attack along the banks of the river (where the defences were at their weakest) because he thought it would expose the infantry to cannon fire from fortified outworks of the town. Five times in May the Tsar sent urgent messages to Paskevich, stressing the importance of taking Silistria. A captured fortress would make the Austrians think twice before threatening intervention, Nicholas argued.[16]

It was while these exchanges were in progress between St Petersburg and the Danubian front that the allied generals reached Varna and met Omar Pasha for the first time. The Turkish commander-in-chief was born in Croatia in 1809 and, as Michael Lotis, became an Austrian army cadet but, while still under twenty, deserted and crossed the mountains into Bosnia. There he apostasized, took the Moslem name of the second caliph, was commissioned in the Ottoman army and attracted the attention of Sultan Mahmud II who appointed him a military instructor. The British first encountered him in Syria and Lebanon and respected his ruthless qualities. The Austrians did not, and repeatedly made their objections known to the Sultan. He made a poor impression on Saint-Arnaud (*'un homme incomplet'*) although he conceded that Omar was 'remarkable enough for his adopted country'. On the other hand, Raglan and his staff were 'much pleased' with Omar and his men: twice they had sent the Russians reeling; and even now they were forcing the invaders back into the hinterland behind Varna.[17] Raglan had no hesitation in recommending to his French colleague that the allied force should be sent up to Varna as soon as possible, so as to relieve Silistria and throw the Russians back across the Danube.

So long as he was in the battle zone Saint-Arnaud fully agreed with Raglan. He arrived back at Yenikoy on Thursday, 25 May, still determined to have 12,000 Frenchmen supporting Omar at Varna by the following Friday. But over the weekend doubt set in. Was the allied force ready to gain the victory which public opinion in Paris and London demanded? The Marshal travelled down to the French camp at Gallipoli: he was short of artillery, short of cavalry horses, short of ambulances and short of provisions. Moreover, as he told his brother, the 'English Army is in no better state than ourselves'.[18] Over the following week there was no sign of French transports sailing for Varna, only of General Bosquet setting off from the Gallipoli peninsula with a long column of green-turbaned Zouaves on a hundred-mile march northwards to Adrianople and the southern outposts of the Balkan Mountains. Better to cover the valley routes to the key passes than send an expedition up to the Danube and risk some indecisive action, perhaps even defeat.

Saint-Arnaud was right in one respect. The British contingent at Scutari was not yet ready for a Balkan campaign. Two letters to the Prime Minister made that abundantly clear. Lord Aberdeen's second son was serving with the Guards in the Duke of Cambridge's division. On 10 May, little more than a week after reaching Scutari, Alexander Gordon let his father know of the confusion at headquarters. Why, he wondered, were they encamped on the wrong side of the Bosphorus for Varna? 'Nothing is yet known of our ultimate destination or when we are to move, which I fear is not likely to be soon as we have the greatest difficulty in getting baggage animals. Not a single cavalry officer has yet arrived (except Lord Lucan).' Three weeks later, after Raglan's return from Omar's headquarters, things were little better: 'We are ready to go up to Varna, but the commissariat is not,' Gordon wrote on 30 May. 'They have no horses or mules for the transport of tents, provisions and baggage – and instead of setting to work to get them they are engaged in objecting to every thing proposed and thwarting Lord Raglan in everything. Until you send out an order that Lord R. is to command the army and not Commissary General Filder we shall not get into ready working order.'[19] There was a sound argument against sending the troops forward too soon.

At eleven at night on the following Saturday (3 June) Colonel Trochu, Saint-Arnaud's chief aide-de-camp, arrived at Raglan's headquarters at Scutari to tell the British commander that the Marshal had decided against sending any substantial contingents to help Omar relieve Silistria. Only a token French force under General Canrobert would go to Varna. He proposed that the main Anglo-French army should hold the Balkan Passes, and stand on the defensive. But Raglan, though always courteous, was firm: the Light Brigade had embarked for Varna on the previous Monday; he was winning the battle of Scutari, against Filder and the sluggards in the commissariat; and ten steamers and nine sailing vessels were standing by to move another 6,000 men and horses up the Bulgarian coast at the first opportunity. Nothing that Colonel Trochu or Marshal Saint-Arnaud might say could make Lord Raglan change his mind.[20]

On 9 June a British brigadier-general hurried across the Bosphorus with a message for Lord Raglan. Fifteen months before, Colonel Hugh Rose had sought to summon Admiral Dundas's squadron to these waters. Now, released from Lord Stratford de Redcliffe's service, Brigadier-General Rose enjoyed higher rank and less executive authority as principal liaison officer at Saint-Arnaud's headquarters. And on that Friday morning he informed Raglan that the Marshal was reverting to his original plan. On Thursday evening the largest steamer in the world, the commandeered P. & O. vessel *Himalaya*, anchored off Constantinople. 'She bore within her iron ribs a burden of more than 2,100 souls,' *The Times* reported. More prosaically she had brought the 5th Dragoon Guards from southern Ireland in eleven days and three hours. As soon as Raglan received Saint-Arnaud's message the *Himalaya* was ordered up through the Bosphorus to take men and horses direct to Varna. Action seemed imminent. Raglan established his field headquarters on the outskirts of Varna on 21 June; and General Bosquet, whose division at Adrianople had risen to almost 12,000 men, began to march them another 150 miles through the mountains towards Varna and the coast. But the journey took them more than three weeks; and by the end of June the military situation was changing out of all recognition.[21]

The beginning of the month had brought an intensification of Russian preparations for an assault on Silistria. Paskevich himself went forward into the battle zone to see how, during the short hours of darkness each night, the trenches were creeping nearer and nearer to the outlying bastion of Arab-tabia. On 10 June the Turks spotted a group of staff officers who had come across the river to study the effects of the Russian bombardment; and the artillery of the fortress opened up. A Turkish shell landed near Paskevich, but no one in the group of officers thought he was hit by any fragments. Suddenly, however, the old Marshal complained of a pain in his shoulder. He was taken back across the Danube; a carriage bore him out of the campaign and, as some believed, out of history too.[22]

When he heard of the incident, Tsar Nicholas was sympathetic: Paskevich was, after all, the military hero he had created. The Russian press announced that the Prince of Warsaw needed a long convalescence to recover from a wound sustained while directing the assault on the Turkish stronghold. To Nicholas's considerable satisfaction, effective command in the field thus passed to Prince Michael

Gorchakov. Within three days the Prince was able to send the Tsar detailed proposals for storming Silistria and meeting any challenge offered by an allied expedition to Varna. General Gorchakov argued that it would be better to give battle to the British and French in a region inhabited by Turks, Bulgars or Roumanians than to allow the enemy to land further along the Black Sea coast and carry the war to Russian towns and settlements. Nicholas was delighted with the General's plans and accepted his reasoning: the Tsar's only worry was the attitude of the Austrians, who in the second half of May began to concentrate newly raised armies in Galicia and along the borders of Transylvania.[23]

For several weeks General Gorchakov's men had held high ground on the right bank of the Danube, above Silistria. From a vantage point in Governor Mustapha Pasha's delightful gardens, a 25-year-old Russian artillery lieutenant looked out day after day over the islands and river banks to the town and citadel beyond, with the individual forts of Silistria clearly visible, 'as if in the palm of your hand'. 'It is an odd kind of pleasure, seeing people kill each other, and yet each morning and evening I would get up on my cart and spend hours at a time watching, and I was not the only one. The spectacle was really beautiful, especially at night,' the lieutenant wrote in a letter home a month later. 'At Silistria . . . I saw so many interesting, poetic and affecting things that the time I spent there will never be erased from my memory,' he added; and twelve years later, in writing about Borodino, the ex-lieutenant placed Pierre Bezukhov on just such a knoll where he, too, was 'spellbound at the terrible beauty' of the unexpected panorama beneath him. But, unlike Pierre, Second Lieutenant Count Tolstoy was not simply a distant observer of events. On 19 June he was down in the trenches in attendance on a general whom he greatly admired, Prince Gorchakov – 'a slightly ridiculous figure, very tall, standing with his hands behind him, cap on back of head, bespectacled, and speaking like a turkeycock'. Late that afternoon, as Gorchakov and his staff waited in the trenches, there was a great explosion from the outer walls of the Arab-tabia fort. After nights of tunnelling the Russians succeeded in exploding what Tolstoy described as 'a mine of 240 poods' (8,000 lb) of gunpowder under the most obstinate defensive bastion of the town. The roar of the explosion could be heard at Raglan's headquarters outside Varna, sixty miles away; and it was assumed that the decisive assault on Silistria was about to begin. Five hundred Russian guns rained shells and shot against Silistria all night.[24]

Twenty-four hours later the assault troops were in position. Dawn approached, the period when (as Tolstoy explained in his letter) 'fear at the thought of attack' gave way to expectant exhilaration 'the nearer the moment came . . . when we would see a cascade of rockets giving the signal to attack'. But on that morning of 22 June, the rockets were not fired. An hour before the assault was to begin, a senior member of Paskevich's staff rode down to General Gorchakov with orders to raise the siege of Silistria. The Austrian ambassador had delivered what was, in effect, an ultimatum at St Petersburg, demanding that Russia should withdraw from the Danubian Principalities. An army pinned between the sweep of the Danube and the Bulgarian coast was liable to be cut off by the powerful Austrian force poised in Transylvania.[25]

As a first move towards safety, General Gorchakov pulled his troops back across the Danube within thirty hours of receiving his new orders. Seven thousand Bulgarian families were ferried across the river, too, for fear of savage reprisals from the Turks. At his new headquarters near Bucharest a letter reached the Russian commander from the Tsar: 'How sad and painful for me, dear Gorchakov, that I had to agree to the insistent arguments of Ivan Fedorovich [Paskevich] as to the danger threatening the army, from the faithlessness of Austria, whom we had saved.' It was said that, in the Winter Palace, Tsar Nicholas was so angry with his fellow autocrat in Vienna that he turned a portrait of the Emperor Francis Joseph to the wall and scrawled on the back of it, in German, 'You ingrate!'[26]

Rumours of the Russian withdrawal reached the British advance camp at Devna on Friday, 23 June. At first no one believed them. But riders exercising their horses that morning sensed something uncanny and realized that the sides of the valley were no longer throwing back the pounding iteration of preceding days. By Sunday morning the news was confirmed and Raglan at once ordered Lord Cardigan to take some 200 troopers from the 8th Hussars and the 13th Light Dragoons and find out 'if the Russian Army was still on this side of the Danube'. For sixteen days this reconnaissance patrol scoured the Bulgarian country-side, going right up to the banks of the Danube, where they at last saw – and were seen by – a Russian force across the river. But it was a strange affair. 'We marched 150 miles without ever seeing a human being, nor saw a single house in a state of repair or inhabited, and not an animal to be seen except those which inhabit the wildest regions,' Cardigan declared in a public speech in London eight months later. North-eastern Bulgaria seemed to him 'a perfectly wild desert'. There is no doubt that Cardigan drove his men and their horses too hard in hot weather through a region where he was surprised to find little water and no forage. A Hussar officer's wife, who watched the horses staggering back into Varna on 11 July, was appalled by this 'cruel parade of death'. Mrs Fanny Duberly, a vivacious 24-year-old horsewoman more perceptive than her husband and his brother officers, was unsparing in her comments on the Light Brigade's commander: 'I hope and trust that Cardigan – whom all abhor – will get his head into such a jolly bag that he will never get it out again,' she wrote home to her sister in Hampshire. Her indignation was fully justified. Almost a hundred first-rate chargers were lost to the Light Brigade, from an exercise which had little value except to expose the general's ignorance of the terrain in which they were still planning to give the enemy battle.[27]

Or were they? As early as 25 June three British frigates, patrolling off the mouths of the Danube, spotted a force of 500 cavalry on the march northwards along the coast.[28] Soon it began to look as if the Russians were not just retiring north of the Danube, but evacuating Wallachia and probably Moldavia as well. Saint-Arnaud, already angry with the Russians for pulling away from Silistria and robbing him of what he believed was certain victory, made it clear to his brother that he was in the dark over what would happen next. He thought, from messages reaching him from Paris, that the Austrians would come into the war and expect the Anglo-French forces to advance on their right flank; but there was so much talk going on in Vienna that he mistrusted them. He would do nothing until he heard that the Austrians were definitely on the move.[29] Meanwhile the battered bastions of Silistria awaited inspection, British troops were ready for review ('none of you can have any idea of the friendliness, sense of unity and sympathy between the two armies'), and there were always new French regiments over whom a tired and sick commander must somehow project the magnetic aura of a Marshal of France.

In retrospect it seems strange that Raglan and Saint-Arnaud lingered so long at inhospitable Varna once the Russians had pulled back from the Danube in that fourth week of June. London, after all, knew well enough what it wanted. An article in *The Times* on 15 June spoke with single-minded clarity: 'The grand political and military objects of the war cannot . . . be attained so long as Sebastopol and the Russian fleet

are in existence . . . We hold, therefore, that the taking of Sebastopol
and the occupation of the Crimea are objects which would repay all the
costs of the present war, and would permanently settle in our favour the
principal questions of the day.' Legend maintains that in this leading
article 'the journal . . . embodied the soul of the nation'; and Kinglake,
who first attributed to *The Times* such authoritative influence, goes on to
recall a fortnight of press thunder, culminating in a memorable post-
prandial cabinet meeting at Pembroke Lodge, Lord John Russell's
home in Richmond. Kinglake's pen-portrait of the Duke of Newcastle
reading to acquiescent and somnolent colleagues his orders for Raglan
to besiege Sebastopol has found a place in almost every subsequent
narrative of the Crimean War.[30]

The truth is less dramatic. Sebastopol had beckoned the more
warlike cabinet ministers ever since they had heard news of Sinope.
Graham, who had told Admiral Dundas to keep his eye on Sebastopol
at the start of the year, seems almost to have become obsessed with its
importance. 'The operation which will be ever memorable and decisive
is the capture and destruction of Sebastopol,' he wrote to Clarendon
three and a half months before the famous *Times* leader. 'On this my
heart is set, the Eye tooth of the Bear must be drawn,' Graham added
and, lest the parallel be missed, he wrote on the back of the copy which
he retained of this letter, '*Delenda est Carthago*'.[31]

Occasionally, in cooler moments of reflection, the ministers shrank
from proposing an assault on so powerful a fortress, as they had after
reading Burgoyne's original memoranda in January. Vice-Admiral
Dundas feared that, if his wooden warships came close enough inshore
to be effective, Russian batteries would fire 'red hot shells at them'; and
Captain Drummond, who in January had brought HMS *Retribution*
into the Bay of Sebastopol, considered the fortress impregnable,
although he thought 'the north side' of the bay 'presented some
favourable points for the disembarkation of troops under the ship's
guns'.[32] But any note of optimism from the war zone swiftly swung
ministerial opinion in favour of an expedition to the Crimea. Graham
thus attached great importance to a letter which his friend, Rear-
Admiral Lyons, sent from his flagship, *Agamemnon*, on 6 April arguing
that 'too much is thought' of the defences of Sebastopol and that the
destruction of Russia's naval base must be the prime objective in any
Black Sea campaign. 'To me the bare idea of our not striking a
successful blow at Sebastopol is painful. It haunts me in my solitary
evening walks on the deck of this splendid ship.'[33] Graham circulated

Lyons's letter and wrote back to him, urging him to make his views known among the other senior officers at Constantinople while, at the same time, trying to discover all he could about the fortress and its defences. On 13 June, two days before the *Times* editorial, Graham again wrote to Lyons, this time confirming to him that the cabinet as a whole thought other enterprises of secondary importance compared to the seizure of the great Russian base.[34]

It is therefore clear that plans for the investment of Sebastopol were considered individually by ministers and by the cabinet as a whole long before the celebrated midsummer night's session at Richmond. Palmerston completed the last of several memoranda recommending a landing in the Crimea on the morning of the *Times* editorial and even the naturally cautious Gladstone had come to accept Graham's reasoning by the beginning of the fourth week. Only the Prime Minister himself held back, hoping that a general peace would follow Russia's withdrawal from the Danube; and he had recognized the need for an attack on the naval base at a cabinet meeting on the previous day.[35]

Despite the licence with which Kinglake described events at Pembroke Lodge, his narrative is accurate in one respect. There was, that summer, a 'rare concurrence of feeling' in London on the need to deprive the Tsar's fleet of its principal base in order to ensure lasting peace around the Black Sea. This was known, and appreciated, in Paris, and the allied commanders had received letters from England and France emphasizing the importance of a landing in the Crimea. It would accordingly be wrong to assume that the orders to attack Sebastopol, which reached British headquarters on Sunday, 16 July, took Raglan by surprise. Yet, in a sense, he had feared their coming: for he knew next to nothing about the geography of the Crimea, let alone the details of its forts and garrisons.

There were three attributes which Wellington used to praise in this loyalest of aides-de-camp: his intelligence, his truthfulness, his obedience. Now Raglan was in a dilemma. Tradition bound him unquestioningly to accept the instructions sent by the Government in London. Instinct made him doubt the wisdom of the whole enterprise. 'A commander-in-chief', Wellington once told Major-General Lord Beresford, 'must not be beaten; therefore do not undertake anything with your troops unless you have some strong hope of success.'[36] But what if you knew so little of your enemy that you could not confidently predict success or failure? Sebastopol, everyone said, was a tough nut to crack; but, as Saint-Arnaud remarked, the Russians were 'an enemy who had pulled away'. After their retreat from the Danube, it was hard to look upon the Tsar's 'million strong' army as a formidable force.

For three days Raglan hesitated: at seventy-six no one would take a quick decision over so grave a matter. On Monday he sent for his senior divisional commander, General Sir George Brown, a martinet who had fallen back on Corunna with Moore forty-five years before and who had seen as much active service as the Commander-in-Chief. But Brown was little help. Like Raglan, he thought of 'the Great Duke'. Wellington would have wanted more information before embarking on such a venture, Brown said; but, he added, if London believed Raglan was procrastinating, 'they' would simply send out another commander in his place.[37] It was, no doubt, the best advice Raglan could expect from a youngster of sixty-six.

Fortunately Raglan could turn elsewhere, for Saint-Arnaud, too, had received orders from Paris. It is a tribute to the good sense of the British and French Commanders-in-Chief, and to the growing trust between the unexpected allies, that the whole enterprise was at once referred to a joint council of war which met under Saint-Arnaud's chairmanship on Tuesday, 18 July. The Marshal had been uneasy about the Sebastopol project in recent weeks because he was short of good cavalry horses, and heavy guns were still awaiting shipment from Toulon. But that Tuesday found him in an optimistic mood: his confidence was boosted by the arrival, on the previous Saturday, of the first consignment of siege equipment; there were, the Marshal told his brother, 'a few cases' of cholera in the army, but he was 'taking precautions and the storm will pass'. He would himself speak for the French army, and Raglan for the British; most of all he wished to sound out the seamen – Admirals Dundas and Lyons of the Royal Navy, and the French Admirals, Hamelin and Bruat. Six men only would do the talking. But, at this conference and at later ones, the principal participants were briefed by other senior officers not admitted to the conclave; Dundas, for example, looked for advice on how to handle the French to the officer-diplomat whom he had scorned in the spring of 1853, Brigadier-General Rose.[38]

Rose's personal journal provides an interesting insight into the troubled minds of his eminent colleagues in this critical week. For some days they had known that a decision over invasion of the Crimea was imminent; and several of them were unsure of the wisdom of such an enterprise. Yet they hesitated over tendering unpopular advice. On Sunday, 16 July, Admiral Dundas showed Rose a letter from the Duke of Newcastle which emphasized the importance of landing close to

Sebastopol before making a decisive assault on the great naval base. Rose, who for the past three years had studied closely every military report from the Black Sea region, thought the operation ill-timed. In conversation with Dundas, he 'urged very much making a feint and capturing Theodosia', in the eastern Crimea, thus confusing the enemy and drawing troops away from Sebastopol. The septuagenarian admiral was, however, strongly opposed to any expedition whatsoever: army and navy were weakened by cholera; and he doubted if the fleets could give the troopships adequate protection. But what ought he to say at the inter-allied council of war which, he assumed, would take place later in the week? 'I advised him, as a friend, at the Council not to give an opinion against taking the Crimea,' Rose wrote in his journal that Sunday. 'There would be those at the Council who would be glad to shift the responsibility of not going there on him. If he gave an adverse opinion it would be noted down.' Advice of this character – not dissimilar to the warning Brown gave Raglan – hardly made for strong and resolute leadership. 'Aren't you coming?' Rose was asked on the Tuesday morning. He was not invited, and had to content himself with giving Admiral Dundas a memorandum on the Crimea's defences.[39]

It was, Saint-Arnaud wrote next day, 'a great and lengthy conference of absorbing interest'. There would be 'a daring enterprise', for it was not right that 'two fine armies, two fine fleets should remain inactive and let themselves fall victim to disease [*dévorer par les fièvres*]. Both commanders were more concerned with ways to implement the instructions from London and Paris than with challenging their good sense. The Admirals were less sure of themselves. Dundas, in the end, did not conceal his qualms. Even Sir Edmund Lyons, consistently a champion of an assault on the Crimea, was subdued by the enormity of the task which now confronted the two navies: they were expected to embark a huge army from open sandy beaches and land it on enemy shores close to a garrison which had long anticipated its coming. The French Admirals seemed similarly divided: Hamelin was reluctant while his deputy, Bruat, favoured the expedition. But, despite doubts, there were no divisions. The conference was a success. General Brown, General Canrobert and the Admirals constituted an informal planning committee to look for suitable invasion points and the navies agreed to extend their reconnaissance patrols to the shores of the Crimean peninsula. The war would be fought and won in Russia, not in the Balkans.[40]

On 19 July Raglan duly acknowledged receipt of the Duke of

Newcastle's orders. The allied commanders were beginning preparations for an invasion of Russia, but, as he told the Duke, they were acting more in deference to the views of the British and French Governments than to their own judgement.[41] After letting London know of this one qualification, Raglan never again allowed any doubt or difficulty to weaken his determination to mount an invasion. On at least two occasions in the following six weeks, Saint-Arnaud was to look for a way of escape from an enterprise which filled him with foreboding. But not Lord Raglan: he had long believed that what was resolved must he accomplished. In that simple and dutiful personal philosophy lay his strength and his weakness.

CHAPTER SIX

'When's the Fighting Going to Begin?'

The British public lionized its first hero of 'the War with Russia' long before the shooting started. Vice-Admiral Sir Charles Napier – 'Mad Charlie', 'Black Charley', cousin of '*Peccavi*' Napier who conquered Sind, kinsman of the Laird Napier who invented logarithms – was one of those officer eccentrics whose vanity condemns them to success. Although a strict disciplinarian, he was personally casual over the wearing of regulation uniform, quarrelsome and ambitious. Other flag-officers never liked him, but he cut a good figure with the public, affecting a quarter-deck jauntiness to recall old acts of initiative and daring.

Of these, as even Napier's personal enemies admitted, there were many in nearly a half-century afloat. He had chased French privateers off the West Indies, commanded a Mediterranean frigate in the afterglow of Trafalgar, and, in 1814, fought his way up Chesapeake Bay to attack Baltimore. After losing a fortune pioneering a steamship service on the Seine, he captured Lisbon and won a victory off Cape St Vincent while fighting for 'the liberties of Portugal' in a civil war. Back in the Royal Navy once more in 1838–40 he won Palmerston's backing in the Levant by defiant independence of a conventionally-minded commander-in-chief. 'I hope the "Nelson touch" will not be necessary,' Sir James Graham wrote to the Foreign Secretary from Balmoral in the autumn of 1853, 'but if unhappily it should be so, Charles Napier is the Boy to advocate it.' By an odd coincidence, 'the Boy' (aged sixty-seven) was, on that same day, assuring a public meeting that, if he held command at sea, 'instead of reviewing a grand fleet at Spithead, I would treat the Russians to the old Nelson trick in the Baltic'. On the following Saturday *The Illustrated London News* was circulating Napier's remarks to a hundred thousand homes.[1]

'Most men of sixty are too old for dash and enterprise', a flag-officer on half-pay had written anonymously three years before, as he surveyed critically 'the Present State of the Navy'.[2] Now, in 1853, that same flag-officer was eagerly campaigning to lead a fleet into the unfamiliar waters of northern Europe. 'I held out to him only a distant prospect of a possible command of a Baltic Fleet, and he rushes at once to the last extremity of warlike conclusions', Graham told Clarendon after meeting Napier at the end of the first week in December.[3] By Christmas 'Black Charley' had the backing of *The Times*. Some members of the cabinet, notably Russell, needed to be convinced that there was no younger admiral, competent and more responsive to government control; but the First Lord of the Admiralty reassured them. Later, when bitter disputes separated the two men, Graham encouraged the accepted belief that he had recommended the Admiral against his better judgement, but from his surviving papers for the winter of 1853–4 it is clear that he had high hopes of Napier. Only in a tactful letter to ensure the approval of the Queen and her consort to the appointment of a seaman who 'on shore has', through his speeches, 'given just cause of complaint' is there a hint of apologetic reluctance. And, even then, Graham was also concerned with explaining the reasons why the cabinet passed over the claims of that 'adventurous spirit' but 'uncontrollable' gallant officer, Admiral Lord Dundonald, who was aged seventy-nine.[4]

'If you have not entire confidence in the strength of the combined forces of France and England, you had better say so to me at once, and decline to accept command!' the First Lord told Napier; but the exclamation mark indicates the response he anticipated.[5] The appointment to the Baltic command was made public on 15 February 1854. There followed a fortnight of extraordinary adulation. As a geographical concept, the Baltic was better known to the British people than the Black Sea: ships had sailed regularly in the summer months from British ports to Riga and St Petersburg for more than 120 years, and Tsar Peter's island citadel of Kronstadt had first aroused concern at the Admiralty half a century before Catherine the Great approved plans for the building of Sebastopol. When Admiral Napier was reported as saying, 'Within a month of entering the Baltic I shall be in Kronstadt, or in Heaven', people knew what he meant. His mood was echoed in a warning jingle addressed to the Tsar and published on the first weekend in March:

> Ere you feel the summer breezes,
> You may thank your lucky stars
> If you do not yield to Napier,
> And his gallant Jack Tars.[6]

The Admiral was feasted at a Reform Club banquet in Pall Mall on Tuesday, 7 March, with the Home Secretary in the chair. 'I never saw a man in my life who calculated so many moves before hand as Sir Charles Napier', Palmerston declared as he toasted the guest of honour. In reply, Napier pointed out that 'we are still in a state of peace', but he hoped that when he reached the Baltic 'I shall have an opportunity of declaring war'. Sir James Graham thereupon assured 'the gallant Admiral on my left' that 'I, as the First Lord of the Admiralty, give him my full consent to do so.'[7]

These speeches excited comment. On the following Monday Fitzstephen French, the Radical member for Roscommon, challenged the First Lord's remarks in the Commons. Graham's response, doubting if any MP might 'put down a question with respect to what passed after dinner at the Reform Club', angered John Bright. Such 'reckless levity', he complained, was 'discreditable to the grave and responsible statesmen of a civilised and Christian nation'. There were angry exchanges: Palmerston mocked both Bright and Cobden; and Disraeli sought to laugh off the whole affair. But it was Bright who won the day. 'I heard Bright say everything I thought', his old political adversary Macaulay noted; and, in Dublin, Father John Henry Newman pasted a copy of the Quaker dissenter's speech into a scrapbook. There was still a public conscience, after all.[8]

By the time of these Commons exchanges, Napier was already at sea. The first of the 'terrible squadrons' which, the reading public was told, would 'swamp the Baltic' left the Solent on Saturday, 11 March. That morning Victoria Pier, Portsmouth, was 'literally black with struggling people' eager to catch a glimpse of the Admiral as he embarked; 'the water was thronged with craft of all kinds' and, at Southsea, 'as far as the eye could reach, the shores were covered with spectators'. From the royal yacht *Fairy* the Queen and Prince Albert saw 'our noble fleet', manned by 9,390 seamen and marines, 'passing us close by and giving us three hearty cheers'. A privileged reporter, dropping astern of the flagship as she sailed into open seas, 'saw the Admiral pacing the stern-galley outside his cabin'.[9]

If Napier was deep in thought that afternoon, it is hardly surprising. Great things were expected of him. 'We have a deuce of a job in hand . . . with a raw squadron to attack an efficient fleet in their own waters', he told Captain Paget of the *Princess Royal* a few days earlier in a moment of realism. But, as Paget later recalled, 'by the time he had finished half a dozen cigars, he had informed me of such bloodthirsty resolves that . . . I slept little that night'.[10] A more experienced officer sensed the emptiness behind Napier's bombast. On the Sunday before the Reform Club banquet, Napier called on the last surviving commander who had served with the Royal Navy in the Baltic during the Napoleonic Wars. The octogenarian Admiral Sir Byam Martin was astonished to find Napier ignorant of what were to him elementary navigational hazards in the inland northern seas: 'Try by every means to tempt or persuade the Russian fleet to come out and meet ours in deep water, but even in that case be prepared for great annoyance from the gunboats which are numerous and heavily armed', Sir Byam advised Napier. So disturbed was Sir Byam that he prepared 'a memorandum while the conversation is fresh in my recollection' and sent it to the Admiralty. Of the Baltic fleet's chosen commander, he wrote, 'It was clear to me that he was by no means at ease, but on the contrary very nervous'.[11]

When war was declared, Napier's flagship, the *Duke of Wellington*, was already with the main fleet off Kiel; and on that day the First Lord of the Admiralty felt sufficiently in command of events to give the Foreign Secretary an unsolicited lesson in grand strategy. 'We have Napier in the right place at the right time', Graham wrote to Clarendon. 'In concert with France we must make every effort to reinforce him; and neither ships nor troops ought to be wanting. If we can drive Sweden into line, we shall press the Czar much nearer home than on the Danube; and more decisive results may be obtained in the Baltic and with greater ease than in the Black Sea. The northern allies are of better stuff than your Mahometans . . . I am eager in the Baltic cause.' And again, four days later, in a second letter to Clarendon, Graham declared: 'My hopes rest on Sweden.'[12]

Soon Lord John Russell and Palmerston were following Graham's lead, hoping that the Swedes would supply troops to support Napier. Palmerston favoured a promise to Sweden of the retrocession of Finland, thus weakening the Tsar's Empire 'for the future security of Europe'; but Russell wanted no offer of a 'bribe' to the Swedes, declaring that 'they must take the fortune of war'. Aberdeen and Gladstone were unenthusiastic, the Chancellor of the Exchequer preferring a subsidy offered to Austria rather than Sweden. The debate within the cabinet over inducements for Sweden dragged on and on throughout the brief Baltic campaigning season of long summer days and ice-free ports.[13]

In France, too, there was great interest in the Baltic, with the Emperor as eager for a Swedish alliance as Graham. Napoleon III made much of the dynastic associations linking Paris and Stockholm. The reigning sovereign, Oscar I, was a son of King Charles XIV John (formerly Marshal Bernadotte) and of Queen Desideria (Desirée Clary, General Bonaparte's 'first love'), who was still alive. Moreover he was married to Napoleon III's first cousin, Josephine de Beau-harnais. King Oscar even owed his unusual regnal name to the whim of his godfather, the great Napoleon, who had encountered it in his favourite reading, an Italian translation of the legends of Ossian. It is not surprising that, as soon as war was declared, Napoleon III made secret approaches to Oscar to tempt Sweden into the war. But Oscar prided himself on his statecraft: he was on amiable terms with Tsar Nicholas, with whom his wife had ties of kinship; he was reluctant to rekindle dying antagonisms by reviving Swedish rule over the Finns; and he possessed all the old Bernadotte family instinct for good diplomatic timing. In London and Paris Oscar seemed exasperatingly devious: 'The King of Sweden appears to be rather shy of our Ministers and entirely to distrust his own', Lord Aberdeen commented in a note to Clarendon.[14] From the allies Oscar sought a subsidy, an assurance of worthwhile territorial gains, and a guarantee that Austria, too, would enter the war against Russia. And, as a first step towards Sweden's entry into the war, he looked for some sign that Napier's 44 ships and 2,200 guns were capable of triumphs more dramatic than the successful enforcement of a blockade. This was not forthcoming.

The odyssey of the Baltic Fleet in 1854 is no epic of naval history. At the outset, for some three weeks, the campaign promised well. Russia's warships and merchantmen were closely confined in the Gulfs of Bothnia, Riga and Finland, there was no danger of a Russian sally into the North Sea, and Napier seemed poised 'to undertake the hostile operations' left impressively vague in his formal orders from the Admiralty. It was assumed that he would attack one or more of the four key fortresses: the island citadel of Sveaborg, off Helsinki; Bomarsund, in the Aaland Islands, protecting the town now known as Maarian-hamina; the much weaker Estonian fortified port of Reval (now Tallinn); and, most important of all, the citadel of Kronstadt, two hundred miles up the Gulf of Finland. It was left to the Admiral's 'abilities and judgement' to select his objective. Along the coast from St Petersburg to Peterhof the Russians daily expected to see the masts of allied warships through the summer haze.[15]

At the end of April Sir James Graham admitted to Clarendon 'an apprehension . . . sometimes felt that Napier may be driven for fear of the Press into some rash act of desperate daring, which may lead to a great disaster'; and he added, 'I shall endeavour to counteract this dangerous tendency'.[16] He need not have worried. Napier had no intention of risking vessels in waters so shallow that they might run aground within range of fortresses bristling with artillery. Sveaborg and Helsinki, Napier informed Graham in late May, were 'unattackable by sea or Land'; he said nothing of Kronstadt.[17] Meanwhile Russian gunboats beat off assaults on the small forts of Hangö and Abö, the British contenting themselves with raids on fishing settlements on both sides of the Baltic. By midsummer *The Times* was printing accounts from Sweden of hardships inflicted by Napier's men on the small communities along the Gulf of Bothnia and around Abö: 'One shriek of woe sounds all through Finland', a correspondent reported. But when, in the Commons, the Manchester radical Milner Gibson protested at the navy's activities, Graham maintained that Napier's squadrons had every right to search and destroy enemy vessels and harbours so long as the Russian Baltic fleet declined to come out and give battle at sea.[18]

It is not surprising if Gibson's humanitarianism received rough treatment in the Commons, for the House had even failed to respond to John Bright's noble speech condemning the war at its very outset. The British public accepted the coming of war as a dutiful obligation. When a 'National Day of Fast and Humiliation' was proclaimed on Wednesday, 26 April, Bright was affronted by what he considered a spectacle of mass hypocrisy, 'much like a gang of burglars seeking the Divine blessing upon their guilty enterprises'.[19] But few agreed with him. Churches, chapels and synagogues were full throughout the land; and Thursday's *Times* devoted four pages of small print to details of the sermons preached in 119 London parishes, 10 other places of worship in the capital, and selected cathedrals and minsters elsewhere. The Dean of St Paul's chose as his text the first verse of Psalm 71: 'In thee, O Lord, do I put my trust: let me never be put to confusion'. Nine weeks before, in a letter to his aunt in the Netherlands, the Tsarevich had selected that same passage, assuring her that, as 'in 1812', it was 'the prayer that every Russian heart pronounces'.[20]

By June in 1854 the mood of anticipatory elation which had gripped the British public in the spring was giving way to impatient criticism of the Government, inside and outside Parliament. Ministers were not waging war vigorously; some, notably Lord Aberdeen, were believed to be hankering after an armistice. The Prime Minister was attacked, in particular, for defending the reputation of the Tsar in the House of Lords against accusations of perfidy and the planning of a war of aggression. So indignant were Lord John Russell's London constituents that they petitioned the Lord Mayor to summon a meeting at the Guildhall to press for a resolute prosecution of the war. Russell warned the Prime Minister privately that 'the position of the Government has become precarious'. And in the last week of June, *Punch*, suspecting that Russell was prodding the Prime Minister, published a full-page cartoon depicting Aberdeen and Lord John as laundresses around a tub; the smaller washerwoman, Joanna, turns to the larger and asks, 'When's the fighting going to begin, Georgeana?'[21]

For the moment it looked as if the answer might soon come from the Baltic, after all. Napoleon III was anxious for a success in northern waters, hoping that Sweden could still be encouraged to join the allies. A formidable army was concentrated around Boulogne to await transport in British vessels to the Baltic. Meanwhile Admiral Deschenes, who as a fifteen-year-old *aspirant* (midshipman) had served aboard the French flagship at Trafalgar, brought a squadron of fourteen vessels to join the British fleet in mid-June. On 20 June Admiral Napier felt able to inform their Lordships of the Admiralty that 'the steam-squadron under my command . . . will sail tomorrow or the following day for Cronstadt, in company with the French Admiral and six of the line'; but, in a private letter to Sir James Graham, Napier indicated that he had little hope of the Russians coming out and accepting the challenge of a naval battle. He also thought it unlikely that he would be able to get close to Kronstadt itself.[22]

Twenty-two allied vessels duly sailed into the Gulf of Finland and took up positions south of Kronstadt on 26 June; and, from the balcony of a waterside villa near the palace of Peterhof, 'the entire enemy fleet was clearly visible' to the imperial family 'for several days'. Napier reconnoitred the fortress carefully before reporting back to London that 'the difficulties of approach are great' and that any assault 'appears to me, with our means, perfectly impossible'. He thought, however, that the citadel might be attacked from the rear – provided that an army was first landed on the coast to seize St Petersburg itself. Napier also reported that Captain Hall in the small steam-vessel *Hecla* had bombarded Bomarsund on 21 June and he commended the courage of the steamship's mate, Charles Lucas, who had picked up and thrown overboard a fused and live shell which had fallen on deck. At the same time Napier added that he was reprimanding Captain Hall for his assault on Bomarsund since he had chosen 'to throw away all his shot and shell against stone walls'.[23] By contrast, Napier's formidable allied squadron left the waters between Peterhof and Kronstadt on 4 July, without a shot being fired. This cautious fleet commander was not the legendary 'Black Charley' whose forthcoming triumphs the Reform Club had celebrated four months before.

Napier's report from off Kronstadt reached the Admiralty on 10 July. Next day he was assured that the Lords Commissioners had every confidence in him and ordered to look for other points where the enemy 'may be more vulnerable'. Already Graham had suggested that a landing might be made in the Aaland Islands so as to capture and demolish Bomarsund. It was essential to make good use of 9,000 French troops who were to sail from Calais at the end of the week, watched by their Emperor in person.[24] But Graham, Palmerston and other members of the Government all recognized that Kronstadt, like Sebastopol, was the name that counted with newspaper readers in the country as a whole; and it was therefore with particular interest that the First Lord studied a memorandum sent to him by the retired Admiral Lord Dundonald, soon after the news was made public that the allied warships were sailing back down the Gulf of Finland.

Thomas Cochrane, tenth Earl of Dundonald, was the son of a Scottish peer who lost his personal wealth by indulging a scientific curiosity for chemical experiment. Cochrane, like Napier, had shown great enterprise as a captain in the Mediterranean during the Napoleonic Wars, but he fell foul of authority for criticizing naval administration and was imprisoned for twelve months in 1815 on a dubious charge of fraud, for which he was dismissed from the service and deprived of a knighthood and a seat in the Commons. His reputation was made in South American waters: he commanded the Chilean navy in 1817 and the Brazilian navy six years later. By 1827 he was founder-admiral of the Greek navy, though with less spectacular success. Eventually, during Sir James Graham's first period of office at the Admiralty, Cochrane secured his reinstatement in the Royal Navy, receiving a free pardon in 1832, ten months after he succeeded his father in the earldom; and sixteen years later he became commander-in-chief of the squadron in the Atlantic, 'the North American station'.

Among Cochrane's earlier exploits was an attack on the French fleet in Aix Roads in April 1809, using fireships and vessels filled with high explosive, and in the winter of 1811–12 he proposed to the Admiralty experiments with a primitive form of poison gas. It was this project which Dundonald elaborated in July, 1854, sending to Graham what he described as 'a simple yet effective plan of operations showing that the maritime defences of Kronstadt (however strong against ordinary means) may be captured and their red hot shot and incendiaries, prepared for the destruction of our ships, turned on those they protect'. Dundonald proposed, in the first place, that a landing be made by allied troops under cover of 'smoke vapours more obscure than the darkest night'. The smoke screen would be laid by specially modified shallow-draught steamers and would 'conceal the ships from the batteries until they arrive at a proper position for beaching'. At a later stage 'sulphurous craft' would belch out fumes which would overwhelm the defenders of Kronstadt and, carried on a prevailing westerly wind, would also cause panic among the citizens of St Petersburg itself, sixteen miles away. Dundonald added that he was prepared to embark for the Baltic and serve there in any capacity to supervise preparations for the use of this secret weapon.[25]

Graham at once referred Dundonald's plan to Admiral Sir Byam Martin, whom he invited to preside over a committee which would evaluate the project. Martin, whose health was poor, consulted the army's Inspector-General of Fortifications, Sir John Fox Burgoyne, who had returned from Turkey in April. The General, however, was a traditionalist, with little liking for new-fangled weapons of war, and he did not rate the chances of success highly; Burgoyne was especially concerned over the fate of assault troops should the wind suddenly change. Martin then turned for advice to the most eminent British scientist of his day, Professor Michael Faraday, at the Royal Institution. On 7 August Faraday confirmed that Dundonald's proposals were 'correct in theory': 'dense smoke will hide objects'; 'burning sulphur will provide fumes . . . able to render men involved in them incapable of action, or even to kill them'. But he reminded Admiral Martin that 'defenders could provide respirators' if 'they thought it was coming'. Martin's committee were troubled by what they considered the inhumane character of Dundonald's proposals; but, before the committee could reach a decision, its president was taken gravely ill and died in October. The icing up of the Baltic and the consequent retirement of the allied fleet enabled the Admiralty, with some relief, to shelve the Dundonald project. Chemical warfare was not to their liking.

When next Dundonald offered his plan, almost exactly a year later, a different government was in office and it was Fort Malakoff that he wished to destroy.[26]

While the Martin Committee was considering Dundonald's secret weapon, Napier and Deschenes were at last able to give the allies their one success of the year in the Baltic. A combined sea and land assault was launched against Bomarsund, the 'Gibraltar of the Aaland Islands', on 9 August. A force of three thousand Frenchmen was landed four miles south of Bomarsund and another detachment of the French, supported by British marines, engineers and gunners, went ashore at a cove two miles to the north, so as to invest the fortress. By dawn on Sunday, 13 August, the French had several 16-pounder guns in position and were shelling the town, while four British vessels and the French flagship engaged the outer defences. Next day the French suffered the only serious casualties of the operation, when they occupied Fort Tzee, the westernmost tower of the citadel, only to find that it had been heavily mined and blew up beneath them. A battery of British 32-pounders was ready to breach the walls of the inner defences (Fort Nottich) but by Tuesday evening it was clear that the citadel would not need to be stormed. On Wednesday morning – 16 August, a day on which *The Times* in London informed its readers of the formidable defences of this bastion of the Aaland Islands – Napier ordered seven of his ships to turn their 10-inch guns on the centre of the fortress, with the injunction, 'Give them a shot and shell every five minutes'. The weight of fire-power from the ships and from the British and French shore batteries proved too much for the defenders. White flags of truce were flown from the casements and by the early afternoon more than two thousand of the garrison, almost all of whom were Finnish, had passed into allied captivity, together with many of their families.[27]

Thanks to the use of the electric telegraph from Danzig, the fall of Bomarsund became known in London and Paris by Saturday. Its significance was inflated by the newspapers so that the public could celebrate the victory for which they had waited ever since 'the finest fleet that has left these shores' had sailed from Spithead in March. 'The capture of Bomarsund and the eighty inhabited islands of the Aaland Archipelago . . . is not meant to be a mere lash of the whip, but a mortal thrust', *The Illustrated London News* declared on 26 August; and there followed more than a week of detailed reports of the engagement and speculation on where Napier would strike next. As late as 4 September a leading article in *The Times* assumed that news would soon come of other assaults around Russia's Baltic shore.[28]

On that same Monday, however, the Admiralty sent a peremptory note to Napier asking for information over 'what further operations' he proposed to undertake. For the Admiralty and the War Office were puzzled by Napier's movements. Two senior soldiers serving in the Baltic, Brigadier-General H. D. Jones and General Adolphe Niel, were known by their respective governments to favour an immediate attack on Sveaborg. Napier, on the other hand, was behaving as though the campaigning season was over, while assuring Sir James Graham that 'the French are all in a hurry to get home as fast as they can'. Mistrust of Napier grew rapidly on both sides of the Channel. On the following Thursday the Prince Consort, in France to observe army manoeuvres around Boulogne with Napoleon III, compained that Napier 'pours cold water' on aggressive plans in the Gulf of Finland; and at the end of the week a second broadside from the Admiralty ordered Napier to convene a council of war to consider an attack on Sveaborg before the coming of winter. At the same time the Prime Minister wrote indignantly to Sir James Graham, stressing the importance of Sveaborg and the difficulty of justifying 'to the world' any decision not to attack the Finnish fortress.[29]

But Napier, having gained a victory at Bomarsund, would not risk defeat in front of Helsinki. A council of war, meeting aboard his flagship on 12 September, decided that 'nothing can be undertaken . . . with a chance of success' at such an 'advanced state of the year'. 'I have received many propositions for attacking both Cronstadt and Sveaborg', Napier told the Admiralty, 'but I will never lend myself to any absurd project, or be driven to attempt what is not practicable, by newspaper writers who, I am sorry to say, I have reason to believe are in correspondence with officers of the fleet, who ought to know better.'[30] Three weeks after telling its readers of the 'mortal thrust' at Bomarsund, *The Illustrated London News* was admitting that 'the prevailing impression seems to be that the Baltic campaign is at an end for the season'. And six weeks later still the same journal, whose rhyming couplets had in the spring warned the Tsar of Napier and his 'gallant Jack Tars', was writing scornfully of how

> 'The Baltic fleet, with fifty thousand men,
> Sailed up the seas – and then sailed home again'.[31]

It is easy to understand the Government's frustration in those first days of September. Parliament had gone into recess on 14 August in an angry mood, with attacks in both houses on the Prime Minister personally and on the failure of his Administration to wage the war effectively. In private Lord Palmerston was bitterly critical of Aberdeen's apparent reluctance to weaken 'Russia anywhere or at all', while the Prime Minister complained that he was receiving little verbal support in the Commons or the cabinet from fellow Peelites like Graham and Gladstone. His letters show that he was close to a nervous breakdown. Granite willpower alone kept him in office; Queen and Country must be saved from the Whig warlords.[32]

News from overseas remained uninspiring. Apart from the capture of Bomarsund there was little to lift patriotic hearts: a blockade of Russia's northern White Sea ports, including Archangel, and a succession of setbacks for the Turks in the Caucasus. Newspaper reports suggested that the war had spread as far as the North Pacific but, as yet, no details were known. Some Russian vessels – including the frigate *Aurora*, whose presence in Portsmouth had caused so much disquiet nine months before – had put into Valparaiso, heading for Petropavlosk, the Tsar's Far Eastern naval base on the peninsula of Kamchatka. It was said that they were being followed northwards from Honolulu by an Anglo-French flotilla commanded by Rear-Admiral David Price, but that several sailing days separated pursuer and pursued. In fact, however, at that very moment, the flotilla was facing defeat. Price's six vessels reached Petropavlovsk on 29 August. Next morning, as an assault on the base was about to begin, the Rear-Admiral went below to his cabin and shot himself, apparently in remorse at not having caught the Russian vessels before they reached their heavily protected anchorage. Inevitably this personal tragedy hampered inter-allied collaboration. The subsequent attack on Petropavlovsk was a disaster, with the British accidentally shelling a French landing party, while a second party was ambushed by a powerful Russian force. The flotilla withdrew on 5 September. Fortunately it took months for news of this defeat in the North Pacific to reach London.[33]

There was equally little cause for the Anglo-French allies to be satisfied with their diplomatic achievements. By the first week in September earlier hopes of bringing Sweden and Austria into the war were rapidly receding. The Swedes, knowing that any hostile move against Russia might soon expose them to an invading army across the frozen northern wastes, showed no interest in an allied offer of the

Aaland Islands. But it was Buol in Vienna who most exasperated the British and French Governments. For, in July, Buol had played a prominent part in drafting the 'Four Points', a definition of allied diplomatic objectives whose presentation to the Russians would, it was assumed in London and Paris, serve as a preliminary to Austrian participation in the war: a European guarantee of the Danubian Principalities, rather than a Russian protectorate over them; free navigation of the Danube; revision of the 1841 Straits Convention, so that movement of warships through the Dardanelles and Bosphorus would be regulated 'in the interests of the Balance of Power in Europe'; and Russian renunciation of any claim to exercise a protectorate over the Sultan's Christian subjects.[34]

These 'Four Points' were, however, soon to become not the basis of an Austrian ultimatum, but a mere programme of war aims. In August Buol found that non-belligerency brought Austria a fine reward, making the Habsburg Empire the first beneficiary from the war, for after the Russians withdrew north of the river Pruth an Austrian diplomatic initiative in Constantinople secured the Sultan's consent to an agreement by which Francis Joseph's army should move into the Danubian Principalities. Austrian forces immediately occupied Moldavia and Wallachia, thereby consolidating effective control over all the navigable Danube and creating a neutral buffer zone between the Balkans and the Ukraine. Despite pressure from a war party in Vienna and some discussion of military plans between top Austrian soldiers and the allied commanders at Varna, the Emperor Francis Joseph repeatedly assured the Tsar's envoys that he would never attack Russia. In these assertions he was perfectly sincere: for the Habsburg Empire was wracked by a chronic financial crisis; even the cost of preventive mobilization and of moving troops into the Danubian Principalities left the Austrian Finance Minister convinced that bankruptcy lay only a few months away. The best hope for the allies in making common cause with Austria against Russia lay in Nicholas I's furious temper, for when the Austrians began to garrison Danubian towns so recently vacated by his army, Nesselrode and Orlov had difficulty in persuading the Tsar not to send Francis Joseph an ultimatum which he had already drafted in his own hand. Relations between St Petersburg and Vienna had not been so strained for forty years.[35]

In London and Paris, too, government ministers complained of Habsburg trickery. Austria would deserve no consideration at the eventual peace conference, since Buol was freeing Gorchakov's 50,000 men to fight elsewhere, Russell told Clarendon. But, on reflection, both Palmerston and Russell saw advantages in the Austrian move into the Principalities, for they had always feared that Lord Aberdeen would either use Buol as an intermediary 'to agree to a suspension of hostilities' before the allies had achieved any of their objectives or commit himself to having 'our troops . . . die of fever in the marshes of Wallachia'.[36] Now the options facing the British Government were narrowed. There would be no campaigning along the lower Danube or the Pruth; nor could there be a winter war in the Baltic. Everything must depend on what was being settled at allied headquarters in Varna. 'If our expedition to the Crimea sets out, it is sure to succeed', Palmerston told Clarendon on 5 September, 'and if it succeeds, we are sure to have Austria with us.'[37] But, by then, more than nine weeks had already passed since the 'sleeping cabinet' at Richmond had approved the orders for an assault on the Crimea, and there was no word that the allied force had sailed from the Bulgarian coast. What if Sebastopol proved as elusive an objective as Sveaborg and Kronstadt? Still Mr Punch's washerwomen could ask each other, 'When's the fighting going to begin?'; and still no one in the Government could give a confident answer.

CHAPTER SEVEN

The Allied Armada

Uncertainty over what was happening at Varna made Lord Aberdeen's ministers carpingly critical of the commanders in the field. The French leaders fared worst, especially Saint-Arnaud: Palmerston wondered how 'a man who has passed his Early Life as an actor could all of a sudden become a great General'; and Clarendon thought he 'ought to be hung' for ordering three of his best divisions northwards into the disease-ridden Dobrudja in response to faulty intelligence reports of a new Russian crossing of the Danube. The Duke of Newcastle, the Secretary of State for War, shared his colleagues' contempt for Saint-Arnaud. But the frustration of having to remain in town after Parliament rose in August made him doubt the qualities of the British Commander-in-Chief as well. Newcastle could not forget that Raglan had spent most of the last quarter of a century in Whitehall, first as military secretary to Wellington and recently as Master-General of the Ordnance. 'I fear Raglan is but seldom seen,' he wrote to Clarendon at the end of August. 'I wish he would devote less time to his desk and more to his saddle, but long use at the Horse Guards has made his fingers tough and his bottom tender.' A week later, with some inconsistency, Newcastle was grumbling to the Prime Minister of the 'singularly meagre' character of the letters Raglan sent home from that over-burdened desk at headquarters.[1]

Such cavilling was unjustified. It minimized the formidable task imposed on Raglan and Saint-Arnaud. They had to improvise the invasion of a peninsula 300 miles across the sea, geographically unfamiliar to them, and defended by an enemy whose strength might be as low as 45,000 or as high as 140,000 men. Anxiously they awaited assessment from their informal planning committee, who sailed for Crimean waters in the fourth week of July aboard HMS *Fury*. It was as dawn was breaking on 25 July that the frigate crept into the approaches to Sebastopol; and in the clear, early morning sunshine Generals Canrobert and Brown studied the fortifications in detail before the defenders opened fire, forcing *Fury* to raise steam and sail off northwards. There the two generals noted good landing-places around the mouths of the Katcha and the Alma rivers, about seven and fifteen miles respectively from Sebastopol itself. The planning committee was back in Varna for a conference at Saint-Arnaud's headquarters on 28 July; and it was still hoped, on that Friday evening, to embark the expeditionary force of some 64,000 French, British and Turkish troops for the Crimea within a fortnight.[2]

This date was totally unrealistic. Already disaster was striking at the heart of the allied force. In a letter to his brother on 13 July Saint-Arnaud mentioned, almost casually, that he had a few cases of cholera in the army. By the end of that week a rush of cholera cases was overwhelming the French field hospitals; soon the disease was ravaging both armies. The French high command had known, as early as the first week in July, that there were over a hundred cases in the reception camp outside Gallipoli. But, for several weeks, the generals at Varna insisted that the awful scourge was spreading southwards; some even wondered if it was the reason why the Russians had broken off the siege of Silistria, for General Luders's corps was known to have suffered from the disease. The fate of the French force which Saint-Arnaud despatched to the Dobrudja, the region lying between the Danube and the Black Sea, seemed to confirm this source. On a march which lasted for almost three weeks, only two Cossack raiding parties were sighted, too distant to be engaged; but, from the second day out, the Dobrudja force suffered heavy casualties, all of them from cholera or typhus. Within a week the French 1st Division (commanded, in Canrobert's absence, by General Espinasse) had 5,000 cases, one-third of them fatal.[3]

'It is almost beyond belief that of the 3 divisions the French sent towards the Dobrudja, 7000 have died of cholera and putrid fever,' Lord Aberdeen's son, Alexander, wrote to his father from a camp west of Varna on 10 August. 'Seven thousand! A pleasant country to make war in! One regiment alone buried 760 in the lake near Kustendij.' And the news of the British expeditionary force was little better: 'Preparations are being made for our embarking on the 12th. The bay is full of shipping for transport, all victualled and watered, but I cannot think we shall go to Sebastopol to undertake the greatest siege ever attempted at the end of the summer, typhus fever and dysentery in our camp . . . You seem to think we are on the Danube. I wish we were . . . Even now it is not too late to get to Bucharest this winter if we set to work.'[4] But long before the Prime Minister received this grimly realistic letter, all London knew of the cholera's mounting toll in the British camps. 'It is useless to alarm friends and relations at home by talking of the number of sick or by giving their names, but it is evident that we are in a very unsatisfactory state as regards health', wrote the great war reporter, W.H. Russell, in a despatch sent from Varna six days before Alexander Gordon's letter and published in *The Times* of 18 August. A few days later Russell gave 'friends and relations at home' what was presumably a message of mild comfort: 'The cholera ... is sometimes quite painless, there is little or no purging but the sufferer is seized with violent spasms in the stomach, which increase in intensity till collapse is established, and death then quickly follows, attended with but little exhibition of agony.'[5]

Cholera epidemics were not uncommon in continental Europe during prolonged hot weather: hundreds died each day in Paris during the summer months of 1848 and, a little over a year later, Paskevich's invading army suffered gravely from an outbreak in Hungary. Radical reformers in Parliament had sought to clean up insalubrious areas in Britain's sprawling cities ever since the epidemics of the 1830s; and Lord Aberdeen's Government could by now regard cholera as an occasional unwelcome visitor. In general, the health of the British soldiery was better than a decade earlier, and they had fewer cholera cases than their French allies. But some battalions in Raglan's army suffered severely. On 10 August, the day that Alexander Gordon wrote to his father, the Coldstream Guards lost eighty men from cholera. Other letters home mentioned regiments 'more than decimated' in the course of the month. Most units struck camp in the valley of Devna, since it was assumed that all water there was contaminated. They trekked inland, away from Varna where nearly 30,000 men were concentrated in a vast mushroom field of canvas – but away, too, from the transports waiting to embark the great invasion force. Mrs Fanny Duberly, whose husband was a captain in the 8th Hussars, later vividly recalled how, in the last days of July, Lord Cardigan marched the Light Brigade twenty-six miles to the bare and treeless plateau of Yenibazar under a 'blinding sun' and 'intolerable heat' when, as another cavalryman wrote, in a letter home, the thermometer was 'seldom below 90° in the shade, and often much higher'. Tragically the cholera kept pace with the Light Brigade; and within days of reaching Yenibazar sick and dying Hussars and Lancers were filling two huge hospital marquees. 'There are no comforts but scanty medical stores, and the burning blistering sun glares upon heads already delirious with fever', Mrs Duberly noted in her journal. The principal medical officer in the 11th Hussars persuaded the imperceptive Cardigan to forbid further renderings of the 'Dead March in Saul', as falling morale was lowering the resistance of men capable of recovery. At night Lancers kept at bay wild dogs eager to snatch bodies from hastily dug shallow graves.[6]

It was not only the army that suffered. The disease spread alarmingly through the densely packed lower decks of the warships anchored at Balchik Bay, a few miles north of Varna. Many vessels put to sea, hoping to get away from an insalubrious anchorage. But Admiral Dundas's flagship, HMS *Britannia*, had some four hundred cases of cholera while cruising for three days between Varna and the Straits; and over a hundred bodies were thrown over the side, with the most perfunctory burial rites.[7] In five weeks cholera and typhus cost the British and French forces on the Bulgarian coast 10,000 casualties, reducing their effective strength in the field by about one-sixth. And all this without the Russian enemy ever once giving a belligerent's twist to the screw of horror.

On the evening of that same 10 August on which Lord Aberdeen's son had wished his regiment had gone forward to the Danube, Varna was afflicted by the second chronic scourge of campaigning in Eastern Europe. There was a strong inshore wind that Thursday, blowing sand and dust through the improvised bars and cafes which were springing up in the lower part of the little town. At seven in the evening, as Saint-Arnaud was riding back from visits to the hospitals, he saw a column of smoke rising from one of the narrower streets; soon the whole quarter was on fire. As at Smolensk and Moscow in 1812 and Salonika in 1917, the French authorities claimed that enemy agents had started the blaze, which they believed flared up 'in four places at once', and a senior British officer told his wife, with approval, that the French had bayoneted to death five Greeks thought to have been arsonists. But, despite rumours which spread through the camps, the fire seems to have begun in a shop used by the French as a liquor store and may well have been started by a drunken soldier knocking over an oil lamp. After several rainless weeks the low, wooden buildings – many of them little more than shanties – were tinder dry; and for five hours Varna blazed like a copse caught in a bush fire. Such allied encampments and hospitals as remained in the vicinity of Varna were not themselves in danger, for they stood on higher ground, away from the town. But at one moment sparks threatened the three powder magazines – Turkish, French and British – which were placed thoughtlessly close to each other, near the waterfront. Seamen from the vessels off-shore fought the flames throughout the night. 'Ten times I was near despair', Marshal Saint-Arnaud wrote to his wife, back at Yenikoy; but at three in the morning the fire was under control, and by dawn only the embers were smouldering. Lord Raglan was at Balchik Bay with the fleet that night; he returned to find that a warehouse full of boots and a cookhouse full of biscuits had gone up in smoke, and a third of the town lay in ruins.[8]

Although the fire checked preparations for the great invasion, the delay allowed more and more shipments to arrive from Constantinople, with three or four vessels dropping anchor off the Bulgarian beaches each day. Sometimes the steamers brought not merely fresh supplies, but visitors from Britain. On 26 August the indefatigable General Burgoyne returned to the Balkans, having left London at six hours' notice ten days before; and from him Raglan heard at first hand of the mounting anxiety and impatience at Westminster. With the cholera raging so fiercely in Bulgaria, recent reinforcements – including the Scots Greys – were detained at Scutari, ready for direct passage to the invasion beaches of the Crimea. Some distinguished travellers were not encouraged to come to Varna: the archaeologist, diplomat and Whig MP, Henry Layard, reached Constantinople in the first days of September and remained there until he could find a steamer which would enable him to follow the invasion convoy. So, too, did Delane, the Editor of *The Times*. His presence in Varna at that moment would have been embarrassing, for, as W. H. Russell himself wrote on 28 August, there were complaints at headquarters 'that the London journals have done great mischief by publishing . . . correct intelligence respecting our intended movements . . . and preparing the Russians to resist us'.[9] As early as 3 August *The Times* announced that a combined French, British and Turkish army was about to invade the Crimea and lay siege to Sebastopol. Such reports were available for assessment at the General Staff Building in St Petersburg within a week of their appearance in the London press.

Marshal Saint-Arnaud issued a resounding Napoleonic proclamation to his troops on 26 August, promising them that within three weeks the imperial eagle would be flying over the bastions of Sebastopol; and two days later the first French detachments began to embark in the huge armada off the Bulgarian coast. Saint-Arnaud, who was by now dependent on narcotics to relieve the gnawing agony in his stomach, had also contracted a fever in Varna and his staff began to suspect that their commander-in-chief was a dying man. Nevertheless he concentrated his mind on the invasion, telling his wife that he hoped to sail on 2 September; the invasion force would make a feint towards Odessa, assemble at sea between the northern mouth of the Danube and Cape Tarkankhut, and then come down on the Crimea from the north-west. Saint-Arnaud duly boarded the *Ville de Paris* on Saturday, 2 September, only to find that the British were not yet ready.[10]

The French were inclined to scoff at their ally's muddle and mismanagement. On this occasion, however, their scorn was not entirely merited. Although the French infantry contingents out-numbered the British, Raglan had more cavalry and more light artillery; it was difficult to load horses and equipment aboard transports from a small port whose limited facilities had so recently suffered from a major fire. Rafts would bring the horses out to the waiting vessels and the animals were by then so frightened that they lashed out with their hind legs at any seaman or groom seeking to get a sling around their bodies. If there was a ground swell – as on the Sunday morning – this activity became long, slow and painful. Special problems, too, attended the embarkation of officers' wives. Lord Raglan sought to keep Mrs Duberly, Lady Errol and her French maid, and other ladies away from the Crimea, but without success. Cardigan, the commander of the Light Brigade, had come to know Fanny Duberly well at Yenibazar: 'We take wonderful rides with Lord Cardigan, but not often, as I detest him', she had written to her sister, Selina Marx. Now it was Cardigan who told her of Raglan's ban. 'Tired out by the marching and fasting, I burst into a passion of tears', she wrote to Selina before the ships sailed; and Cardigan chivalrously assured her that should she 'think it proper to disregard the prohibition' he would not stand in her way. The challenge to a woman of Fanny Duberly's spirit was irresistible. She was smuggled aboard the *Himalaya* hidden in a baggage boat.[11] Other wives, too, successfully escaped the scrutiny of more dutiful officers and boarded the transports.

At last on 4 September steam tugs began to tow the sailing vessels to join a fleet of 600 ships concentrated in Balchik Bay. Saint-Arnaud, in wretched health and confined to his bunk, ordered the *Ville de Paris* to get under way on Wednesday, but it was not until dawn on Thursday, 7 September, that the firing of three saluting guns aboard the flagship gave the signal for the main invasion fleet to put to sea.[12] A convalescent officer, awaiting later shipment from Varna, watched the convoy head slowly northwards under 'an immense cloud of smoke which extended for many miles'. 'So far as the visible horizon', a senior naval officer later recalled, 'the sea was covered with vessels, half obscured by the smoke of a hundred steamers.' When, on the following morning, the allied warships came together, they could concentrate 3,000 guns on the protection of their convoy. The Russian fleet made no attempt to put to sea and engage the allied armada. Despite Sinope, the overall commander in the Crimea, Prince Menshikov, was reluctant to authorize bold naval sorties. He was confident that his army could expel any invaders who landed near Sebastopol. Not that he believed they would come. Cholera and the Varna fire ruled out the assembling of any invasion force, the Prince wrote to Paskevich and the Tsar. However, 'I remain ready to receive the enemy', he assured St Petersburg.[13]

The allied transports were at sea; but where was their destination? 'Opinions are very much divided whether we are really going to Sebastopol at this season of the year and many think we are going to Odessa for winter quarters', Alexander Gordon wrote to his father soon after embarkation. Colonel Gordon believed that Raglan, who 'very wisely keeps his plans close', intended 'to land 15 miles N. of Sevastopol'; but he added that it would be 'rather hard if it comes on to blow from the N. or NW when we want to land'.[14] This shrewd observation seemed justified on Friday when the wind changed and the sea became rough. With the convoy some thirty miles off Cape Tarkhankut Saint-Arnaud invited Raglan to a council of war. But Raglan, having lost his right arm at Waterloo, could not clamber up the side of a vessel rolling in a heavy swell; nor was Saint-Arnaud fit enough to leave his bunk. This important council, on 8 September, was therefore – apart from the two senior admirals – a gathering of deputies.

Several French commanders were by now opposed to an outright attack on Sebastopol. They therefore proposed sailing southwards around the Crimea to take the enemy by surprise at Theodosia (Kaffa). General Rose, with several years of sifting intelligence reports from this region, had long advocated a landing here. He thought it essential to secure land mastery of the Crimean peninsula before attacking Sebastopol; and two eminent engineer officers, Burgoyne and Brigadier-General Tylden, also favoured a landing at some distance from the formidable fortress, preferably in the east of the peninsula. Theodosia was a hundred miles from Sebastopol, with a direct road to the key fortified inland town of Simferopol. Although it could only offer the seamen open sandy beaches and a small harbour, Theodosia was sheltered from the strong northerly winds. Moreover, since Theodosia enjoyed a milder climate than any town in the west of the peninsula, an army might winter in the vineyard-clustered bay of Kaffa. But other British spokesmen were more sensitive than Rose and Burgoyne to the high expectations held in London: if the name 'Kronstadt' was not to appear triumphantly in the press, then 'Sebastopol' it must be, for 'Theodosia' meant little, except perhaps to donnish clerics lovingly fingering patristic folios. The council of war settled nothing. Saint-Arnaud roused himself and said that he would agree with any decision taken by Raglan. The British Commander-in-Chief soon dismissed all talk of a landing a hundred miles from the expedition's chief objective. He would, he said, cruise down the Sebastopol coast aboard *Caradoc* and choose a landing place in consultation with the allied admirals and generals.[15]

Caradoc's reconnaissance of the coastline on Sunday, 10 September, is a familiar prologue to the Crimean drama; but some details have become confused with the passage of time. It was on Saturday morning – not, as so often said, Sunday – that Admiral Lyons in *Agamemnon* left the main fleet and, supported by a steam frigate and a French corvette, escorted *Caradoc* towards Sebastopol. The flotilla approached the Russian coast overnight until (as Rose noted in his journal) 'a little after 4 a.m. we went on board *Caradoc* to reconnoitre Sebastopol'. Lyons thought that a single vessel so early on a Sunday morning would not arouse undue concern. The flagship therefore remained well out to sea and even the escorts came no closer inshore than three miles. But *Caradoc*, with Generals Raglan, Burgoyne, Brown, Rose, and Canrobert and Admiral Lyons himself aboard, slipped to within 3,000 yards of Fort Constantine, looking formidable on its spit of land to the north of the main harbour. So close inshore was the reconnaissance party that several British officers heard the curious chromatic tintinabulation from the cupolas of the city as Orthodox Russia prepared to observe St Alexander Nevsky's Day. 'We closely examined every part of the coast that the Generals desired to see, approaching sometimes within a few cables' length of the beach', Lyons reported when he rejoined the fleet. 'The fortifications looked of immense strength, and appeared to bristle with guns', wrote Colonel Calthorpe, Raglan's nephew and aide-de-camp. But not a shot was fired. Through telescopes the generals studied the lie of several beaches near to

Sebastopol, but they decided against any landing where the enemy might launch a counter-attack before the troops and their guns were safely ashore. They therefore looked for a low-lying section of coast, within a few days' march of the great naval base. Raglan decided that 'the most eligible spot for the disembarkation of the army' was a beach near a ruined Genoese 'Old Fort', in Calamita Bay, twelve miles south of Eupatoria. Sir George Brown, Canrobert and several other officers would have preferred to land some thirty miles nearer Sebastopol, at the mouth of the river Alma; but, wrote Calthorpe, 'the naval men, both English and French, objected to it, as the bay was far too small for our enormous flotilla'. The Old Fort might be forty-five miles from Sebastopol – and not 'some thirty miles' as several recent books have said – but the General welcomed its relative isolation, the protection afforded by a large inland lake, and the hopes of easily securing the small town of Eupatoria itself as a roadstead and advance base.[16]

By seven on Monday morning Lyons had brought his top-level reconnaissance party safely back to the main invasion fleet which was riding at anchor fifty miles west of Cape Tarkhankut, 'a forest of masts, yet quite out of sight of land'. That evening the fleet moved off slowly eastwards. It was an oppressively humid night, threatening thunder and a possible end to the calm seas of the past two days. The French and Turkish ships could not keep up with the British fleet and Dundas dropped anchor eighteen miles north-west of Eupatoria late on Tuesday afternoon, sending tugs out to bring the slower allied vessels to join him. Provided the weather held and the Russians did not make a sortie from Sebastopol, the allied commanders were confident that they would get their first troops ashore on the beaches around the Old Fort on Thursday, 14 September. Saint-Arnaud noted that this was the anniversary of the entry into Moscow of Napoleon's *Grande Armée*. Rather curiously, the coincidence in timing seemed to afford the invalid Marshal comfort and confidence. General Bosquet, commander of the French 2nd Division, contented himself with wry comments on the unsuitability of choosing a place which the charts showed as 'Calamity Bay' for a landfall.[17]

At ten on Wednesday morning Russian observers, peering out across the sea from precarious platforms above Fort Constantine, spotted the smoke of a fleet on the horizon and alerted their commander-in-chief. But Menshikov was still reluctant to admit that an invasion was imminent. Only two days previously, after HMS *Caradoc* had been seen to approach the harbour and turn away again, he had written to St

Petersburg stressing how recent events justified his assessments: the enemy would not dare make a landing; certainly not so late in the campaigning season. But throughout Wednesday afternoon the wooden arms of the coastal telegraph semaphore at the mouth of the river Alma signalled sightings of a great convoy moving into Eupatoria Bay. It seemed, to Menshikov's amazement, as if more than a hundred vessels had slipped in undetected to the Russian coast. He ordered an enterprising junior naval officer, Lieutenant Vladimir Stetsenkov, to set out for Eupatoria with Cossack outriders, who would bring back intelligence reports for the naval and military high command. That evening the officers of the Sebastopol garrison and their families were enjoying a performance of Gogol's satirical masterpiece *The Government Inspector* when, at the end of the third act, news arrived from Stetsenkov that the enemy was, indeed, about to land near Eupatoria in great force; the theatre emptied rapidly.[18]

Stetsenkov also sent a message to Vice-Admiral Kornilov pointing out that as 'the enemy fleet stood so crowded and in such disorder . . . it might be possible to use fire-ships against it'.[19] This was sound advice, but impracticable. A perceptive commander, intent on turning defence into attack, might well have prepared fireships at Eupatoria to be sent down at night on the prevailing wind if an allied fleet moored off the sandy beaches of Calamita Bay or the mouth of the Alma; but it was asking too much of the Black Sea Fleet to set out from Sebastopol with improvised fireships and sail them northwards for more than forty miles to a heavily protected enemy roadstead. Menshikov – who was both an admiral and a general – regarded the navy as an ancillary defence supporting the army. Until urgent fortifications on the north side of Sebastopol were completed, he wanted the fourteen ships of the line and seven frigates to remain in port rather than risk destruction by the numerically superior allied fleet.

From aboard the *Himalaya* Sergeant Albert Mitchell of the 13th Light Dragoons watched the Russian coastline draw nearer and, being a true man of Kent, was at once reminded of Romney Marsh.[20] The comparison was apt: for, at the point where the Light Brigade disembarked, only a narrow stretch of shore separated the sea from a salt lake, while in the distance a crescent of turfy downland ended in shallow cliffs, not chalky white in appearance but a reddish sandstone. Apart from fleeting glimpses of Cossack outriders, there was no sign of the enemy, who were puzzled by a diversion made by seven British and French steamships off the mouths of the Katcha and Alma rivers.

Throughout Thursday, 14 September, the disembarkation continued: the French landed first, then the 7th Fusiliers, and so on through the day, until rain began to soak officers and men alike and 'a heavy swell setting in from the westward' hampered the landing of tents, guns, stores and horses. That first stormy night the Queen's cousin, the Duke of Cambridge, spent huddled under waterproof covers, tentless like the Guardsmen and Highlanders who comprised his 1st Division.

By Friday conditions had improved and the tents were coming ashore; but Raglan and his staff were acutely aware that their army was short of baggage animals, wagons and drivers, and attempts to make good these deficiencies locally by purchase, cajolery or requisition were not entirely successful. It was galling that the French possessed an efficient transport corps and, as at Gallipoli in the spring, they were quicker in learning to live off the land. Saint-Arnaud, whose health improved once his transports reached Calamita Bay, became impatient. From the *Ville de Paris* he had written to his wife telling her his proposed programme: on the 17th or 18th a battle on the Alma, perhaps another on the river Katcha, and so to Sebastopol by the 25th, with the Crimean campaign over by the middle of October. But on Monday, 18 September, Saint-Arnaud was still at the Old Fort waiting for Raglan to get his troops ready for the march. The Marshal was well-disposed towards Raglan, but the long wait tried his patience, and in the course of the day he resolved that he would move forward 'tomorrow at 7 o'clock and nothing will hold us back any longer'.[21]

The strange inactivity of the enemy was beginning to prey on overstretched nerves in the British camp. On that Monday evening troopers in the Light Brigade could see a glow in the southern sky which might be fields fired by Cossacks to deny the invaders forage, but could also be a reflection of camp fires where a Russian army lay silently in waiting. Suddenly a guard thought he heard, above the sound of frogs and crickets, the rattle of harnesses as horsemen loomed up in the darkness. He fired a warning shot, and at once the whole brigade turned out to meet the enemy – who were soon identified as one of the brigade's own patrols. By now the neighbouring infantry divisions were responding to an apparent alert and they opened a brisk fire in the general direction of the horsemen. Order was restored through the powerful lungs and unmistakable manner of Lord Cardigan. A cavalry officer wounded his own batman in the leg; but, remarkably, no one was killed.[22]

The incident showed it was high time that the army marched on

Sebastopol. At 9 a.m., only two hours later than Saint-Arnaud's proposed moment of departure, the allied armies – six thousand Turks on the right, then the French, with the British on the left – began to move southwards, regimental bands playing as they had when the men left their barracks months ago. Soon, with the temperature fast rising into the eighties Fahrenheit and throats parched as the marching columns climbed up from their encampments to a high, rolling plateau, the fifes, drums and bugles went silent. Weary regiments, still plagued by cholera, trudged slowly on, with no enemy in sight but the sun.[23] It was as if a cumbersome tortoise, three miles long and four miles wide, was ambling forward astride the one good coastal road that ran down from Eupatoria and across five river valleys before reaching Sebastopol itself. None of the rivers was much more than a stream at that time of the year, and although no doubt the primitive bridges would be destroyed, each river was easily fordable. 'A nine days march', the staff officers calculated at headquarters; but that, they conceded, depended on what obstacles the Russians might raise at each of those river crossings.

CHAPTER EIGHT

To the Alma and Beyond

Sebastopol – or, as it might be translated, 'City of Imperial Power' – became a naval base in 1804, two decades after Catherine the Great named her new foundation to celebrate the conquest of the Crimea; and from that year an edict of Tsar Alexander I sought, not always successfully, to keep the port closed to commercial traffic. When war began with Turkey in 1853 there were 45,000 people living in the city, 38,000 of whom were either in the army or navy themselves or were serving men's dependents. Sebastopol Bay was a natural site for a harbour, with the main town – like the old centres of Plymouth and Brest – on raised tableland, sloping steeply down to an inlet four miles long and half a mile wide. Until Nicholas I's reign the city's defences had faced the sea, with six coastal batteries capable of engaging an enemy fleet one and a half miles off the outer anchorage. Since 1825 five more batteries had been completed, three of them in recent months; and Menshikov knew that he could now concentrate 610 guns on any seaborne invaders who ventured up Sebastopol Roads, quite apart from the fire-power of the Black Sea Fleet. It was from this mass of artillery that Menshikov had drawn his confidence all that summer.[1]

But Tsar Nicholas, who inspected Sebastopol in 1837, had long been concerned with the ability of his naval base to withstand attack from the land; and theoretically Sebastopol was defended by an outer ring of eight earthwork bastions, connected by a trench system, and the protection offered by a crenellated wall. On the maps spread out across the tables at the General Staff Building in St Petersburg, these defences looked formidable. Yet, in reality, they were far from complete, the most important redoubts remaining isolated from each other. General Prince Michael Gorchakov, who had spent many months at Sebastopol before taking command in Bessarabia, was acutely aware of the city's defensive weaknesses and, when it became clear that there would be no more fighting along the Danube that year, he ordered his most accomplished engineering officer, Colonel Eduard Totleben, to leave

his headquarters at Kishinev, travel to Sebastopol, and offer Menshikov his services.

Totleben duly reported to Menshikov on 22 August, handing him a
letter of introduction from Gorchakov which spoke highly of the 36-
year-old sapper officer's work at Silistria. But Menshikov, as arrogant
and suspicious as ever, received Totleben coldly. The Prince, who
prided himself on being a true Russian soldier schooled in a crack
cavalry regiment, despised engineers (especially those over thirty years
his junior) and disliked Baltic Germans – and the Totlebens came from
Mitau (Jelgava) in Latvia. Moreover, Menshikov resented the in-
trusion of another field commander's military protégé. 'In his absent-
mindedness, Prince Gorchakov appears to have forgotten that I have a
sapper battalion myself,' he told Totleben. 'I suggest you take a rest,
and then return wherever you came from.'[2] But it was not difficult in
Tsar Nicholas's army for a resourceful officer to extend a period of 'rest'
until days stretched imperceptibly into weeks. Totleben examined
Sebastopol's defences at leisure; and he did not like what he saw,
considering that some of the forts were only fit to beat off Tatars. To the
north of the city was the biggest citadel of all, Fort Severnaya, soon to
be known by the allies as 'Star Fort', from its octagonal shape. It looked
impressive from a distance but Totleben was worried by the astonishingly broad northern arc of dead ground to its guns, by the effect of
earlier years of neglect on its fabric, and by the absence of outer
galleries or protective earthworks, giving contact with the main system
of defence. For here, he was convinced, was the key fortress, looking out
over the whole of the anchorage and the city beyond. Whoever held
Fort Severnaya was master of Sebastopol.[3] Unfortunately for the allied
invaders, Totleben was still 'resting' in the city when, on 15 September,
Cossack riders brought the first detailed reports of the landings in
Calamita Bay. It looked as if the allies intended to follow the direct
coastal road towards the city.

The news was, in one way, reassuring for Menshikov. Had the
invaders split their forces, sending one column inland to Bakchisarai
before turning south-west to approach Sebastopol's defences from the
Simferopol Road, their line of advance would have posed problems for
the Russian commander. As it was, Menshikov could write confidently
to St Petersburg that night informing the Tsar that he intended to take
up advantageous positions along the road from Eupatoria and
Sebastopol and await there the arrival of the enemy. Marshal Saint-
Arnaud had told his wife in a letter written three days before he even

saw the Crimean coastline that he would fight a glorious battle (*'une belle bataille'*) beside the Alma; and Menshikov intended him to do so. Rarely has there been such resigned inevitability in the choice of a battlefield.[4]

Menshikov had often ridden along the Eupatoria Road and knew its contours well. He did not bother to summon a council of war, nor take his senior commanders into his confidence. They sensed what he was planning; for already troops were beginning to concentrate on the plateau between the rivers Alma and Katcha, fifteen miles due north of Sebastopol. On either side of the river's mouth was a sheer rockface of chalk which Menshikov assumed no enemy would attempt to scale: a battalion of infantry and a couple of guns could keep token guard from the top of the cliffs. What interested him were two hills, three miles inland: Telegraph Hill, where a skeletal unfinished semaphore looked more like a gibbet; and, overshadowing it, the bluff of Kourganie Hill, presenting a broad natural platform from which field guns could command the bridge across the Alma and over a mile of the main route towards Sebastopol. To a conventionally-minded general looking for textbook battlefields it was, as Menshikov remarked to Lieutenant-General Kiriakov, 'a fine place'. And Kiriakov – an infantry commander to whom sobriety came as an unnatural condition – looked down on the vineyards upstream and agreed with him.[5]

General Kiriakov's men were first in action, the Tarutinsky Regiment stumbling largely by accident on the vanguard of the Light Division beside the Bulganek river on Tuesday afternoon (19 September). The Russians opened fire, killing four cavalry horses in Cardigan's brigade and wounding their riders. Neither Raglan nor Menshikov wished to risk the losses of a chance engagement on the eve of what each assumed would be a set-piece battle. Kiriakov, obeying the Prince's general orders, accordingly pulled the Tarutinsky and their accompanying Cossacks back, while Raglan – with some difficulty – restrained Lord Cardigan from charging the enemy like Quixote tilting at windmills. 'I don't know how it is, but whatever I propose is always frustrated', one of his horsemen heard their Brigadier complaining. Officially Raglan praised Cardigan's 'spirit' and skill in keeping 'his Brigade under perfect command'; privately he resolved to use his light horsemen defensively as a protective screen, eschewing all flamboyance. At this distance from home good cavalry horses were in shorter supply than competent riders.[6]

The Bulganek encounter also disturbed Raglan on another count.

Cardigan's isolation when he crossed the river drew attention to a widening gap between the British 2nd Division, on the extreme right of his line of advance, and the French 3rd Division under Prince Napoleon, the Emperor's cousin. A French liaison officer, Lieutenant-Colonel de Lagondie, was duly sent by Raglan to Prince Napoleon with a polite request to close the gap. With his mission accomplished Lagondie started back for Raglan's headquarters, but he was so short-sighted that he mistook the Kievsky Hussars for British cavalry, was captured by one of Kiriakov's NCOs, and taken to Menshikov's tent. The Russian staff officers felt so sorry for the poor bungler that they offered to send a horseman, under a flag of truce, to collect Lagondie's personal belongings from the British; but the Frenchman, celebrated at Raglan's headquarters for long yarns of his campaigning days in Algeria, had lost quite enough face for one day. The Russian offer was declined and Menshikov gave orders that Lagondie was to be escorted into Sebastopol and detained in Prince Bariatinsky's house 'since this was the only residence available with a staff of servants and cooks' to attend to his needs.[7] Not all prisoners-of-war could count on such generous treatment. On that same day 180 captives from Bomarsund, some with wives and children, were nearing the end of a long journey from the Aaland Islands to East Sussex, where Lewes Prison had been specially set aside for them.

Captain Chodasiewicz of the Tarutinsky Regiment had reached the heights between the rivers Katcha and Alma late on Friday 15 September. His battalion – there were four battalions in the regiment, each of about 800 men – was therefore awaiting the enemy for four days before Tuesday's skirmish along the Bulganek. Back in Sebastopol the officers had been confident of success, but the distant sight of the allied armada left them in doubt; a fleet of that size must have landed at least 80,000 men, they reckoned. The soldiers in the ranks were fascinated by the spectacle: they had been garrisoning Nizhni-Novgorod until the previous December, when they began a four months' march to the war zone; and most of them had never seen the sea until that spring, let alone a fleet at anchor. Nor perhaps had Captain Chodasiewicz, for he later recalled how, 'At night the forest of masts was illuminated with various coloured lanterns'. But to the Tarutinskys' neighbours, a battalion of the Moscow Regiment, the hundreds of masts suggested church towers in a great city: 'Behold the infidel has brought another Holy Moscow on the waves!' Chodasiewicz heard one awed peasant remark.[8]

Lord Raglan's nephew, Colonel Calthorpe, bivouacked on Tuesday night outside a ruined post-house in the upland south of the Bulganek. Like the Polish captain in the Tarutinsky, he, too, was deeply moved by the scene at night; not the ships behind him, but 'the hundreds of watch and bivouac fires' among the hills. Earlier in the evening Marshal Saint-Arnaud, alert and irradiating a confidence pepped up by narcotics, had ridden across to the posthouse, with the ubiquitous Breton, Colonel Trochu, at his side, and informed Raglan of his general plan: a pincer attack on the Russian positions across the Alma, with the French engaging the enemy's left flank, near the sea, and the British drawing Russian fire in the centre while sweeping round their right (inland) flank. Since Raglan was militarily a pragmatist, convinced that no general can decide on the envelopment of an enemy position until he has studied it on the field, he treated the Marshal and Trochu with his customary courtesy, assured them that France could rely on his army's full collaboration, and made no comment on the plan. On Wednesday, a bright and clear morning, the armies resumed their march, somewhat later than the French had hoped, but without disturbance from the enemy.[9]

It was more than forty years since Raglan had ridden into battle beside Wellington with crumbling dust from the Spanish sierra underfoot and the ochre cupolas of Salamanca on the skyline. Saint-Arnaud was then a schoolboy at the *Lycée Napoléon* and Trochu not yet born, although Menshikov was in the field that day, defending Russia from French invaders somewhere north-east of Minsk. But the terrain around the allied army's line of march was more reminiscent of Leon and Castile than of the low-lying marshland and sandy birch thickets of Byelorussia. And if Raglan's thoughts turned to this earlier campaign rather than to the three weeks before Waterloo, it is not surprising. So much around him was unchanged. The artillery was still smooth-bore; the cavalry still hankered after a mass charge rather than the long-range reconnaissance for which lightly armed horsemen were ideally suited; and infantry tactics remained the same, even if muskets now had percussion caps rather than flintlocks and crack marksmen were armed with the Minié rifles, already common to their French allies. But there were differences, too: no one had doubted in Spain that the military mastermind was Wellington and that the officers of Britain's allies were there on sufferance; and in those days there had been none of these wretched 'TGS', 'Travelling Gentlemen', for although the editor of *The Times* hurried back to Constantinople after a day ashore in

Eupatoria Bay, William Russell was keeping up with the columns on the march and so, despite the vexations of a temperamental pony, was the author of *Eothen*, Alexander Kinglake – who, in contrast to Russell, Raglan thought 'a most charming man'.[10] There was, however, a more serious distinction between the old and the new campaigning. In Spain and Portugal Wellington's army found animals, food, fuel for fires, carts and wagons while the local population looked upon them as liberators, except for those wild drunken days when discipline broke and the 'scum of the earth' pillaged and plundered. The Crimea offered few resources for an expeditionary force accustomed to live off the countryside – only fired villages, scorched earth, and, despite amiable gestures from surviving Tatar settlements, the implacable hostility of a colonizing master race. The British Commander-in-Chief was slow to recognize this difference between warfare in the two peninsulas. Outwardly his failure of perception made little difference to what happened on this day of the Alma, 20 September; but it was to hamper the exploitation of a narrow victory in the field.

Whatever doubts junior officers in the Tarutinsky might hold, nothing could shake Prince Menshikov's conviction that he was about to scatter his imperial master's enemies. He had agreed that a group of eminent civilians from Sebastopol could come out early on that Wednesday and watch his 38,000 men put to rout the 30,000 Frenchmen, 26,000 Britishers and 9,000 Turks marching southwards down the Eupatoria Road. These privileged spectators brought picnics with them as if about to see a review or a tattoo, the ladies wearing elegant clothes and carrying parasols and shawls, for it was, after all, the third week in September and no one could be certain of the weather in the Chersonese uplands so late in the season. They were accommodated in an improvised grandstand close to the unfinished semaphore station where, through opera-glasses, there was no reason why they need miss a single rout.[11] And, soon after one o'clock, the spectacle began. The glint of sun on bayonets helped the eye to focus on the red or dark green coats of British infantrymen advancing towards the riverside cluster of villages and vineyards. Immediately below the onlookers and stretching down towards the sea was a proto-Gauguinesque galaxy of colour – scarlet pantaloons, blue tunics and red burnous – as France's chasseurs, Zouaves and Spahis brought to the Crimea all the military trimmings of North Africa. Close to the onlookers' grandstand, a curling cloud of powder-smoke showed that Menshikov's batteries were seeking to bite into the review precision of

Raglan's troops as they advanced on the Russian centre; and soon the first solitary puffs from low ridges beyond the narrow river anticipated the answering boom from the British 9-pounders. Eighteen miles away, back in Sebastopol, Admiral Kornilov, the energetic Chief of Naval Staff, heard the rumble of opposing guns and knew that a decisive battle to save the city had begun. As senior shore-based officer, he left Colonel Totleben to supervise labour battalions throwing up field-works in front of the Severnaya Fort and ordered a carriage to drive him out to Menshikov's headquarters, for seamen and marines were in reserve to help the army protect the docks, barracks and anchorage of the Black Sea Fleet.[12]

By the time Admiral Kornilov stepped down from his carriage, the scene from Telegraph Hill – so sharply defined earlier on – was confused. For the battle refused to follow any predetermined pattern. Raglan's divisions reached their first line before the French on their right had turned the Russian position around the village of Almatamac. The British infantry therefore lay waiting for some twenty minutes to half an hour almost a mile short of the river, under steady fire from the Russian artillery which, to the dismay of Raglan's gunners, was sited too high in the hills to fall within range of the 9-pounders. When at last Lord Raglan gave the momentous order, 'The infantry will advance', ten thousand infantrymen prepared to go forward, a moving human wall two miles in extent.[13]

But it was as if the Cossacks too had heard Raglan's order, for at that moment the village of Burliuk, ahead of the British centre, burst into flame. Every cottage had been evacuated on the previous day and filled with straw and some explosives. A brigade on the right of the 2nd Division – mainly infantry from Berkshire and Wales – was moment-arily checked, not so much by the flames of the village street as by the choking smoke; Colonel Lysons later describing how the village dogs and pigeons had 'dived . . . through the smoke in evident terror of their lives'. But the dramatic firing of Burliuk hampered the defenders. 'We became blinded by the smoke which drifted back on us,' a Russian officer recalled. 'It would have been wiser, as those with battle experience said at the time, not to have created a smoke screen for the enemy's benefit since this enabled him to fire on us without any loss on his side.'[14] Burning Burliuk blotted out the panorama from Telegraph Hill. It must have been at this point, if not earlier, that the Sebastopol gentlefolk hurriedly evacuated their grandstand, for the battle was creeping closer and closer to them. So precipitate was their departure that next day a British skirmisher found on the hillside an abandoned picnic basket, with six cold chickens ready to be eaten and a couple of bottles of champagne. Close by was 'a lady's bonnet very nicely trimmed'.[15]

Meanwhile, out at sea, Lieutenant O'Reilly of HMS *Retribution* had a clearer picture of what was happening; and he duly sketched it for *The Illustrated London News*. From the frigate's mizzen-mast the white cliffs on either side of the Alma's mouth stood out sharply, reminding O'Reilly of the coastline between Brighton and Beachy Head. Like any other officer in the British or French fleets, he could see what Menshikov had ignored – a winding path up the steep face of the cliffs. It was up this route, beyond the village of Almatamac, that General Bosquet led his veteran colonial campaigners, the Third Regiment of Zouaves, to a plateau some 350 feet above sea-level. Once there, and supported by guns dragged up this precipitous path, the French 2nd Division was in a position to turn Menshikov's left flank at a point where he had left only an under-strength battalion of the Minsky Regiment and half a battery of artillery, sited well inland, to keep watch on the allied warships.[16]

Four miles away, at his headquarters on Kourganie Hill, Menshikov at first refused to believe the horseman who brought him bad news from the clifftop. And when the group of staff officers around the Prince persuaded him that these alarming messages might be true, his first reaction was to wonder why General Kiriakov had not already plugged the gap. Captain Chodasiewicz described how Kiriakov was presiding over a champagne luncheon party when Lieutenant Stetsenkov, Menshikov's most enterprising aide-de-camp, rode over to what should have been the western sector's command post: he had, Kiriakov assured Stetsenkov, the French well in sight.[17] Menshikov, unwilling to wait for Kiriakov, rode off towards the sea, ordering the western sector's reserve battalions and four hussar squadrons to follow him. But the Russian reinforcements came under heavy fire from the ships once they approached Bosquet's plateau; and Menshikov pulled them back, so as to form a defensive line around the two dominant features of the whole landscape, Telegraph Hill and Kourganie Hill.

Like Lieutenant O'Reilly and Sergeant Mitchell, Russell of *The Times* looked for familiar parallels in the strange contours of the Crimea: 'If the reader will place himself on the top of Richmond-hill,' Russell wrote that night, 'dwarf the Thames in imagination to the size of a Hampshire rivulet, and imagine the lovely hill itself to be deprived of all vegetation and protracted for about four miles along the stream, he may form some notion of the position occupied by the Russians.'[18] It was up these heights that General Codrington led the infantry of the Light Division in a frontal assault on the glacis defending the Russian gunners' principal stronghold, the 'Great Redoubt', where 24-pounders and 32-pounders had been throwing iron balls more than six inches in diameter for as much as a mile, with reasonable accuracy. Astonishingly, Russian horse-teams succeeded in removing all but one of the guns before Codrington's men rushed the final earthwork. They were not, however, allowed to remain there: the Duke of Cambridge, ponderously correct in his movements and receiving that day his baptism of fire as commanding general of the 1st Division, had not yet crossed the river, with his three battalions of Guards and three of Highlanders; and before he could begin the ascent to the Redoubt, the Vladimirsky Regiment counter-attacked and forced the Light Division to fall back from the Redoubt. To the British right, Prince Napoleon and General Canrobert had not advanced from their footholds south of the Alma, while Bosquet's assault had lost its impetus. By now it was mid-afternoon; and suddenly the battle seemed to have swung in favour of the Russian defenders.

The great battles of history have never 'swung'; their fate has been settled, one way or the other, by the resolute hand of a natural commander, or the belated arrival of a second army. But on that Wednesday, beside the Alma, there was no outstanding general on either side and no prospect of reinforcements. Both Saint-Arnaud and Menshikov had planned their battle, leaving little to be improvised according to the circumstances of the day. Eye-witnesses describe the opposing commanders in the saddle for hours at a time, riding backwards and forwards along their lines: Saint-Arnaud, tired and gaunt; Menshikov, choleric and suspicious; a couple of aspiring grandmasters, hesitant above their chessboard. But one of Saint-Arnaud's pieces refused to conform to the pattern of the game. Raglan puzzled his allies, deeply though they respected him. The French remained unsure how far he accepted the Marshal's grand design for victory. At the crucial point in the battle – with Canrobert, Bosquet and Prince Napoleon checked and the Great Redoubt again in Russian hands – Raglan and his staff were lost from sight.

Yet, in reality, Raglan was at that moment engaged in the enterprise which made an allied victory certain. As soon as the British infantry obeyed his order to move forward, he rode down to the river bank parallel to their line of advance, but well to the seaward side of burning Burliuk. The approach to the ford over the river had collapsed in the course of the fighting, but the deep water was held back by some rocks, over which Raglan's horse carefully picked his way. His staff followed their commander, and it was remarkable that they were not caught in heavy crossfire from the Russian positions. 'In a minute more', wrote Colonel Calthorpe, 'we were among the French skirmishers, who looked not a little astonished to see the English commander-in-chief so far in advance'.[19] His staff officers then found, by chance, 'a sort of lane with high hedges . . . which gradually rose higher and higher' until it emerged on a promontory, looking out over Telegraph Hill and the Great Redoubt. Quickly two artillery officers on his staff rode down the lane again and returned with a couple of 9-pounders, but no gunners. Briefly staff officers 'dismounted and served the guns themselves', their somewhat random shots convincing the Russian commander in that sector, General Kvetsinsky, that the allied troops – at first he took it for granted that they were French – had, for the second time that day, mysteriously scaled heights up which, it had been assumed, no passable route existed. By the time Kvetsinsky wheeled his defenders to face the new threat, the British had hurriedly brought forward a full battery, whose gunners were in position and firing at the Russian infantry below. One shot hit an ammunition wagon; and in retrospect this stands out as the decisive single blow in the day. For, after such a tremendous explosion, Kvetsinsky determined to pull his troops back, so as to safeguard the next rise of ground protecting the Sebastopol road, known to the allies, rather grandly, as 'the Pass'. At the same time General Canrobert's artillery – and gunfire from the ships – repelled a counter-attack by a battalion of the Moskovsky Regiment, who were also forced back to guard the road to the Pass, taking up a position at right angles with the remaining Russian troops engaging the Duke of Cambridge's division along the banks of the Alma.[20]

By now the brief moment when Menshikov might have snatched victory had come and gone without the Prince recognizing it. The whole allied line moved forward, with the Guards Brigade and the Highland Brigade storming Kourganie Hill and recovering the Great Redoubt. To the Russians, Sir Colin Campbell's kilted Black Watch and Cameron Highlanders seemed an irresistible force, 'the savages without trousers', as the mortally wounded General Karganov called them, with grudging admiration. The Lancers and Dragoons of the cavalry reserve forded the Alma and joined the pursuit, their

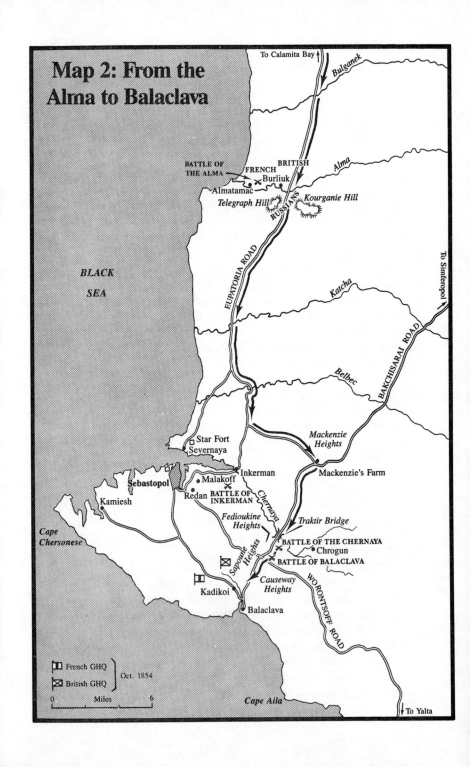

Map 2: From the Alma to Balaclava

To Calamita Bay

Bulganek

BATTLE OF THE ALMA

BRITISH

FRENCH

Burliuk

Almatamac

Alma

Telegraph Hill

Kourganie Hill

RUSSIANS

BLACK SEA

Katcha

To Simferopol

EUPATORIA ROAD

Belbec

BAKCHISARAI ROAD

Star Fort
Severnaya

Mackenzie Heights

Sebastopol

Inkerman

Mackenzie's Farm

Malakoff

Kamiesh

Redan

BATTLE OF INKERMAN

Chernaya

Fedioukine Heights

Traktir Bridge

Cape Chersonese

Sapoune Heights

BATTLE OF THE CHERNAYA

Chrogun

BATTLE OF BALACLAVA

WORONTSOFF ROAD

Kadikoi

Causeway Heights

Balaclava

French GHQ

British GHQ

Oct. 1854

0   Miles   6

Cape Aila

To Yalta

commanding general, Lord Lucan, not waiting for orders from a distant Lord Raglan.[21]

Menshikov had lost the battle. Perhaps he had lost the war. A cavalry staff-captain was sent off at once to St Petersburg to tell the Tsar what he had seen that day, for the Prince could not bring himself to set pen to paper. Desperately the Russian commanders tried to restore discipline in a defeated army pulling back towards the outer ring of Sebastopol's forts. 'The battalions of the reserve began to retreat without orders and our battalion followed them,' Captain Chodasiewicz wrote. 'When we withdrew, nobody knew whether we ought to go to the right or to the left.'[22]

There were still some hours of sunlight left. Raglan, having restrained Lucan's Lancers and Dragoons, proposed to Saint-Arnaud that the allies should send their cavalry, horse artillery and reserve divisions down the Sebastopol road in pursuit of the enemy. The Marshal refused: his soldiers, he explained, must first retrieve their knapsacks, which they had left beside the river when the battle was at its height; he had to ensure that the wounded and the sick received medical attention; and, after four and a half hours of artillery exchanges, his gunners were short of ammunition. Not one of these reasons seemed convincing to the British; and they suspected that Saint-Arnaud was thinking in narrowly French terms rather than in collaborating closely with his ally. It is certainly strange to find him next day writing to his wife, 'Had I possessed cavalry, I would have taken 10,000 prisoners'.[23] For, although Napoleon III would not risk the élite squadrons of the Empire on an overseas expedition, there were mounted troops on the battlefield that evening eager for a pursuit. A thousand British horsemen had spent much of the afternoon in a field of cantaloups, watching and waiting for the order to advance.

For one officer, half Irish and half Italian in parentage, this enforced inactivity was particularly galling. At Raglan's side during much of the day was an aide-de-camp who had served in the Austrian army and studied at first hand the cavalry systems of Russia, France and Prussia; and, on paper, no one in the British army was better informed on the handling of horsemen than Captain Lewis Edward Nolan. His textbook, *Cavalry, its History and Tactics*, supplemented by a manual, *Nolan's System for Training Cavalry Horses*, kept his name before the public on both sides of the Atlantic; his system was introduced at West Point, where Colonel Robert E. Lee was Superintendent; and even Tsar Nicholas knew of Nolan's works. But, like every other officer below the age of fifty-eight, until that Wednesday Captain Nolan had never watched a clash of arms between the great European Powers; and, to his chagrin, on this personally momentous occasion the opposing squadrons of cavalry remained inactive throughout the battle. That evening Nolan poured out his disillusionment to a sympathetic listener, W. H. Russell of *The Times*. Most officers around Raglan followed their commander's example and shunned Russell, taking no more notice of him 'than you would of a crossing sweeper', as he once remarked. But Nolan respected the mounting influence of newspapers – and Russell was, after all, an Irishman by birth. 'There were one thousand British cavalry, looking on at a beaten army retreating – guns, standards, colours and all – with a wretched horde of Cossacks and cowards who had never struck a blow, ready to turn tail at the first trumpet, within ten minutes of them,' Nolan complained. 'It is too disgraceful, too infamous! They ought all of them to be damned.'[24]

Russell did not recount this conversation until he put together a book on the war, after the fighting was over, but the pronominal imprecision of the last sentence is so characteristic of Nolan that it rings true. At the time, Russell's newspaper readers were merely told that 'Lord Raglan had expressed his intention of keeping his cavalry "in a bandbox", and he was apprehensive of getting into any serious difficulty with the enemy at the close of such a day'.[25] This was a half-truth, for Raglan was undoubtably disappointed by the Marshal's lack of response: his instinct had been to exploit every sign of a Russian rout. But he was, indeed, short of cavalry, and the British contingent was not in itself powerful enough to risk an ambush in the failing light from the numerically superior Russian cavalry further along the road to Sebastopol. Tonight therefore the armies would bivouac on the Alma heights, or in what remained of the villages and vineyards along the river. Tomorrow Raglan hoped to convince Saint-Arnaud and Canrobert and the enigmatic Trochu of the need to march directly on Sebastopol.

Casualties at the Alma were not heavy by the standards of earlier or later wars. The French lost 60 men killed, of whom 3 were officers; British dead numbered 362, including 25 officers; Turkish losses are not known, but must have been few; and the Russians finally listed 46 officers and 1,755 other ranks killed, together with 7 officers and 728 men missing. It was the suffering of many of the 6,000 allied and Russian wounded that made the night after the battle hideous. 'Groans', 'piteous cries for water', 'heartrending', 'a horrible scene –

death in every shape and form', in Colonel Calthorpe's words; and a Russian guards officer wrote in almost identical terms of the terrible misery around him: 'The sights I saw will remain vivid in my memory all my days,' he added. Raglan, who surrendered one of his two tents as a casualty station that night, had seen the harrowing face of war before, in the Iberian peninsula and at Waterloo. The ghastly novelty in the aftermath of the Alma was the continuing incidence of cholera, which soon 'swept off many who had taken part in the battle'; among them was Brigadier-General Tylden, commanding the sappers who had marched south from Calamita Bay. And there was, too, a terrible omission: for, unlike the French, the British landed in the Crimea 'without any kind of hospital transport, litters or carts or anything', as the senior surgeon attached to the Light Division noted in shocked disbelief.[26]

On Thursday morning (21 September) Raglan had two conferences with Saint-Arnaud and his staff. There is confusion over what was said. The French have maintained that the Marshal wished at once to press forward on Sebastopol and was held back by Raglan, since it took the British two days to tend their wounded and ensure safe conduct back to the ships off Eupatoria for the Russian prisoners, many of whom were themselves battle casualties. Saint-Arnaud, writing that day to his wife, told her that he intended to resume the advance at seven on Friday morning, expecting to cross the last of the rivers along the Eupatoria Road, the Belbec, on Sunday; he would then send her a letter from Sebastopol. But Raglan appears to have believed that the French were as reluctant to march on the city as on the previous afternoon. The crossings of the Katcha and the Belbec would be as hotly contested as the Alma, they maintained; the Russians must still have some 40,000 men to defend the naval base; no siege artillery had been landed to bombard the defences of Severnaya ('Star Fort'). Better a more cautious approach, probing the outer defences, cutting the route from Simferopol and Bakchisarai so as to deny Menshikov reinforcements, while waiting for more French and British troops (including the cavalry Heavy Brigade) to arrive from Varna and Constantinople. To these arguments were added Raglan's own doubts about the French Commander-in-Chief's health, for Saint-Arnaud's long hours in the saddle on Wednesday were followed by a serious relapse. Whatever the reason for the delay, it was Saturday morning before the advance was resumed along the road southwards from Eupatoria.[27]

'There were not many traces of a beaten army,' Raglan's nephew noted with surprise, as they rode towards the Katcha. 'A good many helmets and knapsacks ... and occasionally a ghastly corpse, but altogether it did not give one the idea of a disorganized force.'[28] But it was a puzzling ride: no sign of the enemy at the Katcha, where the armies spent the night; and no speedily constructed earthworks around the Belbec. All the bridges had been left intact. The vineyards and villages were not fired, and marching soldiery long denied fresh fruit reached out for pears, apricots and melons growing beside the road. So much was unripe that Colonel Calthorpe was convinced the 'men will make themselves ill'. There was something uncanny about the rustic peace of the valleys. In 1812, after Borodino, Napoleon had ridden towards Moscow unmolested by an enemy who seemed swallowed up by the vast emptiness of Russia; in triumph he surveyed this 'Third Rome' from Salutation Hill; and yet, only a few hours later, fire began to consume the heart of the city as the Imperial Guard marched in. Menshikov was a veteran of the 1812 campaign. Now, forty-two Septembers later, were the Russians in the Crimea setting a similar trap to spring on their invaders? The allies did not put the question to the test.

There was no Salutation Hill on the road into Sebastopol, but on the afternoon of Sunday, 24 September, Raglan and his staff rode up to a ridge four miles north of the city and looked down, as Napoleon had done before Moscow, at the prize which had lured the allied expedition into Russia. 'All the buildings were of white stone, and with the sun on them, quite dazzled' the little party on their ridge. From the sea they had already picked out the onion-shaped cupola of the Admiralty, but the green roofs of the private houses were new to them. More ominous was the solid strength of the Star Fort, menacingly silent above the road into the town. Raglan turned away. Saint-Arnaud and General Burgoyne between them had persuaded him that the Russians were obviously waiting for an attack from the north. It would be better to move around the city, find quays for the steamers close at hand and then enter Sebastopol from the south, where there was no Star Fort guarding the approaches. Not one of the redoubts south of the city was yet ready for manning – or so, at least, primitive intelligence reports suggested.[29]

On Monday morning at half-past eight the British columns began to march south-eastwards into heavily wooded country. Now it seemed as if they were heading away from the city whose lights they had seen reflected on the placid waters of the inner harbour the night before.

Morale, so high on Saturday beside the vines and fruit trees of the Belbec valley, began to fall as they stumbled forward through brushwood, the narrow track beneath the oak trees left clear for field guns and horses. Still, it was encouraging to hear that at the end of their flank march the new veterans of the Alma would find a harbour, fresh supplies, and some of those battalions left waiting in the cholera camps of Varna. They were marching, it was said, to an inlet called Balaclava.

News of the Alma travelled slowly. Even Fanny Duberly, separated from her husband when the troops disembarked and now aboard ship off Eupatoria, did not hear of the battle until her maid – a trooper's wife – woke her on Saturday morning with a rumour that the cavalry had been wiped out and that they were all widows.[30] Trustee for the news within Russia was Captain Serge Greig, the cavalry officer sent by Menshikov to give Tsar Nicholas an oral report of the battle; and Greig kept silent for six nights and days as he rode towards the capital. The Court, however, was not in St Petersburg but twenty-eight miles away at Gatchina where Nicholas's father had spent so many months parading his Prussianized soldiery. Isolated in this grim, square-towered fortress, Nicholas did not know if the courier who arrived from the Crimea that Tuesday (27 September) was bringing news of victory or defeat.

Among the officers in attendance on Tsar Nicholas was the future reforming minister of war, Count Dmitri Miliutin, then a colonel; and in his diary he described how Greig was so weary and overwhelmed at the prospect of telling his soldier sovereign that Russia's armies had suffered defeat that he was incapable of giving the Court a coherent account of what had happened. Personal experiences intruded into his stumbling flow of words and he gave Nicholas the impression that his soldiers had lacked courage and fought badly. To Miliutin's consternation, as Greig's narrative rambled on, Tsar Nicholas sank back into a chair and burst into a flood of tears. Then, standing up to his full height, he seized the wretched Greig by the shoulders, shook him violently and bellowed, 'Have you any idea what you are saying?'[31] The news of the Alma was not made public for several days: Russia's newspaper readers were first told that, after an artillery duel between the two armies, Menshikov, finding his troops outnumbered, had ordered a strategic withdrawal to the defences of Sebastopol itself. Only when alarming rumours reached the capital from Berlin and Vienna was it admitted that Menshikov had suffered a defeat.[32]

The earliest news of the Alma reached Paris and London by way of Constantinople, Belgrade and the Vienna telegraph on the evening of Friday, 30 September, but was not made public until the following day. Most ministers were out of town, Lord Aberdeen himself about to leave Balmoral, where he had been in attendance on the Queen, for a few weeks at Haddo, his Aberdeenshire estate. But Sir James Graham made sure that the news was telegraphed to Scotland; and he followed it up with a letter suggesting that the Prime Minister should 'take the tide at its rise' and hold a snap election, no doubt counting on the Alma factor to boost the popularity of the Peelites.[33]

No one doubted that victory in the field would lead to the capture of Sebastopol and probably to peace. Indeed, hard on the news of the Alma came reports from several sources, including Britain's Consul-General at Bucharest, which suggested that Sebastopol had already fallen. When, from the steps of the Royal Exchange, the Lord Mayor announced the victory of the Alma to a cheering crowd of Londoners on Saturday evening, the proclamation only mentioned the battle, despite rumours of the great prize in allied hands. But Napoleon III was less circumspect. On that Saturday he was reviewing troops beneath the great Emperor's Column outside Boulogne, with the young Empress Eugénie beside him and a line of eagle-topped tricolour standards in front. The occasion was irresistible, and the Emperor won easy cheers with the words both sides of the Channel wished to hear. 'At the moment I speak', Napoleon declared, 'I have little doubt that the flags of the allied armies are waving on the walls of Sebastopol.'[34]

The Times proudly announced 'The Fall of Sebastopol' in its Monday edition (2 October), 'confirmed' the report next day, quoted Napoleon III's speech with warm approval, and by Wednesday was wondering when the Baltic Fleet would finish off the war by taking Kronstadt and landing troops to enter St Petersburg. When, at midday on Monday, the saluting guns at the Tower and in Hyde Park fired salvoes celebrating the victory of the Alma, Londoners might legitimately be forgiven for assuming that the cannonade signalled the capture of Sebastopol.[35]

Cabinet ministers spent a few hours circulating notes to each other on what should be done with Sebastopol. Palmerston and Graham were agreed that the port should never be 'returned' to Russia. Graham wanted all fortifications facing the sea destroyed at once, but not the land defences, as the expeditionary force would need to winter in Sebastopol if the war continued. Most of his colleagues agreed with him, and, indeed, the suggestion had already been made by Napoleon III. Palmerston, who even before the expedition landed in the Crimea had told Clarendon that he thought the peninsula should come once again under the Sultan's sovereignty, argued that Sebastopol should remain intact until the peace conference, as a bargaining counter.[36] Far away, at Haddo, Lord Aberdeen showed greater statesmanship. No territory liberated from Islamic rule by a Christian Power had ever been restored to the Sultan, and he personally could not share Palmerston's Turcophilia: 'The Turks really hate us all alike,' he reminded Clarendon on 1 October, echoing the tone of Alexander Gordon's letters from Constantinople. 'With Sebastopol entirely razed, and the fleet captured, I would not give sixpence for the possession of the Crimea in any political view,' he told Clarendon two days later, admitting that he was 'much encouraged by the news'. But the Prime Minister was more cautious than his colleagues down south. It was, perhaps, a little premature to begin disposing of Sebastopol; there was still no official word from Lord Stratford or Lord Raglan that the city was, indeed, in allied hands. 'The suspense is most tantalizing; and this is increased by distance,' Aberdeen added.[37]

All suspense was ended on Thursday, 5 October. An official announcement on the Paris Bourse denying that Sebastopol had been occupied by the Franco-British armies was followed later in the day by reports in London that the allied force had set out on a flank march to 'the port of Balaclava'. By the weekend the press was looking for ingenious explanations of the tale: all the work of stock exchange speculators, said *The Illustrated London News*; some diabolical scheme of Russian agents intended to demoralize the British and French public by raising false hopes, suggested a blandly unembarrassed *Times*.[38]

The origins of the rumour may well have been less nefarious. After the Alma defeat Menshikov left the city with a sizeable force on 24 September, arguing that if the allies knew they had a Russian army on their flank and in their rear, they would not risk an assault on Sebastopol for fear of encirclement.[39] It is probable that garbled tales of Menshikov's hasty departure towards Simferopol reached Bucharest from Gorchakov's headquarters at Kishinev. What would nowadays be called the enforced Russian news blackout encouraged the spread of rumour, for it was obvious that the bells would have rung out had Nicholas's army won a victory in the Crimea. But *The Times* was right to comment on the demoralizing effect of the report. Politicians were accustomed to such buffetings of fortune: the general public was not.

Over the following month there was to be a sharp reaction to the twin disappointments of an unmolested Kronstadt and an untaken Sebastopol.

CHAPTER NINE

The Decisive Weeks

The flank march of the allied army from the Belbec valley to the sea took some thirty hours. The weather was humid by day and foggy after dark; and there was a strange clash of arms on the Monday afternoon when Raglan and his staff, emerging from woodland on the Simferopol Road encountered the rearguard of a Russian force moving away from Sebastopol six miles due east of Severnaya. The horse artillery, reacting quicker than the Hussars, soon scattered the surprised Russian infantrymen and captured some carts filled with food, clothing and delicacies. But Raglan himself was uneasy that night. His artillery was hampered by the narrowness of the pathway through the brushwood; the French were even worse placed, with all their guns parked overnight in what was probably the crater of an extinct volcano. Raglan was much relieved next morning when, four miles after crossing the river Chernaya by a bridge at Traktir, he reached the village of Kadikoi and saw beneath him what looked like a lagoon surrounded by red sandstone cliffs. It was the inner harbour of Balaclava.[1]

Genoese traders had discovered the inlet of Balaclava in the sixteenth century and constructed a small fort at the cliff-top to protect their anchorage. The fort was defended in September 1854 by some seventy militiamen with four brass mortars and they dutifully fired on Raglan and the vanguard of the expeditionary force as it prepared to descend from the Kadikoi plateau to the sea. It was, however, a token gesture of defiance, and Balaclava was taken without loss of life on either side. Already the *Agamemnon*, Rear-Admiral Lyons's flagship, was off the inlet and Lyons sent the frigate *Niger* into the small harbour of Balaclava on Tuesday afternoon (26 September). By that evening a line of white bell tents ringed the edge of the plateau while seamen and marines were ashore along the cart track which served the cluster of sheds and shanties as a village street. With green-tiled cottages half-buried in honeysuckle and clematis, Balaclava was a picture of rustic artistry, the calm, translucent silver of the inlet forming a haven of domesticated peace. On the higher ground there were orchards and, below them, narrow sloping strips of pumpkins and tomato plants. Apart from hanging draperies of Muscatel grapes, it could have been an English West Country water-colour. 'A most beautiful harbour, not more than two miles round – a basin in its shape, where the water is always like a mill-pond, though deep enough for any line-of-battle ship to come within stone throw of the shore', wrote Henry Clifford of the Rifle Brigade to his brother on the afternoon after the British arrived.[2] His letter was cheerfully optimistic: the fall of Sebastopol was imminent, now that siege guns were being landed; and, for the first time in six days, officers and men would be able to enjoy a wash – they might even shed their uniforms, a luxury they had been denied for a fortnight. On both counts, Lieutenant Clifford was wrong: the troops, called suddenly to arms, were sent unkempt and unwashed to bivouac on the heights inland; and another 346 days were to pass before allied flags flew over smouldering Sebastopol.

Balaclava was recommended as an 'admirable siege depot' by Major-General Macintosh when, early in November, 1853, he prepared for the British ambassador in Constantinople the first intelligence assessment on Sebastopol's defences in nearly twenty years; and it was favoured by Burgoyne, who had studied Macintosh's report. But so narrow an inlet could hardly serve both the British and the French. Was it really the best forward base, Raglan wondered? Momentarily he hesitated, for from the Kadikoi Plateau another cart-track ran due west to the twin open bays of Kamiesh and Kazatch, nearer to Sebastopol. He consulted Rear-Admiral Lyons, who had no doubt that Balaclava was the right depot. Kamiesh and Kazatch were north-facing exposed anchorages, rather than harbours. Although steam tugs could manoeuvre sailing vessels more easily in the twin bays, their waters were shallow. A month later with the French building up a larger and better equipped expeditionary force, Raglan's critics began to argue that he should have given them first choice of the quayside. But in September it seemed the right decision. No one believed that the siege would last long, and the British certainly had more vessels than the French plying between Constantinople and the Crimea.[3]

On the evening he reached Balaclava Raglan drafted a precise memorandum for General Rose to pass to the French high command: 'Lord Raglan does not consider it at all necessary that the French army should march upon Balaclava. The English army came here with a view only of securing its communications with the sea. The combined object of the allied armies is to establish themselves on the range of heights [which] may be said to command Sebastopol.' Detailed references marked off segments of the front to be held by the British and by the French, with the Turks in reserve. Siege guns, the French were assured, would be landed speedily. Soon everything would be ready for bombarding the city from the land and from the sea.[4]

Raglan's memorandum reads more like a directive from a generalissimo than a proposal from one allied commander to another; and with good reason. For on this flank march Saint-Arnaud's health had finally given way. His son-in-law, who served as his military secretary, and the omnipresent Colonel Trochu persuaded the Marshal to hand over command of the French forces to the soldier whom Napoleon III had already nominated as his deputy, François Canrobert; and it was to the infantryman whom Raglan persisted in addressing as 'General Kant Robert' that the memorandum was despatched.

Poor Saint-Arnaud resigned his command early on the morning of 26 September, at his overnight headquarters beside the river Chernaya. As soon as he was well enough to be moved, a column of Spahis escorted the mortally sick Marshal down to Balaclava, where it was easier to board a vessel than at Kamiesh. 'I had only one desire – to enter Sebastopol', he told his doctor, as he waited to sail for Constantinople and home in the steamer that had brought him out from Marseilles in the spring; 'Had I been able to carry out my original plan, perhaps I could have done it, but I have been master neither of myself nor of events', he added. Saint-Arnaud had nothing but praise for the British when Raglan went to bid him farewell: a thirty-hour voyage across calm seas to the Bosphorus would speed his recovery, he told his visitor. But six hours before the *Berthollet* was due to pass Madame Saint-Arnaud's waterside Villa at Yenikoy, the Marshal lost his long fight to go on living. An autopsy confirmed a chronic disease of the heart. But in a real sense he was a casualty of his own campaign, for, whatever the clinical cause of death, there is no doubt that he contracted cholera at Varna, later drugging himself heavily so as to rise from his sick-bed and spend those weary hours in the saddle at Calamita Bay and the Alma. The *Berthollet* continued her voyage to France, and on 16 October the Marshal was buried beside the greatest names of French military history in the chapel of the Invalides.[5]

Were it not for an obligatory tuft of imperial beard and vestigial reminiscence of flowing hair about the neck, portraits of Canrobert seem to anticipate Dame Agatha Christie's descriptions of Hercule Poirot. Saint-Arnaud's successor was commendably neat and precise in manner, a short, dapper man with a high, domed forehead and a heavily waxed moustache. It had soon become clear to his British allies that Canrobert possessed many excellent qualities, not least among them the combination of a brisk efficiency with a humane sense of compassion for his men. In three months as liaison officer Hugh Rose, who spoke and wrote French well, had come to understand and admire the astute Canrobert, although his journal shows that he was baffled by the General's lingering attachment to the exiled Orleanists. Such subtleties of loyalty were not apparent to Raglan's staff. 'His bravery is without question', Colonel Calthorpe commented at the time of Canrobert's appointment. Yet there was, none the less, one serious disadvantage for the French in the General's assumption of these new responsibilities. For Canrobert was inexperienced in high command; at forty-five, he was eleven years younger than his predecessor and twenty-one years younger than the British Commander-in-Chief. It is not surprising if, at first, even so gentlemanly an officer as Raglan tended to treat him brusquely.[6]

Not, however, for long. For at the first conference of the allied commanders, Canrobert insisted that he could not order a direct frontal assault by French troops on the Russian positions defending Sebastopol from the south until the forts had been reduced by steady bombardment. Over this question Canrobert had a strong supporter in General Burgoyne, to whom Raglan listened, with respect, more and more once it became clear that Sebastopol was a fortress needing investment. It was settled that no attack would be made until the siege guns were in position and the French ready to open up with a light cannonade on those Russian defences.[7]

Twenty-one days elapsed between the conference of allied commanders and the first bombardment of the city. They were the three decisive weeks of the campaign. For, while the British concentrated first on hauling massive siege guns up from the shore to the heights and then on digging zig-zag approach trenches to extend sunken cover for the attacking infantry, Admirals Kornilov and Nakhimov took advantage of this precious time to ensure that Totleben's genius made Sebastopol unassailable. These three weeks condemned the allied expeditionary force to all the rigours of a war of attrition.

The sight of defeated and dejected troops filing back into their city from the Alma Heights caused dismay among the people of Sebastopol.

Worse was soon to follow when, on 24 September, Menshikov led his main force of soldiers out along the Simferopol Road, leaving the city's defence to the admirals. On the previous afternoon seven Russian warships, moored across the entrance to the harbour, were sunk to prevent the allied fleets from entering Sebastopol Roads, and the admirals could therefore make use of seven ships' crews, together with naval reserves from the barracks, to help ward off an assault by land. Nevertheless, on the day after Menshikov's departure, Admiral Kornilov, who assumed the title of Chief of Staff of the garrison, reckoned he had no more than 17,800 men, including sappers, to hold the city; along the north shore only twelve guns were manned and in position. But, like Suvorov and Kutuzov, Vladimir Kornilov was one of those remarkable folk heroes who, over the centuries, have lifted Russian morale from abject defeatism to a sublime defiance of the enemy. While Totleben drew up the plans for new batteries, Kornilov mobilized men, women and children to work throughout the day, bringing up guns from the ships, deepening trenches, building new protective works for existing redoubts, and making certain that powder magazines were secure. In front of the British position a round tower, the Malakoff, was converted into a formidable redoubt, protected by earthworks and linked to two other bastions, the Great Redan to the south and the Little Redan to the north. The French forces, to the west of the British, faced the improved fortifications of the Old Town – the Flagstaff, Central and Quarantine Bastions. Across the harbour, at Severnaya, the 'Star Fort' guarded the approach from the north. Fort Alexander to the south of the harbour entrance and Fort Constantine to the north remained as sentinels against bombardment by the fleet. To the south and east of the city, lamps and flares were improvised so that work could continue on improving all these defences by night and by day. In one thirty-six-hour period of intense physical labour no less than a hundred guns were placed in position.[8]

The Friday after Menshikov's departure – 27 September by Western calendars – was the anniversary of the coronation of Alexander I, the Tsar who redeemed the burning of Moscow by entering Paris in triumph eighteen months later; and Kornilov resolved to associate the coming battle for Sebastopol with the epic struggles of 1812–14 by an act of solemn religious observance, with Holy Russia consecrating the city's defences. Priests, processing with sacred ikons and banners, sprinkled holy water over the troops, blessing them with the sign of the cross as they knelt beside the fortifications. It was thus that Russia's soldiers had shown their devotion to the Blessed Virgin of Smolensk on the eve of Borodino, under the puzzled scrutiny of Napoleon's staff. British and French officers were watching through their telescopes all the frenzied activity in front of Sebastopol day after day; but we do not know if, on this Friday, they perceived the significance of the strange procession which they must have seen winding along the earthworks and parapets in front of Malakoff tower and the Greater and Lesser Redans.

Although the allies had established themselves in Eupatoria as well as at Balaclava, they did not hold the lower stretches of the road down which they had marched from the Alma, and Sebastopol was not, in reality, cut off. It was thus possible for Menshikov's naval aide, Stetsenkov, to ride up to Kornilov's headquarters on the morning after the religious ceremony. What, he asked on behalf of 'the commander-in-chief', was 'the state of Sebastopol'? And had the Chief of Staff made any assessment of enemy intentions? Kornilov replied crisply that he needed more trained battalions of soldiery since it was clear that the British and French intended to attack the city from the south. Two days later even Prince Menshikov ventured as far as Severnaya and met the Admiral in conference. The Prince told Kornilov that he had received reinforcements from the Caucasus and Odessa as well as from Gorchakov at Kishinev; more men, guns and supplies were on the way south from Moscow. An angry Kornilov even wrung from Menshikov a promise of infantrymen to support his improvised defence force; and during the first days of October the Tarutinsky, Moskovsky and Borodinsky regiments arrived back in the city, while Menshikov himself concentrated his army between the river Belbec and Severnaya so as to give Kornilov support in the rear.[9]

Lord Raglan and Sir John Burgoyne had chosen the day before Menshikov's conference with Kornilov to reconnoitre the Russian position from the heights looking northwards towards the city; and Raglan's nephew leaves us in no doubt that, after their ride, they no longer underrated the strength of Sebastopol's defensive system. 'The more he saw of it', Colonel Calthorpe writes of his uncle's impressions, 'the more convinced he was of the utter impracticability of attacking the town without first reducing the fire of the Russian batteries.' 'Large batteries were constructed on every available spot that could in any way assist the defence of the place,' Calthorpe wrote, with some concern, a few days later. 'When we first sat down before Sebastopol, we saw thousands of men employed making earthworks, and daily fresh batteries sprang up as if by enchantment.'[10]

Slowly and ponderously the British and French prepared for the great bombardment. Raglan worked as closely as possible with Dundas, Lyons and the French Admiral, Hamelin; the prospects for collaboration looked good. It was agreed that there would be a simultaneous cannonade of the Russian defences from sea and land, beginning at half-past six on the morning of Tuesday, 17 October. The most centrally placed of Canrobert's batteries – forty-nine guns massed on a low hill known as Mount Rodolphe – would signal the start of the bombardment by firing three shells; and then the whole tempest of explosive would shake Sebastopol to its foundations. The army would take care of the Malakoff and the Redan; the fleets would silence Forts Constantine and Alexander, as well as any other batteries above the harbour; 'Star Fort' at Severnaya was on the wrong shore, too distant for that day's fighting. All in all, the admirals and generals agreed, it would be the heaviest bombardment the world had ever heard.[11]

Mrs Fanny Duberly had been told on Sunday by General Airey's ebullient aide-de-camp, Captain Nolan, that on no account should she miss being early at the forward positions on Tuesday, so as to be certain of seeing the start of the great bombardment. But she was still asleep in her cabin aboard a steamer in Balaclava Harbour when the first crash of guns echoed in the hills. The sound was, indeed, impressive; but it was not what Raglan or Canrobert or Captain Nolan or the ever-observant William Russell had wished to hear, for, before the French could give their signal, the Russians noticed a movement behind the allied gun positions and themselves began the firing. Perhaps others than Captain Nolan and Mrs Duberly had discussed, too freely, the timing of allied intentions; for the Russians were not taken by surprise and, by later standards, security at Balaclava was appallingly lax. Certainly no one had anticipated that the great bombardment would become a gunners' duel. Moreover, to Raglan's consternation, in all these exchanges there was no sign of any cannonade from the warships clearly visible off the coast. Not until the afternoon were the fleets in action. Admiral Hamelin had decided that he was too short of ammunition for a day-long bombardment; but he was slow to warn the British admirals of his change of plan, and even slower to send the information to Canrobert and Raglan.[12]

Long before the ships opened fire, the French artillery had gone silent. Brigadier-General Rose's diary, written up that evening, contains the cryptic sentence, 'French magazine blew up, 8.48';

Calthorpe, too, mentions 'the great disaster of the day, viz. the explosion of the principal French magazine' on Mount Rodolphe as having occurred 'at 8-45 a.m.'; and in his next letter home Alexander Gordon wrote: 'The batteries opened yesterday morning for both French and British attacks but about 9 a.m. the French fire entirely ceased owing to a terrible explosion in the centre'. Other accounts put the 'thunderous explosion' more than an hour and a quarter later, when a second magazine appears to have been hit. As often in the letters which Lord Aberdeen received from his son, there seems to have been a measure of exaggeration, especially in the phrase 'entirely ceased', for the outer French batteries kept up a steady cannonade until half-past ten when the senior artillery officer, General Thirry, reported to Canrobert that he could not maintain an effective barrage.[13]

Canrobert himself was so unnerved by the earlier explosion that he was convinced the Russians were employing a secret weapon, a shell filled with devastating high explosive. Rose and a French major were sent at once to Lord Raglan with what Calthorpe described as 'this monstrous piece of information and appeared quite astonished when we all said we did not believe such humbug'. Later in the day Rose returned to British headquarters with a written message for Raglan: 'General Canrobert and Colonel Trochu and I were this afternoon in the French Redoubt', it explained. 'The whole magazine of the battery was blown up' after three-quarters of an hour of heavy shelling; it was unlikely that the battery would be able to open up again tomorrow. Perhaps the redoubt would never be rebuilt, he added.[14] Meanwhile, Russian sorties threatened the general position along this sector of the French line. This depressing news was followed by further explosions, as the Russian bombardment again set off French ammunition outside the redoubts. Conversely, soon after three in the afternoon, a Russian magazine at the rear of the Great Redan went up, with 'immense beams of wood and what looked like barrels thrown high in the air'. Here, when this key position was reduced to smouldering rubble, was the moment for which cavalry and infantry had been waiting since soon after dawn. 'We have been saddled all day in expectation of a turn-out,' wrote Lieutenant Temple Godman of the Dragoon Guards to his sister later that day. 'Once the whole army was said to be advancing, and pistols were capped and got ready.' All that the expectant officers looked for was a signal from Raglan or his mounted aides to go forward. It never came; the allied commanders had agreed that the British and French infantry should attack together.

Since Canrobert was in no position to order an advance, Raglan dutifully held his men back.[15]

Raglan's staff, failing to sense the lost opportunities of that October afternoon, were pleased with the success of their gunners and confident that the Russian defensive nut would soon crack under joint Anglo-French pressure. Nevertheless Calthorpe admitted that the Russians had imposed 'their first successful check against a hitherto victorious enemy'.[16] The soldiers were particularly disappointed with the fleet. 'The naval attack yesterday was a complete failure,' Alexander Gordon reported in his letter of 18 October. 'They could make no impression on the Russian batteries. Some lay all the blame on Admiral Dundas for not going nearer than 1500 yards. He might just as well have remained 15 miles off.' Hugh Rose's diary entry is also critical of the naval bombardment for he, too, could not understand why the warships had not come closer inshore; but Rose's jottings were, of course, meant only for himself and not for the perusal of a father who happened to be prime minister.[17] Dundas and Lyons subsequently insisted that the bigger warships could not come closer inshore because of a dangerous shoal off the bluff of land on which Fort Constantine stood. In fact, despite the soldiers' strictures, Admiral Lyons brought *Agamemnon*, his flagship, to within half a mile of Fort Constantine, knowing that he had only a few feet of water under her keel. The combined fleet was able to concentrate 500 guns on the Russian seaward defences, maintaining a constant cannonade from 'about half-past 1 until half-past 6 p.m., when being quite dark, the ships hauled off', Dundas reported to the Admiralty; there had never been so heavy or sustained a bombardment of a fortress from the sea. The Russian forts, whose granite casements suffered negligible damage from such a long-range assault, responded with 'a great quantity of red-hot shot', which started fires aboard Lyons's flagship and three other line-of-battle ships. Two more – *Albion* and *Arethusa* – were so badly damaged that they had to be towed across the Black Sea and repaired at Constantinople. During the five-hour action the British lost 44 officers and men killed and 266 wounded, while the French suffered 212 casualties, 32 of them fatal. Poor liaison between Dundas and Hamelin, together with the dangerous decision to use the vessels as moored floating batteries, contributed to what was virtually a naval defeat.[18]

From prisoners, and from Polish deserters, the allies later discovered that, during the bombardment, the Russians had suffered one great loss. As soon as the artillery duel began, Admiral Kornilov set out from

his headquarters beside the Volokhov Tower, to the north of the
harbour, to visit each of Totleben's forts in the threatened southern
perimeter of the defences. Shortly after eleven o'clock he left the
Malakoff to visit the Borodinsky Regiment, who with their horses were
sheltering from the storm of fire in a ravine to the west of the fort. But he
had only walked some six or seven yards when he was hit by a round
shot and was carried off to the naval hospital, where he died a few hours
later.[19] As Admiral Nakhimov was also slightly wounded that
morning, there was a momentary crisis in command on the Russian
side. But the sight of Kornilov unconscious on a stretcher beside the
Malakoff did not demoralize the troops, as had the fatal wounding of
Bagration at Borodino; rather it intensified their stoical capacity to
endure until they themselves seemed fanatics, as willing as their dying
commander to court a hero's death. Ultimately it was this inspired
courage of Russia's soldiery that cemented the fissures in Totleben's
defensive wall.

'The "weak Front" of Sebastopol turns out to be a very respectable
one', Alexander Gordon commented drily to his father in the letter
which he wrote on the following day. No one doubted, however, that
the cavalry and infantry would go forward soon and scatter the
Russians as on the Alma. When the army went into winter quarters in
Sebastopol, Colonel Gordon told his father, he would, he thought,
come back to Britain for a few months and then return to the Crimea,
accompanied this time by his wife, before next spring's campaigning
season began.[20] But on the Wednesday on which Gordon wrote this
letter came the first warning that the Russians were about to turn the
besiegers inside out. That morning, as Raglan was watching his guns
firing once again at the Redan, a report was brought to him from
Turkish outposts to the north-east of the British positions which
suggested that Menshikov was assembling a large force behind the
river Chernaya and on the hills around the village of Chorgun.[21]

Raglan rode up a track on the edge of the Sapoune Heights from
where he could look due eastwards across the Plain of Balaclava, along
a ridge called by his troops the 'Causeway Heights' – for the ridge gave
the impression of supporting like a causeway the best surfaced route in
the Crimea, the Worontsoff Road, linking Sebastopol to Baidar and
Yalta. To Raglan's left, as he gazed through his field glass along the
ridge, lay the 'North Valley', long and narrow, rising in grass-covered
downland to the Fedioukine hills and almost barred more than three

miles to the east by a humpy knoll running north-south from above the Chernaya to the Worontsoff Road. A hazy gap gave a faint outline of the upland beyond the Chernaya and around Chorgun. There was no sign as yet of any Russian concentration in those hills, and Raglan observed before him all that he had anticipated: a succession of six redoubts on small hillocks straddling the Worontsoff Road, two on the edge of the North Valley and four overlooking the South Valley, and the approaches to the gorge at the foot of which lay Balaclava village and harbour. Of these redoubts only the farthest east and south had been given a name by the allied soldiers – 'Canrobert's Hill', in honour of the new French commander. Each redoubt was armed with 12-pounder British naval guns manned by the Turks. To Raglan all this seemed a strong enough protective crescent: everyone assured him that the Anatolian Turk was a good natural fighter. But, as an additional precaution, he placed the defence of his army's eastern flank under the command of General Sir Colin Campbell, whose 93rd Highlanders were encamped around Kadikoi. The approaches to the Balaclava base were safeguarded by the Royal Marines, with three more batteries of naval guns. Raglan saw no reason to think that his foothold on the Crimean shore was in danger.

For the next week French and British guns continued, day after day, to lob high-explosive shells and red-hot shot against Totleben's defences and into the heart of Sebastopol, bringing house walls crashing down and causing a succession of small fires. But, while Raglan and Canrobert gave their attention to these siege operations, beyond the protective screen of the Fedioukine hills twenty-four new battalions, hurried eastwards by forced marches from Bessarabia, were poised, ready to strike southwards towards the improvised British harbour and base; and two more divisions were on their way. Effectively these troops were under the command of General Pavel Liprandi, one of Russia's ablest soldiers. Back in St Petersburg, Tsar Nicholas and his staff officers had every confidence in Liprandi's force, if only they could instil some confidence into Menshikov and encourage him to take the initiative.[22]

The Prince, however, was unnerved by the events of the past month, and particularly by the confusion at the Alma; his judgement, faulty before the allied landing, was now the prey to every whim of the moment. At a war council which he convened on Monday, 23 October, his subordinate generals could see for themselves Menshikov's difficulty in making up his mind: the weather was worsening, and he needed to be able to send St Petersburg news of a victory before winter set in; he was inclined to order Liprandi to attack the forward British positions facing Sebastopol. The generals urged him to strike instead at Balaclava – but, they said, not yet, for it was essential to wait until the full strength of the Russian army could descend on this weak allied flank. If they struck too soon, said Liprandi, their gains would not be decisive and the allies would have time to strengthen these positions against a renewed assault. Menshikov, however, was in a hurry. The attack must come on that Wednesday. Urgent orders were sent to General Ryzhov, who was three miles south of Bakchisarai, to march some fifteen miles down the road to Sebastopol and concentrate his cavalry, horse artillery, an infantry regiment and four battalions of rifle sharpshooters in the Fedioukine Heights, immediately above the 'North Valley'.[23]

The British knew that there was some Russian activity in the hills. Two days after Raglan's first alert, there was a 'false alarm' soon after dusk when a British outpost heard the sound of Russian reinforcements 'marching in with their band playing' and soon 'the reflection of their watchfires could be seen in the sky over the hill'. All night the cavalry stood ready; a nervous sputter of musketry from one of the Turkish forts was followed 'an hour or two later' by the roar of a naval battery opening up against an imaginary enemy patrol. Another alarm, on Sunday, fetched out the whole of Sir George Cathcart's 4th Division, unnecessarily. After such incidents it is not surprising that when, on the following Tuesday night, Campbell sent Raglan a report that a Turkish spy had seen 20,000 Russian infantry and 5,000 Russian cavalry converging on the Plain of Balaclava, the British Commander-in-Chief merely received the message with a crisp 'Very well', sent no formal acknowledgement to Campbell, and continued discussing with Canrobert the next stage of operations against Sebastopol.[24]

Campbell, however, was so impressed by the Turkish spy's account that he discussed it with the commander of the Cavalry Division, Lord Lucan, who also took the report seriously. George Charles Bingham, third Earl of Lucan, received a poor press for much of his life, and a worse one after his death. His chronic quarrel with his wife's brother, Lord Cardigan (commander of the Light Brigade), was known throughout London society and was a persistent source of embarrassed irritation to Lord Raglan, both at Varna and since landing in the Crimea. Lucan, an unpopular parade-ground martinet who at the age of twenty-six bought command of the 17th Lancers in November 1826 for £25,000, became an ideal butt for would-be army reformers wishing to end aristocratic privilege: had not his own soldiery nicknamed him 'Lord Look-On'? To his fellow officers in the Crimea Lucan was 'the cautious ass', as distinct from his brother-in-law, who was 'the dangerous ass'.[25] But Look-On possessed one advantage over Raglan's other divisional commanders: he had actually served as a volunteer with a Russian army fighting against the Turks. In 1828 Colonel George Bingham had taken temporary leave of absence from the Lancers and been attached to the staff of that same Prince Worontsoff whose Crimean estates were served by the road across the Causeway Heights. Twelve months in Nicholas I's army won Lucan the Order of St Anne (Second Class) and the Tsar's personal approbation for courage: it also gave him some insight into the Russian military mind; and, after talking to the Turkish spy on that Tuesday, Lucan did not doubt that a Russian attack was imminent.

Before dawn on Wednesday, Lucan was in the saddle patrolling the Causeway Heights with two of his staff officers. They trotted past the Light Brigade: Cardigan did not join them; quite apart from the reluctance of the brothers-in-law to speak to each other, he was that night sleeping aboard his private yacht, *Dryad*, which had entered Balaclava Harbour a few days before. But the second-in-command of the Light Brigade, Lord George Paget, rode out to join Lucan, and it was Paget who, in the first clear light of day, noticed something different about the redoubt on Canrobert's Hill. The Turks on that redoubt could see farther east than any other allied observers —and the redoubt was flying two flags, one above the other, the agreed signal that the enemy was advancing in a major assault on the allied positions. While Lucan and his companions were galloping back to turn out the cavalry, the sound of artillery echoed from the furthest heights above the valley: it was shortly after six o'clock, and the Russian attack on Canrobert's Hill had begun.[26]

To the British, that Wednesday was 25 October, St Crispin's Day, the 439th anniversary of Henry V's victory at Agincourt; but by the Julian Calendar it was 13 October, the 42nd anniversary of Malo-yaroslavets, the battle celebrated in Russia as the beginning of Napoleon I's 'rout and ruin'. On both counts it was a poor anniversary for Canrobert's compatriots.

CHAPTER TEN

The Day of Four Cavalry Charges

For Lord Raglan's staff, Wednesday, 25 October, began with an unusually exigent reveille. By now they were used to the regular boom of siege artillery on the plateau. But, alarmingly, on this morning the sound of a heavy cannonade came from the other direction three miles up the valley. Almost simultaneously Raglan received a report of Lucan's cavalry reconnaissance and a warning, brought from French headquarters by Hugh Rose, that one of Bosquet's patrols had sighted 'a large Russian force threatening Balaclava'. There could be no doubt that, exactly five weeks after their drubbing on the Alma, the Russians had gone over to the offensive. As Henry Duberly scribbled in a note to his wife, 'The battle of Balaclava has begun and promises to be a hot one.'[1]

Lucan's cavalry, 'on parade as usual . . . an hour before daybreak', were in the saddle soon after their divisional commander's return from his reconnaissance. They cantered forward across the plain to within half a mile of the redoubt on Canrobert's Hill, while Campbell's Highlanders took up positions in South Valley, intent on guarding the route down to the harbour. But when Raglan discovered the ferocity of the Russian assault, he became uneasily conscious of his eastern flank's exposed weaknesses. The Duke of Cambridge's 1st Division and Cathcart's 4th Division were ordered to leave their trenches facing Sebastopol and march to the plain so as to strengthen the shield around Balaclava. They could not, however, reach their new positions for another two hours and, as an immediate safeguard, Raglan brought Lucan's cavalry back. They would help defend the western end of the South Valley, facing north-east towards the Causeway: Lord Cardigan's Light Brigade was on the left; Brigadier-General Scarlett's Heavy Brigade of dragoons were a hundred yards away, on the right. Raglan also approached Canrobert. But the French Commander-in-Chief, far from showing interest in the fate of the hill named after him, was militarily obsessed in the duel with the Sebastopol forts. Only with reluctance did he agree to spare some reserve battalions of infantry and the Chasseurs d'Afrique from General Bosquet's 1st Division. It was after ten o'clock before Hugh Rose rode out to Raglan's observation post on the edge of the Sapoune Heights to inform the British commander that Bosquet's troops would soon be moving into positions immediately beneath him, between the Sapoune escarpment and the first slopes of the Fedioukine Heights.[2]

No doubt tactically this defensive deployment of British and French troops was eminently sound. It was, however, demoralizing to the third ally, 'Johnny Turk'. For over an hour the thousand Turkish defenders of Canrobert's Hill kept the Russians resolutely at bay, half of them perishing in one of the unsung epics of the campaign. But when the Russians finally scaled the inner earthworks Turkish resistance crumbled 'all along the range'. Russell of *The Times* arrived at the ridge which was to serve as his observation post for the battle too late to see the Turks' heroic stand but in time to record, with 'inexpressible disgust', the flight of the survivors. The Sultan's troops in the second, third and fourth redoubts – who were said to be Tunisians and not Anatolian Turks – did, indeed, take to their heels at the approach of 'the Cossacks', fleeing in the general direction of the harbour. 'We were much annoyed at seeing the Turks come flying down past us crying, and calling upon "Allah" ', Sergeant Mitchell of the 13th Hussars later recalled, with that endearing meiosis which runs throughout his reminiscences. 'Our men called out "No Bono Johnny" but that made no impression on them, for soon they were off as fast as they could go to Balaclava.' Mrs Fanny Duberly met them shortly afterwards. Alerted at eight o'clock by the message from her husband, she was riding up to a vantage point in the hills when, to her indignation, she 'found the road blocked by Flying Turks'. 'Had I known of their *brutal* cowardice', she wrote two days later to her sister Selina, 'I should have ridden over them all.' Such drastic action proved, however, unnecessary. Fanny reached her husband safely, only to find that he was 'striking tent' and that 'mounted Cossacks . . . were making straight for where I stood'. She was witnessing, in the most alarming manner, the first of the four cavalry charges of that historic Wednesday.[3]

Fortunately, between the tents and the Cossacks were Sir Colin Campbell's 'Highlanders', defending Kadikoi. This famous body of men was, in fact, a scratch force of 550 Sutherland Highlanders from the 93rd Regiment, together with a leavening of Turks and 140 men from other British regiments, hastily rounded up in Balaclava base by

Sir Colin's aides that same morning. Two civilians, as well as Mrs Duberly, saw the Russian charge brought to a halt by the steady volleys of Campbell's imperturbable infantry. Kinglake, myopically peering across the plain to follow the twists and turns of a fast-moving battle, was to recall the glory and tragedy of Balaclava in measured prose more than a quarter of a century later; but William Howard Russell had to write a despatch for *The Times* while the menace of enemy sabres was still vivid in his eyes; and on that day he first employed a phrase which, emasculated into 'thin red line', passed rapidly into patriotic folk cliché. 'The Russians', Russell's readers saw in their newspaper columns twenty days later, 'drew breath for a moment, and then in one grand line dashed at the Highlanders. The ground flies beneath their horses' feet; gathering speed at every stride, they dash on towards that thin red streak topped with a line of steel. . . . But ere they come within 150 yards, another deadly volley flashes from the levelled rifle, and carries death and terror into the Russians.' The attack was repelled; and for the remainder of the day General Liprandi's troops stood on the defensive, eager to safeguard their commanding position on Canrobert's Hill and save, if possible, the redoubts taken in that lightning thrust along the Worontsoff Road.[4]

Liprandi was reluctant to credit 'enemy rifle fire' with driving off his horsemen. Next day he reported that the Russian cavalry charge – undertaken not solely by 'Cossacks', but by General Ryzhov's fourteen squadrons of the Kievsky and Ingermanlandsky Hussars as well – was checked simultaneously by infantry on the flank and 'English cavalry from the front'.[5] This, however, is a misleading version of events. General Scarlett's dragoons were already heading westwards to protect the Turks when they sighted the glint of Cossack lanceheads above the ridge of the Causeway, as the main Russian cavalry force bore down on Kadikoi. Scarlett, who at fifty-five had never before fought in any battle, halted the advance; he was beginning to dress his three squadrons into line when Lord Lucan galloped up and ordered the Heavy Brigade at once to charge the Russians who had by then crossed the Worontsoff Road. Although Scarlett was reluctant to be hurried by an over-excited divisional commander, he seems to have ordered the trumpeter to sound the 'Charge' so suddenly that brigadier and aide-de-camp were well in front of the Greys and Inniskillings, who formed the first line of galloping horsemen. It chanced that at this moment Ryzhov's cavalry were stationary, for their general was about to redeploy them after the frustrating check imposed by Campbell's 'thin red streak'. The Heavy Brigade therefore fell upon their enemy with all the ferocity of armoured knights in the Middle Ages, the second and third lines – the 4th and 5th Dragoon Guards and the Royals – soon adding their weight to the hand-to-hand fighting, which had taken the Russian Hussars by surprise. 'In forty-two years of service and ten campaigns, among them Kulm, Leipzig and Paris, never before have I seen such action, with both sides cutting and thrusting at each other for so long', the veteran General Ryzhov was to recall in old age.[6]

No doubt to General Ryzhov the action did, indeed, seem to last a long time; but to Raglan and Russell and Kinglake and Fanny Duberly, watching this second cavalry charge of the morning from their vantage points on the Sapoune Heights, only eight minutes elapsed between the braying trumpet call to 'Charge' and the cheers which 'burst from every lip' as the Russians were seen to retreat. Although casualties in the Heavy Brigade were light – eight killed outright and some seventy wounded – Scarlett's squadrons were too disorganized to pursue the Russians. But Cardigan's Light Brigade, deployed as neatly as on a parade ground a quarter of a mile up the valley, were eager and unscathed. 'We all felt certain', writes Sergeant Mitchell, 'that if we had been sent in pursuit of them we should have cut up many of them, besides capturing many prisoners.' So, too, thought Captain Morris, the acting commander of the 17th Lancers. He asked his brigadier's permission to charge the flying enemy. Cardigan, however, refused. He had convinced himself that ambiguously worded orders from Lucan required the brigade to remain inactive; and he would not risk yet another accusation of impetuosity. 'Well done the Heavy Brigade', came a message from Raglan to Scarlett. No words either of reproach or instruction were as yet sent to the commander of the Light Brigade.[7]

For perhaps as long as half an hour the fighting seemed to have died away. In his talks with Menshikov two days before, General Liprandi had never rated highly his chances of breaking through to Balaclava itself, and after the rebuff to Ryzhov's cavalry he was inclined to regard the battle as ended. While the Russian cavalry reformed in the shelter of the hills, Liprandi placed Colonel Prince Obolensky's field battery, eight guns manned by Don Cossacks, in a commanding defensive position at the eastern end of North Valley. As it now seemed doubtful if the Russians could hold the string of ex-Turkish redoubts, the Odessky Regiment, with supporting ancillaries, was ordered forward to the most western redoubt, so as to neutralize the defences and remove the captured British naval 12-pounders.[8]

This lull in the action was not, however, to Lord Raglan's liking. Only now was Cathcart's division moving into position beneath the Commander-in-Chief's vantage point 600 feet up on the edge of the escarpment. Cambridge's 1st Division was still not in sight, for the Duke was as methodically slow that morning as at the Alma. But Raglan had no doubt that he would shortly have enough troops to clear the Russians from the valley. General Canrobert, with his escort of Spahis, and General Bosquet had recently joined Raglan at his post in the Sapoune Heights. So, too, had the British liaison 'commissioner' with the French army, Brigadier-General Rose; and it is Hugh Rose's long-neglected diary, written up that evening in a hand still shaking with the impact of all that he had witnessed, which throws fresh light on a historically familiar day, helping to fit isolated happenings into a coherent pattern.[9]

When Rose arrived at Raglan's observation post he found the Commander-in-Chief concerned for the fate of the valiant defenders of Canrobert's Hill, those Turkish allies for whom he had as yet done nothing. For Raglan did not share the arrogant contempt of so many of his countrymen for the Ottoman Empire's regular army; he admired the fighting qualities of the infantry. 'We must set the poor Turks right again, get the redoubt back,' Rose heard Raglan say. An order was sent to Lord Lucan: the cavalry must take advantage of any opportunity to recover the Causeway Heights and would be supported by infantry advancing on two fronts. But nothing happened: Lucan could see no sign of infantry support and therefore decided that the 'opportunity' had not yet come. Through field-glasses, Raglan and his staff were watching, with mounting impatience, the first Russian attempts to remove the British 12-pounders. It was at this point, more than half an hour after his previous order to Lucan, that Raglan turned to his quartermaster-general, Sir Richard Airey, and gave verbal instructions which Airey wrote out in the famous order to Lucan: 'Lord Raglan wishes the cavalry to advance rapidly to the front – follow the enemy and try to prevent the enemy carrying away the guns – Troops Horse Artillery may accompany – French cavalry is on yr. left –Immediate'.[10]

Transmission of the order, signed by Airey, posed a minor problem. Should it be carried down to Lucan by the Commander-in-Chief's duty aide, Captain Thomas Leslie, or by Airey's aide-de-camp, that Irish-Italian hotspur, Captain Nolan? According to Hugh Rose, Raglan handed the 'bit of paper to Nolan'. This was sensible, for Nolan was a good horseman who would not need to pick his way slowly down the steep and rough path to the plain. But, Rose adds, Nolan was 'much excited'. He was, after all, a cavalry specialist. An hour earlier he had expressed deep contempt for Cardigan's inactivity. Now it seemed as if there would be an even more impressive cavalry manoeuvre than the charge of the 'Heavies': Scarlett had moved at the gallop for little more than a hundred yards; to stop the guns being carried away, the cavalry would have to cover well over a mile before clashing with the Odessky Regiment around the Second and Third Redoubts. Yet Nolan seems to have feared that the brothers-in-law whom he so despised, Lord 'Look-On' and Lord Cardigan, would through caution or incompetence muff the assault. 'I'll lead them myself, I'll lead them on', Rose reports Nolan as calling out when he began to spur his horse in a reckless descent to the plain.

It seems improbable that if Nolan did use these words, he meant them to be taken seriously. He was, to some extent, still on sufferance in the expeditionary force, for, although General Airey might rate his abilities highly, Captain Nolan remained no more than a seconded squadron commander from a hussar regiment which was never called to serve in the Crimea. His duty was to return to the group of staff officers once he had delivered Airey's message. There was no reason why he should participate in the Charge, let alone attempt to upstage Cardigan as the Murat of Balaclava. Yet it is clear that he had no intention of riding back up the escarpment. Once he reached the plain, there followed the famous exchange with Lucan, in which the cavalry's divisional commander showed perplexity over Airey's written orders. Down in the valley, 600 feet below the line of vision of Raglan and Airey, he could not see the captured British guns. 'What guns, sir? Where and what to do?' he asked Nolan testily. And Nolan, with a casual gesture pointed vaguely westwards, in the direction where from the Heights he had seen the redoubts along the Causeway: '*There*, my Lord! *There* is your enemy! *There* are your guns', he said with fatal insolence. But Lucan was not only 600 feet lower than the observers on the escarpment; he was also facing slightly north of west whereas Raglan's post faced slightly south of west. The only guns Lucan could see, with the sun glinting on their polished barrels, were the 6-pounders of Obolensky's battery, facing down the valley. He assumed that these must be the cavalry's objective. As Lucan and Cardigan conferred over the meaning of Airey's message, Nolan asked Captain Morris if he might ride that day with his 17th Hussars. Cardigan, accepting his divisional commander's assumption 'that there was no choice but to obey', was positioning his regiments in line for the Charge when he heard that 'young fellow' Nolan muttering disparaging remarks about the slowness of his preparations and he immediately threatened him with court-martial. Then Cardigan, resplendent in his blue and cherry-coloured uniform with gold trimmings across the chest and shoulder, took up his proper place ten yards ahead of the brigade, and ordered 673 men and horses to advance. It was, William Russell meticulously noted, ten minutes past eleven.[11]

As the three lines of Hussars and Lancers, 400 yards apart and 200 yards across, moved forward up the North Valley, they had to pass immediately beneath a Russian battery on the Fedioukine hills and were soon within range of another battery to their left, along the Causeway Heights. Before the Russian cannon opened up, Captain Nolan moved out of position, cutting from left to right across the advancing line, sword drawn upraised, pointing towards the redoubts with their captured British guns. Some survivors said that they thought he shouted 'Come on': it seems as if, realizing that Cardigan was leading the brigade to the wrong objective, he sought both to correct the error and to fulfil his boast to 'lead them myself'. But, no sooner had Nolan crossed to the right flank than a shell burst close to him and his body was pierced by a splinter of metal. 'He uttered a fearful cry', Sergeant Mitchell recalled several years later;[12] and the officer who brought the cavalry's scribbled orders down to the plain became the Charge's first casualty.

'Fearful' was the adjective most readily conjured up that day. 'A more fearful spectacle was never witnessed than by those who, without the power to aid, beheld their heroic countrymen rushing to the arms of death,' Russell reported to his readers in a famous *Times* despatch which described how '30 iron mouths . . . belched forth . . . a flood of smoke and flame' to thin 'our ranks'. It was 'fearful', too, for Fanny Duberly, the only allied officer's wife at that moment in the Crimea, as she stood powerless among the onlookers on the escarpment. 'Ah, even now my heart turns sick', Fanny wrote to her sister two days later, with 'I have a letter of disastrous news' as her opening words. So many of the riders and their horses were known to her: only two and a half weeks before, Lord Cardigan had lent her 'Ronald', the chestnut charger with two white fetlocks on which he was now mounted; and the 8th Hussars, her husband's regiment, were riding in the third line – although with one section short, for regimental orders, posted long before the battle, had assigned Captain Henry Duberly's troop to serve on 25 October as personal guard and escort to the Commander-in-Chief.[13]

For the first quarter of a mile it was possible for the onlookers to follow the Light Brigade quite clearly with the naked eye. Then men and horses were lost in the dust raised by their hooves and the smoke of explosives around them. But not before the group around Raglan sensed that something was wrong. 'Cardigan must have lost his head', was Hugh Rose's horrified reaction to the sight of the Light Brigade advancing on the distant guns at the end of the valley between two ridges bristling with enemy artillery. General Bosquet was close to the British liaison commissioner when he declared that what they were seeing was 'magnificent, but not war', adding in a sentence which the tactful rarely quote, 'It is madness' (*C'est de la folie*).[14]

So, too, at first thought the Russians at the other end of the valley, although Liprandi believed that the British must have made their riders drunk with spirits before they would follow a madcap leader on such an enterprise. General Ryzhov later described how, while his cavalry were reforming on the slopes above the Chernaya river, he went forward to talk to Prince Obolensky, when suddenly the Cossack gunners became excited by what looked like a cloud of dust bowling along the valley. Two minutes later, the Don Cossacks realized that these English horsemen were heading for them. They replied with shot, shell and case-shot, while Ryzhov tried to bring up his cavalry to protect the battery. But the enemy was on them, slashing with sabres and spiking the guns. Providence seemed to protect their leader, whom a Polish aristocratic officer recognized from his days in London society as the Earl of Cardigan, for his chestnut charger carried him through the battery and down towards Ryzhov's Hussars, who had been slow to respond to their general's call to arms. It was an extraordinarily confused mêlée around what was left of Obolensky's battery.[15]

By now casualties were thinning out the Light Brigade. The assault lost all impetus. Lucan, moving up more cautiously with the dragoons of the Heavy Brigade on Cardigan's right, was checked by the fire from the redoubts; and the third line of the Light Brigade reached the battery only to find dazed survivors from the first line beginning to pull back. To Fanny Duberly, still trying through her husband's field glasses to make out details from the plateau two miles away, there seemed to be some skirmishers among the Russian guns. With horror, she realized that she was looking at what was left of the Light Brigade.[16]

Mrs Duberly missed seeing the fourth cavalry charge of the day, as indeed did most of the onlookers, for Bosquet had not contented himself with coining a famous epigram. Airey's note had told Lucan, 'French cavalry is on yr. left'; and it was Bosquet who made certain that the British did indeed have support from their ally in that quarter. A mile and a half behind the 'Heavies', and therefore rather more distant than Airey's words suggested, the Fourth Regiment of Chasseurs d'Afrique moved forward at a steady trot. Under the inspired leadership of General d'Allonville they swung sharply left up the northern slope of the valley and wiped out that Russian position on the Fedioukine escarpment which had rained down shot and shell on Cardigan's men as they began their advance. Without d'Allonville's action it is doubtful if any of the survivors from the Light Brigade's Charge could have found the protective cover which enabled them to return to the British lines.[17]

For survivors there were. 'At 11.35 not a British soldier, except the dead and the dying was left in front of these bloody Muscovite guns,' *The Times* told its readers on 14 November. Yet things were not quite so bad as Russell reported at the time. Wandering in front of the guns were some of the riders whose horses had been shot beneath them. Among them was Sergeant Mitchell, who tried in vain to calm and mount one riderless horse: 'I was getting tired, for we had been out since 4 a.m.,' he wrote in his memoirs. Some survivors took protective clothing from the bodies of dead colleagues: 'From the day on which we landed, 15 September, until the 25 October, we had not had a change of linen, or hardly any opportunity of washing anything,' Mitchell shamefacedly explained. Human endurance was reaching breaking point. 'You had better make the best of your way back as fast as you can, or you will be taken prisoner,' Lord Cardigan called gruffly down to the Sergeant as he rode past him. Many were too weak to avoid capture. But, with the aid of a generous swig of rum, Mitchell reached the British lines, and throughout the afternoon dazed survivors struggled back to safety. At last, at five o'clock, there was a roll call. Of the 673 who set out on the Charge, only 195 were fit six hours later. 'You have lost the Light Brigade!' Raglan said with icy reproach to Lucan when they met that afternoon.[18]

The final casualty list gave 113 men killed and 134 wounded. But reality was grimmer than these figures suggest, for with few tents on the plain there was little immediate comfort for the survivors. 'A bitter cold night', Mitchell recorded, 'with a sharp white frost' in the small hours. Fanny Duberly, although grieved to find that her maid's husband was among the dead, was almost as affected by the sufferings of the horses. Four hundred and seventy-five perished, either in the battle or at the hands of farriers seeking to put those gravely injured out of misery. Yet there were as astonishing survivals among the animals as among the men. Sergeant Mitchell knew of one wounded horse which went through the rest of the campaign, returned to England and was still appearing regularly on parade when he left the army in 1862; and 'Ronald', as unscathed that morning as his rider, outlived the Earl of Cardigan by several years.[19]

Militarily the Charge of the Light Brigade was a futile act of heroism which achieved nothing except the destruction of a Don Cossack battery. The immediate effect of this tragic disaster was to check Raglan's plans for a counter-attack on the redoubts. He could not hope for cavalry support that afternoon, for the 'Heavies', too, had been severely mauled. Moreover if the infantry divisions of Cambridge and Cathcart recaptured the lost Turkish positions, good British regiments would have to keep them manned throughout the following weeks, reducing the effectiveness of the allied assault on Sebastopol itself. It was this argument which Canrobert hammered home in long talks with the British Commander on that Wednesday afternoon. Did it matter if Liprandi's men held the three eastern redoubts along the Causeway Heights, provided that adequate defences were thrown up around Kadikoi? The allies, Canrobert insisted, must not be distracted from the primary objective of the campaign, the need to destroy Russia's Black Sea naval base.[20]

As if to emphasize Canrobert's point, the Russians made a sortie from Sebastopol on the afternoon of 26 October, hoping to find the British sector weakened by the previous day's withdrawal of troops to deal with the threat from the Heights seven miles away. At one point a Russian column, some 700 strong, was checked by a detachment from the Brigade of Guards, but further along the line only heavy artillery fire prevented a Russian breakthrough. 'Little Inkerman', as this action was called, helped Raglan make up his mind. The infantry divisions moved back to the plateau before Sebastopol, while British sappers gave every attention to the defences covering the approach to Balaclava. Within six days they were ready for inspection and for the verdict of a veteran specialist in such matters: 'I have this day gone carefully over the entire position round Balaclava and consider it one of very great capabilities for defence throughout,' General Burgoyne wrote confidently to Raglan on the last day of the month. He added, however, that it was 'too extensive for the forces covering it'. Ten thousand more men were needed, Raglan reckoned, when he wrote that week to the War Secretary in London; and they were needed speedily. He was thinking now, not simply in terms of besieging Sebastopol, but of ways of enduring a siege of Balaclava by the combined forces of General Liprandi and his ally, the Russian winter.[21]

CHAPTER ELEVEN

Sisters of Charity and Mercy

Midway through a Friday afternoon in October 1854, a 32-year-old nurse was walking a group of orphans from Devonport up to the high ground at Stoke Damerel, where children always enjoy counting the warships moored in the Hamoaze. The nurse, Sarah Anne Terrot, belonged to an Anglican religious nursing Order, founded six years before by a naval commander's daughter, Priscilla Seddon, and generally known as the 'Devonport Sisters of Mercy,' or more simply the 'Seddonites'. Sister Sarah Anne, a woman of high intelligence fluent in French, was accustomed to discipline and obedience and she was not surprised when her walk was interrupted by an urgent message calling her back to the 'Abbey' in Plymouth. By five o'clock she was on the overnight mail train to Paddington with two other nursing Sisters; a fourth joined them at Totnes; a fifth at Bristol. When they reached London at 4 a.m. on Saturday, 21 October, the Seddonite nurses thought they had been summoned to help combat some cholera emergency in the capital. Within a few hours they were at the Secretary at War's home in Belgrave Square, where they met Florence Nightingale and agreed to serve under her at hospitals in Turkey. Two days later, at ten past eight on the Monday morning, eight Seddonites were among a party of thirty-three nurses who left London Bridge station for Folkestone, Paris and the East; and on 4 November, just fifteen days after looking down on those familiar mastheads in the Hamoaze, Sister Sarah Anne was gazing at 'great imperial Constantinople', in the rain. 'Giddy and confused, we could hardly realise that these painted houses, gay gardens and glittering minarets were not a vision or panorama', she wrote in her journal.[1]

It is small wonder if Sister Sarah Anne was 'giddy and confused' that day, for Florence Nightingale swept into Victorian legend with the awe-inspiring spontaneity of a whirlwind. At the start of October she was 'Superintendent of the Establishment for Gentlewomen during Illness' in Upper Harley Street, no more and no less. She was a solace to sick governesses and a person already feared and respected in Whig society for the persistence with which she fulfilled her vocation, but to the wider public who read the fivepenny dailies and sixpenny weeklies she remained unknown. Three weeks later, as she lay prostrate with sea sickness in a French mail steamer tossed by heavy seas off Sardinia, hers was a household name. By that last weekend in October even so radical a weekly as *The Examiner* could print a biographical portrait in which this 'proudest and purest' of 'England's daughters' was delineated with all the inventive fervour of a mediaeval hagiographer; a 34-year-old saint was, it appeared, on her way to tend the sick and the dying in the hospitals along the Asiatic shore of the Bosphorus.[2]

Tradition maintains that 'England rang with the story of Scutari because with the British Army was the first war correspondent, William Howard Russell'.[3] This tale distorts the facts, for Russell knew nothing at first hand of the tragic chaos in the hospitals beside the Bosphorus: he remained on the Balaclava front throughout the winter of 1854–5; and although his despatches after the Alma emphasized the hardships of the soldiery and criticized the lack of ambulance wagons, he spoke highly of the improvised medical services in the Crimea itself. In the second week of October *The Times* did indeed print a succession of reports publicizing the hospital inadequacies at Constantinople; this journalistic enterprise was, however, the work not of Russell but of the editor, John Delane, who arrived home in London from his brief visit to the Crimea and Turkey in the first days of the month. In crossing back to Constantinople from Eupatoria Bay, Delane experienced all 'the horrors of a ship where hundreds died from its being overcrowded with invalids'; and he made sure that what had touched his eye with pity on the Black Sea was soon made known throughout Britain in a succession of editorials from his desk in Printing House Square. The despatches themselves were datelined 'from Constantinople' and were the work of the correspondent with whom the editor had talked in the Turkish capital, Thomas Chenery, a Barbadian-born Etonian barrister, then aged twenty-eight. It was Delane who, drawing on his personal experiences, wrote the leading article of 12 October, regretting that 'there are no nurses at Scutari' and suggesting that the British people might wish to set up a fund for 'sending a few creature comforts' to the sick and wounded. Next day the newspaper printed the famous despatch from Chenery which is almost invariably attributed to Russell:

The worn out pensioners who were brought out as an ambulance corps are totally useless, and not only are surgeons not to be had, but there are no dressers or nurses to carry out the surgeon's directions, and to attend on the sick during the intervals between his visits. Here the French are greatly our superiors. Their medical arrangements are extremely good, their surgeons more numerous and they have also the help of the Sisters of Charity, who have accompanied the expedition in incredible numbers. These devoted women are excellent nurses.[4]

Delane's editorial produced an instant response. The same issue of the newspaper which printed Chenery's despatch carried a letter from Sir Robert Peel, son of the former prime minister, offering £200 towards Delane's fund; and over the following fortnight the British public contributed so generously that the initial target of £10,000 was reached by 25 October. There was a response, too, to Chenery's report praising the efficacy of French nursing services in contrast to British inadequacies. On Saturday, 14 October, a querulous letter demanded angrily, 'Why have we no Sisters of Charity?'

There *were* Sisters of Charity in Britain in 1854, following, like their French counterparts, the non-conventual nursing precepts laid down by Vincent de Paul and Louise de Merillac two centuries before: the Seddonites at Devonport, with their London home in Osnaburgh Street, St. Pancras; the Roman Catholic 'Sisters of Mercy' at Bermondsey and Norwood; the Anglo-Catholic sisterhood of St John's House, Westminster; a Protestant nursing order founded by the great Quaker social reformer, Elizabeth Fry, in 1840, five years before her death; and others, too. What was lacking was not charitable sisterhoods, but a common standard of nursing and the presence of a woman of character who could impose her will on professional helpers from the hospitals and yet hold these sectarian groups together at a time when deviations in ritual habitually fired embers of bigotry within the faithful. That paragon, it was hoped, was Miss Nightingale.

Delane and Chenery impressed Florence Nightingale so deeply that on Saturday, 14 October, she wrote a letter to her friend, Mrs Sidney Herbert, wife of the Secretary at War, explaining that, although she did 'not mean to say' that she believed *The Times* accounts, she was convinced that she could do something for the 'wounded wretches'. Why should she not take out 'a small private expedition of nurses' to Scutari? But the Secretary at War himself had other plans. While several of his cabinet colleagues discounted *The Times* reports as alarmist, Sidney Herbert was convinced that something was gravely wrong in the hospitals beside the Bosphorus, for private letters seemed to substantiate newspaper stories. On his own initiative he sent Florence Nightingale a 1,500-word letter in which he invited her to organize and superintend a female nursing service in Turkey. Cabinet approval followed on 18 October and next day Florence Nightingale received a directive defining the Superintendent's responsibilities and authorizing her to draw funds for fitting out some forty nurses and meeting their travelling expenses to Constantinople.[5]

Throughout that third week in October Florence Nightingale and her friends were engaged in a frantic search for capable nurses. Some episodes stand out from the records of the time: a blank response from Elizabeth Fry's successor; the despatch of five nuns from Bermondsey, who had to wait in Paris for the rest of the party; delicate negotiations over safeguards for the spiritual welfare of the St John's House, Westminster, sisterhood; and the telegram to Plymouth that brought the five Seddonites up on the mail train to Paddington. And at Sidney Herbert's private house in Belgravia there were long interviews with the Sarah Gamps of London as the Dean of Westminster's sister, Mary Stanley, looked for professional nurses of skill, sobriety and probity: 'I wish people who may hereafter complain of the women selected could have seen the set we had to choose from', she wrote. Yet by Saturday, 21 October, fourteen nurses from the capital's hospitals were ready to join the twenty-four nuns and sisters who had said they would travel to Constantinople. Among the Nightingale Papers in the British Library is preserved a signed document in which the lay nurses acknowledge an advance of three pounds 'received from the hands of Miss Nightingale' on 21 October. Only two signatures are written with the easy confidence of someone accustomed to hold a pen.[6]

Sidney Herbert also persuaded his colleagues to accept the appointment of a three-man 'Commission of Enquiry into the State of the Hospitals and the Condition of the Sick and Wounded'. Yet most of the cabinet continued to deplore what Clarendon called 'the infinite mischief' done by *The Times* correspondent in 'his descriptions of wounds & sufferings & hospital deficiencies'.[7] Sir James Graham did indeed show concern over hospital ships: 'Distressing accounts, probably exaggerated, of the sufferings of the sick and wounded after the battle of Alma, on their passage to Constantinople, have produced a painful impression in England', he wrote to Vice-Admiral Dundas on the day of Balaclava, and he ordered him 'to have one or two of the large steam-transports fitted' for the carriage of the sick and wounded 'without delay'; but so tardy was the elderly Rear-Admiral responsible for Black Sea transports, Edward Boxer, that little improvement had been made by the end of the year.[8] Constantly the service ministers in Aberdeen's cabinet were puzzled by these complaints of hospital inadequacies. The Director-General of the Army Medical Department in London, Dr Andrew Smith, could point to long lists of medicines and supplies sent out to Scutari since the spring; and he received letters from Dr John Hall, the inspector general in the field, and from the principal army dispenser at Scutari maintaining that 'the hospital establishment has now been put on a very creditable footing' and that there was enough 'lint, linen, bandages, dressings and necessary medicines' for 'any emergency'.[9]

John Delane, having seen the hospitals in the third week of September, had no time for such complacency. He did, however, discover why supplies known to have left England were not available in Turkey when he was there. 'The absence of medical supplies and comforts which was deplorable when I left is at last explained,' he wrote to his friend Monckton Milnes, the Peelite MP, on the day that the Nightingale nurses set out from England. 'They had all been sent to Varna, while the sick and wounded were sent to Constantinople.'[10] Earlier campaigns – notably Moore's expedition to Corunna in the winter of 1808–9 and the landing on Walcheren a few months later – were marred by similar administrative incompetence; but in the Napoleonic Wars newspaper editors remained at their desks and pioneer special correspondents had not developed the investigative sixth sense of a Russell or a Chenery.

Not that there was, in 1854–5, any common approach by the British press to the fatuities of a muddled campaign or the chaos in Constantinople. A newspaper war within a war rumbled on throughout that winter and into the following summer.[11] Professional jealousy of Delane, the influence and facilities which he secured for his correspondents, their speed in getting the news through to London, and the mounting fame of Howard Russell distorted editorial comment on events around the Black Sea in contrast to reports from the Baltic, over which there was a shared feeling of hopes dashed to disappointment. No editor questioned the heroism of the Queen's soldiers and sailors in the Crimea or the Baltic, but treatment of Britain's allies and of the supporting ancillary services away from the war zone varied from paper to paper.

Every leading London journal sent at least one correspondent to Balaclava. The ablest of them were Nicholas Woods of the Tory *Morning Herald*, who seems to have kept a cabin aboard what was virtually the headquarters ship, HMS *Caradoc*, and Joseph Archer Crowe of *The Illustrated London News*, who, being an excellent artist, also supplied his journal with drawings that could be speedily turned into wood-engravings. Crowe attached himself to Sir George de Lacy Evans's 2nd Division, just as the correspondent of the *Morning Chronicle* attached himself to the cavalry division, an interesting association for a reporter representing a newspaper with radical traditions. Both Woods and Crowe distinguished themselves as journalists in later years, Crowe also earning a knighthood for his perceptive analyses of German society while serving as British Consul General. But all that lay in the future. In 1854 even Crowe was liable to suffer humiliation at the hands of his editor. Having spent Balaclava Day under fire on the right flank of the army while Russell observed the battle in Olympian detachment from the Sapoune Heights, it was no doubt galling for Crowe that on 18 November *The Illustrated London News* – without acknowledgement – lifted Russell's account of the charge of the Light Brigade word for word from Tuesday's *Times* and printed it on the journal's second page, while relegating to a separate supplement Crowe's painstakingly judicious report of the same action ('I am not aware whether any discretion was left to Lord Lucan to obey or disobey . . . I know not whether the causes of the disaster of the day will ever be explained', etc., etc.).[12] The truth was that in 1854 no other correspondent – except perhaps Chenery at Constantinople – came anywhere near to possessing Russell's gifts of descriptive imagery or his Irish turn of phrase.

The motives of *The Times*, both in reporting the miseries of Scutari and in opening a 'Fund for the Sick and Wounded', were questioned by other dailies, notably the *Daily News* and the *Morning Post*. At the same time an official 'Patriotic Fund' for widows and orphans was set up under the presidency of Prince Albert and established so speedily that it seemed to be competing with the charity sponsored by Delane and the initial generosity of Peel. *The Illustrated London News* singled out for attack Delane's fund and scoffed at a newspaper, 'cursed with too much zeal and too little discretion', for 'lustily calling . . . for the subscriptions of the wealthy and tender-hearted to alleviate the misery said to be suffered in the General Hospital at Scutari by our wounded soldiers'. It condemned 'these rumours' as 'either grossly exaggerated or totally destitute of foundation', and hoped 'for the sake of truth, the interest of the public service, and the national character that such reports should not be circulated by British newspapers'. The journal's editorial insisted that 'British benevolence . . . will have ample and noble work before it' in supporting the Patriotic Fund, made 'under the sanction of the Queen in Council'; and it hoped that Delane's appeal 'will fall dead with the contradiction of the false statements on the truth of which alone it would have been justifiable . . . to respond to it'.[13]

Despite this robust salvo in the newspaper war, *The Illustrated London News*, like every other daily and weekly, supported the principal immediate beneficiaries from *The Times* Fund, the Nightingale nurses, if now and again a little oddly. Thus the issue on sale when the nurses left London Bridge station welcomed reports that 'Mrs Nightingale' (*sic*) was taking 'Sisters of Charity and Mercy' to Scutari, the editor assuring his readers that once they were there the English ladies would be able to 'compete with the French . . . in the generous rivalry of good works'; and a fortnight later a half-page engraving depicted 'Boulogne fishwomen carrying the luggage of the nurses for the East' from ship to train above a report of the 'demonstrations of sympathy and respect' which accompanied the 'self-devoted band' down to the Mediter-ranean.[14] This slightly puzzled and slightly patronizing tone in the London press foreshadowed many of the social difficulties ahead of the Nightingale mission. What even its leader did not apprehend, however, was the depth of professional resentment she would meet on the Bosphorus and outside Sebastopol.

But Florence Nightingale's first enemy was not bureaucracy and red tape. It was filth. 'The strongest will be wanted at the wash-tub', she had told an enthusiastic nurse as the new arrivals waited to be carried in caiques from the mail-steamer to the landing pier. The sprawling yellow walls of the Selimiye Kislasi barracks still survive, on their eminence across the waters from the Topkapi Palace; and, with an avenue of cypresses behind them in an old cemetery, the barracks make an impressive skyline along the Asiatic shore of the Bosphorus. But in 1854 there was nothing attractive about this former headquarters of the Sultan's artillery corps. In 1854 the Nightingale nurses found the Selimiye Kislasi in an even worse condition than the gloomiest newspaper reports had suggested. It was not until September that the buildings began to be used as a hospital and some parts of the barracks were still serving as a transit depot when the nurses arrived. Walking patients or orderlies were faced with an uphill climb from a ramshackle landing stage before they reached the three-storeyed rectangular block, where lines of verminous beds stretched down four miles of corridors which the Hospital Commissioners later described as 'a sea of sewage'. There was a shortage of doctors, a shortage of drugs, a shortage of lamps and candles, a shortage of basic domestic furniture. Sister Sarah Anne, one of the more restrained chroniclers of those early weeks on the Bosphorus, was told on arrival that 'there was not a table in the Hospital, even for operations'.[15] Rain penetrated the roof and on bad days caused the latrines to overflow and flood the wards; and sometimes when a gale swept down the Bosphorus rickety windows would blow in on the sick and wounded as they struggled to survive. Surgeons carried out amputations without anaesthetic within sight and sound of those next awaiting attention, making the filthy corridors as hideous as the cockpits below gundecks aboard Nelson's warships in action half a century before. One of Florence Nightingale's first purchases was 'a Screen for the amputations' in the hopes of beginning to lift morale among those 'poor fellows' awaiting 'the knife'. 'You Gentlemen in England, who sit at Home in all the well-earned satisfaction of your successful cases, can have little idea from reading the newspapers of the Horror and Misery (in a Military Hospital) of operating upon these dying, exhausted men,' she wrote to a Harley Street friend after her first ten days in Scutari; 'A London Hospital is a Garden of Flowers to it,' she added.[16]

Florence Nightingale at once drew on *The Times* Fund for basic necessities. 'I recollect one of the first things she asked me to supply was 200 hard scrubbers and sacking, for washing the floors, for which no means existed at that time,' recalled John Cameron MacDonald, the newspaper's Manager, who was sent out to Constantinople as the Fund's first almoner and travelled in the same ship as the nurses.[17] From her own purse she found cash to augment the limited food resources of the hospital in these early days. Help would come from the ambassador, Sidney Herbert had assured her, on the Foreign Secretary's prompting. Stratford de Redcliffe did, indeed, send his First Secretary to Scutari on the day the nurses arrived, with an enthusiastically phrased letter of welcome from his wife. Lady Stratford would not herself come to the hospital as the stench made her feel unwell, but she ensured that her husband supplied 'articles of comfort' for the sick and wounded which the medical authorities did not at that time possess. But the Stratfords' ideas of what was needed by a military hospital were so unimaginative that relations soon became strained between the strong-willed ambassador and the strong-willed Superintendent.[18]

Sister Sarah Anne recalls that on the day she arrived at Scutari, 'Miss N. sat down with us, and told us the last news from the Crimea, the wonderful charge at Balaclava'. It was the first any of the nurses had heard of the battle, which had taken place ten days before, and in their innocence they did not realize that a 'wonderful charge' would be followed by a stream of casualties to a hospital not yet ready to receive them. Next day what Sarah Anne called 'the wreck of the Six Hundred' were 'landed and carried up to the Hospital'.[19] This influx of casualties, followed four days later – and at half an hour's notice – by more than 500 wounded from Inkerman, brought the total number of patients in the Selimiye Kislasi to 2,225, with another 650 men housed in the General Hospital, a purpose-built Turkish institution where accommodation was less cramped than up the hill. Had the Nightingale Mission left England a month earlier, it is possible that at least the sanitary conditions in the hospital might have been improved before the wounded hundreds began to arrive from the Crimea. As it was, roofed and tiled wash-houses, clean kitchens and effective latrines had to wait until the spring. The Superintendent's energy was absorbed in a constant battle to secure for her patients the basic medicines, drugs, ward fittings, and clean clothing and, by the end of the year, she had achieved wonders, at the cost of her own health and that of many of her assistants. Even so the mortality rate rose rather than diminished in the critical weeks which followed the nurses' arrival. In the last month of 1854 two thousand British soldiers died in the Scutari hospitals.[20]

No doubt the hidebound regulations which required doctors' signatures for anything requisitioned for hospital use delayed effective improvements; and it is clear that, even before the nurses left England, the medical authorities at Scutari were finding it difficult to induce the civilian Purveyor (a muddle-headed Peninsular War veteran named Ward) to keep his stocks up. But there was never any prospect of the senior doctors and the Superintendent of Female Nurses working together to cut through the red-tape of officialdom. Biographers of Florence Nightingale rightly emphasize the hostility she encountered from Dr Duncan Menzies, the senior medical officer at Scutari, and Dr John Hall, Chief of Medical Staff of the British Expeditionary Army in the Crimea. On the day after the nurses reached the Bosphorus, Menzies wrote to the Duke of Newcastle in London giving his 'settled opinion that the admission of women, whether wives or not, was an unwise indulgence, unfavourable to medical discipline and the recovery of the patients'; and it was Hall who told London that nothing was lacking in the base hospitals, now 'on a very creditable footing.' Hall or Menzies seem momentarily to have even convinced Chenery that 'the present state . . . is by no means unsatisfactory',[21] for they were desperate to keep out the nurses. Both doctors would have resented the interference of *any* woman in the running of the army's medical service. Florence Nightingale, however, was especially unacceptable to them; for she had behind her the Press and in particular *The Times*, the newspaper which had shaken their world with its reports from Scutari. Close contact with MacDonald enabled Florence Nightingale to use Delane's Fund to advantage, so that, as the 1855 Select Committee of Parliament reported, 'the first real improvements in the . . . Hospitals . . . are to be attributed to private suggestions, private exertions, and private benevolence'.[22] This was sour reading for the misogynists who remained Miss Nightingale's immediate superiors.

There was no comparable outcry in the French press. If there was corruption in the commissariat, it was no more marked in the Army of the East than in garrisons at home or in North Africa. The ambulance service and the work of the Sisters of Charity were known to be efficient and well-organized. Closer acquaintance with the French medical service made Florence Nightingale more critical than the praise lavished on it by Russell, Chenery and Delane might suggest: female nurses were not allowed in the Crimea but were expected to remain in the ring of base hospitals around Constantinople; and to the English Superintendent they seemed more like 'comforters' (*consolatrices*) than ward sisters.[23] But, while the war made no great change in the French system of nursing, it had considerable effect on hospital administration in Russia, where developments seem at times to have run almost parallel to what was happening in Britain.

During the Russian campaign against Turkey in 1828–9 the Tsar's army had suffered heavy casualties from epidemics, the mortality rate soaring because of poor nursing. This experience led Nicholas I to encourage the development of military hospitals, and he visited them from time to time on surprise tours of inspection. The Tsar retained, under his wife's patronage, a charitable body of women hospital helpers established by his mother, Dowager Empress Marie Feodorovna, during the Napoleonic Wars and known as the 'Compassionate Widows'. Nicholas I also took a particular interest in the Military-Medical Academy, established by his father as early as 1798, in the

Viborg district of St Petersburg. By the 1840s the Academy possessed a first-rate professor of hospital surgery, Nicholas Pirogov, who spent nine months with the army in the Caucasus in 1848–9 pioneering improved medical services in the field and using ether as an anaesthetic for the first time in a military campaign.

Nevertheless the allied landings in the Crimea, unexpected so late in the year, took the Russian military-medical authorities by surprise and exposed weaknesses in their system. Ghastly tales reached St Petersburg after the battle of the Alma. Pirogov, who thought poorly of the professional value of the Empress's 'Compassionate Widows', at once sought support from the vigorous and intelligent Grand Duchess Elena Pavlovna, in whose palace had taken place the famous 'sick man on our hands' conversation. The Grand Duchess showed interest; her concern for Russia's sick and wounded was deep and genuine, but there was, too, a personal reason why she was especially pleased to become founder-patron of the Orthodox Sisters of Charity. She was a Wurttemberger princess, like the late Empress Marie Feodorovna who was both her mother-in-law and her great-aunt; but the Empress had treated her so badly as a young bride that the Grand Duchess had no fond memories of her. It gave Elena Pavlovna particular satisfaction that her nursing Order would undertake duties for which the ladies of the 'Compassionate Widows' were unsuited. The Grand Duchess called on Russian women to serve, for one year in the first instance, as military hospital nurses in the 'Order of the Exaltation of the Cross'. They would wear a habit to emphasize their religious calling and receive no pay, their reward being the spiritual fulfilment of a vocation for patriotic self-sacrifice; but the Grand Duchess undertook to maintain the Sisters out of her private funds.[24]

The effective Superintendent of the nursing Order was Alexandra Stakhovich, who had influential contacts at court, but from its inception the Order was dominated by Pirogov, who arrived in Sebastopol early in November 1854. Ekaterina Bakunina, daughter of a governor of St Petersburg, wore the brown habit for six years and, having briefly walked the wards of a Moscow Infirmary, she was accepted as a nursing sister after only four further days of training. Most of her companions gained their experience of nursing from spending a fortnight in October working in clinics around Moscow or the capital, their period of 'training' almost coinciding with the journey of the Nightingale Mission from England to Turkey. But although there was such a close coincidence in timing for the formation of these

British and Russian nursing societies, the Grand Duchess's Order was hampered by a problem which had not troubled Florence Nightingale. Apart from a day spent on the Rhone covering the railway gap between Lyons and Valence, her nurses had completed their 2,000-mile journey by rail and steamer without great difficulty, although often buffeted by stormy seas. The thirty members of the Order of the Exaltation of the Cross who travelled speedily along the Nicholas Railway from the capital to Moscow at the beginning of November found that it took another month to complete the journey southwards to Simferopol in the Crimean hinterland. Five years later Alexandra Krupskaya – member of a liberal gentry family better-known after 1917 than before it – wrote their Odyssey, describing how horse-wagons, ox-carts and finally Crimean camels carried them down flooded roads and along dirt tracks until they reached Simferopol, where they were able to tend the wounded for the first time on 13 December. Another seven weeks went by before the first batch of nurses were working under Dr Pirogov in beleaguered Sebastopol.[25]

Pirogov himself succeeded in making the fifty-mile journey across the Yaila Mountains from Simferopol to Sebastopol about the same time that Florence Nightingale's nurses were completing their voyage to the Bosphorus. Some of the problems he reports from the Sebastopol hospitals make familiar reading: the same shortages, the same appalling hygienic conditions; 'more than 2,000 wounded, mixed up together, lying on filthy mattresses soaked in blood', he wrote in one of his earliest letters from Sebastopol. At one point he calculated that he was performing operations for ten hours a day ten days running.[26] Almost certainly Pirogov was the ablest surgeon of Nicholas I's reign, with a military-surgical experience and a national standing unmatched by any British or French army doctor, and he could speak with an authority which Florence Nightingale only attained in later years. Yet, even so, he found himself battling constantly against the prejudice of the older generation of Russian officers. Prince Menshikov in particular was opposed to new-fangled ideas: he mistrusted the use of ether as an anaesthetic; and he was totally opposed to the employment of nursing sisters in the hospitals. He feared, so he told Pirogov, that it would increase the incidence of syphilis. Another high-ranking officer said bluntly that the men 'will rape them right away'. Privately Pirogov suspected that the real reason why the military establishment were so hostile was a fear that intelligent and devoted nursing sisters would expose the knavery of hospital administration. He was fighting thievery and corruption as much as entrenched prejudice.[27]

Pirogov had his way. The nurses came to the Sebastopol hospitals, some seventy of them in four escorted groups. They remained there, amid the sagging gutted houses of a ghost city, throughout the grimmest months of bombardment. Many travelled slowly back with ambulance convoys across the terrible roads of southern Russia. There were feuds within the nursing Order, with bitter conflicts between the matrons, just as there were also in Scutari. But the Russian soldiery respected the honour of their Sisters of Mercy just as the British sailors and soldiers respected the group of nurses who had come out with Florence Nightingale. If the wearing of a holland scarf, embroidered 'Scutari Hospital' in red, was said to be a guarantee of protection on the waterfront of Constantinople, so a brown habit with golden pectoral cross safeguarded Russia's nurses in Sebastopol, Kherson and Simferopol. Not the least curiosity of the Crimean War is the almost encouraging circumstance that, unlike later campaigns, humanity's brutalization by battle failed to corrupt the spirit.

Tsarist Russia, although respecting Pirogov's achievements and recognizing the philanthropy of Grand Duchess Elena Pavlovna, never found a heroine of the war. There was too much in-fighting within the Order of the Exaltation of the Cross for Alexandra Stakhovich or Ekaterina Bakunina or Alexandra Krupskaya to win acceptance as legendary figures. Moreover, though literate Russians avidly read newspapers and periodicals reporting the heroism of the Tsar's troops, journalism in St Petersburg and Moscow did not become politically influential until the sudden ascendancy of Michael Katkov's Panslav *Moskovskiya Vydemosti* a decade later. In Paris, too, the press remained inhibited by political censorship, enhancing the reputation only of those on whom the sun of imperial approval smiled benignly.

By contrast, there is no doubt that in those last four crucial months of 1854 Britain's newspapers and journals shaped public opinion as never before. With Parliament not sitting between 14 August and 12 December the press built up heroes and heroines of its own choosing while denouncing inefficiency wherever it was to be found. Three of the four memorable phrases of the war years owe their origin to reports in *The Times*, the odd one out coming from Bright's apocalyptic Commons speech in the last week of February 1855. Indeed the issue of *The Times* which printed Russell's famous account of the light cavalry charge not only included his description of the 'thin red streak tipped with a line of steel', but also a report sent several days earlier of how a road up to the British batteries facing Sebastopol was so exposed to 'fire that it has been called "The Valley of Death" ' – an image which Tennyson borrowed and transferred five miles eastward to the Causeway above Balaclava.[28] It was *The Times*, too, which spread the most familiar picture of Florence Nightingale. Shortly before he left Constantinople, MacDonald, the almoner of the 'Fund for the Sick and Wounded', sent home a report from Scutari which finally placed the Superintendent of Female Nurses on her pedestal:

Wherever there is disease in its most dangerous form, and the hand of the spoiler distressingly nigh, there is this incomparable woman sure to be seen; her benignant presence is an influence for good comfort, even amid the struggles of expiring nature. She is a 'ministering angel', without any exaggeration, in these hospitals; and as her slender form glides quietly along each corridor, every poor fellow's face softens with gratitude at the sight of her. When all the medical officers have retired for the night, and silence and darkness have settled down upon those miles of prostrate sick, she may be observed alone, with a little lamp in her hand, making the solitary rounds.[29]

Thus did 'The Lady with the Lamp' make her entry into folklore. For months ahead, popular prints and verses would feed on MacDonald's sentimental imagery. Nor was it only the British who were moved. Across the Atlantic, in the quiet serenity of Harvard, Longfellow had a vision of 'heroic womanhood' in Scutari. Lifting doggerel into poetry, he idolized the heroine of mid-Victorian London in the moving stanzas of *Santa Filomena*, an obscure early martyr whom in 1854–5 it was fashionable to venerate in France and Italy.

The parallel was inappropriate. The Florence Nightingale of Sister Sarah Anne's vivid journal is a woman of character, a compassionate fighter, suggesting a literate Joan rather than some nebulous waif from the catacombs. The 'Lady with the Lamp' cult was treated by Miss Nightingale with embarrassed impatience. To Sidney Herbert she confessed that she could see no good in this talk of 'our self sacrifice, heroism and so forth' when around her were 'men who are neither gentlemen, nor men of education nor even men of business' but men 'whose only object is to keep themselves out of blame'.[30] At Scutari she had discovered what she had long suspected, that she was engaged in a battle against obdurate male prejudice which would continue long after the guns fell silent.

CHAPTER TWELVE

A Victory and a Disaster

In later years Florence Nightingale used to head letters written on the anniversary of her arrival at Scutari, 'November 4th (Eve of Inkerman)'. The parenthesis bore testimony to the importance she attached to the battle whose casualties so nearly overwhelmed her nurses in those terrible first weeks in Turkey. Yet in one sense the dateline was misleading. Most great battles in fluid campaigns – Agincourt, Lützen, Austerlitz, Borodino, to pick names at random – are preceded by days or nights of expectancy, with rival troops bracing themselves as their commanders find high ground from which to survey the terrain. Even in static trench warfare ominous signs suggest a coming attack: watchfires glow in the night sky; harnesses rattle, wagons creak; and it is enough to make forward troops stand-to for false alerts, as in the week before Balaclava.

Inkerman, however, was one of those rare engagements for which there was little preparation on either side. The main body of the Russian assault troops knew nothing of the ground, having only arrived on the previous day from Bessarabia; and if there were warning signals of increased activity in the enemy camp, no British staff officer was perceptive enough to recognize them. Letters from England, based upon titbits of information picked up by British diplomats in the German states, had suggested that the Russians wished to launch a full-scale attack to relieve the pressure on Sebastopol. But the besiegers were both confident and complacent. They took little interest in what the Russians were doing: Menshikov had probed the flank of the British position in the hills on 26 October, only to pull back badly mauled by the Guards. He was, it seemed, as cautious as ever. 'We can see that large reinforcements are daily arriving to the Russian army', Raglan's nephew noted, but he was sure that the enemy did not have 'determination and courage enough to overcome British firmness and French gallantry'.[1] The allies went ahead with their plans for an assault on Sebastopol, having reached the stage where scaling ladders were stacked ready on the Balaclava quayside, where any spy might note their presence. At Raglan's farmhouse headquarters, midway between the harbour and Sebastopol itself, there were no 'Eve of Inkerman' premonitions.

Throughout Saturday, 4 November, it was raining heavily in the hills behind Sebastopol, just as it was on the nurses disembarking off Constantinople. The clay soil in the valleys became a morass of mud and it was slow going for carts and wagons on the tracks up to the high ground. In the morning Lord Raglan rode the short distance to Canrobert's headquarters for a council of war at which it was resolved that on the following Tuesday a final effort should be made to break into Sebastopol before the grip of winter tightened on the peninsula; the two commanders agreed that they would meet again on Sunday evening and settle details of the attack.[2]

Late on the Saturday afternoon Brigadier-General Pennefather – temporarily in charge of De Lacy Evans's 2nd Division, whose commander had recently fallen from his horse – rode to the southern end of the mile-long ridge which the Russians called Cossack Mountain. From an outpost on 'Shell Hill', the furthest hump in the ridge, Pennefather noticed some excitement along the road that formed 'besieged' Sebastopol's remaining link with Simferopol and the interior. The drizzle made it difficult to focus his field-glasses but he could just make out a brightly coloured yellow carriage hurrying into the city; the Tsar's third and fourth sons, the Grand Dukes Nicholas and Michael, had arrived to bolster the morale of the defenders. More interesting to Pennefather was what seemed to be a mass of troops across the marshland of the river Chernaya. He sent two officers down into the valley to take a closer look at the enemy; but they could see nothing remarkable.

That night, as a raw mist clawed into the forward pickets on the edge of Cossack Mountain, their commanding officer took pity on them and pulled them back into the shelter of Shell Hill's crest. Next morning, well before dawn, the church bells of Sebastopol began to ring out. To the detachment on Shell Hill that seemed nothing unusual: it was after all a Sunday, merely Guy Fawkes Day to the British, but no doubt for Orthodox believers one of those occasions which call for a mighty din at an early hour. At six o'clock the young officer commanding the furthest picket post was pleased to see reliefs looming up through the heavy mist. All thirteen men turned out to greet them – and were at once taken prisoner, for the newcomers were a company of the Tomsky Regiment, who had scaled the ridge in the mist and darkness, with the carillons deadening the clatter of their approach. In all, three regiments – with twenty-two field guns – had made the difficult ascent and within minutes were ready to open fire on Pennefather's advanced command post, 1,200 yards away on a slightly higher hillock known as 'Home Ridge'.[3] This initial Russian success by the 10th Infantry Division was a remarkable achievement, not least because General Soimonov, their commander, had arrived in Sebastopol from Kishinev less than twenty-four hours before and had only received his somewhat confused operational directive from Prince Menshikov on the previous evening. Most of the ensuing battle was fought over this saddle of Cossack Mountain, separating Shell Hill from Home Ridge. Important actions also took place in the ravines which cut deeply into the 400-foot-high spur of the mountain. To the west, coming out from the bastions of Sebastopol itself, was the Careenage Ravine, with an offshoot known as the Mikriakov Gully at the foot of Shell Hill and another offshoot, the Wellway, which ran eastwards and northwards beneath Pennefather's camp on Home Ridge. To the north of Cossack Mountain, cutting south-westwards into it from the marshy mouth of the river Chernaya, were four other, smaller, ravines – Georgievsky, Volovia, Quarry and St Clement's. Of these only Quarry Ravine had a significant distinguishing feature, the old post road from Bakchisarai to the port. Across the Chernaya marshes ran a causeway leading to Menshikov's field headquarters near the overgrown village of Inkerman, where a cluster of towers and ramparts survived from a former Genoese settlement. Inkerman itself, five miles from the centre of Sebastopol, was on rising ground which faced, beyond the river, Quarry Ravine and the mountain saddle forming the battlefield that was to appropriate the village's name.

Menshikov's battle plan looked good on paper.[4] No less than 60,000 men and 234 guns, with a considerable force held in reserve and the promise of covering fire from two Russian warships, would go over to the offensive, mounting a series of attacks, first on the British positions on Cossack Mountain and then seven miles to the east, from the direction of Chorgun. The Sebastopol garrison would engage the British forward trenches, while on the extreme right of the Russian line a foray against French siege positions would threaten to cut Canrobert's supply route from his base at Kamiesh. Detailed development of Menshikov's orders were left to his second-in-command, General Dannenberg, to the generals who had recently arrived from

Bessarabia (Soimonov of 10th Division and Pavlov of 11th Division), to General Moller in Sebastopol, and Generals Paul Gorchakov and Liprandi on the eastern sector. The plan, which needed precise and accurate timing if it were to succeed, thus assumed good co-ordination between the garrison of Sebastopol, the Black Sea Fleet and four Russian commanders who were separated from each other by high ground and by the enemy. Poor visibility, on top of heavy rain, made the plan almost unworkable from the start.

Prince Menshikov, having sketched this grand design, took little part in its execution. Indeed he appears to have seen nothing of the battle. Next day the Grand Duke Nicholas, in a letter to his brother Constantine in St Petersburg, described how he and their brother Michael had been waiting for Menshikov on the causeway across the Chernaya when the first firing began. But the commander-in-chief did not leave his house until half-past six. He then rode with the Grand Dukes to the Georgievsky Ravine where he had decided to await reports from his generals. No message reached him; and the Grand Dukes, whose presence with the army in the field had been well publicized, heard the din of a great battle up on the heights and the boom of artillery echoing from more distant hills, but saw nothing of the morning's action. At last, about one o'clock, Menshikov rode off in search of news. Apparently by chance he met the deputy whom St Petersburg had foisted on him, General Dannenberg, a veteran of the Napoleonic Wars who detested the Prince almost as much as the Prince detested him. It had been a hard morning's struggle, Dannenberg explained; in fact he had just ordered a withdrawal, since otherwise the army would have been totally destroyed. 'After this', Grand Duke Nicholas wrote, 'the Prince became completely unnerved.'[5] Not until much later did it become clear to Menshikov that victory had come within reach of his troops on Cossack Mountain that Sunday morning.

The British response to the sound of the first exchange of firing on Shell Hill was slow, for reports reached headquarters thick and fast of activity on one sector after another. Even as Raglan hurried off north-westwards from his headquarters, he was, as his nephew wrote, 'doubtful for a moment as to which point he should go' since news had reached him that Liprandi was also on the move in the east. Which was the genuine attack and which was the feint? Or did Menshikov think he was now strong enough to squeeze the invaders with a pincer embrace? Surely no commander-in-chief would attempt to launch a co-ordinated counter-offensive in such atrocious weather? 'The fog and vapours of drifting rain became so thick . . . that one could scarcely see two yards before one', Russell told his *Times* readers.[6]

For more than an hour and a half General Soimonov was able to attack in strength, with twenty-two guns maintaining a steady cannonade on the 2nd Division camp, behind Home Ridge. At the same time a column penetrated the Mikriakov Gully while two battalions of the Ekaterinburgsky Regiment groped their way up the Wellway under cover of the fog. Suddenly, at the crest of the hill the Ekaterinburgsky found themselves faced by a composite force from Sir George Brown's Light Division, hurriedly formed up at their camp from such battalions as were not then in the trenches.

There followed a sharp engagement which was typical of the day's confused fighting. General Buller, moving a group of no more than 260 infantrymen as quickly as possible through the brushwood, 'guided only by the sound of the firing', had to be convinced by his aide-de-camp, Lieutenant Henry Clifford, that the shadowy figures looming up ahead of him in such vast numbers were the enemy. Bayonets clashed and, on the left, the British pulled away until Clifford himself led a charge which forced the Russians to retire and they then came under fire from a patrol of Grenadiers.[7] This marked the start of a series of British counter-attacks, which pushed the Tomsky and Ekaterinburgsky Regiments back on to Shell Hill. Unexpectedly the fog lifted briefly, making the whole spectacle clear to British sharpshooters. Within minutes General Soimonov, his two deputies and his artillery commander were picked off by riflemen and left dead on the field. But in the general confusion three battalions of Russians occupied a small, improvised and empty position known as 'Sandbag Battery' on a spur above St Clement's ravine and some half a mile to the north of Home Ridge. Over the following two hours the militarily valueless Sandbag Battery – no more than a half-built protective shield ten feet high, with two gaping embrasures for field guns which were not there – became the scene of the most intense hand-to-hand fighting in the whole campaign. Pierre Bosquet, France's toughest general in the field, was accustomed to the sickening carnage of North African campaigns. But when, later that day, he stood on the spur above St Clement's Ravine and saw the ghastly layers of Russian, French and British corpses grotesquely intertwined around what remained of the Sandbag Battery, the sight pierced his mask of impassivity. '*Quel abattoir!*' (What butchery!), he exclaimed with crisp revulsion.[8]

Nothing had gone right for the Menshikov plan after the unfortunate

Soimonov's initial success. Over in the Chorgun sector there was no more than a desultory exchange of cannon fire and a token demonstration by Liprandi's troops that deceived neither the French nor the British; and the fog made nonsense of the proposed sorties by the Sebastopol garrison. It was almost ten o'clock before Major-General Timofiev was able to send four battalions of the Minsky Regiment out from the protection cover of one of the southern bastions to break into the French siege works between Sebastopol and Kamiesh Bay. In this sector, more than four miles from the grim combats around Sandbag Battery, there was heavy fighting for more than two hours before Timofiev pulled back, with a third of his force dead or wounded.[9]

But, apart from Timofiev's attack, the day's fighting was concentrated on Cossack Mountain, or the 'Inkerman Heights' as the British inaccurately called this massive spur of rocky scrubland, with its thorny bracken and stunted oaks. Here, too, General Dannenberg – who assumed effective command about half-past seven – had difficulty in preventing the Russian columns from acting in dangerous independence of each other. The weather, the terrain, the massive numbers of men concentrated in a small area, needed a great natural commander to improvise a victory once Menshikov's plan had become an irrelevancy; and Dannenberg was new to the terrain, old and indecisive.

From the start, Dannenberg was puzzled by the way in which the battle was unfolding. The 10th Division should have pressed forward towards Home Ridge almost side by side with Pavlov's 11th Division, but there was still no sign of Pavlov's gunners or infantry when Soimonov was killed. The 11th had been given the task of approaching the mountain up the Volovia and Quarry Ravines. So indeed they did; but at least an hour later than the timing on the original plan. Captain Chodasiewicz's Tarutinsky battalion, who were protecting Pavlov's engineers as his gunners made their way to the heights, found such confusion in the 10th Division after Soimonov's death that Russians were firing on Russians; the battle-weary men of the 10th were too demoralized to obey officers who sought to stop the senseless firing.[10] Yet, remarkably, Dannenberg restored some sort of order at the very moment when it looked as if the arrival of the Guards regiments from the Duke of Cambridge's 1st Division would tilt the balance decisively in favour of the defenders of the ridge. But there was that day a dangerous sense of rivalry between the Scots Guards, the Scots Fusiliers, the Grenadiers and the Coldstreams. Successive charges

proved so costly that the Duke was soon anxiously seeking reinforcements. And at that critical moment – still only about half-past eight in
the drizzle of a November morning – Dannenberg was concentrating
some 8,000 men and 100 guns against the weakest point in the British
position – 'the gap' an area of some 700 yards of unfortified scrubland
south-west of the Sandbag Battery. If the Russians broke through there
they might easily outflank Home Ridge and the whole British position.
'Who can plug that gap?' the British commanders asked each other
urgently.[11]

Strictly speaking, the question should never have been posed, for
Raglan was on the ridge himself. But one of the oddities of Inkerman as
a battle is the absence of clear orders from the commanders-in-chief,
allied and Russian alike. The fog, of course, was partly to blame,
although it began to lift on the Heights about nine o'clock. But the real
reason for the heavy responsibilities assumed by divisional commanders was the sense of having been surprised into an emergency
unforeseen by councils of war. Surviving letters home from the officers
attached to various regiments tell similar stories: fire of musketry heard
from the outposts of the 2nd Division, a mustering of 'all we had in
camp', and a march in the general direction of the firing. Pennefather,
in the 2nd Division lines south of Home Ridge was therefore joined by
two senior generals – Sir George Brown with the Light Division and Sir
George Cathcart with the 4th Division – as well as by the Queen's
cousin, Lieutenant-General the Duke of Cambridge, with the 1st
Division. Sir Richard England, with the 3rd Division, remained in
reserve protecting the British siege works, although he sent individual
units to the Heights. Pennefather, a competent hard-fighting and
hard-swearing brigadier who had two horses killed under him that day,
needed every reinforcement available, but, it could be argued, his
position would have been easier had Raglan, with his senior rank,
issued effective orders or if the divisional commanders could have held
in check their dangerously contentious ardour.

Sir George Cathcart, who had fought at Waterloo as a 21-year-old
subaltern, came out to the Crimea with a reputation for courageous
initiative won in campaigns against the Kaffirs in southern Africa. It
had not, as yet, been enhanced in the Crimea. On that Sunday morning
he committed a fatal blunder which, in its impetuosity, matched the
decision to charge Obolensky's battery beside the Worontsoff Road
eleven days before. As soon as the 4th Division reached the Heights
Cathcart assigned his Rifle Brigade to Pennefather. He refused,

however, Cambridge's request to support the Brigade of Guards by plugging that widening gap. Nor would Cathcart change his mind when General Airey rode up with a verbal order from Lord Raglan that his infantry should help Cambridge. His fellow commanders, Cathcart decided, were over-cautious. Six hundred of his men – an ominously familiar number – were told to discard their greatcoats, so as to move more freely in the brushwood. They then followed their Brigadier in a downhill charge, intended to bite deeply into General Pavlov's leading column, the Okhotsky Regiment, on the Russian flank. Cathcart, who was mounted, followed them and the charge threw the Okhotsky into disorder. The apparent success of Cathcart's charge induced the Scots Fusiliers, contrary to the Duke of Cambridge's orders, to rush pell-mell down the slopes into St Clement's Ravine, shouting and firing, with bayonets at the ready. But the Jakutsky and Selenginsky Regiments, who had advanced up the Quarry Ravine with the Okhotsky, were now able to cut round on to the high ground vacated by Cathcart's men. With the mist suddenly giving way to wintry sunshine, the red coats of the British infantrymen stood out as conspicuous targets and, once they were down in the valley, they could be picked off easily by the Russians who had closed in above them. Cathcart himself was shot through the heart. In all, his 4th Division suffered 500 casualties, dead or wounded, that day.[12]

The rash charge left the group of Grenadiers around the Sandbag Battery desperately outnumbered. The Duke of Cambridge's horse was killed under him and he was fortunate to escape with his life. With some 9,000 men held in reserve, Dannenberg seemed close to a spectacular victory. Russian shells began to land close to Lord Raglan, killing his senior gunner, General Strangways. At this point the dashing young Béarnais general, Charles Bourbaki, induced two hesitant French regiments to go forward, take the Russians in the flank and force them to break off the engagement at the Sandbag Battery and fall back to regroup in greater numbers for another attempt, later in the morning, to clear the allies from Home Ridge.

After nearly four hours of fighting the sheer weight of Russian numbers forced the British and the small French detachment back southwards until, about ten o'clock, the leading column of the 11th Division advanced up the old post road to Simferopol and captured three guns at the southern edge of the Home Ridge. Fortunately they seem to have been too elated by their trophies to have realized their key position on the field, and their hesitation was decisive. For at last two

18-pounders, ordered from the siege park by Raglan when the battle began and dragged up the steep escarpment by 150 men, were brought into action; soon afterwards twelve French heavy guns arrived to support them. Moreover, General Canrobert, who had joined Raglan at the height of the battle for Cossack Mountain, brought General Bosquet's troops into action; and the arrival of 2,000 fresh French troops, many of them Zouaves from North Africa, checked the impetus of Dannenberg's latest assault. Bosquet was greeted by the un-emotional stone-faced Raglan almost as warmly as the great Duke had welcomed Blucher at Waterloo. The crisis was over. 'Au nom d'Angleterre, je vous remercie,' Raglan said formally to Canrobert at his side.

The arrival of the French reinforcements alerted Dannenberg's latent instincts of caution. The sight of those newly committed columns was a sign that no thrust or feint in any other sector had succeeded in pinning down Raglan's chief ally. He believed, rightly, that even more French regiments were on their way to the Heights and he therefore held back sixteen battalions of Russian infantry. For some two hours Dannenberg tried to secure by entrenchment the positions won on Shell Hill earlier in the morning. Throughout that time the struggle swayed backwards and forwards along the westward end of Home Ridge and around what was left of the Sandbag Battery. Raglan, however, was determined not to allow the Russians to retain Shell Hill. Soon after midday Lieutenant Acton rallied a company of his 77th Regiment (later the Middlesex) and, under cover of an artillery barrage, stormed forwards towards Shell Hill. The Russians, believing that Acton's charge would be followed by a wave of advancing bayonets, hurriedly sought to get their own guns away from Shell Hill. It was at this moment that Dannenberg decided to pull back his survivors, under cover of artillery fire from two Russian warships anchored high up the inlet of Sebastopol Harbour.[13]

Raglan would have liked to pursue the Russians, but the British had lost more than 2,500 men dead or wounded in the eight-hour battle, more than half of their original strength on the Heights. The Brigade of Guards had suffered particularly badly. The Duke of Cambridge had brought 1,300 Guardsmen with him to the Heights that morning, and by the time Bosquet's troops intervened there were only some 200 still fit to fight. 'My company went into action 52 men, and came out only 21; and all other companies in about the same proportion', one of the unwounded survivors in the Scots Fusiliers, Strange Jocelyn, wrote

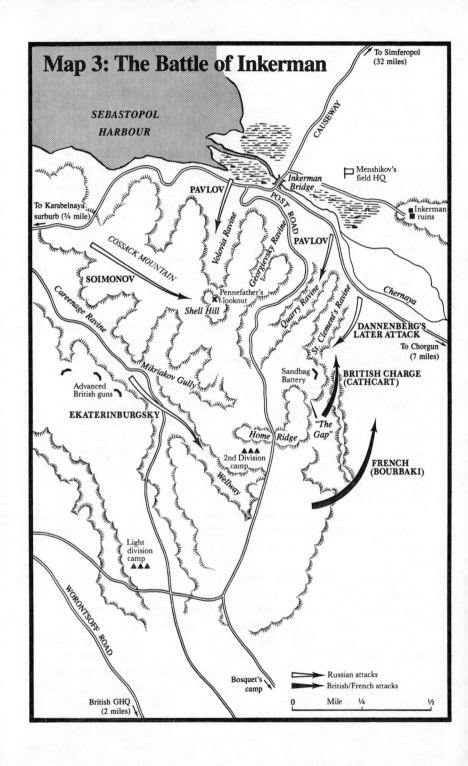

Map 3: The Battle of Inkerman

SEBASTOPOL
HARBOUR

To Simferopol
(32 miles)

CAUSEWAY

Menshikov's
field HQ

Inkerman
Bridge

PAVLOV

To Karabelnaya
surburb (¾ mile)

POST ROAD

Inkerman
ruins

COSSACK MOUNTAIN

Volovia Ravine

Georgievsky Ravine

PAVLOV

SOIMONOV

Chernaya

Careenage Ravine

Pennefather's
lookout

Shell Hill

Quarry Ravine

St. Clement's Ravine

DANNENBERG'S
LATER ATTACK

To Chorgun
(7 miles)

Mikriakov Gully

Sandbag
Battery

BRITISH CHARGE
(CATHCART)

Advanced
British guns

EKATERINBURGSKY

"The
Gap"

Home Ridge

2nd Division
camp

FRENCH
(BOURBAKI)

Wellway

Light
division
camp

WORONTSOFF ROAD

Bosquet's
camp

British GHQ
(2 miles)

Russian attacks

British/French attacks

0   Mile   ¼   ½

home to his father next day. 'Our Regiment now numbers only about 280 men, instead of the 1,100 that left England,' he added.[14] If there was to be a pursuit on that Sunday afternoon, it would have to be undertaken by the French. Canrobert, however, declined – and rightly. The French, too, had suffered casualties: he did not know precisely what had happened either in the Chorgun sector or between the southern bastions and Kamiesh; but he could see the weariness of his troops here on the Heights. Moreover, he did not believe that anything would be gained from harassing the Russians back to their lines, thereby exposing his men to cannonades from Totleben's guns in the forts as well as from the two warships. Far better to harness one's strength for that long-planned attempt to break into the city, he argued. The battle was over; news of victory should be sent swiftly to Paris and London.

The fifth of November, once but too notorious in the annals of civic dissension, has been made memorable for ever by the splendours of one of the greatest victories ever achieved by this nation over a foreign foe. The field of Inkerman and the 5th of November will henceforth be linked in glory on the page of European history.

So began the leader article in *The Illustrated London News* three weeks later, when details of the battle became known in Western Europe. The editor, taking pride in 'the dreadful glories of war', rejoiced that the Queen had created 'the illustrious soldier', Lord Raglan, a field marshal in honour of his feat of arms. There was a conviction, in the British and French press, that Inkerman would stand out as the decisive victory of the campaign. And so, in a sense, it does – but not as the newspaper editors saw it in November 1854, for Inkerman was soon recognized as a negative, defensive success rather than a memorable triumph. The outcome of the battle settled two questions: the Russians, despite their reinforcements, could not eject the French and the British from their commanding positions above Sebastopol; and, although they were slow to admit it, the allies did not have the men or material to come down from the Heights and capture the city before Christmas. Inkerman imposed a stalemate on the opposing armies.

The earlier pages of that same issue of *The Illustrated London News* gave a more sober account of Inkerman. In three long columns, written on the Wednesday after the battle, Crowe gave a detailed and accurate account of the fighting, finishing up on a personal note. He described how shells burst in his tent, in the 2nd Division lines 'where I was standing just before': 'I never had such narrow escapes of life as on that day. The scenes on the battle-field were awful. I sickened over them, and have been ill ever since.'[15] Crowe was not the only one revolted by the carnage. The Duke of Cambridge, who had shed tears after the Alma, collapsed after Inkerman and went aboard ship for Malta and England a few days later. Fanny Duberly, having watched the 'melancholy train of ambulances winding down to Balaclava' on Sunday afternoon, irritated her insensitive husband by refusing to join him in a tour of the battlefield next day; the prospect of such an undertaking made her feel sick.[16] Shattered or twisted bodies lay strewn among the scrubble and brushwood. Turkish labourers continued burying the Russian dead for another three days. Around the Sandbag Battery and on the slopes leading down to the adjoining ravines more than eleven hundred corpses were counted, most of them Russian. Some 35,000 Russian troops were engaged in the battle, and nearly 11,000 of them were killed or seriously wounded.

Menshikov was not prepared to recognize the magnitude of his defeat. His first message to the Tsar did not mention his original plan for a sustained offensive in successive sectors of the front, merely adding in the last paragraph that his troops had also carried out 'a strong demonstration against Kadikoi'. The despatch simply described how nine regiments had made a sortie from Sebastopol, captured the English fortifications and spiked eleven guns. Menshikov admitted that 'the enemy had won' the battle, a success which, he explained, was due to the superiority of their rifles, the greater range of their siege artillery, and their 'numerical superiority'.[17] This was, at best, a misleading account of a battle in which the Russians, for the only time in the Crimea, had far more men and far more guns than their opponents. Privately the Prince told his sovereign that Dannenberg was to blame for the failure to exploit the early success of the sortie. The Tsar was given a father's satisfaction in reading of the fine example of 'calm courage' set by his two sons when they 'were in the midst of this terrible fire' and Menshikov urged that they should receive decorations. After the frustrations of the morning the Grand Dukes did indeed risk their lives when they sought to hearten the Russian infantrymen as they fell back towards Sebastopol with shells crashing down among them; and the Tsar subsequently created both of his sons Knights of the Order of St George (Fourth Class).[18] But if Menshikov believed that flattery would silence the Grand Dukes he was mistaken. Their letters to St Petersburg roundly blamed the Prince for the defeat, emphasizing his incompetence and his failure to organize an effective headquarters staff. Nor was it only the Grand Dukes who exposed Menshikov's failings. Dr Pirogov, appalled by the disorder in the hospitals, never minced his words when writing to the Grand Duchess Elena Pavlovna; and she had been notoriously outspoken at court for more than twenty years. Over the following two months a powerful party in St Petersburg began to urge the dismissal of Menshikov.[19]

Paskevich, Nesselrode and Orlov were all convinced that only a new commander could save Sebastopol. However, the Tsar, who spent longer and longer in the comparative isolation of Gatchina, was perplexed. If he dismissed Menshikov, who would replace him? Had Nicholas's health been good, he would have acted with the old decisive authority which had safeguarded the throne from the Decembrists at his accession. But he was by now in a state of physical collapse: he could not sleep; he could not eat; he could not resolve the problems facing him. His eldest son, Alexander, had no doubt as to what should be done with the Commander-in-Chief; but obstinately Tsar Nicholas ignored all demands for Menshikov's dismissal. Gatchina was gloomy and silent, a young maid-of-honour noted in her journal; and as for the Tsar, he seemed to her 'like an oak, weakened by the gale, an oak which can no longer bend but only die in the midst of the tempest'.[20]

In Sebastopol itself morale was higher than at court. The soldiers and sailors despised Menshikov, looking on him as a useless outsider. They saw little of him. His headquarters were twelve miles away, on the Belbec river; occasionally he would come down to Fort Severnaya and he spent the night before the battle on Cossack Mountain even nearer to the city, but he remained a remote figure, little more than a name to them. Most of the dead at Inkerman had come from the relief regiments he had summoned up from Bessarabia. Inside Sebastopol the defenders were proud and confident. Lieutenant Count Leo Tolstoy arrived in the city a fortnight after Inkerman and found 'the spirit of the army beyond all description'. It was, he assured his brother, 'a wonderful time' to be in Sebastopol; and he thanked God that he had enjoyed the privilege of seeing such heroic people.[21]

By contrast, there was little elation over the Inkerman victory among the British troops in the peninsula, only a feeling that 'the staff know nothing of the enemy until they see him' and that, on the whole, they were 'a moderate lot'. What rankled most was the slow reactions of Raglan himself to moments of crisis and the apparent lack of any strategic vision. 'We are doing nothing with the siege, and there are great doubts if we shall take the place,' wrote Temple Godman despondently three days after Inkerman.[22]

More senior officers than Lieutenant Godman had doubts, too. After Inkerman the allied generals met in two councils of war at Raglan's headquarters in the Nikolayevka House on Monday and Tuesday, 6–7 November. It was agreed that Bosquet should deploy 2,000 French troops on the Heights, alongside what remained of the British 2nd Division, and that once the Turkish labourers had disposed of the Russian bodies they should construct a system of redoubts to strengthen this whole sector. The second meeting was held on Tuesday morning at an hour when, three days before, it had been assumed that the combined might of the allies would be hammering the city's defences. Now, after Inkerman, General Canrobert ruled out any such attack: the allies lacked the men and guns to be certain of a victory. Raglan was disappointed, but he had to admit that at that moment the British expeditionary force could muster only 16,000 fit infantrymen. Reinforcements were on their way from England and from France; reluctantly Raglan agreed with Canrobert to postpone the great assault on Sebastopol. Huts must be found for the troops, for it would now be necessary to winter in the hills around the city. Privately – and not at the council table – two generals who were about to leave for England proposed more drastic courses to Raglan: the Duke of Cambridge thought the British should raise the siege and establish defensive lines around Balaclava, on the model of Torres Vedras, emerging to defeat the weary Russians when spring returned; and the sick and incapacitated General De Lacy Evans argued that Sebastopol was too hard a nut to crack and that the army should be evacuated. Neither proposal appealed to Raglan; it was unthinkable that 'our allies be left in the lurch'.[23]

The Prime Minister's son, Alexander Gordon, was by now Assistant Quartermaster-General and was therefore well placed to inform his father of the true state of affairs. Three days after Inkerman he wrote:

You will have heard that we have had another terrible battle in which we were at length victorious but with a loss which we can ill afford. Owing to the mercy of God, I again escaped unhurt, although my horse was shot under me. The battle lasted 9 hours and hard fighting most of it. You need not expect to hear of the fall of Sebastopol this winter, the utmost we can do is to protect ourselves in our present positions and we shall be very fortunate if we succeed in that.

The Russians, he explained, had received considerable reinforcements because the Austrians as yet showed no sign of taking the field against them.

I hope you were not an advocate of this expedition although of course you must have sanctioned it. You must prepare another army to carry on the war next spring for I do not think you will get much out of this, or rather what will be left of it by that time. You should immediately order several hundred waggons for the conveyance of ammunition and commissariat supplies in the next campaign. Do not waste time but copy the French which is excellent.[24]

These problems seemed so pressing to an officer at headquarters that Alexander Gordon reverted to them again in a letter to his father on the following Monday (13 November). Heavy rain had fallen throughout the weekend; roads and tracks were broken up, and it was difficult to move supplies or ammunition from the base to the front line. To the chronic shortage of horses was now added a desperate lack of fit and able troops. 'Unless you send out 10 or 12,000 men, militia or anything *immediately* we shall not be able to keep our position here through the winter,' he wrote. 'You should also send out several shiploads of hay because the horses are fast dying of starvation and cold. Why was not winter clothing sent out sooner? Do not be surprised if the siege is raised and we fall back on Balaclava.'[25]

This letter, which must have reached Lord Aberdeen by the end of the month, was intended not merely for the Prime Minister but also for Prince Albert, who had presented Alexander Gordon with one of the horses he took with him to the war. Already the Prince had received at least one private letter sent soon after Inkerman. His kinsman, Prince Edward of Saxe-Weimar, who was serving with the Guards Brigade, had repulsed a Russian patrol which reached a spur of land above the Wellway at the height of the battle. But Prince Edward, 'still under the excitement of that fearful scene', evidently wrote less of himself than of the British commanders; and so critical was his tone that he felt the need to write contritely three weeks later to the Queen. 'Reflections on our Commanders . . . are at all times wrong,' he confessed.[26] Yet, whatever niceties loyal obedience might demand, Prince Edward and Alexander Gordon rendered their brother officers a service by speaking out. So, too, did Major-General Bentinck, who was wounded in the arm during the terrible tussle for Sandbag Battery and subsequently invalided home. By 2 December he was fit enough to travel to Windsor and give the royal couple a personal account of the horror he had witnessed less than four weeks earlier. Thus did the truth about Sebastopol begin to puncture illusions of glory within the Castle's precincts. Well before Christmas, Victoria and Albert could judge for themselves the wretchedness of seeking to improvise a victory in the Crimea. Soon the Queen's cousin, George, Duke of Cambridge, would be at hand to add his weight of enlightened experience to their understanding of the war.[27] But not so soon as the Duke anticipated, for before he left Balaclava poor Cambridge was delayed by the worst natural disaster of the campaign.

He had embarked in the steam frigate HMS *Retribution* which was about to sail for Constantinople when a strong gale sprang up from the south-west soon after dawn on 14 November. By nine o'clock the wind was so fierce that spray was breaking against cliffs several hundred feet high and falling as rain on the crowded inner harbour, which was seething with foam. It seemed as if ships at the quayside would be crushed against each other while those offshore in the harbour would be lifted by huge waves and dashed against the rocks. *Retribution* lost two rudders and would have capsized had not her commander jettisoned her upper guns, enabling the frigate – and her distinguished passenger – to ride out the storm. There was little hope for vessels in the outer harbour or waiting at sea anchorages: seven large and fourteen smaller vessels were totally wrecked on the rocks off Balaclava; five transports, protected by Dundas's squadron at the mouth of the river Katcha were driven aground, Cossack snipers firing at their crews; and, further north, terrible damage was done to the vessels in the bay of Eupatoria (where the town was still occupied by an allied force, mainly Turkish). Some vessels were undamaged, Lord Cardigan's yacht *Dryad* among them. But less compact ancillaries were battered to pieces. The *Rip van Winkle*, a familiar sight in Balaclava harbour, was lost with all hands. Aboard her was Richard Nicklin, a commercial photographer sent out by the army in May to make a visual record of Raglan's campaign. Any prints Nicklin may have made went down with him and his equipment.[28]

The worst single disaster of the gale was the sinking of the new 2,700-ton steamship *Prince* off Balaclava. She had arrived four days earlier, having transported the 46th Foot from Southampton. The troops disembarked on the Saturday but congestion within the harbour prevented the unloading of a mass of munitions and supplies put aboard her in the first week of October when London first learnt of the desperate shortages in the Crimea and at Scutari. The *Prince*, having lost two sheet anchors, was pitched broadside on to the rocks; only six members of the crew of 150 were saved. It has sometimes been suggested that the value of the *Prince*'s cargo was later exaggerated so as to hide deficiencies in the administration. But Crowe's report, which reached London three weeks after the gale, shows that the gravity of the disaster was appreciated immediately at Balaclava:

> With the exception of the troops everything remained in her when she was dashed on the rocks. The whole of the winter clothing for the men went down – 40,000 suits of clothes . . .; vast quantities of shot and shell; and, not least in consequence, the medical stores sent out in consequence of the deficiencies which formally existed. The latter were, with not uncommon negligence, stowed away under the shot and shell and could not be landed at Scutari.[29]

On shore the gusts of the gale suddenly reached hurricane force. 'We had just got our morning dose of cocoa and the soldiers their rum when, about seven o'clock, the squall came down on us,' Colonel Sterling wrote in a letter three days later. 'All the tents fell in about three minutes'; and the Colonel's official papers were caught by the whirlwind and scattered 300 yards away. Temple Godman, with the 5th Dragoon Guards above Balaclava, was peeved that a three-week-old copy of the *The Illustrated London News*, which had arrived with a letter from his father on the previous day, was carried away by the wind before he had read little more than a page of it; but worse was to follow: 'Every hut was levelled, and all our things drenched . . . One officer's air-bed I saw flying high away, over the Turkish camp', he wrote three days later.[30] It was far worse on the Heights south of Cossack Mountain, for within a few hours a blizzard followed the hurricane and the heavy rain. 'We had no shelter whatever,' Strange Jocelyn wrote home from a Scots Fusiliers bivouac in the hills. 'I never knew what misery was before. Nor our poor, starved men, only half clothed in rags.' After twenty-four hours guarding an isolated battery, Captain Campbell, who had so recently come out with the 46th Foot aboard the ill-fated *Prince*, had to march fifty exhausted men five miles back to camp through the blizzard along a route 'difficult to find' in the pitch dark; and when the exhausted men reached 'home', their comrades were 'endeavouring to shelter themselves under the wet canvas as it lay on the ground'. Captain Campbell records that ten men in the 46th Foot perished that night, presumably from hypothermia. Next morning, from the Rifle Brigade camp, a fatigue party was sent out to help bring in the 'wretched parties in the trenches . . . they being quite unable to carry their rifles and water-bottles'.[31]

The French sustained heavy shipping losses but, as letters home to England constantly emphasized, their men were better accommodated for a winter campaign than their ally's troops. The Russians, too, suffered little. Lieutenant Tolstoy, who was in Sebastopol during the gale, does not mention it in a very detailed letter written soon afterwards; but on Wednesday, 15 November, the day on which the besiegers were rescuing frozen and frost-bitten patrols stranded on the Heights, he appears to have had no difficulty in leaving the city by the Inkerman Causeway and travelling to an outlying battery four miles away, at Eski-Orda.[32] Had the allied army entered Sebastopol in October – as its commanders had assumed it would when the army began that 'nine day march' south from Calamita Bay – gales and blizzards need have left little mark on the troops: the army would have sheltered in stone buildings while the ships rode out the storm at safe anchorages. As it was, this disastrous visitation of nature exposed the British expeditionary force's greatest weaknesses. A tattered army, cold, frustrated and angry, saw no reason to keep silent. There was no censorship of letters from the battle fronts in 1854. Soon after the troops heard that they were to receive campaign medals John Leech was to capture the mood of the moment in *Punch* with the greatest of his satirical drawings. Two ragged soldiers crouch in a snowbound Crimean outpost: 'Well, Jack! Here's Good News from Home,' one of them remarks. 'We're to have a medal.' And Jack replies, 'That's Very Kind. Maybe one of these days we'll have a coat to stick it on.'[33]

CHAPTER THIRTEEN

Hard Times

On 9 December a London weekly, *The Examiner*, published the stanzas by the Poet Laureate which immortalized the Light Brigade's charge of seven weeks earlier. The poem became so popular that it was soon printed on thousands of sheets and given by wellwishers to the serving soldiery as a tribute to the army's courage and unquestioning sense of discipline. But Tennyson's poem, as originally published, was something more than a patriotic ode: the line 'someone had blundered' – omitted when, nine months later, the poem appeared in book form, alongside *Maud* – faithfully caught the mood of indignant uncertainty which spread across Britain in those closing weeks of the year 1854; to many it seemed time to call the Aberdeen Government to account.

Yet, despite the war news, Queen Victoria opened Parliament on 12 December with customary splendour, a troop of Life Guards escorting the ten-carriage procession from Buckingham Palace to Westminster. 'The debates which ensued ... will ring trumpet-toned throughout Europe', *The Illustrated London News* proudly reported four days later. What was said in the two houses, the journal predicted, would multiply 'the meed of praise with which History will hereafter record the deeds of the present Administration in a crisis of unexampled peril and difficulty'.[1]

Few members of the Government shared the optimism of the *'Illustrated'*, for the strains of war were weakening the coalition of Peelites and Liberals over which Aberdeen had by now presided for two uneasy years. Lord John Russell, in particular, frequently threatened resignation if his cabinet colleagues shelved his proposals for winning the war. The Prime Minister personally had been in no hurry to fetch MPs back to Westminster. But, in the week that brought news of Inkerman to London, he accepted the need for a pre-Christmas session, largely at the prompting of a youthful Lord Privy Seal and a buoyant Home Secretary. The Duke of Argyll and Lord Palmerston argued that it was essential to boost the nation's confidence by presenting a list of measures being taken 'to invigorate our troops'. They seem, too, to have been looking for a safety-valve; in ten days of debates, followed by another month's adjournment, the disgruntled might let off steam without imperilling the life of the Coalition.[2]

In one sense Argyll and Palmerston were right. The Government ministers emerged well from the debates, with safe majorities every time the division bells rang. A mass of statistics proved that reinforcements were steadily leaving the British Isles for the East and that clothing and stores were on their way to replace what had been lost when the *Prince* foundered. Parliament was told of new measures to prosecute the war energetically: militiamen, traditionally local defenders of the English shires, would be encouraged to transfer to the regular army; and a force of fifty-four navvies was at Birkenhead about to leave for Balaclava, where the men would build a railway from the quayside to the siege works. There were few objections to a Militia Bill to permit the sending of militia regiments to free garrison troops in Gibraltar, Malta and Corfu for service in the Crimea; but a Foreign Enlistment Bill that would allow the Government to recruit in Germany, Italy and Switzerland as well as from among refugees in England aroused considerable mistrust.[3]

The origins of both the Militia Bill and the Foreign Enlistment Bill may be traced to a memorandum sent by Prince Albert to Lord Aberdeen in mid-November which emphasized the need for effective reinforcements and pointed out that many recent army recruits were 'mere boys, unfit for foreign service'.[4] But nothing was said of the Prince's initiative when these proposals came before Parliament; this was a wise precaution, considering the latent xenophobia of the English middle classes. As it was, the mere prospect of a British Foreign Legion excited narrowly patriotic prejudice, especially in the Commons. 'A calamity and a degradation to this country', said the backbench member for Leominster; exiles and malcontents would ruin discipline in the army, other critics complained. Richard Cobden, on more general grounds, condemned the immorality of enlisting 'mendicant Germans' to fight for a cause for which they felt no call of sentiment; to employ them was 'wholesale assassination'.[5] But, despite the misgivings of individual MPs, both the Militia Bill and the Foreign Enlistment Bill became law; and, by the following August, Victoria and Albert were able to review a British-German Legion and a British-Swiss Legion at Shorncliffe Camp on the eve of their departure for Scutari and Smyrna.[6]

Yet, although the Aberdeen Coalition weathered this pre-Christmas buffeting, several speeches contained a threat of storms ahead. Nothing could reconcile Cobden and Bright to the war; and both orators spoke at the end of the brief session, lifting the level of debate with pleas for the Government to 'err on the side of humanity' by concluding an early peace.[7] Of more immediate concern were the accusations that ministers were failing to wage war effectively.[8] 'You have attacked Sebastopol', complained Disraeli on the opening day of the session. 'It might have been a questionable proceeding at any period of the year; but you have chosen the very worst period – a winter campaign, in a country in which of all others a winter campaign ought to be avoided. You have commenced this, the greatest of blunders, without having provided for the next blunder. Your huts will arrive in the middle of January, and the furs in time for the suns of May.'[9] But it was Henry Layard who, having returned from the Crimea only nine days before, posed questions which no minister answered. If Sebastopol were captured, was that in itself anything more than a single step in toppling the power of Russia? Why had the great commercial port of Odessa been spared? Why had there been no effective demonstration of power in the Baltic? There was, Layard argued, only one way to overcome Russia, 'and that was to meet her in Europe, and to erect Poland into a kingdom'.[10]

Layard's speech was an embarrassment for the Government on several counts. Lord Clarendon had no wish to see the Polish Question raised at that moment, for on 2 December Austria, one of the traditional despoilers of the old Polish kingdom, had formally joined the Anglo-French alliance. There was still no guarantee that the Austrians would declare war on Russia and fight alongside their allies, but the three governments could now work together politically. Moreover Clarendon had every hope that the Austrians would check pro-Russian sentiment at Berlin. Francis Joseph and his ministers might even tolerate Polish patriotic propaganda, provided it was specifically anti-Russian in character. But Clarendon was, at the same time, following up hints of intervention in the war from Count Cavour, the Piedmontese prime minister, a natural enemy of Austrian pretensions in Italy. The attraction, for the British and French, was the evident willingness of Cavour to send some 15,000 men from Sardinia-Piedmont's efficient little army to fight in the Crimea itself. Yet it is hardly surprising if, in private, Lord Aberdeen confessed that he found his Foreign Secretary's pursuit of a Sardinian alliance on top of the

Austrian alliance 'rather strange'.[11] Clarendon was not so skilled a diplomatic juggler that he could handle the intensely nationalistic Polish exiles at the same time.

Had the Poles depended entirely on the goodwill of their compatriot, Count Walewski, Napoleon's ambassador in London, Clarendon might, even so, have found a place for them in his act. The danger for those who shaped British and French policy lay in the close links of exiled Poles with exiled Hungarians. Three days before Austria joined the allies, the twenty-fourth anniversary of Poland's anti-Russian insurrection was celebrated in London with a speech from the Hungarian patriot, Lajos Kossuth, in which he criticized Britain and France for concentrating on the entrenched camp of Sebastopol rather than seeking to rouse the 'oppressed nationalities' against Tsar Nicholas's despotism. The Peelite members of the Aberdeen Coalition consistently mistrusted Kossuth, but there remained widespread sympathy for the Poles, and the cabinet had already given some thought to raising a Polish Legion. The proposal worried the Secretary of War: 'We must get men where we can', Newcastle wrote to Clarendon on the day after Inkerman, 'but I have very little faith in Poles of the English and French refugee class. They are great rogues'; and the Prime Minister agreed with him.[12] So long as Aberdeen presided over his Coalition cabinet, British policy was more interested in checking Napoleon's enthusiasm for national revolutions than in sponsoring the Polish cause. Already, however, Palmerston, the most European-minded member of the Government, was convinced that not only Britain and France but Austria and Prussia too should 'restore a substantive Kingdom of Poland'; and, as he had told Clarendon in September, he found it hard to believe that Aberdeen 'can have discouraged the idea'.[13]

Yet it was another passage in Layard's speech which threatened to rock the cabinet, for Layard mischievously urged Lord John Russell 'as the head of the great Liberal party . . . to prevail upon his colleagues to adopt, ere it be too late a policy . . . more consistent with the honour, the true interests, and the immortal traditions of this mighty empire'.[14] To those members of the Government who did not belong to the 'great Liberal party', Layard seemed to be trying to break up the Coalition by flattering its most restless and quarrelsome member. Lord John hardly needed encouragement from a back-bencher with a personal interest in foreign affairs. He could now convince himself that he commanded a following in the Commons, even though twenty-one Liberals had voted against the Foreign Enlistment Bill and there remained a rift between Russellites and Palmerstonians. Uncertainty over Russell's intentions marred the satisfaction of Aberdeen's fellow Peelites – Gladstone, Graham and Herbert, in particular – at the size of the Government's majorities.

On the morning that the parliamentary session closed, a change in policy by the editor of *The Times* emphasized this weakness. Eleven days earlier the paper had come down firmly in favour of the Government: 'Never was war prosecuted so vigorously and resolutely as this one at this moment', a leading article declared on 12 December. But, while the debates were in progress, extracts from more and more letters home were forwarded to the editorial offices at Blackfriars, and the first sick or wounded heroes were welcomed back to their London clubs, coming 'with an awful budget of stories', as Thackeray noted after meeting one of them.[15] The testimony of these letters and the tales of the returned veterans corroborated Howard Russell's mounting list of failings. Disparities between reports from the battle front and the bland assurances of ministers in Parliament suggested a 'cover up' for Raglan and his staff. Accordingly, on 23 December, *The Times* sent its readers off to Christmas with a thunderous leading article. Nobody in authority was spared, least of all Lord Raglan, a commander-in-chief of whom 'with the extremest reluctance', the article said, 'no one sees or hears anything'. The festive mood at home was contrasted with the plight of 'the noblest army ever sent from these shores': 'Incompetence, lethargy, aristocratic hauteur, official indifference, favour, routine, perverseness and stupidity reign, revel and riot in the camp before Sebastopol, in the harbour of Balaklava, in the hospitals of Scutari, and how much nearer home we do not venture to say.' By printed prose, by verse, by letters from the post and by word of mouth the British public was not allowed to forget this Christmas that 'someone had blundered'. And in the New Year they were to seek the reason why.[16]

Before Sebastopol the weather was fine and frosty but it remained a wretched Christmas. Apart from occasional night alarms and a curious sortie by 'about 300 men all well primed with Brandy and three parts drunk' on 12 December, there had been little action since the blizzard. But by now the siege of Sebastopol was largely nominal. There were reports of British troops so preoccupied with fighting the Russian winter that they grew careless, exposed themselves to enemy fire or were surrounded while on outpost duty and captured or killed. On

Christmas Day itself an extra ration of fresh meat was distributed; 'We made a pudding after a fashion', Temple Godman wrote unenthusiastically to his father a few days later. Conditions were better for the vessels remaining in Balaclava harbour: Assistant Surgeon Henry Taylor, who was being sent to Constantinople for a month's convalescent leave, had 'a capital Christmas dinner' aboard the steamship *Australian*, still unloading her cargo several days after she should have sailed. Captain Duberly and his wife were able to give a small Christmas dinner party, 'which somehow was prolonged long into the night'; but it cannot have been the cheeriest of gatherings, for there was no heating whatsoever aboard the depot ship *Star of the South* in which Mrs Duberly had her cabin.

A generous supply of Christmas gifts had left England for the East in good time; and officers' letters home mention the safe arrival of bottles of old port, fur boots, socks, hampers from Fortnum and Mason, books and magazines. But there are also references to long delays in unloading ships at the quayside. 'The "Royal Albert" has arrived but as yet we cannot find out where she has sent her parcels', Strange Jocelyn told his father three days after Christmas. There was a general conviction that troops under canvas around Balaclava fared better than the infantry regiments up in the hills. 'Comforts of all kinds arrive daily at Balaclava for the men, but we don't see much of them in camp', Captain Clifford wrote from 2nd Division headquarters on the Heights. Earlier that month Henry Clifford, like many other bored officers, had been reading 'Dickens's new work *Hard Times*'. 'I wish he could sit, with my pen and paper, and write a book, "Hard Times" in the Crimea', he added ruefully. 'Only just what is passing in front of the door of my comfortable little tent would give him plenty of matter.'[17]

Already, before Christmas, many officers who had come from Varna and marched south to Balaclava had left the Crimea. Some, like Lord Lucan and Henry Taylor, were content with a short spell of leave in Constantinople. But a considerable number returned to England, some as invalids, others on compassionate grounds, and some on a flying visit to settle business affairs, for those who sailed out in the spring had assumed that they would be home again before the end of the year. The Duke of Cambridge finally got away on 25 November in the steamship *Trent*, refusing to come aboard this time until the vessel was about to leave for the Bosphorus. General De Lacy Evans MP, the Peninsula veteran and titular commander of the Light Division, was on his way home before the end of the month. Lord Cardigan asked for sick leave five days after the November hurricane, was pronounced unfit on 3 December, and sailed off in his yacht *Dryad* on the following Friday. He lingered in Constantinople and was a guest at Stratford de Redcliffe's New Year's Eve Ball where, to their mutual annoyance, he met Lucan. But Cardigan was back in London by the middle of January; and five days after his return he entertained the royal family by re-enacting his charge (unmounted) down the Long Corridor of Windsor Castle. By contrast Lord George Paget, who on Balaclava morning first spotted the warning signals from the Turkish redoubt, was cold-shouldered by London society as though he were a deserter. Ironically, unlike Cardigan, Paget had every intention of returning to the Crimea, and was back with the Light Brigade by early summer, accompanied by his young wife.[18]

For less fortunate officers and men, who were left to face the worst weeks of a Crimean winter, there was something demoralizing about this exodus. Apart from the Rifle Brigade, all pride in regimental dress and all sense of cleanliness seemed to disappear. Deep resentment festered among men who believed that there was a privileged caste at General Headquarters. As early as 12 December Captain Duberly (whose prose style was far clumsier than his wife's) was bitterly hostile to Raglan and his staff. Henry Duberly told his brother-in-law: 'I know of a letter that goes by the mail from one of the Guards, part of it was read to me and, as sure as it goes it will be read by Prince Albert, and I know of many other letters from men out here whose relatives have great influence in high places and so I expect that people's eyes will be opened as to the shameful mismanagement here.' The toughest and loyalest officers began to complain of those 'lazy, idle, drinking and swearing fellows' who filled 'that nest of noodles', otherwise known as Lord Raglan's staff. The fact that five of the Commander-in-Chief's aides-de-camp were blood relations and that Raglan himself seldom left his 'comfortable farmhouse' angered an aristocratic Guards officer like Strange Jocelyn; and Colonel Alexander Gordon, who disliked most journalists (and *Times* reporters in particular), told Lord Aberdeen some weeks later that, in one respect, '*The Times* was right, and it *is* worth being related to the Commander-in-Chief'.[19]

Yet what annoyed Major Jocelyn even more than nepotism at headquarters was the 'falsehoods' of ministers in Parliament during the pre-Christmas session. On 12 December Sidney Herbert had told the Commons, with impressive precision, that when the troops on their way and awaiting embarkation had reached Balaclava, 'no fewer than

54,736 officers and men would, from first to last, have passed under the command of Lord Raglan'. But these figures were received with cynical incredulity when newspaper reports of the speech reached the Crimea. 'It makes me so angry to read them,' Strange Jocelyn told his father on 10 January. 'After all the drafts sent out to us, three weeks ago and many before, what is my Battalion on Parade? Only 280 men, including servants and Corporals; the same with the Coldstreams. . . . The 9th and 63rd Regiments have actually not a dozen men left in each regiment.' 'England does not know what we are come to, by mere mismanagement', Jocelyn added, '. . . The wooden huts, people in England took so much trouble and expense about, are littering about the Streets of Balaclava, and mostly used as planks for crossing through the mud.' There was widespread disappointment over the huts, whose provision had been given such prominence at Westminster and in the newspapers. Colonel Gordon, writing home a day after Major Jocelyn, reported that the huts had arrived from England, but were too heavy to be moved to the Heights along muddy tracks rendered almost impassable by rain and sleet. Six days later Captain Duberly felt certain 'there are not 12 wooden huts at present erected in the Crimea'.[20]

When, over the first five weeks of 1855, *The Times* published extracts from letters sent by officers in the Crimea, many people asserted that they could not be genuine; this bitter catalogue of ill-natured grievances must surely be a weapon in the private vendetta of Delane and the army authorities, they claimed. But the tone and content of the letters is so similar to genuine correspondence that there is no reason to question their authenticity. The *Morning Herald*, the *Manchester Guardian* and the *Daily News*, as well as *The Times* published articles which used the evidence of the letters to ridicule an antiquated military system. The Queen was indignant at the presumption of the newspapers in attacking *her* army. She had long been at odds with them over their treatment of Lord Aberdeen for whom she possessed a protective affection, quite distinct from her feelings for other favourite prime ministers. A few weeks previously Aberdeen's 25-year-old son and private secretary, Arthur Gordon MP, was accosted by his sovereign during a visit to Windsor. 'Why do you let Lord Aberdeen read all these attacks on him in the newspapers?' the Queen demanded. 'It can do no good and I know it worries him.' 'It is not with my goodwill be reads them, Ma'am,' Arthur Gordon explained, apologetically. 'But you should take them all away and put them in the fire – say I told you', the

Queen replied. 'It is really no use, and Lord Aberdeen has public and private anxiety enough without those scribblers. I am quite annoyed at it'.[21] If Arthur Gordon passed the Queen's remarks on to his father, it made no difference; the articles were read, and inwardly digested.

Often the anonymous extracts from people's Crimean correspondence must have made familiar reading to the Prime Minister, for they seem to voice in stronger language Colonel Alexander Gordon's complaints. The four letters which Aberdeen received in December and January gave him a clearer indication of the mood of Raglan's army than any judiciously phrased despatch from headquarters to the War Secretaries. It was Alexander Gordon who let his father know of Sir George De Lacy Evans's farewell conversation with the commander-in-chief, two months before the General – who was a Member for Westminster – arrived back in the Commons: 'His parting advice to Raglan was "My Lord, Save your Army, and raise the siege",' Colonel Gordon reported, and he added, 'I believe the same advice would be given by every General and Officer of Experience in this Army, *if his opinion were asked* '.[22] Fresh food remained scarce because of the rain, mud and lack of transport, the Prime Minister was told in the first week of December; 'Our cavalry are dying fast', a letter reported ten days later; boots, newly arrived from England, were so small that the men could not wear them in the trenches and were suffering from frost-bite; and illness had left some batteries so short of sentries that some guns would have to be spiked and abandoned.[23] All these misfortunes were known to Lord Aberdeen long before they appeared in the evidence of any committee of inquiry.

But the most impressive messages for the Prime Minister from a soldier son of undoubted personal courage were pleas for a negotiated peace, an end to a war whose character he doubted whether the Government had ever begun to understand. A rumour spread through the army at Christmas that peace talks had begun. 'We hear we are to have peace directly,' Alexander Gordon wrote on Boxing Day. 'The whole army would be delighted if so for they are suffering very much from cold and wet. We hear from good authority (Lord Stratford) that the only difficulty about peace is the indemnity. I hope no such petty consideration will interfere to prevent it and it will be as well to bear in mind that we are not in Sebastopol yet – and that the place is five times stronger than on 17th October when we fired the first shots.' Four weeks later the Colonel sent home a stark assessment of the situation: 'If put to the vote in the army we should have peace immediately, for the men are suffering severely from wet and cold – about 200 become non-effective every day, of whom 50 or 60 die . . . Our infantry effectives in the camp before Sebastopol today are 10,504. Deaths in the last 24 hours, 64. Total sick here and at Scutari 16,588'; and he sent a final blunt and brief message on 2 February: 'My humble opinion is that you had better make peace as soon as you can and not be too particular over the terms.' But by then his father was no longer prime minister.[24]

Fanny Duberly, too, had picked up the Christmas peace rumour: 'Here is a report come from Lord Raglan's that peace is proclaimed in London. Can this be true?' she wrote to her sister on Holy Innocents' Day.[25] But, whereas Colonel Gordon thought the army would be thankful if the war were brought to a speedy end, Mrs Duberly was horrified. Had all these sacrifices been in vain, then? A peace short of victory would make the 'English people rise up and denounce the idea', she believed. The report was, to say the least of it, premature, but by the end of the first week in January there seemed a better prospect of peace than for many months. The Russians informed Buol, the Austrian Foreign Minister, and the British and French ambassadors in Vienna that they were prepared to discuss a peace settlement based upon the Four Points, provided that it did not impose any conditions concerning Russia's position in the Black Sea which would wound the Tsar's 'honour and dignity'. Napoleon III was less interested in a compromise peace than in forcing Russia to break off negotiations, thus provoking Austria into active participation in the war alongside her allies. Palmerston, who had visited Napoleon in Paris at the end of November, was sympathetic to this policy, and so too were several British diplomats. But not Lord Aberdeen. Arthur Gordon describes in his diary for 8 January 1855 how on hearing of Russia's willingness to discuss peace, his father 'not a little rejoiced thereat'. The Prime Minister's only doubts were whether the Tsar was sincere and whether he personally had enough standing in Britain to get away with a compromise settlement. Palmerston, he suspected, could gain acceptance of peace terms which the country would never allow him to consider.[26]

Parliament reassembled, after the Christmas recess, on Tuesday, 23 January, in weather as bleak as the reports from the Crimea. There was freezing fog in London and ice on the railway track hampered communications with the court, which remained at Windsor until 2 February. On Monday evening (22 January) Arthur Gordon wrote in his diary that, for his father, 'things look better': Russell, 'quite alone' in the cabinet, had given up scheming for the moment; it 'suited Palmerston's game' to wait upon events; Clarendon, although insincere and devious, was personally loyal to Aberdeen; and Gladstone, though impulsive, did not mind if there was 'a rupture with Lord John'. The Duke of Newcastle, Arthur Gordon said, wished to resign in favour of Sidney Herbert but Palmerston was the only possible war minister who would 'give real confidence'. Among his father's cabinet colleagues it was Graham who worried Arthur Gordon, for he was 'at once rash and timid . . . a warm friend and a dangerous adviser' whom Aberdeen consulted too readily.[27] Yet, however astute this character analysis of the cabinet may have been, as a current political assessment it was singularly complacent, for tempers were already strained at Westminster, 'deeply moved' by reports from the Crimea and from Scutari. And on the first day of the session the plain-speaking patriot Radical MP for Sheffield, John Arthur Roebuck, gave notice that he intended to propose the appointment of a select committee of the House of Commons to inquire into the condition of the army before Sebastopol.[28]

That Tuesday night Lord John Russell sent in his resignation: he said that he could not oppose Roebuck's proposed motion; as it censured his colleagues in the War Departments, he would have to leave the cabinet. There followed an extraordinary political crisis, in which the Queen urged Aberdeen to stay on in office and rebuked Lord John for deserting his leader. Roebuck, a diminutive Yorkshire terrier, proposed his motion in the Commons on the following Friday but was unable to speak for more than ten minutes because he was racked with pain from a stomach ulcer. It made little difference. Others took up the challenge to the Government, notably Layard again and – when the debate was resumed on the following Monday – Augustus Stafford, the much-respected Conservative MP for Northamptonshire North, who had spent several weeks at Scutari helping Florence Nightingale. The best speech in defence of the Aberdeen Administration was made by Palmerston, who as nominal Home Secretary had little to lose and much to gain if the vote went against the Government. When the House divided on that Monday night, Roebuck's motion was carried by the surprisingly large majority of 305 votes to 148.[29] 'They . . . sent us down with such a whack that one heard one's head thump as it struck the ground,' Gladstone remarked to the defeated premier on Tuesday morning. That afternoon, as 'large damp snow flakes fell slowly, thickly and sullenly' around him, the Earl of Aberdeen walked up the hill from Windsor railway station to tender the Coalition Government's resignation to a sovereign who was deeply distressed at parting with 'so kind & valued and dear a friend'.[30]

The Queen sent for Lord Derby to see if he could form a Conservative-dominated coalition; but Derby, to Disraeli's disgust, thought the task beyond him. She tried the aged Lord Lansdowne and the able Lord Clarendon, but without success. Curbing her indignation at his disloyalty, she even sent for Lord John Russell who found that, apart from Palmerston, none of his old colleagues would serve under him. At last, on 4 February, she invited Palmerston himself; and he, with the fallen prime minister encouraging the Peelites to back him, had a government to present to the Queen by the following evening. Clarendon, Graham and Gladstone kept their old posts. The two War Departments were at last merged into a single Secretaryship of State for War held by Lord Panmure, a shambling giant of a Whig peer, hitherto nicknamed 'Bison' but now to enjoy greater dignity as 'Mars'. Sir George Grey took Palmerston's place as Home Secretary and Sidney Herbert became Colonial Secretary. Lord Palmerston kissed hands as the Queen's chief minister at Buckingham Palace on 6 February.[31]

That same evening, three miles away, the Lord Mayor was presiding over an annual banquet at which the Corporation of London entertained guests of particular distinction. This year a wave of patriotic sentiment had broken over the City: the banquet would honour the Queen's fighting men. As the one admiral who had brought a fleet back to Britain, 'Black Charley' Napier responded to the toast of the Royal Navy; but to speak for the Army the hero of the hour had to be Lord Cardigan, who rode through the City astride Ronald, the horse which had carried him in the great charge at Balaclava fifteen weeks before. On that occasion Ronald had been lucky to keep his life; on this he was lucky to keep his tail, for as the Earl arrived at the Mansion House he was surrounded by an excited crowd eager to pluck a hair from the most famous chestnut charger in the world.[32] *The Times* thought the whole evening had a flavour of Madame Tussaud and *The Illustrated London News* ignored the occasion entirely. Cardigan spoke egotistically, although no doubt the tears he shed on mentioning the losses in his Brigade were genuine signs of grief; but the remarkable speech of the evening came, yet again, from Admiral Napier. He denounced the officers and men of his Baltic Squadron for giving him less personal loyalty than he might have expected; he denounced the Admiralty

Board; and, most of all, he denounced Sir James Graham for having ordered him to strike his flag and return to civilian life while the laurels of victory were still eluding him.

To attack a First Lord of the Admiralty at a time when he had just been confirmed in that office by a new prime minister was bound to cause a sensation, and Graham's opponents in the Commons followed up Napier's speech with a series of questions. Graham would say nothing that might be of value to the Russians, for 'naval preparations' were 'about to be resumed in the Baltic'; and, as for Napier himself, 'the gallant officer . . . has proclaimed himself a hero . . . but it is not my intention to allow him to dub himself a martyr as well as a hero'.[33] The nation, in these first days of Palmerston's premiership, thus had an opportunity to discuss, not only shortcomings in the Crimea, but also the failure of Aberdeen's ministers to give the people those victories in the Baltic which they had so confidently expected ten months before. So far from welcoming the advent of a new war leader, the Mansion House banquet made it harder for him to hold together the coalition which he had inherited.

In Parliament the Government made a shaky start. Palmerston at once appealed to the Commons to give up the idea of a committee of inquiry into the conduct of the Crimean campaign; and the Commons refused. Roebuck explained that some of the guilty ministers were still there, in the cabinet; and he intended that the committee should assist 'the Noble Lord in infusing new vigour into the constitution of the country'. Layard went further even than Roebuck, attacking aristocratic inefficiency at home and overseas and urging that investigatory MPs should be empowered to travel to the Crimea and dismiss on the spot incompetent administrators or commanders.[34] This proposal was too reminiscent of the French Revolutionary Convention to satisfy most members of the Commons, and Layard was left to wage his campaign for 'the right man in the right place' outside the House. But Palmerston was forced to give way to Roebuck, and the Sebastopol Committee came into being. Thereupon the three Peelite survivors in the cabinet decided that their prime minister was weak and inconsistent; and accordingly on 21 February Gladstone, Graham and Herbert resigned. Russell agreed to come back into the cabinet as Colonial Secretary, but was at once appointed First Commissioner to the proposed conference in Vienna. The rest of Palmerston's team was not impressive, although Sir Charles Wood, who replaced Graham at the Admiralty, did at least possess nine continuous years of experience in office, mainly concerned with Indian affairs. 'We have replaced a Cabinet of All the Talents by a Cabinet of All the Mediocrities', scoffed Disraeli.[35]

To the nation as a whole, however, Palmerston gave an impression of vigorous war leadership. He no longer made memorable speeches in the Commons: that was the prerogative of John Bright, who on 23 February brought tears to members' eyes by the simple grandeur of his finest peroration – 'The angel of death has been abroad throughout the land; you may almost hear the beating of his wings.' Occasionally, too, Palmerston misjudged the public temper: thus the decision to institute a second National Day of Fasting and Humiliation at the end of March 1855 won little support and was satirized in *Punch*. But, for the most part, Palmerston offered the country action, not sackcloth and ashes. Over the next twelve months, like Churchill ninety years later, he concerned himself with the smaller details of campaigning and with operational sideshows as well as with the main theatres of war. Significantly the first returned officer he interviewed after becoming prime minister was General Channon, who had been in command of the Anglo-Turkish base at Eupatoria only six weeks before; and he never lost interest in what was happening elsewhere around the Black Sea. As early as 22 February he was warning Raglan, 'If no proper precautions are taken before the sun's rays begin to be felt, your camp will become one vast seat of the most virulent plague.'[36] Palmerston also examined proposals for improved weaponry, especially rifles, mortars, and 'steam guns'; he was interested in plans for 'a submarine vessel'; and when, later that year, James Cowan took out a patent for a steam-driven, four-wheeled, armoured 'locomotive land battery fitted with scythes to mow down infantry', this proto-tank aroused the Prime Minister's interest. But Cowan's ingenuity was never put to the test. An armoured chariot, like Dundonald's sulphurous fumes project, was thought needlessly brutalizing to warfare.[37]

Almost as soon as Palmerston became prime minister conditions in front of Sebastopol began to improve. The reinforcements and supplies assigned to the Crimea by Lord Aberdeen's ministers in the closing weeks of the previous year were at last reaching their destination; and on this occasion they were spared a hurricane. Moreover, the less severe weather helped earlier projects to come to fruition. 'Our railway is growing fast', Fanny Duberly wrote to her sister on 17 February; and other letters home, too, commented on this track that British navvies, Croats, Montenegrins, Albanians and Turks between them were thrusting forward up the hill towards Kadikoi and the forward bases of the army. It did not reach the plateau until the end of March, and by then a Land Transport Corps had been improvised, to bring some order into the movement of supplies by horse cart, mule and dromedaries. The railway, however, meant more to officers and men than improved communications: it was a sign that Raglan and Canrobert were determined to organize a carefully planned assault on Sebastopol. When in mid-Febraury Lord Lucan was curtly recalled to England, there were some who hoped that 'Raggles' and his staff would follow him.[38] But by now the defeatism and self-pity of December and early January were out of fashion in the Crimea.

Human endurance was still strained at Scutari, in the hospitals beside the Bosphorus. Despite Florence Nightingale's devoted work, and the improved sanitary conditions, the mortality rate at the Selimiye Kislasi barracks was still two out of every five men admitted in February 1855, and higher still at neighbouring hospitals. An earthquake on the last day of February caused no casualties in the wards but 'created great fear'; Sister Sarah Anne records that 'many who had shown no emotion in battle were crying and trembling, and left the bed to which they had been confined though too feeble to return unassisted.' Strained relations between Florence Nightingale, the army medical staff, Lord Stratford de Redcliffe and a second group of nurses brought out to Turkey by her friend, Mary Stanley, hampered the smooth running of the hospitals. Lord Raglan was reluctant to allow any female nurses to land in the Crimea itself. But he relented during the January crisis weeks and the first eight women nurses from England went ashore at Balaclava on 29 January. The Commander-in-Chief still forbade them to attend the field hospitals within range of enemy fire, but on 3 February he rode down to Balaclava and was gratified to find 'the eight nurses in full employment'. 'With the exception of the three ladies, they are none of them young,' wrote Raglan's nephew, ungallantly, 'all rather fat and motherly-looking women, and quite up to one's idea of orthodox nurses.'[39]

That night of 3–4 February was the coldest of the winter, with the thermometer at Raglan's sheltered headquarters dropping to 10° Fahrenheit (−12°C). But thereafter, climatically, the 'hard times' were over. Before the end of the month, three vessels chartered by *The Times* had berthed at Balaclava with comforts for the troops. No matter that flannel shirts, sheepskin coats, and knitted hats were being unpacked under sunshine which held promise of an early spring; what delighted the troops were the beer, sweets, biscuits and other forgotten luxuries.

The gifts were distributed free or sold cheaply in shops which opened at Balaclava itself or up the hill at Kadikoi. It must have been late in that same month, although the precise date remains unknown, that Mrs Mary Seacole arrived in the harbour, having paid for her passage from her native Jamaica to England and thence out to the Black Sea. Soon this fifty-year-old Creole, with 'good Scotch blood coursing in my veins',[40] was serving the expeditionary force both as an unofficial nurse and as a sutler; and within two months she had opened the 'British Hotel', near Kadikoi, where there was an officers' club and a good, clean canteen for the troops. Lord Raglan's veto on women rendering assistance at the battle front did not inhibit Mrs Seacole from riding forward with her small, personal mule train of medicaments, food and refreshment. By the summer of 1855 Mary Seacole was regarded by the troops as part-heroine and part-mascot. If Scutari had its Lady with the Lamp, Balaclava could offer romantic legend a Creole with the Teamug.[41]

Militarily there remained little activity in front of Sebastopol in the opening months of 1855: a Russian feint attack on 10 January; an allied probe across the river Chernaya on 20 February, which was frustrated by a late snowstorm; and, at the end of the month, a four-day tussle between the Russians and the French for control of a hillock known as the 'Mamelon Vert', which Totleben was able to secure as an advanced redoubt in his improved defensive system to the east of the city. The main Russian assault in the Crimea during February was further north, a determined effort by some nine thousand men, with support from over a hundred field guns, to eject the Turks, British and French from their base at Eupatoria; but the attack was beaten off by Omar Pasha's troops, supported by gunfire from six French and three British warships.[42] In front of Sebastopol, the French gradually took over more trenches from the British. Shortly before the political crisis at Westminster led to his resignation, the Duke of Newcastle had written to Raglan insisting that, now French numbers had doubled, Canrobert should extend the French sector of trenches; and the recently promoted Major-General Rose recorded in his journal for 29 January an amicable council of war on closer Franco-British collaboration. Raglan seems at times to have taken French assistance for granted; French commanders, notably Bosquet, thought Canrobert too accommodating to 'England's needs'.[43]

By early March it was clear that the allies would soon intensify the siege by bombarding Sebastopol once more. Raglan was presiding over a council of war on 7 March when a telegram reached him, forwarded by steamer from Constantinople and enclosing a telegram handed in at Berlin by Lord John Russell on 2 March saying that Tsar Nicholas I 'died this day at 10 minutes past 12'.[44] At first the generals were sceptical, no doubt puzzled why such information should have come from such a person in such a place. A similar message reached Canrobert twenty-four hours later; but there was still much doubt at headquarters. There had already been many rumours flying around the camps, particularly about the Russian imperial family: only seven weeks before, a well-authenticated report had maintained that the Tsar was dying, although Polish deserters said he was expected soon in Sebastopol itself. 'Some will not yet credit it', Henry Clifford wrote to his brother on 11 March. But when no denial came of Lord John's message and when press reports indicated that he had, at that moment, been in Berlin on his way to Vienna for peace talks, hopes were high that the war would soon be over. It was resolved that the batteries would shortly open up on Sebastopol, provided the fine weather held; but it might not be necessary to storm those formidable defences. So often the conflict had been over-simplified as 'the Tsar's war' that there seemed no reason why it should continue. 'His eldest Son, they say, is most anxious for Peace', Henry Clifford wrote.[45] Moreover, it was surely a good sign that a British cabinet minister was travelling once again to confer round a table at Metternich's old chancellery in Vienna. On 22 March even so cautious an observer of high politics as Hugh Rose went so far as to write in his journal, 'I think there must be Peace'.[46]

CHAPTER FOURTEEN

New Management

Prince Menshikov had remained at his headquarters on the Belbec over Christmas and throughout January 1855. Ever since Inkerman his private contacts in the capital had kept him informed of the whispering campaign which was blackening his name at court; and he knew he was dependent for support on Tsar Nicholas's obstinate reluctance to give way to any pressure group, either in his family or among his closest advisers. As he never came under enemy fire, it was difficult for Menshikov to follow the example of Paskevich and retire wounded from the war zone. Moreover, pride still drove him to hope that he might, somewhere soon, snatch a victory on the cheap. At last urgent prompting from St Petersburg induced him to order the attack on Eupatoria in mid-February; he might, he felt, recover lost credit by liberating a Crimean town which was held mainly by the despised Turks. But when news reached him that the naval guns of the defenders had repelled the attack and that the Russians had lost nearly eight hundred men, Menshikov sensed that his military career was over; and he was right. His despatch reporting the failure at Eupatoria reached St Petersburg on 24 February. Three days later – Tuesday, 15 February by the Russian calendar – Tsar Nicholas dismissed Menshikov from his command, appointing Prince Michael Gorchakov to succeed him as Commander of the Army of the Crimea while retaining responsibility for the Southern Army, stationed in Bessarabia.[1]

Significantly the order dismissing Menshikov was signed, not by Nicholas I, but by his eldest son, Grand Duke Alexander, writing in his father's name; 'the health of the sovereign is not good', he explained to the disgraced Commander-in-Chief. On the previous Saturday the Tsar had attended the wedding of a leading court functionary's daughter; he appeared well, although his face looked weary. 'Influenza ... has taken hold here. I have been near to it for a few days', he admitted in a letter to his sister, Anna, that night. He was not, however, worried about his health, for he added that, if danger continued to threaten his empire, he would shortly be joining the army in the field.[2] Meanwhile, despite bitterly cold weather, he did not cancel his engagements. Next morning he inspected troops at the cavalry school, where an icy wind blew straight off the frozen Neva into the city. Two days later he thought that, like so many members of St Petersburg society at that time of year, he was suffering from a feverish cold. Even when he took to his bed on Tuesday there was no great concern at court. Not until the small hours of Friday morning (18 February/2 March) did his physician realize that the Tsar's lungs were badly congested. Nicholas died later that day, technically from pneumonia. According to his widow, he insisted that 'the heroic defenders of Sebastopol' should be assured that he would continue to pray for them in the next world.

Rumour immediately created a mystery from the suddenness of the Tsar's death, as so often in Russia's history. He died, it was said, from a heart broken by the failure of his troops to inflict a decisive defeat on the enemy. More sensational stories recounted how he had committed suicide: he had shot himself, said some; he had swallowed poison, said others. But almost certainly Nicholas I died a natural death. That generation of Romanovs had never been robust. Although only fifty-eight, Nicholas lived longer than his three brothers and five of his six sisters; and he had always found difficulty in relaxing from the cares of government. His last private letters reflect his intense irritation with Menshikov and his renewed anger with Francis Joseph for Austria's ingratitude in concluding an alliance with Britain and France. But they show, too, that he had every intention of continuing to prosecute the war vigorously, unless his enemies were about to offer favourable terms. Of this he had little hope.[3]

Russia's new sovereign, Tsar Alexander II, was thirty-six when he came to the throne. By temperament he was not so autocratic as his father and in July 1853 he had strongly opposed the decision to march into the Danubian Principalities; but he was proud of the army which had schooled him, and he was determined not to begin his reign by accepting a shameful peace. Foreign observers who thought the Grand Duke's accession would bring a speedy end to the war were soon put in their place. On the day following Nicholas's death Alexander II gave the assembled diplomatic corps a clear indication of the policy he advocated for the conference about to open in Vienna, seeking a peace based on last August's 'Four Points'. Alexander told the diplomats that, like his father, he wished for an end to the conflict; but he emphasized that if the conference did not produce an honourable settlement, 'I, and my faithful Russia, will go on waging war' since 'I would rather perish than surrender.'[4]

The immediate fate of Russia was, largely by chance, in the hands of two first cousins that month: General Prince Michael Gorchakov travelled from Kishinev to Crimean Army headquarters on the Belbec; and Prince Alexander Gorchakov, having emerged in July 1854 from thirty years of small-power diplomacy to become ambassador in Vienna, was responsible for rejecting any humiliating terms which Russia's enemies might put down on the conference table. The principal British spokesman, Lord John Russell, reached Vienna at the end of the first week in March, travelling by way of Paris and Berlin. Preliminary conversations with the Conference's president, Count Buol, went smoothly; and by 10 March Lord John was almost ready to concede that 'an equilibrium of forces in the Black Sea' might afford 'enough security' for the Powers. 'I doubt, however, whether people in England would be satisfied, they have tasted blood, and must be gorged with the garrison of Sebastopol before they are ready for peace', noted the Foreign Secretary's nephew, Thomas Lister, who was attached to the Russell mission.[5]

When formal sessions began, on 15 March, Gorchakov made little difficulty over defining what was meant by the first two of the Four Points, and Lister was able to write in his journal: 'The first conference on the 15th was very satisfactory.' But within a week there was trouble over Point Three, with its stipulation that the movement of warships in and out of the Black Sea should reflect the European Balance of Power. Gorchakov at once insisted that Russia would not permit any naval restraints in the Black Sea. 'Of course, on this rock the Conference must split,' Lister commented. 'In England I hear that everyone says that the destruction of Sebastopol must be a condition of peace. And Russia won't even tolerate a limitation of her warships.' But Lord John was not so impetuous as his young attaché. Rather than allow the Conference to break up, he proposed that the Russians should themselves define how a balance of power might be achieved in the Black Sea. So serious a problem required reference back to St Petersburg; and the Conference went into recession until mid-April.[6]

Neither Palmerston nor Clarendon held high hopes of the Vienna Conference. They saw it as a useful talking-shop which, if the Russians rejected Buol's proposals, would persuade Francis Joseph to impose armed mediation on Alexander II, just as the failure of the Prague Conference in 1813 had persuaded Francis I to impose armed mediation on the great Napoleon. The Vienna talks had a secondary importance, too, both for the British statesmen and for the leading advisers of the Emperor in Paris: so long as there was a prospect of a sudden armistice in the East, followed by the drawing up of a comprehensive peace settlement for Europe in general, Napoleon III needed to be at the centre of affairs. If the talks broke down, it would be harder to prevent Napoleon III from carrying out an idea he had cherished since the previous July – to go to the Crimea himself, and take command of the armies in front of Sebastopol.[7]

Marshal Vaillant (the French Minister of War), the Empress Eugénie and other members of the imperial family, Napoleon's Foreign Minister, and several of his oldest supporters all tried to persuade him that an Emperor's place was in Paris, not in the Crimea. Those with longest memories gave the gravest advice. Marshal Boniface de Castellane, who had been at his sovereign's side when Moscow was burning, bluntly told Napoleon III that a military reverse could prove disastrous if the Emperor were there in person; and another veteran of 1812–13, the Comte de Flahault – Talleyrand's natural son – sought out the British ambassador and asked if Her Majesty's Government could not persuade Napoleon III to stay away from the Crimea.[8]

From the War Office, Lord Panmure wrote to Raglan on 2 March saying that he believed Napoleon would 'positively go to the Crimea' and that Raglan would find him 'a more sincerely disposed co-operator than ... his generals'. But 'Mars' Panmure was alone among Palmerston's cabinet ministers in favouring the idea; it was felt that public opinion at home was not ready for a campaign in which British troops and seamen would be serving as auxiliaries to a Bonaparte Emperor. Clarendon hurried across to Boulogne on 3 March, saw Napoleon III, and persuaded him that the time was not ripe for new imperial management in the Crimea. If the war was not ended by the Vienna talks it would be better, Clarendon argued, to wait for 'le dernier coup de main', and then ride into Sebastopol in triumph. Meanwhile perhaps the Emperor and Empress of the French would like to exchange state visits with the British sovereign and her consort? If Napoleon and Eugénie came to Windsor in April, they could entertain Victoria and Albert at Saint-Cloud in August. Such a programme would, of course, make it difficult for the Emperor to fit in a campaign against the Russians. By 16 April, when the French imperial visitors stepped down from their train at the Bricklayers' Arms (careful preparations being taken to avoid roads, stations or bridges which commemorated Waterloo), Napoleon was no longer inclined to go out to the Crimea. But he was in no hurry to tell his hosts that he had changed his mind. The possibility of French imperial leadership remained a convenient weapon to prod the British into closer collaboration and his generals in the field into positive action.[9]

By now Napoleon III had more than 80,000 troops in the Crimea and there were new faces under the gold-braided *képis* at French headquarters. Canrobert remained in command, although there was a feeling in Paris that he lacked the iron will of a victorious campaigner; but in the second week of February General Pélissier had arrived at Kamiesh from Oran, to take charge of what was now called the 1st Army Corps, with the 2nd Corps entrusted to Bosquet. At the same time Napoleon III sent a personal representative to Headquarters, General Adolphe Niel, who had distinguished himself at Bomarsund in the previous summer. These appointments increased the distrust at headquarters, where there was already much ambitious jockeying for position – or, as some maintained, for the marshals' batons which the Emperor would, no doubt, distribute once the tricolour was flying in Sebastopol. Pélissier was fifteen years older than Canrobert, who regarded him as a ruthless soldier, inclined to make personal enemies very easily.[10] Niel, little known a year before, was mistrusted on three counts: he was an engineer; he had never commanded troops in action before the attack on Bomarsund, although he had been under fire in North Africa; and he was, in a sense, the Emperor's personal spy, entitled to communicate directly and confidentially with Napoleon. In reality, Niel was a remarkably able organizer and administrator in the tradition of Carnot; and he brought a fresh eye to the problems of the Crimea. But this, too, did not make him popular at headquarters.

Although Raglan and Sir George Brown stayed on, there were also changes in the British command. The Admiralty had always intended that Sir Edmund Lyons should succeed Sir James Dundas at the end of December 1854; and this transference of authority was duly carried out. Lord Rokeby arrived in January to take the place of the Duke of Cambridge at the head of the 1st Division, while in the 2nd Division Sir George De Lacy Evans had been succeeded, first by General Pennefather and, later, by General Markham. After Lucan's recall to London, the Cavalry were entrusted to Sir James Scarlett, who had commanded the Heavy Brigade on 23 October. Panmure would have liked other changes, and his earliest despatches to Lord Raglan were so hostile that a more temperamental field marshal would instantly have asked to be relieved of his command. But Raglan, although distressed that the politicians were taking their cue from what he regarded as ill-informed newspaper reports, possessed an almost inhuman calm: patiently he rebutted each complaint from Panmure, staunchly defending what Palmerston privately called 'that knot of incapables' who were his closest advisers. Raglan insisted, in particular, that Burgoyne should remain at headquarters, to give advice on the preparations for the coming spring's siege operations. But Panmure decided that he, too, needed the benefit of Burgoyne's experience; and on 20 March the old war horse, by now in his seventy-fourth year, left Balaclava for home. Four weeks later he was at Windsor giving his views on grand strategy to a war council in which Napoleon III, Prince Albert, Palmerston, Panmure, Clarendon, and Marshal Vaillant also participated.[11]

Panmure succeeded in imposing a new chief-of-staff on Lord Raglan. Lieutenant-General Sir James Simpson, a lowland Scot who served as a Guards subaltern under Wellington in the Peninsula and at Waterloo, reached Balaclava a few days before Burgoyne sailed for home. At first he was treated with suspicion: if Niel was Napoleon's spy, then no doubt Simpson had come as Palmerston's spy. But Simpson, a good professional, was not politically receptive. Within a month of his arrival he felt able to report to Lord Panmure that he considered 'Lord Raglan the most abused man I ever heard of', served by 'a very good set of fellows at Headquarters', and with 'no staff officer objectionable in my opinion'.[12] Panmure evidently found this message reassuring, for he began to treat Raglan more generously, perhaps because by now the War Office was in closer contact with headquarters in the field, for by the third week in April a submarine electric cable at last linked Balaclava with Varna and thence by way of Bucharest and Vienna with Europe's rapidly spreading telegraph system.

Theoretically, from the spring of 1855 onwards, a message put into cipher at Balaclava could reach London and be decoded at the Foreign Office and brought to the attention of the War Secretary within twelve hours. There were, of course, the customary technological teething troubles, one of which was caused by typically Crimean mismanagement: although an electric cable had reached the Crimea, standard cipher books had not. Shortly after the installation of the cable, Panmure informed Raglan: 'Your telegraph message which arrived this morning is utterly unintelligible at the Foreign Office. From its length we deem it to be of importance, but we must wait in patience for a solution of it from yourself . . . Ask General Rose to help you as he is fully acquainted with the Book cipher of the Foreign Office'.[13] A cipher book, Panmure assured Raglan, was on its way, by sea; and by early May the telegraph link was working effectively.

Yet, despite the efforts of London and Paris to inject a vigorous fighting spirit at headquarters, the allied commanders still seemed reluctant to tighten the grip around Sebastopol or to unleash a new bombardment of the city. At a series of war councils, the French argued that if the guns opened up on Sebastopol, it would provoke Gorchakov into a major attack; and neither Canrobert nor Niel thought that the allies as yet possessed the numerical strength to contain a determined Russian thrust. Sardinia-Piedmont had indeed declared war on Russia at the end of January, but the Italian expeditionary force would not arrive until mid-May. Meanwhile Canrobert was reluctant to risk a general engagement, unless the bulk of the Turkish troops which had fought so well at Eupatoria in February could be shipped to Balaclava. Raglan did not agree with his ally: he was unenthusiastic over the merits of Turkish support, but he was also deeply conscious that by now the British were the junior partners. There were eight full-strength French divisions in the Crimea, with more troops promised by the early summer; and Raglan had only six divisions, with their numbers depleted by sickness. Both Raglan and Simpson realized that it would be difficult for the British to impose their views on Canrobert and his staff, however good their personal relationship might be.[14]

Events at Easter emphasized the difficulties. Now that the Balaclava Railway could keep ammunition supplied to the batteries on the Heights, Raglan proposed that Sebastopol should be bombarded for the first time that year: the guns would open up at dawn on 6 April, an allied assault following once the outer defences were reduced to rubble. Canrobert appeared to agree, but on 4 April he insisted on postponing the bombardment: the date chosen by the British Field Marshal was Good Friday, which in 1855 was observed on the same date by both the Latin and Orthodox Churches. On the previous Orthodox Good Friday (7 April, 1854, a week ahead of the Latin observance) there had been a naval bombardment of Odessa, and Tsar Nicholas subsequently denounced the barbarity of Christian nations whose missiles fell on good churchgoers at such a time. Raglan accepted the postponement, although his staff believed that Canrobert's scruples were linked with the imminent arrival of powerful Turkish reinforcements. But the people of Sebastopol were at least allowed to celebrate Easter in deceptive peace. There was even a military band concert on the Sunday evening in the Mitchmanski Boulevard, while a few miles away Russia's enemies were welcoming the arrival of Omar Pasha, with a contingent of 13,000 Turks from Eupatoria.[15]

Next morning, at a quarter past five, nearly 400 French and 123 British field guns and mortars began their bombardment of the outer forts; and for six and a half hours the boom of cannon and whistle of shells echoed along the ravines around the city. In theory the Russians could reply with 900 well-sited guns but, uncertain of what would follow this thunderous bombardment, they dared not waste ammunition and their response was therefore muted. Inexplicably the allied guns fell silent well before noon on that first Monday; and no attack followed. For ten days the bombardment continued, intermittently. Each night Totleben was able to bring up labourers to repair the most dangerous gaps in the defences. The Russians assumed that the allies would send in their infantry after the first days of bombardment, as indeed Raglan had wished. But Canrobert argued that any attack against so formidable a position would lead to a heavy toll in lives needlessly cast away; he thought that the artillery should continue to pulverize Totleben's improvised fortifications, until a shattered city silently admitted the enemy at its gates.[16]

Wars of attrition rarely bite so deeply or decisively as their advocates expect. During the bombardment the Russians lost more men than at the battle of the Alma, most of the casualties being infantrymen stationed in the front line to await the assault that never came. Yet materially the 200 tons of ammunition fired each day against Sebastopol inflicted relatively little lasting damage. Only the southern-most fort, the Flagstaff Bastion, was put out of action. Even so, Tolstoy, who was stationed there for nine of the ten days, wrote in a letter to his aunt that 'the bombardment wasn't as terrible as most people describe it'. When it was over he found accommodation in an apartment on the boulevard, where there was music every afternoon and he could bathe in the sea.[17]

It is hard to see what the allied generals gained from the ten-day bombardment. Since any defences which were knocked out all lay in the southern sector, this massive expenditure of ammunition brought no nearer the investment of the city from the north, an essential prerequisite for any effective siege. Napoleon III repeatedly put forward a more ambitious plan: a holding force would man the siege-works and trenches; a British corps would advance northwards from Kadikoi on Bakchisarai; and the French would make a new landing at Alushta so as to march through the coastal mountains and capture Simferopol. These operations would secure for the allies control of the two supply centres for the southern Crimea. Having cut off both Sebastopol and Gorchakov's relief army, the allied march would force the Russians to sue for peace. This essay in grand strategy was pastiche early Bonaparte, with the nephew showing that he had studied his uncle's campaigns at least as far as November 1796. General Niel liked the plan; Canrobert was uneasy about its implementation without total unity of command; and Bosquet thought (rightly) that it took little account of the Crimean terrain. Back in London, Burgoyne considered the plan, at best, risky: it would weaken the army in front of Sebastopol; and it might require the transportation through the mountains of a siege-train, if Simferopol was turned into an armed camp. That same septuagenarian caution which, after the Alma, ruled out a direct march on Sebastopol now shelved the first imaginative concept of the campaign.[18]

Throughout April 1855 there was, however, a strong possibility that no army would need to march on Simferopol or fight its way into Sebastopol. During the fortnight when the Vienna Conference stood suspended (2–17 April) it seemed likely to the allies that Russia's new Tsar would send instructions to his ambassador to end the war. Lord John Russell remained in Vienna to represent Britain's interests and he was joined by the French Foreign Minister, Drouyn de Lhuys. Nevertheless it was felt in London that there was a need to let the Austrians and the Russians know that Britain and France would continue to wage war if Alexander II rejected the revised Four Points as a basic for peace. Already the advance division of a new Baltic Fleet had sailed from Spithead, and the main squadron followed at the end of the first week in April. This spring there was no flamboyant Napier in command, for he had been succeeded by the former Second Sea Lord, Rear-Admiral the Hon. Richard Dundas; but the departure of the Baltic Fleet was once more trumpeted in the newspapers, with a clear warning to the Tsar that 'the force is stronger and the duty more terrible than last year'.[19] News of the ten-day bombardment of Sebastopol was also interpreted in London as serving Russia notice of the massive fire-power which the allies could now concentrate on a single objective.

But when Prince Alexander Gorchakov returned to the conference table on 17 April, Drouyn, Russell and Buol found that the Russians would make no concessions. Buol, however, was ready to save the talks. He suggested that the Four Points be modified to enable Russia to keep as large a fleet in the Black Sea as before the war while Britain and France would be allowed to deploy warships in the Black Sea to act as a 'counterpoise'. At the same time Buol gave an impression to both Russell and Drouyn that, if the Russians rejected 'counterpoise', Austria would enter the war. Russell and Drouyn accepted the plan, with modifications, and returned to London and Paris to win support from their respective governments. But Napoleon III, Marshal Vaillant, Palmerston and Clarendon were all opposed to the idea of 'counterpoise'. 'Were we to adopt Buol's plan', Clarendon told the British ambassador in Vienna, 'none of us would feel safe from attack in the streets, and serve us right.'[20]

Drouyn was so angry at the refusal of his government to reach a compromise with Buol and Alexander Gorchakov that he resigned office, and was succeeded by Walewski. At first Lord John Russell sought to stay in Palmerston's cabinet as Colonial Secretary, but newspaper attacks on his apparent willingness to appease the Russians forced him out of office early in July; he remained on the back-benches for the next four years. Technically the Vienna Conference stood adjourned until 4 June, when Alexander Gorchakov announced that the Tsar would not accept any peace which imposed limitations on the size of the Russian fleet. The British and French ambassadors at once broke off all talks. Austria, however, did not declare war on Russia; for Buol and Francis Joseph convinced themselves that their Western allies had deliberately sabotaged the conference in the hope that Austrian military intervention would induce the Russians to accept harsher terms of peace.[21]

Failure to reach agreement at Vienna made both Napoleon III and the British Government eager for a victory in the field. Napoleon used the telegraph several times each day at the end of April in an effort to force Canrobert to go ahead with his plan for a march on Simferopol. But since the British authorities knew that Raglan, too, wished for an early military success, they made no attempt to cajole him. It was the British commanders, Raglan and Sir Edmund Lyons, who on 29 April persuaded Canrobert to agree to a plan by which a combined Anglo-

French force would make a lightning raid on the seven Russian batteries at Kerch, which kept the Sea of Azov closed to allied warships. The expedition, under Brown's command, sailed from Balaclava at sunset on 3 May, heading out towards Odessa so as to confuse the enemy. But that night Canrobert received two telegrams from Napoleon III: he was to send vessels to Constantinople to convey 40,000 more French troops to the Crimea; then he would concentrate all his forces, 'and not lose a single day', preparatory to landing an expedition at Alushta, as the first step towards realizing the Emperor's grand strategic plan. After reading the first telegram Raglan persuaded Canrobert not to interfere with the raiding force sailing for Kerch. But the arrival of Pélissier, Niel and the electric telegraph had destroyed Canrobert's confidence. Ever since Easter his vacillations had led wits at British Headquarters to nickname the French Commander-in-Chief 'Robert Cant'. Now, within an hour of leaving Raglan, the second telegram made Canrobert change his mind yet again. Without consulting Raglan he ordered a fast despatch boat to sail after the Kerch expedition, which turned back within sight of its objective, its commanders having 'under very propitious circumstances, considered success certain', as Lyons telegraphed to the First Lord.[22]

The recall of the expedition was 'a vast disappointment', Raglan told Panmure with his customary understatement on 8 May. Four days later a council of war, attended by Omar Pasha as well as by the principal French and British commanders, scrutinized the Emperor's plan in minute detail. Canrobert, with Niel dutifully at his side to support Napoleon, found opinion rapidly hardening against the Alushta expedition. At one moment he even tempted Raglan with a proposal that the British Field Marshal should command the whole operation. But in the end the war council decided that 30,000 more good front-line troops were needed to maintain the pressure on Sebastopol and safeguard the allied bases before any troops marched into the interior of the Crimea. Wretchedly distraught, Canrobert decided to resign his command; a semi-official account, partly dictated by Canrobert himself, says that he even went down to the trenches and stood up, in full dress uniform, so that a Russian sniper could end his military career with glory. But not a shot was fired. Next day he handed over his responsibilities to Pélissier, gladly returning at his own request to his old division, now organized as the 1st Division of Bosquet's 2nd Army Corps.[23]

Pélissier was a rough and tough officer, the antithesis of the gentlemanly Lord Raglan. He respected Niel as an engineer and as an organizer, but he would stand no nonsense from him as Napoleon III's mouthpiece and observer: nobody was to communicate with the Emperor except through the Commander-in-Chief; and if Niel found this prohibition intolerable, he could return on the ship to Marseilles. Pélissier also made it clear that he would not be intimidated by those laconic, and often incomprehensible, messages that the cipher department brought to him from that 'newest enemy' of a good general, the electric telegraph. What he did not wish to know became crumpled paper in his pocket.[24] If Admiral Lyons and Lord Raglan sought to carry the war to the Sea of Azov, Pélissier would not stop them.

A second expedition accordingly sailed for Kerch on 22 May and gained command of both sides of the Strait leading into the Sea of Azov three days later. Over the following fortnight the smaller British and French warships swept the Sea of Azov clear of Russian vessels, destroyed a succession of supply bases and landed British, French and Turkish troops to hold strategically important posts in the eastern Crimea. Roger Fenton, the photographer, accompanied the expedition – although without his cameras and equipment – and his letters home chronicle a disgraceful tale of plunder and pillage along the eight miles which separate the historic town of Kerch from the old fortress of Yenikale; but, while appalled by what he saw, he recognized the 'immense value' of the operation to the allies. So long as they held the Strait, no men or material could reach the Russians in the Crimea from Taganrog and the other harbours in the Sea of Azov. Militarily the Kerch expedition was recognized as the first totally successful enterprise in the war against Russia.[25]

But Pélissier, Raglan and Lyons himself knew that Sebastopol remained the great prize. Back in London ingenious minds considered new ways of taking the city. Navvies who were no longer needed to build the railway might be employed, not merely to dig trenches, but to man them as a holding force while an allied attack was in progress, Panmure suggested. If untrained in the use of firearms, the navvies could always be issued with pikes, he explained. And, on this occasion looking to the future rather than the past, he put forward another proposal in mid-May: 'I do not like to write about it officially', he diffidently told Raglan, 'but it appears to me that, if you are to assault, a reconnaissance on a quiet day, by means of a balloon let up to a certain height and retained in position would be a means of ascertaining the inner defences and the obstacles which you may have to encounter. I shall have all ready, so that if you telegraph for one it shall immediately go to you'.[26]

No request was made for the balloon, for aerial reconnaissance was not needed. Through field-glasses from the Heights it was possible to see by daylight the smallest details of the city and the antlike movements of Gorchakov's troops. On May Day Roger Fenton, 'basking in the sun' on slopes covered with 'a mass of wild flowers', could pick out 'a piquet of Cossacks along the Tchernaya and a regiment of infantry being drilled about two miles off'. The promontory above the Worontsoff Ravine where the British generals killed at Inkerman were burried was now known as Cathcart's Hill; the headquarters of Sir John Campbell's 4th Division were on its crest, and looked out towards the centre of Sebastopol, about one and a half miles distant. From the Mortar Battery, some 500 yards north-west of Campbell's headquarters, there was a good view down the ravine to the fortress of the Redan, little over a mile away. Here, at the start of the second week in May, Florence Nightingale was shown a hazy white vision of Sebastopol at her feet, as soldiers rushed from their tents and 'cheered to the echo with three times three', while her officer escorts presented her with a bouquet of wild lilies and orchids.[27]

By now official visitors were beginning to arrive from the Bosphorus: the British ambassador to Turkey; the Anglican Bishop of Gibralter, who wished to consecrate the war graves; and, later in the summer, the Duke of Newcastle, whose orders had first sent the expedition to the Crimea. Lord and Lady Stratford de Redcliffe were received with a guard of honour of Highlanders as they disembarked from HMS *Caradoc* in what Stratford called 'the picturesque harbour of Balaklava' on 26 April. For over a week the Great Elchi, his wife and a company of distinguished dignitaries and their ladies were escorted around the battlefields, often by the Commander-in-Chief in person. It was, however, more of a grand tour than an inspection: the route of the Light Brigade's Charge as seen from the hills, not down in the valley where five weeks later both Fanny Duberly and Roger Fenton, on separate riding excursions, still found 'many skeletons half buried'; the French Army in review order, not manning the trenches; while a distant night prospect of Russian musket flashes and a brief cannonade rounded off the visit with a touch of what later travellers might welcome as *son et lumière*.[28] It was left to Miss Nightingale a week later to see inside the hospitals, where she was received with suspicious hostility by the medical authorities. She thought the Balaclava General Hospital dirty and inefficiently run; and as her original instructions gave her no direct authority outside Turkey, some of the nurses treated her insolently. Unfortunately, soon after her arrival at Balaclava, Florence Nightingale collapsed with a bout of 'Crimean Fever' and was herself gravely ill for more than a fortnight. Not until a second visit to the Crimea, in November, could she leave any mark on its hospitals. Even then she accomplished far less than she had hoped in the spring.[29]

Some who made the voyage from Constantinople stayed on at Balaclava. Colonel Lord George Paget had already returned from England to serve in the Rifle Brigade, and the Stratfords invited the young and beautiful Lady George Paget to sail with them aboard *Caradoc* so that she could join her husband; and, as it happened, cheer Lord Raglan by her company.[30] Of greater importance for the army as a whole was Florence Nightingale's travelling companion, Alexis Soyer. The chef of the Reform Club had come out to Turkey with government backing but at his own expense, in order to show how the cooking of food could be improved and the rations stretched further. Printed recipes distributed throughout the regiments not only gave instructions on such problems as how to cook a rice pudding when there are no eggs or milk, but enabled camp kitchens to offer such dishes as 'Camp Pot au Feu', 'Stewed Salt Beef and Pork à la Omar Pacha' and 'Cossacks Plum Pudding'. *Soyer's Culinary Campaign*, which was published in book form two years later, recorded his experiences, included special recipes, and pioneered ways of providing meals for huge numbers of men economically. The book also described Soyer's inventions for use on active service: a field stove, 'baking stewing pans' (casseroles), and a tea percolator. 'A material point I had in view was that no fire should be seen when used in the trenches', he explained.[31] No one had ever taken camp cookery seriously in the British Army, and there was still a tendency among the junior officers to look upon M. Soyer as one of the pleasanter jokes of the war – 'a great swell' who 'sang some good songs and made himself very agreeable,' Temple Godman wrote to his father after the chef of the Reform Club had been a guest in the cavalry mess at Kadikoi.[32] But, however much he might be treated as a 'comic opera Frenchman', there is no doubt that by his assault on the army's traditional dietary chaos Soyer dramatically checked the incidence of sickness in the later months of the campaign.

'My time passes pleasantly', Roger Fenton wrote to his wife during one of those early summer days when the war seemed wrapped in silence and the sun had not yet scorched the wild flowers on the slopes above the Chernaya. But, like every other visitor to the Crimea, he could sense the impatience of the troops with the long wait for action. During the Vienna Conference 'officers and men in the batteries were', as Henry Clifford told his brother, 'reluctant to make a sacrifice of life and limb at a moment when report said Peace was probable'. 'I hope the war will be settled this summer because I am getting tired of it', Trooper Coombs wrote to his sister in his first letter home for six months. However, once it was known that the Conference had broken down, there was a return of the previous autumn's eagerness to force an end to the war. By the beginning of June a succession of rumours – 'shaves', as they were called in the camps – built up such excitement that officers sought to cool their men's enthusiasm. Everyone was convinced that a major assault on the two key forts, the Malakoff and the Redan, was imminent. The army, anticipating Dickens, had progressed from hard times to great expectations.[33]

CHAPTER FIFTEEN

Into Sebastopol

The third great bombardment of Sebastopol began, unlike its predecessors, in mid-afternoon. At three o'clock on Wednesday, 6 June, almost 600 French and British guns opened fire, concentrating on the narrow sector, hardly more than a mile from east to west, which separated the Little Redan from the point where the Worontsoff Road turned down towards the dockyards. The principal forts in this district were the Malakoff and the Redan, but ahead of them the Russians had fortified a mound known as the Mamelon and some diggings, 'the Quarries', which gave cover for sharpshooters. Around these two strong-points had been planted a field of fougasses, primitive land mines charged with powder and filled with stones. Pélissier and Raglan were agreed that, after persistent pounding by the allied gunners, the French would storm the Mamelon while the British would seize the Quarries. Then, once these gains had been consolidated, the armies would move against the Malakoff and the Redan. Everyone remained convinced that Sebastopol would be untenable if these two forts were in allied hands.

Spectators, civilian and military, journeyed up to Cathcart's Hill, much as the Russians had flocked to the slopes above the Alma in September. Lord Raglan was accompanied by Lady Paget, while Roger Fenton and Fanny Duberly (who was cultivating favour with the French now that more British officers' wives were at Balaclava) attached themselves to General Bosquet's Corps. The firing ceased as darkness fell, but it was followed by a thunderstorm which kept the night sky alive with flashes until the deeper boom of the mortars gave notice that the bombardment had resumed.

Shortly after five o'clock on that Thursday morning Pélissier and Omar Pasha came to Raglan's headquarters. Roger Fenton was there to take a photograph of the French, British and Turkish commanders as they sat studying a map in the clear, early morning sunlight: Omar glances suspiciously at Péllisier, as if seeking to lipread his exposition of the day's plans; while Raglan wearily rests his arm on the table, a vast sun hat draped with a white scarf giving the Commander-in-Chief more than a passing resemblance to Miss Matty as Mrs Gaskell depicts her, hesitating over the merits of red and white silk in the shop at Cranford.[1] A strange timelessness hung over military operations that Thursday. Onlookers again took up positions in the hills; this time the band of the Rifle Brigade played popular tunes as troops and spectators waited while the temperature rose higher and higher under the June sunshine. At last, soon after six o'clock a signal rocket led to a quarter of an hour's intensive bombardment. Then the French emerged from their trenches, dashed some 500 yards to the slopes of the Mamelon, and took the position without much difficulty. So elated were the Zouaves that they continued to pursue the Russians as though they were charging into the Malakoff itself. 'God in heaven they have got the Mamelon and are going to take the Malakoff with all those guns! How the Malakoff fires! Flash and smoke leaping from it every moment', Fanny Duberly wrote to Selina. 'Look once more through the glasses, Frenchmen certainly, but running under that tremendous fire, running for their lives away from the Malakoff and the Mamelon.' But it was not so bad as she feared. The French held on to the first defences they had captured.[2]

As soon as the British saw the tricolour flying from the Mamelon, two columns of infantry advanced on the Quarries, avoiding the field of fougasses by a flank assault. Here, too, the initial attack was successful and some of the British infantry reached the parapets of the Redan in pursuit of the enemy. The Russians were not prepared to see either of their positions remain in enemy hands. Before dark they counter-attacked and briefly recovered the Mamelon; and there was a grim tussle for possession of the Quarries through the night and into the next morning, both sides suffering casualties from the fougasses. But by noon on Thursday it was clear that the allies had secured their two objectives, although at heavy cost. Nearly half the British troops engaged in the struggle to gain and hold the Quarries were killed or wounded.[3]

All was quiet again by Friday morning; and at midday a Russian emissary under a flag of truce proposed that there should be an immediate suspension of hostilities so that each side could bury its dead. Colonel Calthorpe rode down to the battlefield and watched British and Russian fatigue parties carrying away the mutilated corpses. Enemy officers were there, too. A young 'civil and polite'

Russian told Calthorpe that the loss of the Mamelon was not of great importance to them. As the two men were in conversation, a 'tall handsome man' rode by. 'His uniform was like that of the officer with whom I was talking, except that he had a broad gold strap upon his shoulders: his cap also had a certain quantity of lace upon it', Calthorpe wrote later that week. The young Russian saluted him and then told Calthorpe that the horseman was Totleben, by now promoted to acting general. There followed a curious incident. Calthorpe, a nephew of the Commander-in-Chief, walked up to 'the man who has most distinguished himself in the Russian army during the war' and chatted with him and with two French officers in a ravine where 'bodies covered with ghastly wounds met the eye all around'. 'He appeared to treat the capture of the Mamelon with perfect indifference . . . He also intimated that we were no nearer taking the place than before', Calthorpe noted. 'I suppose he felt himself bound to appear cheerful on the occasion', the colonel reflected.[4]

Totleben was confident that the main defences would hold and that, in seizing these outworks, the allies had exposed their advanced troops well beyond their support trenches. Inside Sebastopol there were by now 45,000 soldiers and 9,000 naval gunners, while there were another 21,000 men and over 100 field guns on the Belbec, to say nothing of the army east of Chorgun. If more troops promised from southern Russia reached the Belbec, reinforcements could be sent to augment the garrison and it would not be difficult to recover the Mamelon and the Quarries. But Totleben's optimism was not shared by Prince Michael Gorchakov, who seems to have inherited Menshikov's defeatism as soon as he reached the Belbec. Already, before the allied attack, he had written to the Minister of War to tell him that he did not see how he could retain the south bank of Sebastopol, the shore on which stood the city and the dockyard. Now, on the Friday that Totleben and Calthorpe had their macabre encounter, Gorchakov wrote to Tsar Alexander II, 'I am at present thinking of only one problem: how Sebastopol is to be abandoned without losses which may mount to 20,000 men. We cannot even consider saving our ships or artillery.' But when the Tsar replied, a week later, he was adamant: Gorchakov was to hold on to the fortress until further divisions could be sent south.[5]

In St Petersburg, however, the Tsar was faced by a familiar dilemma: how many regiments from Russia's northern armies might safely be despatched to the Crimea? A fleet of twenty-one British and four French warships appeared off Kronstadt in the last days of May.

By now the island fortress and the approaches to St Petersburg were protected by the earliest naval minefield. The explosive devices themselves were not powerful, for in June three British warships – *Firefly*, *Merlin* and *Vulture* – detonated mines without suffering serious damage. Nevertheless the new invention convinced the Russians that there was even less danger of a direct assault on the capital than when Napier had brought his fleet into the Gulf of Finland twelve months before.[6] But the death of Nicholas I had not silenced Paskevich, and the old Marshal persistently warned Alexander II of the dangers of weakening military establishments in the Baltic provinces and Finland for the sake of the Crimea.

On the other hand, better news reached St Petersburg from the south-western frontiers. Two days after the Sebastopol garrison had lost the Mamelon and the Quarries, the Emperor Francis Joseph ordered the demobilization of reservists sent earlier that year to augment his army along the Russian border – a line which, since Austria's occupation of Moldavia and Wallachia, now extended for some 700 miles from the Carpathians to the Danube delta. From his accession Alexander II had made it clear to Francis Joseph that, like his father, he regarded Austria as Russia's faithless friend, but at least this partial demobilization allowed the Tsar to reduce his concentration of troops around Kishinev.[7] Even so, he was not sure whether the regiments now freed from service in Bessarabia should undertake the relatively short journey to the Crimea or be moved to the Caucasus. There the Viceroy and Commander-in-Chief, General Nicholas Muraviev, was about to launch an offensive against the fortresses of Kars and Erzerum, which were garrisoned by the Turks, with a leavening of British officers. But Paskevich had no intention of letting troops go from Bessarabia or Poland to the Caucasus, for he had long regarded Muraviev as a personal enemy. Reluctantly, Paskevich agreed that three reserve infantry regiments should be sent from Kishinev to Sebastopol.[8]

There was, however, little prospect that the reinforcements would reach the city until the first days of August; and it was clear that the allies would never wait so long before launching their principal assault on the city. Raglan wished the offensive to begin as soon as possible, but Pélissier needed more time to concentrate his troops. On 15 June an allied council of war decided that the French would put 25,000 men into the attack and the British 8,000; and, in the hope of bringing new significance to a historic date, Monday, 18 June, the fortieth anniversary of Waterloo, was chosen as the moment when the allied armies would make their bid for a decisive victory.[9]

The weather was unbearably hot by now, the ground hard and burnt-up. As at Varna a year before, there were outbreaks of dysentery, and cholera became once more a scourge; one in twenty of the Italians in the advance party from Piedmont succumbed to cholera within a month of their arrival. On 17 June, while another great bombardment was giving notice of allied intentions, the waiting troops suffered from the glare of the sun, from smoke and dust, from a plague of flies, and from dehydration. Fenton, in his next letter to his wife, commented on his terrible thirst that Sunday: 'I took seventeen tumblers of liquid, nine of which were tea, two champagne and the rest beer.'[10] To these natural torments were added extra dangers for the gunners, for it soon became clear that much of the allied artillery was overheated: one 68-pounder naval gun burst, not 'from any symptom of weakness' but because 'like all the others' it 'had been fired much oftener than it is warranted to bear'.[11]

The response from more than 700 Russian guns was, at first, determined and sustained. Three British warships received direct hits during the small hours of Sunday morning; and Admiral Lyons's son, who was in command of HMS *Miranda*, was so gravely wounded that he died a few days later in hospital at Therapia, on the Bosphorus. By Sunday evening, however, the waiting troops noticed that enemy guns which had troubled them earlier in the day were silent. It was assumed that they had been knocked out by the allied bombardment. No one seems to have wondered if the guns were being moved to new positions or if the defenders were conserving ammunition. Morale among both the French and the British was high: officers speculated on the chances of there still being restaurants in Sebastopol where they might dine on Monday evening.[12]

Pélissier was as confident as his junior officers. He had rejected Niel's plan for an all-out offensive against the whole perimeter of the city's defences, Bosquet's suggestion that tunnels should be dug right up to the edge of the Russian forts, and Raglan's proposal of a diversionary attack in the south, on the Flagstaff Bastion. His plan was simple: 'successive assaults and limited combats'; the French to concentrate on the Malakoff first, and then the British to storm the Redan. A furious row between Pélissier and Bosquet on the eve of the assault weakened French effectiveness; Pélissier accused Bosquet of retaining for his own use a captured plan of the Malakoff, and in a fit of rage he refused to

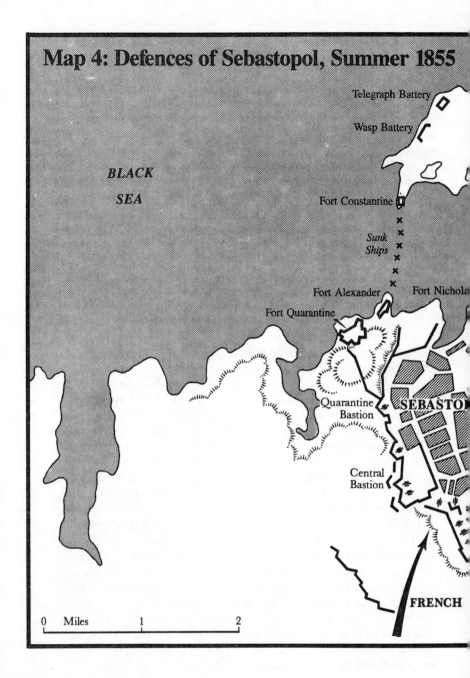

Map 4: Defences of Sebastopol, Summer 1855

Telegraph Battery

Wasp Battery

BLACK

SEA

Fort Constantine

Sunk
Ships

Fort Alexander   Fort Nichola

Fort Quarantine

Quarantine
Bastion

SEBASTO

Central
Bastion

FRENCH

0   Miles   1   2

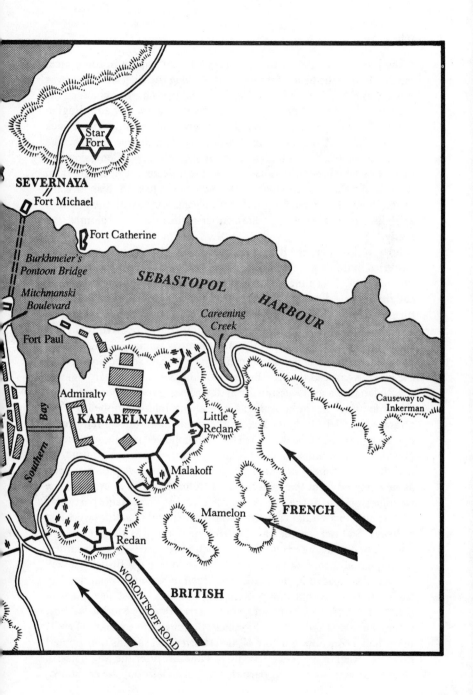

Star
Fort

SEVERNAYA
Fort Michael

Fort Catherine

*Burkhmeier's
Pontoon Bridge*

*Mitchmanski
Boulevard*

Fort Paul

SEBASTOPOL

*Careening
Creek*

HARBOUR

Causeway to
Inkerman

Admiralty

KARABELNAYA

Little
Redan

Southern

Bay

Malakoff

Mamelon

FRENCH

Redan

BRITISH

WORONTSOFF ROAD

allow the commander of the 2nd Corps to participate in the attack, putting him at the head of reserve troops along the Chernaya. Nor was this Pélissier's only act of folly. Late on Sunday evening he changed the moment of attack, advancing the time by two hours to 3 a.m. Raglan did not learn of this modification in the agreed plan until he rode back to headquarters from an evening inspection of his forward troops. The timetable for attack was therefore wrong from the start. Confusion was made worse by French advance troops who mistook a trail of light from the fuse of a shell for the signal rocket which was to send them forward at zero hour. The French right therefore went ahead with their assault at about a quarter to three, before either of the other two columns was ready.[13]

So well sited were the Russian guns at the Malakoff and its adjoining batteries that not a single Frenchman was able to cross the defensive ditch and begin scaling its ramparts. Hundreds of infantrymen were caught in crossfire and perished from grapeshot. Individual units turned the Malakoff's defences on the left and found themselves in the streets of one of Sebastopol's suburbs, but no one supported them and they were soon mopped up by Russian infantry. Raglan, seeing that the French were heading for defeat, conferred with Sir George Brown; and the veterans agreed that the British would have to go forward against the Redan to draw off Russian fire at dawn, even though the assault was timed for later in the morning. General Sir John Campbell led the attack on the left, Colonel Yea on the right. Both officers required a covering party of riflemen to dash forward, followed by sailors from the Naval Brigade and sappers with ladders and other siege equipment, and then by the main storming party. But Campbell was killed as soon as he emerged from the trenches, and Colonel Yea as he reached the wooden stockade at the foot of the earthworks. The assault party was soon caught in a similar crossfire to the French; and casualties were just as heavy. So brief was the battle of 18 June that it was all over by half-past eight in the morning. The French sustained 3,553 casualties, nearly half of them fatal; and almost one in four of the British soldiers and sailors engaged in the battle was killed or seriously wounded.[14]

On this fortieth anniversary of the day on which he lost his right arm, the Commander-in-Chief watched the battle from the Mortar Battery, where the troops had cheered Florence Nightingale five weeks before. 'I never had a conception before of such showers of grape as they poured upon us,' Raglan wrote wretchedly to Panmure after the tragic fiasco. 'The greatest mistake is the partial attack of Sebastopol', he explained, for it allowed the Russians to concentrate reserves in the suburb of Karabelnaya, immediately behind the Malakoff and the Redan; 'If the attack had been general, the enemy's troops must have been scattered,' Raglan added. He complained of the changed hour of attack, while Brigadier-General Rose in a despatch to the Foreign Secretary regretted the tension between the French generals and, in particular, Pélissier's furious exchange of words with Bosquet.[15] The British tended to blame the French while the French blamed the British and the Italians and Turks blamed them both.

When Raglan discussed with Pélissier the reasons for the allied failure, the two commanders agreed that they had dangerously under-estimated the strength of Russian artillery and over-estimated the damage caused by the allied bombardment.[16] Neither was prepared to admit the basic folly of an operational plan which required two thousand troops to dash across sloping ground exposed to enemy grapeshot for almost a quarter of a mile, scale a rampart of felled trees with outward facing branches, cross another ditch or sunken road, and then find themselves at the foot of a heavily defended escarpment. 'A ditch and a wall require that a breach should be made, and that the guns should be silenced before an assault is given,' the Prime Minister wrote in a note to Panmure a few days later; and, recalling events in Spain when he was himself Secretary-at-War, Palmerston added, 'This seems to have been similar to the mistake made by the Duke of Wellington in his first attempt on Badajoz'.[17] But what made good military common sense when analysed in a room looking out over London's Green Park eluded the Badajoz veteran plagued by ill health in the Crimean uplands.

'Do you not see the change in Lord Raglan?', a Guards officer asked a group of staff officers on 19 June: 'Good God! He is a dying man'.[18] The remark struck those closest to the Commander-in-Chief with great force, for they had not recognized that 'Raggles', who always looked frail, was now gravely ill. Their lack of perception is hardly surprising; so many senior officers were collapsing around them that June. General Estcourt, Raglan's Adjutant-General and personal friend, died from cholera on the Sunday after the attack; and Generals Pennefather and Sir George Brown were invalided home, although Brown did not sail until the end of the month. Raglan remained at his headquarters, trying to weld differing allied plans together, patiently defending the British from French complaints that they were unimaginative and slow to respond to emergencies. As late as 24 June he could still entertain Lady Paget and her husband to dinner, but his physical strength was ebbing away. Four days later, just three weeks after Fenton photographed him in conference with Omar and Pélissier, Lord Raglan succumbed to the disease which had killed so many hundreds of his men.

The news was telegraphed to London that same Thursday. At once General Simpson was ordered to succeed Raglan. But Simpson had no illusions about himself: he was a very old sixty-three, sound and sensible as a Chief of Staff, but far too set in his ways to snatch a victory in the Crimea. He made a strong bid to prevent Panmure confirming his appointment. 'I sincerely trust, my Lord, that a General of distinction will be sent immediately to command this Army,' he wrote to Panmure two days after Raglan's death. 'My health is sure to give way, as I have constant threatenings of gout in spite of all the care I take, and it may come some day too hard for me to bear!'[19] Apart from his health, Simpson's chief worry was the 'irksome and embarrassing' task of having to handle 'these Allies'. Fortunately Rose was well able to manage the French by now and, if necessary, Stratford de Redcliffe in Constantinople would intervene with the Sultan to force Omar Pasha to toe the line. The Piedmontese commander, General La Marmora, was technically subordinate to Simpson, as the Italian contingent was attached to Raglan's army as soon as it disembarked; La Marmora was eager for his troops to be given a chance to show their mettle but, unlike Pélissier or Bosquet, he was not personally ambitious. Queen Victoria thought Simpson too despondent to carry on with the command. His appointment was nevertheless confirmed on 18 July, while the cabinet looked around for a younger successor, if the task ahead proved beyond Simpson's powers.[20]

Both besiegers and besieged were by now weary of the campaign. The repeated allied shelling of the city's defences in July accounted for about 250 men's lives each day, 'a frightful massacre', as the Tsar himself commented. The senior Russian general inside Sebastopol, Count von der Osten-Sacken, was an extremely devout Baltic German who, although regularly interceding for the Almighty's blessing on Russia's just cause, was not in himself an inspiring leader; he made a practice of going up to the bastions from his headquarters at Fort Nicholas, down by the water's edge, only in the quieter moments of the conflict. Totleben, a gifted engineer greatly respected by the officers of the garrison, remained something of an outsider; and, after the third major bombardment of the city, he had to leave Sebastopol to recuperate on the Belbec from a serious wound. But the Mikhailovs and Volodya Kozeltsevs of Tolstoy's perceptive *Army Tales* had, ever since the first days of the siege, been heartened by the example of the naval commanders: originally Kornilov; then, through the winter months, Rear-Admiral Istomin, who was killed by a shell in the middle of March; and thereafter Admiral Nakhimov, the hero of Sinope. Nevertheless Nakhimov became bitterly depressed by the defeatism around him: he knew that neither Gorchakov nor Osten-Sacken had any confidence in Sebastopol holding out until the enemy abandoned their assaults. To raise morale Nakhimov would let himself be seen in full uniform by the troops manning the defences. Gold epaulettes, however, could be spotted from a distance; and on 10 June he was shot by a French sniper while observing the allied positions from the Kornilov Bastion. Three days later he died. Just as allied observers noticed how Russian guns remained silent while poor Raglan's coffin was borne down to HMS *Caradoc*, so Nakhimov's compatriots commented on the 'respectful silence' of the enemy's batteries when the Admiral was interred on St Vladimir Hill.[21] It was the same mood of mutual respect between opponents in adversity which prompted Tolstoy to tell his brother what 'fine fellows' the British and French prisoners were, 'morally and physically a gallant lot'.[22]

The news of Admiral Nakhimov's death induced Tsar Alexander to prod the defeatists even more vigorously. A single victory in the field would allow Alexander's emissaries to seek a compromise peace, with honourable terms which would save the new reign from beginning with a humiliation. On 25 July and again exactly a week later the Tsar urged Prince Michael Gorchakov to go over to the offensive at once; he was to consult his generals and decide where best to strike at the enemy. A military council of senior Russian officers in the Crimea accordingly met under the Prince's chairmanship at Fort Nicholas on 9–10 August: Osten-Sacken wished to evacuate the naval base and the southern shore – 'downtown Sebastopol', as it were; but a majority of those officers present favoured a diversionary offensive in the hills. Against his better judgement, Michael Gorchakov prepared plans for an attack on 16 August against the extreme east of the allied line, in the Fedioukine hills, close to the valleys along which the cavalry had charged on 'Balaclava Day'.[23]

Russian security was, however, remarkably lax. Reports from Polish deserters in the Crimea were confirmed by intelligence assessments telegraphed from Berlin to the Foreign Office in London and forwarded

– again by telegraph – to General Simpson. The allied commanders were left in no doubt that a Russian offensive was imminent; and troop movements noted early in the third week of August concentrated their attention on the river Chernaya. The Russians could even be seen constructing pontoon bridges. At least one French commander thought the preparations so obvious that he began to wonder if they were a decoy, intended to conceal a major sortie from the city itself.[24]

Earlier in the campaign such matters would have concerned, first and foremost, the intelligence department of the British army; and in October 1854 almost all the high ground looking out over the Chernaya towards Chorgun had been held by Raglan's men and 'Johnny Turk'. But now, ten months later, the nearest British force was Scarlett's cavalry division encamped at Kadikoi, although in an emergency the Highland Brigade could have moved forward from Balaclava itself. The Sapoune Escarpment and the Fedioukine hills were occupied entirely by French and Piedmontese, but with Turkish infantry detachments held in reserve and some of Omar Pasha's artillery on the more distant hills. Since this contest for mastery of the Chernaya banks was a predominantly Franco-Italian engagement, it has been neglected by most English-speaking commentators on the Crimean campaign; and the most renowned historian of the British Army, Sir John Fortescue, even dismisses the battle of the Chernaya as 'a little affair'. Contemporaries were less arrogantly insular. Panmure and Simpson realized at the time that the battle was decisive for the fate of Sebastopol. A Russian victory would guarantee that the allies remained confined to their small foothold on the peninsula: a Russian defeat would make it certain that the invaders had the power to strike inland, cut the city's last supply lines and finally make the siege of Sebastopol a grim reality.[25]

Although Gorchakov was pessimistic about the outcome of the battle, he took personal tactical command of the whole operation. He instructed General Read of Russia's Third Corps and General Liprandi of the Sixth Corps to 'await the order of the commander-in-chief' at each stage of the battle before moving forward to their next objective. This direct involvement of the commander-in-chief – which was in striking contrast to Menshikov's conduct at Inkerman – convinced his corps commanders that Gorchakov knew clearly where he intended his troops to make their main effort and how he was going to see the battle as a whole at any one moment. But Gorchakov, whose ideas had been clear during the fighting on the lower Danube, was by now so tormented by doubts that he became a muddled thinker. Not once did he explain to Read or Liprandi what he hoped to gain by an offensive in the Fedioukine hills. Did he intend to follow it up with an attack on the allied siege works, as Pélissier and Simpson anticipated? He was not sure. Was his principal thrust across the Chernaya to be against the French on his right flank or the Italians on his left? He could not make up his mind. Nor could Gorchakov find a single command post whence to observe the unfolding of a battle in which his 24,000 infantrymen were deployed along a two-and-a-half mile front broken by outcrops of high ground. Good clear summer weather might have made some form of semaphore visible from a particular high point. But at dawn on Thursday, 16 August, the hills were covered with a heavy mist; and Gorchakov spent much of the following two hours riding between Read's and Liprandi's headquarters, trying to assess the enemy's strength before determining where to deploy the forty-eight squadrons of cavalry he was holding in reserve.

At first all went well for Liprandi and the Sixth Corps; the Piedmontese fell back from their outposts in the hills. At the same time Read's Third Corps forced the French to retreat quickly across the Traktir Bridge over the Chernaya, and Read was able to order up pontoons to speed the Russian advance beyond the river and over a canal which ran close beside it. But thereafter the attacks lost impetus. Liprandi's troops, obeying Gorchakov's original directive, consolidated their early gains in the face of Piedmontese artillery fire and awaited further orders. Read's Third Corps was left to scale the green downland slopes of the Fedioukine hills which, when the mist lifted, gave them no protection from the French crossfire. On the left of his position, Pélissier assumed command himself, not allowing his troops to charge the Russians until they were two-thirds of the way up the hill. French field guns raked the enemy support troops, shell splinters killing General Read and the Tsar's personal emissary, General Vrevsky. When, soon after eight in the morning, Gorchakov arrived at the Traktir Bridge to take over the Third Corps he was at once forced to order his staff officers to disperse and seek cover from the relentless French bombardment. An urgent appeal to Liprandi to shift his line of assault from the Piedmontese to engage the French right flank came too late to check the allies, for General La Marmora had himself seen the need to plug the dangerous gap which separated his troops from Pélissier's main force. By ten in the morning the Russians were once more on the north bank of the Chernaya, leaving thousands of dead and wounded on the slopes above the river and the canal. Gorchakov, blaming the dead General Read for bungling the attack south of the Traktir Bridge, ordered his cavalry to pull back to the plateau known (after one of Catherine the Great's Russo-Scottish admirals) as the 'Mackenzie Heights'.

The total allied casualties in the battle of the Chernaya were less than 1,700; and only 14 Italians were killed that morning. But the defeat cost the Russians more lives than any other engagement except Inkerman. Gorchakov reported that he had lost 2,273 dead, with 1,742 missing and almost 4,000 wounded. In the hope of treating casualties more effectively than at the Alma or Inkerman, fourteen Sisters of Mercy had been sent from their field hospital on the Belbec to establish first-aid posts on the Mackenzie Heights. Alexandra Krupskaya, who was one of these nurses, later described their terrible burden of work, sixteen days of caring for the wounded without once having the opportunity to change their own clothes.[26] In St Petersburg Marshal Paskevich, who was gravely ill, prepared a bitter indictment of Gorchakov, alleging that the casualties were even higher than he admitted and that this needless battle ruled out the possibility of any subsequent offensive against the invaders. Tsar Alexander, however, knew of the mutual bitterness felt by Paskevich and Gorchakov since the siege of Silistria; he loyally supported his commander in the Crimea, not least because he knew that he had urged him to go over to the attack in the first place. Gorchakov, for his part, no longer disputed his sovereign's wishes. Early in June he had told Alexander that his only concern was to avoid the heavy losses which would follow any withdrawal from Sebastopol. Now, ten days after the defeat, a letter from Gorchakov's headquarters assured Alexander that he was determined not to evacuate the south bank of Sebastopol; if he could hold on for another ten weeks, the allies might seek a compromise peace rather than suffer a second winter in the Crimean hills. These words struck that note of stubborn defiance which the Romanov Tsars habitually expected from their generals in the field.[27]

Although Scarlett's cavalry and some heavy field guns moved up from Kadikoi to support the Zouaves and Chasseurs who recaptured the Traktir Bridge, the British played no direct part in the battle of the Chernaya. Simpson's army remained concentrated on the Heights overlooking the Redan and the Karabelnaya district of Sebastopol itself, in anticipation of a major sortie from the city. Morale, low after the failure at the Redan and the death of Raglan, picked up again with a change in the weather, thunderstorms at the end of July relieving the heat and giving way to what seemed to veterans from Varna like a good English summer. Newcomers continued to go down with cholera or dysentery but there was a more relaxed atmosphere in several British camps. Race meetings had been held on several occasions and on the day after the battle of the Chernaya there was a cricket match between the Guards Division and the 'Leg of Mutton Club', a scratch team of officers from other regiments. One of the Guard's batsmen, Sir John Astley, remembered that leisurely Friday many years later, but his account is more informative about Mrs Seacole than the cricket, for he best recalled that 'we had a capital lunch on the ground, provided by an old blackwoman who kept a sort of eating-house on the Heights'.[28]

There was good precedent for cricket on the eve of a great battle, for the Duke of Wellington had watched his Guards playing at Enghien six days before Waterloo. And while the Leg of Mutton's bowlers were seeking to get the Guardsmen's wickets, more sinister projectiles were being lobbed into the beleaguered fortress four miles away. Indeed the cricket match must have taken place against a background din of constant explosions, for on that Friday – 17 August – 800 guns and 300 mortars began a methodical bombardment of the city and the Karabelnaya suburb which was to continue intermittently for ten days. The Russians were left in no doubt that Pélissier and Simpson were determined to secure Sebastopol before mid-September, and the first anniversary of the allied landing in Calamita Bay.

Momentarily Pélissier appears to have hoped to gain the city not by a costly assault, but by saturation shelling, for the August bombardment differed from its predecessors. The largest mortars, firing 10-inch shells sighted on particular targets, could continue their work of destruction by night as well as by day, thus preventing the defenders from carrying out repairs as they had done on previous occasions. A thousand Russians a day were killed or seriously wounded by this August bombardment. Some of the Grand Duchess Elena Pavlovna's 'Sisters of Mercy' remained in Sebastopol itself, with a makeshift casualty clearing station in a deep casemate at Fort Nicholas, where they could treat men wounded by shell splinters or rescued from the debris of fallen buildings. For eight weeks before the battle of the Chernaya allied observers had been puzzled by the movement of ox-drawn wagons from the Belbec to the northern waterfront of the bay, but soon they realized that Gorchakov was constructing a bridge of boats across a thousand yards of sea from Fort Michael on the north shore to Fort Nicholas. This major engineering feat, supervised by General Burkhmeier, necessitated the linking of eighty-six pontoons, each secured to the sea bed by a pair of anchors. The bridge was completed in the last week of August. 'We are on the tip-toe of expectation to know what is the object of building it,' Henry Clifford wrote to his father. Occasionally some round shot hit the bridge, Clifford reported, even though through his field-glasses he had 'observed . . . some of the fair sex honouring it with little feet'. But it was noticed that the bridge traffic moved almost entirely out of Sebastopol. The Burkhmeier Bridge was intended for evacuation, not the arrival of a relief force.[29]

Apart from Pélissier, few people of eminence on the allied side seem to have believed that Sebastopol would fall like an apple pecked by the birds. The Russians continued to offer spirited resistance. A shell hit a French magazine in the Mamelon on the night of 27 August, causing an explosion which killed more than a hundred Frenchmen and scattered wreckage as far away as the north shore of the Bay and the British camps around Balaclava. In London both the Prime Minister and the War Secretary continued to look for ingenious ways of getting the troops into Sebastopol: Palmerston was even prepared to sanction the Dundonald project for smoking the enemy out of Sebastopol with sulphurous fumes – if the octogenarian admiral would himself go out to the Crimea 'to superintend and direct the execution of his scheme'.[30] But Napoleon III and Marshal Vaillant believed that Sebastopol would fall only when the assault troops made one final effort. Napoleon explained his views to Queen Victoria and Prince Albert when they made their state visit to Paris in the third and fourth weeks of August: 'The Emperor is full of anxiety and regret about the campaign,' the Queen noted in her journal on 22 August. 'Ten thousand shells have been thrown into the town within the last few days, and they are in want of more!'[31] Napoleon was convinced that the Second Empire needed the prestige of a battle honour, a French military victory achieved preferably at little cost. The British Government, too, was still looking for that 'sudden making of splendid names' which the Poet Laureate had anticipated in *Maud*. Rear-Admiral Richard Dundas, whose Baltic fleet was reinforced in July by a flotilla of block-ships, shallow-water steam gunboats and mortar vessels, could no more achieve a spectacular success than Napier in the previous summer: Kronstadt remained too formidable; Fort Svartholm, off the Finnish town of Lovisa, was captured by a raiding party from HMS *Arrogant* and its guns blown up; and the island fortress of Sveaborg, three miles south-east of Helsinki, was bombarded on 9 August, with further attacks by mortars and rockets over the two following days. Considerable damage was done to the dockyards and powder magazines, but the bombardment left the guns worn out and needing new mountings before any further attacks could be launched in the Baltic.[32] None of this made exciting reading in the British press. By now people in Britain were no longer talking of 'our war with Russia', but of 'the Crimean War'; and they were waiting, with mounting impatience, for what they assumed would be the climax of the campaign, news of a triumphant feat of arms at Sebastopol.

Pélissier was not surprised by the mood in Paris and London. It coincided with views shared by several of his own generals and by Simpson and his staff officers. Moreover, professionally Pélissier remained a conventional Saint-Cyrist whose campaigning days in Algeria had taught him that enemy positions were there to be captured, not forced to capitulate. If officers whom he had known in Oran had wives with them at Kamiesh – the young and sultry Mme Soledad Bazaine, for example – they would be invited to dine with the Commander-in-Chief at his headquarters. There the guests might watch Pélissier's dog obediently jump over a row of chairs at its master's command, never once failing to do precisely what was expected of it. Pélissier was not a man of subtlety; and to some the inference seemed obvious. If only his divisional generals would perform their party pieces so dutifully and reliably, the war would soon be over and they could all enjoy a hero's welcome home in France or Algeria.[33]

During the saturation shelling of August Pélissier had therefore continued to press forward with all the preparations for an eventual assault on the Malakoff. By the end of the month French sappers had advanced their trenches ('parallels') to within twenty-five yards of the great fort; and on 3 September Pélissier presided over a council of war which resolved that an attempt should be made to seize Sebastopol and the whole of the southern shore five days later, on Saturday, 8 September.[34] Unlike the abortive attacks on the Malakoff and the Redan twelve weeks before, Pélissier's new plan provided for that general offensive which poor Raglan had vainly urged in June. The front covered more than six miles of the Sebatopol defences, but the principal assault was still to be made against the Malakoff, 'the only objective', General Niel noted at the time. No fewer than 25,000 French troops were assigned to this sector of the Front, as well as a brigade from the Sardinian-Piedmontese Expeditionary Force. General Bosquet, back in favour with Pélissier, was given the command denied him in June; under him, leading the 1st Division which was to break into the Malakoff itself, was a newcomer to the Crimea, General Patrice de MacMahon, who arrived on 18 August as a successor to Canrobert, recalled by Napoleon III for 'special service' on behalf of the Emperor.

While great attention was given to the details of the French operation, the British contribution was left as a matter for General Simpson to decide. No one at French headquarters had much respect for Simpson, as even General Rose's journal shows. He did not possess Raglan's natural authority and dignity, nor was he fluent in army French. He was physically and mentally exhausted and never sought the responsibilities of high command, constantly hoping that Panmure would recall him on grounds of ill-health. Through much of the council of war on 3 September Simpson is reported to have slept, his head nodding rhythmically as though in agreement with everything those Frenchies around him were saying. Subsequently his staff discovered that the British were committed to another assault on the Redan, seeking the success which had eluded them on 18 June. It was agreed that Simpson would put his men on the alert the moment the tricolour was seen flying from the Malakoff. They would move forward when their general ordered the firing of four signal rockets.[35]

On 8 September zero hour was fixed, not at dawn when the enemy might expect an attack, but at twelve noon. Originally it was intended that the fleet should support the attack with a bombardment of the shore batteries, but there was a north-west gale blowing on that Saturday morning and, as heavy seas made it impossible for the warships to concentrate their fire on any particular objective, only Admiral Lyons's six mortar vessels went into action.[36] But the gale made no difference to the gunners ashore; and at noon, after forty minutes of intense artillery fire, the Zouaves in MacMahon's Division sprang out of their trenches. Dashing over the twenty-five yards of open ground in a few seconds, they were inside the parapets of the Malakoff before the Russians realized that the infantry attack had begun. Within ten minutes of MacMahon's forward troops leaving their trenches, the tricolour was fluttering from the top of the Malakoff. Repeated Russian counter-attacks failed to dislodge the French; but at times their situation looked desperate to Pélissier (who, Rose reported, 'was very nearly killed, during one of the heaviest cannonades I ever heard'). Simpson, too, was worried, for he did not wish to commit his men prematurely to the assault on the Redan by firing off the signal rockets. A quarter of an hour after the tricolour streamed out in that north-west gale, Simpson decided to find out exactly what was happening at the fort. It was therefore an English officer – Captain Biddulph – who went forward through the trenches and into the captured fort to ask MacMahon the famous question, 'My General wishes to know if you can hold your position.' 'Tell your General', MacMahon replied with laconic simplicity, 'that I am here and that here I stay.'[37]

Simpson need not have sent Biddulph forward to MacMahon, for the attack on the Redan was already in progress. The British assault troops had been waiting in their trenches for many hours and, on seeing the tricolour over the Malakoff, they rushed over the parapets without any formal order to go forward coming from Sir William Codrington, who was in the advance trenches as commander of the Light Division. Lieutenant Ranken of the Royal Engineers was in charge of one of the parties of eight men who were to carry 24-foot ladders across two hundred yards of open ground ready to scale the defences of the Redan. Ranken's account, published less than two years later, describes what happened:

We were ordered not to advance till a decided success had been achieved; but, as it were, in a second the dreaded Malakoff had fallen into the hands of the French. Our men could no longer be restrained; before there was time to get the ladders to the front ... they rushed in a straggling line over the parapets, and dashed onwards to the salient. I hurried up my sappers as fast as I could, shouting to them till I was nearly hoarse, and ran forward with them and the ladder party, with a sword in my hand (my scabbard and belt I left behind).[38]

Once again the advancing troops were raked by enfilading fire in a repetition of that storm of grapeshot which had horrified Raglan in June. Nevertheless, despite heavy casualties, the outer works of the Redan were taken.

After half an hour of what Simpson called 'a most determined and bloody contest' the French and British commanders were confident of victory. Elsewhere along the front the French and Italian attacks had been checked; but no sector matched in importance the heavily fortified salient beyond the Karabelnaya suburb, and here MacMahon and Bosquet were establishing a commanding position on the Malakoff, while the Redan seemed close to capture by the British. General Codrington sent up reinforcements, but suddenly found that this second wave of infantry, many of them youngsters new to the Crimea, lacked the spirit of the assault troops. Henry Clifford reckoned that six hundred men were congested in the angle of parapet before the inner defences of the Redan, and 'nothing the Officers could say or do would induce the men to make a dash over the Parapet'. Many were killed as they lay under inadequate cover, and when the Russians exhausted their ammunition they 'began pelting them with stones'. Clifford and other officers drew their swords and 'implored them . . . to stand and not to run', but in vain. The British attack on the Redan, begun in over-enthusiastic disorder, ended in an appalling rout. 'What almost breaks my heart, and nearly drove me mad, I see our soldiers, our English soldiers that I was so proud of, run away,' Henry Clifford wrote to his family next day.[39]

The Redan was therefore never captured. Simpson could have brought up the Guards Brigades and the Highlanders, who were held in reserve that day; but he did not, perhaps because too much scaling equipment had been destroyed to warrant an improvised attack in the late afternoon. Sir Colin Campbell was, however, ordered to prepare for yet another assault on the Redan next morning. It was not needed. The Russians counter-attacked time after time against the Malakoff, but could not dislodge MacMahon's troops. In the late afternoon General Prince Gorchakov came forward to the second line of his defences, overshadowed by the Malakoff itself. There, soon after 5 p.m., he gave orders for the evacuation of Sebastopol; he knew he could not hope to save the southern shore once the Malakoff was lost, and he hoped that the allied armies would be so exhausted by the day's fighting that they would not interfere with the withdrawal. The first regiments pulled back over the pontoon bridge just seven hours after the Zouaves had launched their assault.[40]

Not a man was lost during the evacuation; 'A masterly retreat that does great credit to Russian military genius and discipline', wrote an American major sent to the Crimea to observe the war.[41] Throughout the night fires shot up from different parts of Sebastopol. From his flagship, off the approaches to the Bay, Admiral Lyons 'at early dawn observed that the fortifications on the south side were in flames, and that the six remaining ships of the line had been sunk at their moorings, leaving afloat no more of the late Russian Black Sea fleet than two dismasted corvettes and nine steamers, most of which are very small'. At 9.22 on the Sunday morning Lyons was able to telegraph to the Admiralty, 'Allied troops in the dockyard'. Already British troops were standing in what remained of the Redan.[42]

A telegram from Simpson announcing that 'Sebastopol is in the possession of the Allies' was deciphered in London at a quarter to five on Monday afternoon, 10 September. There was jubiliation that evening in London and in Paris. The news reached Queen Victoria and her family at Balmoral 'when we were sitting quietly round our table after dinner'; and at once they lit a bonfire on the top of a hill which had been prepared 'last year when the premature news of the fall of Sebastopol deceived every one'.[43]

Fanny Duberly recalled that false dawn of hope when, a few days later, she wrote to her sister, Selina, describing the reaction in the French camp. *'Sebastopol est prise,'* she began her letter. 'The cry was echoed in Paris months ago. Now it rings through every crevice and valley of the camp – *Sebastopol est prise.* And yet, strange to say, there is no elation – no cheers – no drunkenness, no bonfires except the vast bonfire of the smouldering blazing city which obscures the whole horizon and which fills the air with a smoke as heavy and black as the hearts of the Russians themselves.'[44] The flames were still burning in Sebastopol next morning; and explosions continued intermittently over several days, for the Russians had planted between thirty and forty booby traps which took a heavy toll among the first French troops, looking for plunder. The speculation in June on whether or not there would be restaurants open when the city was captured seemed ridiculous now, in retrospect. There were, in fact, only two sources of refreshment: looted wine cellars, and the indefatigable Mary Seacole who, having badgered Major-General Garrett into issuing a special pass for herself and her attendants, borrowed mules from the Land Transport Corps and became the first woman to go into Sebastopol on Sunday morning. 'Every step had a score of dangers', she wrote eighteen months later, 'and yet curiosity and excitement carried us on and on. I was often stopped to give refreshments to officers and men, who had been fasting for hours.'[45] Apart from some drunks who had looted wine cellars, the general mood was sombre. On that same Sunday morning Henry Duberly stood beside an Anglican chaplain outside the Redan as he read the funeral service over 700 shattered bodies lying in trenches which became their grave when the earth was shovelled in upon them. The stench of putrefying corpses and a piled-up heap of human bodies outside the Customs House greeted the Duberlys when they were allowed 'actually in Sebastopol' four days later.[46] Over the following few weeks, letters home conveyed the ghastliness of victory in all its tortured glory.

In London and Paris there was elation, a sense among the general public that the prime objective of the war was achieved. But, when the troops were at last allowed freely into the ravaged city, they became aware of the limits of their success. The southern shore of Sebastopol Bay, with its ruined barracks, sunken ships and derelict dockyard, was now in allied hands; but across the Bay, in Severnaya, Gorchakov retained a powerful army. To watchers on the Sebastopol waterfront, Forts Constantine, Michael and Catherine were low outlines, stone walls protecting tiers of black-muzzled artillery. Above them, almost concealed from view but known to be far more menacing, loomed Star Fort with its 120 guns mounted in positions as formidable as anything in the Malakoff or the Redan. It was hard to believe that the end of the war could be in sight so long as the Russian imperial flag flew defiantly over so commanding a fortress.

CHAPTER SIXTEEN

The Second Winter

The city of Paris was illuminated to celebrate the fall of Sebastopol on 10 September; and next day Napoleon III ordered his Minister of War to inform Pélissier that, in honour of the victory, he was 'raised to the dignity of Marshal of France'. But Parisian delight at the news from the Crimea was not entirely a manifestation of patriotic pride. In the first months of the war there had been a good response to the Government's appeal for subscriptions to a war loan, with most of Napoleon's radical and socialist critics approving a campaign against Tsarist tyranny. By the summer of 1855, however, there was widespread disillusionment. The war never became a crusade against either Orthodoxy or Autocracy; it produced no striking feat of arms, no flashes of strategic vision; and there was an influential group at court who favoured an early end to the conflict in the hope of winning the new Tsar's patronage for French commercial ventures. The capture of the Malakoff and the fall of Sebastopol were therefore welcomed as a sign that peace was close at hand. French national honour was satisfied, for, after forty years, military glory was once more uplifting the imperial eagles.[1]

In Turin opinion was divided. Victor Emmanuel II was pleased by the performance of his troops at the Chernaya and in the final assault on Sebastopol; and Cavour knew that, if Austria remained neutral, further military success would give Sardinia-Piedmont greater influence at the conference table. But what if Austria entered the war? Peace now would allow him to enjoy the status of a combatant in any discussion over the re-shaping of Europe's political frontiers. There was much to be said for striking an early bargain with Napoleon III and Palmerston.[2]

Sultan Abdul Medjid, on the other hand, was content that the war should continue: the Turks knew that they had little real chance of recovering the Crimea, and they had lost interest in what happened at Eupatoria or Sebastopol. The Caucasus was another matter; in that region the Sultan hoped that an allied victory would permit him to move his frontiers northwards. Throughout much of July and August Omar Pasha had been seeking permission from Simpson and Pélissier to withdraw Turkish units from the Crimea in order to relieve the allied forces locked up in Erzerum and Kars. As the French mistrusted Omar and as Simpson felt that the Sultan's contingent could not be spared from the Crimea, Lord Stratford again came up to Balaclava from Constantinople to argue with the Turkish commander. However, once Sebastopol fell, there seemed no good reason for retaining his troops. If an offensive to relieve Erzerum and Kars was the only way to keep alive Turkey's interest in the war, the British argued that Omar should be given a free hand. But Pélissier refused to let the Turks sail from the Crimea until the last days of September. Familiar complaints were voiced in Paris of British intrigues in Constantinople which were hostile to France's best interests.[3]

Foreign observers were constantly puzzled by the changing mood in London. Recruiting, high when war was declared, had declined dramatically by the close of the year and never picked up again. Tennyson, writing his long epic *Maud* in the spring of 1854, made the romantic hero narrator of this curious monodrama find spiritual re-awakening 'to the better mind' in answering a call to serve his country 'by the side of the Black and the Baltic deep'. But when the poem was published fifteen months later the Poet Laureate found himself attacked as a militarist glorying in 'a rampant and rabid blood-thirstiness of soul'.[4] At times the conflict into which the British people had entered with such intense patriotic fervour in the spring of 1854 seemed to recede altogether from their collective consciousness, the public showing an extraordinarily parochial concern with matters of little interest to Europe as a whole. Thus at four successive weekends at midsummer in 1855 there were violent clashes in Hyde Park against a private member's bill to 'prevent Sunday trading in the metropolis'; the Government had to persuade the bill's sponsor, Lord Robert Grosvenor, to withdraw his measure in order to check rioting in the capital. The widespread indignation with the mismanagement of the Crimean campaign, which had enabled the belligerent Palmerston to become prime minister in February, found a safety-valve in Roebuck's Select Committee. Day after day from early March to early June the Committee probed military muddle and aristocratic privileges 'in front of Sebastopol'. Public attendance at its hearings declined sharply as the war entered its second year, and the Prime Minister remained untroubled by its activities or by the attacks of the short-lived Administrative Reform Association on sloth in the civil service. His constant concern remained the vigorous prosecution of the war.[5]

In one respect, however, Palmerston took advantage of the call for administrative reform. When Parliament went into summer recess in 1855 he set up an informal four-man War Committee, which could meet more easily and frequently than the full cabinet and bring cohesion both to the overall strategy against Russia, naval and military, and to the making of peace. Naturally the Prime Minister was chairman of the committee. The other members were Wood (First Lord of the Admiralty), Panmure (the War Secretary) and Earl Granville (the Lord President of the Council), and senior naval and army officers in London could be co-opted by the four ministers. It is clear from a report of the first meeting, which Granville sent to Clarendon on 21 August, that the Lord President worked closely with the Foreign Secretary, a collaboration which assumed great importance in the weeks ahead because of sudden shifts of policy by both France and Austria. An article in *The Times* of 1 September welcomed the coming of this executive innovation, explaining to readers that the four men would come together each week 'to superintend the operation of the war'. There had been criticism of Palmerston's idiosyncratic style of leadership both inside and outside the cabinet; and it was hoped that the establishment of the committee would ensure a sense of 'order' and 'regularity' at the head of affairs. Yet to some extent the innovation was a sop to the newspaper's Cerberus. After forty-eight years in Parliament Palmerston was at last, as Wood called him, 'the new chief'; and he had no intention of delegating responsibility to ministers whom, in his more generous moments, he grudgingly acknowledged as well-intentioned advisers.[6]

A letter from Palmerston to Dr Sumner, the Archbishop of Canterbury, sent a few days after news of Sebastopol's fall reached London, throws light on his approach to the war that September. The surrender of the Russian naval base, the Prime Minister told the Archbishop, should be observed not by a weekday set aside for thanksgiving, as Waterloo had been, but by special services on a Sunday, the practice followed by the Church in 1812 and 1813 after Salamanca and Vitoria; for no one should assume that the capture of Sebastopol was so decisive a victory that peace was in sight.[7] Palmerston remained much concerned over the need for the allied forces to press forward against the enemy. Simpson, however, insisted that the Russians had withdrawn to an unassailable position on the north shore of the bay, where Star Fort seemed as impregnable as Gibraltar.

Immediately after a cabinet meeting on 16 September Panmure sent a bluntly worded telegram to Simpson, following it up with a private letter, rich in mixed metaphor: the General was 'not to rest on his oars', nor 'play second fiddle to Pélissier'; but Panmure conceded that 'so much must depend on your own information that all we can really say is, "Don't waste yourself in idleness"'.[8] When full details of the abortive attack on the Redan reached England, both the Queen and Palmerston were deeply worried by the Commander-in-Chief's unimpressive leadership. 'The assault in September appears to have been made almost identically in the same manner as that of June', Palmerston commented in a note to Panmure. Even stronger pressure was put on Simpson to take the initiative; and at the end of the month he decided to resign: 'The turmoils of a command like this are too much for my age and health', he told Panmure. The cabinet accepted the General's resignation on 3 October, but he was persuaded to stay at his post for another five weeks, because the débâcle at the Redan had also raised doubts over the abilities of the general designated his successor, Sir William Codrington. But whose reputation remained unsullied? On 11 November Codrington duly took over the command.[9]

'Pélissier and myself are both of one opinion that the electric telegraph is our greatest enemy! worse even than the newspapers, which publish to the enemy everything we are doing', Simpson wrote to Panmure in a final fling three days before he left the Crimea.[10] The French Commander-in-Chief had suffered less from the press than his British colleague, but far more from telegraphic interrogatives. Should Sebastopol be razed and the Crimea evacuated? How many men would be needed to hold Sebastopol, if most units were brought home or sent elsewhere? Ought the allies to seize the Perekop Isthmus? Or would it be better to take Kherson, eighteen miles up the river Dnieper, or the base of Nikolayev, on the lower Bug? What were the views of the Commander-in-Chief on an offensive against Simferopol from the Mackenzie Heights? Or from Eupatoria? Or from Theodosia (Kaffa)? And would a seaborne invasion of Bessarabia with a force of a hundred thousand men be militarily practicable?[11] Pélissier referred all such questions to his staff-officers, telling them to emphasize the difficulties of any operation which might be suggested in Paris. But clearly something had to be done to stop those relentless wires buzzing. On 29 September an inter-allied conference attended by Pélissier, Simpson,

Admiral Lyons and the French naval commander, Admiral Bruat, decided on an expedition to destroy the fortress of Kinburn, which controlled entry to the Dnieper estuary and the approaches to two of the possible objectives mentioned by Napoleon III, Nikolayev and Kherson. On 7 October 10,000 troops, 4,000 of whom were British, were embarked in seven ships of the Royal Navy, three French warships and two transports. Six French gunboats, with mortar batteries, sailed in support of the expedition. The overall command was entrusted to General Achille Bazaine, of the Foreign Legion, Marshal Pélissier courteously consoling Madame Bazaine by a personal visit on each afternoon of her husband's absence.[12]

The Kinburn expedition was an outstanding success. French and British troops and marines landed north of Kinburn on 16 October, so as to cut off the garrison from support; and the British and French warships then bombarded the Russian positions until the fort surrendered next day. Across the estuary the fort of Ochakov – whose acquisition by Catherine the Great had brought Britain and Russia close to war in 1791 – was blown up by its garrison in anticipation of an allied assault. Naval command over the estuary left the allies with an option of striking inland at Nikolayev or Kherson in the following spring. No attempt, however, was made to bombard Odessa, a city in which French concerns had invested heavily earlier in the century.[13]

It is clear from their reports to Paris and London that Pélissier, Simpson, Lyons and Codrington suspected the Russians of preparing a counter-offensive before winter set in again. The Tsar's proclamations to the Russian people after the fall of Sebastopol had rung with proud defiance. He at once left St Petersburg for Moscow. Once Alexander was in residence in Russia's traditional capital, he invoked inspiration from what had happened in that other September, forty-three years before. On the anniversary of the day Moscow went up in flames around the *Grande Armée*, he sent a personal message of encouragement to General Gorchakov filled with a sense of the past: 'Do not lose heart. Remember 1812 and put your faith in Providence. Sebastopol is not Moscow, the Crimea is not Russia. Two years after the firing of Moscow, our troops marched in the streets of Paris. We remain the same Russians, and God is still with us'. Alexander informed the General that he was sending to his headquarters in the Crimea the holy ikon of St Sergius, which was with Peter the Great when he gained his victory at Poltava and with the Moscow militia in the darkest days of the Napoleonic invasion.[14] The Tsar then summoned a military council to meet in the Kremlin at which it was agreed to defend the Crimea and prepare for a counter-offensive in the following spring. After a week in Moscow, Alexander II began a long and slow journey south to Nikolayev, where he remained for several weeks, and on to Simferopol early in November. A report which Codrington received from an intelligence agent on 13 November suggested that the Tsar was reviewing troops at Korales, halfway between Bakchisarai and the Mackenzie Heights, and that the Russians might launch an attack on the allied positions from the north-east. The allied commanders thought it too late in the year for any serious military operations, but they remained puzzled as to the Tsar's intentions.[15]

So, indeed, was everyone else. Outwardly there was a show of patriotic pride in St Petersburg, matching those fine words proclaimed so defiantly from Moscow.[16] But at least one experienced public servant wanted the war to end before worse calamities hit Russia. Nesselrode was still serving as the Tsar's Chancellor; no parallels struck in 1855 could incline him to equate what was happening in the Crimea or the Baltic with those epic days of 1812 when he had been at Alexander I's side in Vilna, riding back with his sovereign to Moscow and St Petersburg as secretary in charge of diplomatic correspondence. In the week after Sebastopol was evacuated, the Chancellor told foreign envoys that Russia would listen with interest to any peace proposals made to her. For the moment, however, nothing happened. So long as Alexander II was with his troops in southern Russia, there was little overt diplomatic activity in St Petersburg. It was assumed that the Tsar was consulting his generals in the field, searching for one point where the allies were so vulnerable that Russia could snatch a victory before negotiating peace.[17]

When Nesselrode was a young diplomat in Paris in 1809, he had won Talleyrand's grudging admiration for his ability to forge unofficial links between Russia and France. The gift had not deserted him. Another great survivor of Congress diplomacy, Princess Dorothea Lieven, willingly served as an intermediary between Paris, where she had settled in 1835, and her Russian homeland.[18] But Nesselrode, who always distrusted the Princess, possessed even better contacts. Throughout the Eastern Crisis of 1853 and the subsequent war one of Nesselrode's daughters was living in Brussels, as the wife of a diplomat; but more valuable still was a second daughter, Baroness Seebach, who was married to the King of Saxony's envoy in Paris. On several occasions the Seebachs had been useful to Nesselrode, and he could be certain that peace feelers would win active support from the Baron's nominal superior in Dresden, the Saxon Foreign Minister, Count von Beust. This Saxon connection became especially important in mid-October 1855 when two kinsmen of Napoleon III made secret approaches to the Russians. Count Walewski – who, besides being Foreign Minister, was known to be Napoleon I's son – told Seebach that it was time the Russians put forward peace proposals which the Emperor could persuade Palmerston to accept;[19] and the Duc de Morny, Napoleon III's half-brother, established contact with Alexander Gorchakov in Vienna through an Austrian banker, offering to meet him at Dresden. So closely involved were the Saxons in these diplomatic exchanges that Beust, with Nesselrode's encouragement, personally travelled to Paris to see Seebach and Walewski in an attempt to get peace talks going in earnest; and, in the fourth week of November, it seemed from a letter sent by the Russian Chancellor to Beust that there was a good prospect of a direct exchange of views between Paris and St Petersburg.[20]

These hopes were dashed by the return of Alexander II to his capital in the last days of November. He came in a belligerent mood: the satisfaction he gained from ordering defensive preparations at Nikolayev and inspecting regiments ready for action in the Crimea encouraged him to dispute the arguments of Nesselrode and Orlov in favour of peace. By now, moreover, Russian troops had gained the first military success of his reign: for seven months the Turkish garrison at Kars, strengthened by a handful of British officers, had resisted Muraviev's army and in early November it had seemed that Omar Pasha would soon arrive with a relief force; but Omar moved too slowly and Kars surrendered to the Russians on 25 November. News of Muraviev's victory, so far from persuading the Tsar that he might now obtain better terms, intensified his conviction that the allies were in more need of peace than Russia. Reports told him that the French harvest was bad and that there was discontent in Lyons and working-class districts in Paris. Alexander Gorchakov was told to have nothing more to do with Morny; but Nesselrode took the opportunity of inviting his son-in-law, Seebach, to St Petersburg for the Russian Christmas.[21]

Both Alexander Gorchakov and Walewski had already made it clear to Nesselrode that the Austrians were once again contemplating entry into the war if Russia did not make peace soon. Similar information reached St Petersburg from Berlin, the King of Prussia warning

Alexander II that he would have difficulty in preserving his neutrality, let alone maintaining friendly relations with the Tsar's court, should there be an Austro-Russian conflict.[22] Quite apart from this German threat, Napoleon III was sharpening another diplomatic weapon. General Canrobert had arrived back from the Crimea in August ready for 'special service on behalf of the Emperor'. The first of these services was to charm Queen Victoria during her state visit, sitting next to her at dinner at St-Cloud, 'talking with much gesticulation' of 'the trenches where I was a fortnight ago'.[23] But a harder task awaited the General. In November he was sent to Sweden to persuade King Oscar that the allies were prepared, in 1856, to shift the emphasis of their military effort against Russia from the Black Sea to the Baltic. Although Palmerston was by now suspicious of many aspects of French policy, he warmly approved the renewed approach to Sweden. A Swedish alliance, he explained to his Foreign Secretary a month before Canrobert left Paris, should be seen 'as part of a long line of circumvallation to confine the further extension of Russia'.[24]

The Canrobert Mission has not received the attention from historians which it merits.[25] The General saw King Oscar on 17 November. He gained Swedish agreement to a formal treaty, signed four days later, which although outwardly defensive in character secretly provided for joint military action on both sides of the Gulf of Finland. A Russo-Swedish dispute over grazing rights for reindeer in Lapland, together with Russian naval incursions into Swedish waters, would give an excuse for the British and French to come to King Oscar's assistance. Canrobert would be entrusted with overall command of a force of 165,000 men drawn from the armies of France, Britain, the kingdom of Sweden and Norway, and, it was hoped, Denmark. This army would force the Russians to evacuate Finland and raze the fortress of Kronstadt, while diversionary operations south of the Gulf would threaten Riga and Reval (Tallinn). The Swedes were assured that special gunboats and floating batteries were being built in British and French shipyards for operations in the Baltic.

Although details of the military plan were kept secret, many aspects of Canrobert's Mission were leaked to a Belgian newspaper. Subsequently the report appeared in *The Times*, whose columns, so everyone asserted at Westminister, were regularly scanned by the Tsar and his ministers. The press stories concentrated on an alleged conference between Canrobert, Rear-Admiral Richard Dundas, and the French Rear-Admiral, Charles Pénaud, which took place in the

Danish port of Kiel on the last day of November. Apart from putting greater emphasis on landings in Russia's Baltic provinces than on operations in southern Finland, assigning the conference to Pénaud's flagship instead of Dundas's, and saying that it lasted for four hours instead of eight, the report was substantially correct.[26] It was certainly accurate enough to alert St Petersburg, as Napoleon intended; and, since the Swedes duly informed Nesselrode that they had concluded a defensive alliance with Russia's enemies, the threat was taken very seriously in the Tsar's capital. On 16 December, eight days after the report of the Kiel conference appeared in *The Times*, Napoleon sent for Baron Seebach and asked him to emphasize to his father-in-law during his visit to St Petersburg that it would be extremely foolish of Alexander II not to make peace now, before the might of this new coalition was brought to bear on Russia in the coming year.[27]

On that same Sunday, Count Valentin Esterhazy, Austria's ambassador to the Tsar, left Vienna with new demands for a peace settlement which had been drawn up in consultation with the French and, belatedly, the British. If these terms were rejected by Russia, Austria would break off relations. But this latest threat did not immediately strengthen the hand of the peace party in St Petersburg. Throughout the last three months the pace of allied diplomacy had been set in Paris rather than in London, to the chagrin of both Palmerston and Clarendon, who had delayed Esterhazy's departure by several weeks through their insistence on modifying the original Franco-Austrian draft.[28] This rift between Paris and London – characterized by a speech by Prince Napoleon in which he spoke about the Crimean campaign without mentioning the presence in the peninsula of the British – was well known in other European capitals and exaggerated in St Petersburg. The Tsar clung to the hope that, so long as there was no outward weakening in Russia's resolve to continue the war, he might detach the French from their British partners and, by breaking up the allied coalition, secure a good peace for his Empire. 'Never will I accept humiliating terms,' he wrote to his Commander-in-Chief in the Crimea. 'It only remains for us to make the sign of the Cross, march straight ahead, and defend our homeland and our national honour by our united efforts.'[29]

Lord Panmure used less exalted language when he let General Codrington 'know confidentially the political aspect of affairs': 'You will no doubt be inundated with many vague reports from all quarters, and dark hints from Pélissier as to the future,' he wrote. 'There can be no doubt that the Emperor of the French is tired of war at so remote a distance from France, and he is fast making up his mind to no more in the Crimea.'[30] Codrington had clear evidence around him of the declining French interest in the campaign. Generals Bosquet and Niel were back in Paris before Christmas, and many of the best regiments returned home. Apart from occasional skirmishes, there was little action. So surprised was Marshal Pélissier by a sudden eruption of fighting in the second week of December that he sent Brigadier-General Rose over to British headquarters to report that the Russians had made an unsuccessful raid on one of the most distant French outposts, nine miles east of Balaclava. It is characteristic of a winter in which the Commander-in-Chief's despatches were concerned with leaky hut roofs, the state of the roads, and a temperamental locomotive on the Balaclava Railway, that when Rose rode over to headquarters, General Codrington was not there to see him.[31]

Codrington was, however, commended at Windsor and Westminster for the clarity and frequency of his reports. He was prepared to do all that was required of him in the captured city. 'The destruction of the South Side of Sebastopol, its docks and forts, is in our power', he wrote to Panmure on 8 December, 'but the enemy holds as much control over the harbour as we do: we have not possession of it at all in a naval point of view; it is a large mutual wet ditch under fire from both sides.' The delay in blowing up the docks was caused partly by heavy rain which flooded the holes in which explosives had been sunk, but over the New Year the work of destruction went rapidly ahead.[32] Codrington, too, withdrew veteran troops, so as to avoid having men and horses spend a second winter in the Crimea; but most units did at least remain in the theatre of war, ready for another campaign in the spring. Thus the Duberlys, wife and husband, left Balaclava with the 8th Hussars on 7 November for Turkey, so that the Light Cavalry could winter their horses in well-protected quarters at Izmit, fifty miles south-east of Scutari. They did not doubt that they would return northwards once the Crimean snowline receded. By contrast, in France on the last Saturday of the old year, there was a triumphant parade through the streets of the capital, as if the fighting were already over.[33]

At St Petersburg, two evenings later (1 January, 1856), Alexander II convened a special council of ministers at the Winter Palace to decide whether, in view of the threatening attitude of Austria, the war was to continue.[34] The Tsar, who had seen both Esterhazy and Seebach over the weekend, read out the Austrian demands: acceptance of the old and familiar Four Points as a basis of agreement, but with two important additions – a 'Fifth Point' in which the belligerents reserved a right to bring forward at a peace conference other 'special conditions, in the interests of Europe', and an amplification of the First Point (the future of the Danubian Principalities) requiring Russia to withdraw from southern Bessarabia and lose all sovereignty over the banks of the Danube. Alexander personally made no comment on these proposals, but he sought the opinions of Nesselrode, Orlov and three widely experienced ministers. None favoured the continuance of the war; yet none wished to accept these Austrian demands. Count Bludov, the President of the Imperial Council, wondered if the situation was as desperate as it seemed and made an emotional appeal to think of Russia's honour. Others, however, emphasized Russia's financial weakness and the danger of insurrections should the war drag on. All agreed that Alexander Gorchakov in Vienna must seek withdrawal of the Fifth Point, on the grounds that it was too vague to merit acceptance; and he should emphasize that Russia would not allow her frontier to be pushed back from the Danube. Gorchakov himself suggested to Nesselrode that Russia could ignore the Austrians and make a direct personal approach to Napoleon III; for the ambassador was convinced that the French were so tired of the war that they would prefer a speedy peace which left Russia on the lower Danube to a protracted diplomatic wrangle over the future of Bessarabia.[35]

Although Nesselrode, who disliked all the Gorchakov family, was slow to respond to the ambassador's proposal, it made good, shrewd sense. For Napoleon was embarking on a tortuous policy which could be eased by direct Russo-French contacts, rather than by counting on the Austrians. He had welcomed a British suggestion that the allies should hold a Grand Council of War in January to plan an overall strategy for the new year. But, whereas the British delegates and the French soldiers at the council table wished to consider specific military objectives, Napoleon hoped to persuade them that a wider war would impose greater burdens in manpower, money and resources than Britain or France could afford. Since there was a Piedmontese delegate to the Grand Council, but nobody from neutral Vienna, it would be convenient for Napoleon if he could bring peace nearer by direct links with Russia, which ignored Austrian susceptibilities entirely. A deviously worded letter to Queen Victoria explained that public opinion in France would never understand a conflict which was allowed to drag on simply 'in order to obtain some wasteland in Bessarabia'.[36]

The Grand Council of War, which met intermittently in Paris under the Emperor's presidency from 10 to 21 January 1856, was a typically Napoleonic showpiece. It fulfilled its function admirably, by attracting maximum attention and postponing every decision to a speculative future. The British ambassador (who had first proposed the convening of the Council) was joined by the Duke of Cambridge and two lesser military luminaries from the Crimea, Generals Airey and Jones, as well as by Admirals Lyons and Richard Dundas. General La Marmora had been fetched back from Balaclava to speak for Sardinia-Piedmont, but, as so often in these allied deliberations, there was no spokesman for the Turks. The French delegates were a collection of military heavyweights: Marshal Vaillant and Generals Bosquet, Niel, Canrobert and Martimprey (Pélissier's chief of staff), together with three admirals and a transfusion of Bonapartist blueblood – Count Walewski; Prince Napoleon; and the septuagenarian Marshal Prince Jerome, the great Napoleon's surviving brother, once King of Westphalia and, for three undistinguished weeks forty-four years in the past, commander of the Third Army in the invasion of Russia. Much of the discussion around the conference table seemed suddenly irrelevant. There was talk of using Eupatoria as the best base in the Crimea for striking inland, but more interest was shown in plans for a Baltic campaign, in which even Sardinia-Piedmont now wished to participate. Yet here, too, concentration wavered. On 12 January Canrobert began to read a paper that he had prepared on ways of capturing St Petersburg, but before he had finished his exposition he abandoned it, with profuse apologies for having wasted the Council's time on so impracticable a project. Peace was in the air and everyone knew it; although the Duke of Cambridge took care 'to urge upon the Emperor' the need to press on vigorously with the war 'should the pacific turn that affairs have momentarily taken not be continued in that direction'.[37] Napoleon, interested in summoning an even more prestigious gathering in the French capital, hurriedly agreed with His Royal Highness, who returned to London somewhat confused by what his cousin, Queen Victoria, felicitously called 'the cancans at Paris'.[38]

Meanwhile, on the fifth day of the Grand Council's deliberations, an important and less publicized conference took place in the Winter Palace. The Austrians had refused to tone down their demands, and the King of Prussia had again warned the Tsar that Berlin would almost certainly have to follow Vienna's lead in breaking off all relations with Russia. Esterhazy, the Tsar told his ministers, would leave St Petersburg for the last time on 18 January, three days ahead. What was settled in this second Imperial Council in a fortnight would therefore be decisive. Nesselrode read a memorandum prepared by the Ministry of Foreign Affairs which insisted that, if the Russians did not now accept the Franco-Austrian terms, they would be forced to accept even harsher ones sooner or later. Other ministers expressed fears of revolt in Finland and Poland, complained of a shortage of munitions, and conjured up the spectre of national bankruptcy. Long before the meeting ended, the Tsar was nodding his head in approval every time it was suggested that Russia should accept the Austrian demands and hope that private contacts in Paris would offset their harsh character. Far more bitterness was felt towards Francis Joseph than towards Napoleon III. [39]

Alexander Gorchakov informed Count Buol in Vienna in the early evening of 16 January that Russia unconditionally accepted the allied conditions for peace. An enterprising journalist, T.O'M. Bird, telegraphed the news to *The Times* three hours later, and a special edition was on sale in the City by eleven o'clock on the morning of 17 January.[40] But for the remainder of that month and for most of February there was still uncertainty, particularly in London. After a cabinet meeting on 28 January Panmure wrote urgently to Codrington insisting that although 'peace looks more definite . . . you are not to relax any preparations'. Eleven days later he was still discussing with Codrington the coming campaigning season: would 'one great and vigorous effort to sweep the Crimea' really 'be as bloody an affair' as the General contemplated, he wondered?[41] By then, in Vienna, the Russian, British and French ambassadors and the Austrian Foreign Minister had agreed that peace delegates, with plenipotentiary authority, would assemble in Paris not later than 25 February to conclude an armistice and prepare a final treaty.[42]

The war was not yet over. Suddenly, on 29 January, in a final gesture of belligerency, all the Russian guns in the tiered emplacements from the northern shore up to Star Fort had begun a bombardment of the amputated city and the Karabelnaya district. But, apart from the dull thud of explosions as the British demolished the quays and the French blew up Fort Nicholas, there was for the most part a brooding silence around the Sebastopol Heights throughout February. Living conditions for British troops were far better than in the previous winter.

But the French, whose standards of sanitation and medical care had been so high under Canrobert, suffered heavy losses in these weeks of inactivity. Nearly 53,000 soldiers were admitted to the fourteen French hospitals around Constantinople in the first three months of 1856, and another 5,000 died on transports between the Crimea and the Bosphorus. Typhus was the greatest scourge, but cholera, too, continued to claim its victims; and there is no doubt that neglect, and a shortage of medical staff, forced the death toll to rise even higher. Unexpectedly those Frenchmen who survived the ravages of disease began to see that, while returned veterans were feted in Paris, those left in the Crimea had become a forgotten army.[43]

Eventually, on 28 February the electric telegraph brought news that an armistice, valid until 31 March, had been signed two thousand miles away, in Paris. Next morning at ten o'clock Major-General Timofiev, an elderly artilleryman, rode down with his staff and an escort of Cossacks under a white flag to the Traktir Bridge, where mounds of improvised graves recalled the summer slaughter twenty-eight weeks before. At the same time a brigade commander from the 3rd Division, General Barnard, together with a group of British, French and Sardinian-Piedmontese officers, came down the slopes towards the Chernaya to greet them. The allied delegation crossed the bridge and began detailed talks to ensure that no more shots were exchanged. More and more officers from both sides wandered curiously forward to the bridge: the Russians carried white kid gloves, some even wore patent leather boots, a British observer noted with surprise. At last Timoeev, Barnard and their staff remounted their horses and rode together through a line of troops on both sides of the bridge. Salutes were exchanged; and 'our friends, the enemy' turned back across the river.[44] The campaign, anticlimactic to the end, was over.

CHAPTER SEVENTEEN

The Coming of Peace

Most European statesmen referred to the forthcoming assembly in Paris as a 'conference'; they envisaged a series of meetings to draw up a treaty of peace between rival belligerents. Napoleon III had grander ideas. He wished to settle the affairs of all Europe, not simply to seek the latest answer to the interminable Eastern Question; any gathering of foreign ministers and diplomats in the capital of his Empire must therefore follow the precedents set in 1814 at Vienna, on his uncle's downfall. Visiting diplomats were left in no doubt of the dignity of the occasion for, in the last week of February, the official gazette announced the imminent opening, at the new Foreign Ministry on the Quai d'Orsay, of the 'Congress of Paris'.[1]

As at Vienna, the host country's Foreign Minister took the chair, although Walewski never won the authoritative prestige possessed by Metternich in 1814–15. France also supplied the Secretary General, Vincente Benedetti, the diplomat who had summoned the French fleet to Turkish waters at the start of the Eastern Crisis, three years before. Four foreign delegates were already resident in Paris: the British ambassador, Lord Cowley, was his country's second plenipotentiary; and the Austrian, Sardinian-Piedmontese, and Turkish envoys participated in all the preliminary discussions, too. No seat was set aside at the Congress for a Swedish delegate, despite the recent showy bluster of the Canrobert Mission; and the Prussians, who had consistently rebuffed British efforts to tempt them to march against Russia, were only admitted to the discussions in the fourth week of the Congress, as signatories of the 1841 Straits Convention.

The Austrians sought to exclude any representatives of Sardinia-Piedmont because, as Buol complained to Clarendon, to 'erect Sardinia into a first-class Power . . . could disturb the settled order of things in Europe'. But the British public admired their Italian ally; letters home from the Crimea mentioned with affectionate tolerance the 'Sardines' who wore a 'kind of wide-awake hat with feathers in it' and 'General

Marmalade', their Commander-in-Chief, who looked so extraordinarily like the Emperor of the French. La Marmora, Queen Victoria declared, was 'a universal favourite' when he visited Windsor in January. 'The Queen has the greatest respect for that noble little country', she wrote to Clarendon, adding that she rejoiced 'to hear Count Cavour is coming to Paris'.[2] Throughout the Congress, the British warmly supported the Piedmontese, partly from genuine sympathy with Cavour's anti-papist liberalism and partly from self-interest, for an Italian commercial dependency would offer good markets for trade and investment. Before setting out for Paris, Clarendon told the French ambassador in London that as Sardinia-Piedmont had fought not for narrowly territorial gains but for the cause of Europe, King Victor Emmanuel's envoys had a right to discuss matters of concern to the Continent as a whole.[3]

The first plenipotentiary to reach Paris for the peace talks was Baron Brunnow, who had been serving as the Tsar's envoy to the German Diet at Frankfurt since his departure from London two years before. The British Foreign Secretary arrived soon afterwards, on 16 February, and two days later Lady Clarendon could write to her niece that 'George is glad that he came here', as his presence 'has a salutary effect on Walewski . . . of whom he has nothing to complain, he tells me'. Lady Clarendon also commented on how curious it seemed 'to meet and almost to fall into Brunnow's arms tonight', dinner *chez* Walewski promising the renewal of old friendships rent asunder.[4] This, however, was a superficial judgement. Neither Clarendon nor 'the chief' in London trusted Walewski and deep suspicion and resentment continued to separate the British and French throughout the Congress, especially when the Tsar's principal plenipotentiary, Prince Orlov, arrived later that week.

Had Clarendon possessed the relative independence enjoyed by Castlereagh at Vienna or by Wellington at the Congress of Verona, his task might have been easier. But railways, steamships and the electric telegraph were bringing Paris nearer to Westminster. Almost daily the Foreign Secretary received precisely worded letters of advice and instruction – often ten pages or more in length – from his Prime Minister. When this rich source of unsolicited experience began to dry up, there followed a stream of cipher telegrams. If constitutional precedent had allowed the head of a British government to attend a protracted summit conference abroad, Palmerston would have come to Paris in person. He remained a convinced Russophobe, anxious to check the power of the Tsar's army and navy in the Baltic and the Caucasus, as well as in south-eastern Europe. 'The main and real object of the war', he had already told Lord Cowley, was 'to curb the aggressive ambitions of Russia'; so far as the Ottoman Empire was concerned, Britain had fought 'not so much to keep the Sultan and his Mussulmans in Turkey as to keep the Russians out of Turkey'; and Clarendon was warned against Orlov, who 'is civil and courteous externally, but his inward mind is deeply impregnated with Russian insolence, arrogance and pride'.[5] These feelings were reciprocated. Nesselrode, for his part, no longer had any illusions about the British: 'England is and will remain our chief and implacable foe', he wrote in the draft instructions prepared for Orlov before the Prince set out from St Petersburg in the second week of February.[6]

The Congress began in the pristine marble splendour of the Quai d'Orsay on 25 February. Over the following seven and a half weeks there were, technically, twenty-four sessions for the ministers and diplomats seated at the round green table of the Salon des Ambassadeurs. The Peace Treaty itself was signed on 30 March but diplomatic exchanges over the future of Italy, problems of maritime law, and international arbitration continued until 16 April. But, as at earlier congresses, most vital decisions were reached in private talks outside the Salon, many of them depending on conversations with the Emperor at the Tuileries. Napoleon's plans had by now gone beyond any idea of a simple prestigious victory over Russia. He sought recognition as arbiter of Europe, redistributing territories according to principles of nationality which, though confusing to other statesmen, were clearly set out in his mind. Unlike Palmerston, he was not interested in the Caucasus, nor would he concern himself with Sweden and Finland if there was to be no more campaigning against the Russians. But there were three regions on which Bonapartist sentiment and the Paris Bourse concentrated his thoughts. He wanted to 'do something for Italy' and restore some form of Polish state; he would have liked an excuse to win for France the left bank of the Rhine; and he was responsive to an influential pressure group in his capital who reminded him that the Roumanian inhabitants of the Danubian Principalities were a Latin people claiming national recognition. As for Pélissier's army in the Crimea, the sooner what remained of those 150,000 men returned to France the better: 'The Emperor himself admitted to me', Clarendon wrote to Stratford de Redcliffe when the Congress was over, 'that with 22,000 men in hospital, and likely to be more, peace had almost become a military as well as a financial and political necessity for him.'[7]

Palmerston wanted no appeasement of the Russians. He even hoped to set up autonomous Georgian and Circassian principalities, which were apparently to acknowledge the Sultan's suzerainty.[8] Clarendon, however, sensed the dangers of isolation as soon as the Congress began, for Orlov wanted to link the return of the captured fortress of Kars to the Turks with concessions over Bessarabia. The French and the Austrians were willing to negotiate over these matters. Clarendon sought fresh instructions from London, warning Palmerston, 'We may in the next forty-eight hours find ourselves standing alone and having to decide the grave question of peace or war.' But the chief was in what the Foreign Secretary regarded as 'his jaunty mood': 'Faint heart never won fair Lady', Palmerston replied on leap-day's eve. 'Fortune is the Lady, and our stoutness will win her in spite of all difficulties among friends and bluster from our opponents'; the most that the Prime Minister would admit was that it would be a mistake to 'press Austria to make war in the event of hostilities being renewed in consequence of our refusal to let the Russians off about the Bessarabian frontier. This would be a sure way to go over to the side of Russia.' Clarendon thereupon lost patience: 'When you talk of "we" and of "our" going on with the war if the Russians are intractable, you are probably thinking of the France of two years ago, whereas it is no such thing,' he replied. 'Except the Emperor and Walewski, who does not care to act contrary to the Emperor's orders, we have nobody here who is not prepared to make *any* peace.' There was too, as Clarendon warned Palmerston, a danger that Napoleon would become an emperor of the revolutionaries, seeking to liberate all the oppressed nationalities of Europe, not merely Italians and Poles, but Roumanians, Hungarians and South Slavs as well. This was far too radical a crusade to be welcomed by a Whig flying liberal colours; and, faced by murmurs of dissent within his cabinet, Palmerston became less insistent on securing the unattainable.[9]

Meanwhile Orlov successfully toned down the allied demands.[10] Nothing more was said about autonomous Caucasian states, and with a show of magnanimity the Russians agreed to hand back Kars in return for major concessions in Bessarabia. The Tsar was still forced to accept withdrawal from the banks of the Danube, but Russia retained more than two-thirds of the region in Bessarabia which the allies had originally sought to detach from his Empire. The small segment of southern Bessarabia which was handed over to the Danubian Principality of Moldavia was the only territory lost by Russia in the peace settlement. Only one minor change was made in northern waters: a separate convention signed by the plenipotentiaries of Britain, France and Russia on the same day as the Treaty of Paris provided that the Aaland Islands would no longer be fortified, nor would any military or naval establishment ever again be established in the archipelago. But, although Bomarsund might be a neutralized historical relic, the Tsar's troops continued to garrison Kronstadt, Sveaborg and the other fortresses which had defied Admirals Napier and Richard Dundas in the Gulf of Finland until Imperial Russia collapsed in revolution more than sixty years later.

On 4 March the Congress began to consider a vital question for the Russians, the Third Point in the original demands of the allies, neutralization of the Black Sea. Reluctantly Alexander II had recognized, before Orlov left St Petersburg, that there was little hope of saving what remained of the dockyards and fortifications of Sebastopol from destruction. Nevertheless Orlov and Brunnow claimed that the demand for razing to the ground all naval arsenals did not require the dismantling of forts that were not in themselves depots. This argument made little impression on other delegations. Nor did the claim that warships were necessary on the Black Sea in order to check the slave trade and the carriage of dangerous contraband from small harbours in the Caucasus and Turkey's Armenian coast to Western Europe. But the Russians gained more concessions than they had anticipated: against British pleas, the Congress did not specifically include the Sea of Azov in the clauses of the peace treaty which provided for neutralization of the Black Sea; and the Russians were allowed to keep shipyards and forts at the river ports of Nikolayev and Kherson, as well as some small armed vessels for coastal guard duties. Moreover the treaty specifically excluded 'the Flag of War . . . of any other Power' from the waters of the Black Sea; and once again, as in 1841, a revised Straits Convention closed the Dardanelles and Bosphorus to the passage of foreign warships so long as the Ottoman Empire was at peace. It was, however, these Black Sea clauses in Article XI of the Treaty of Paris which most rankled in St Petersburg. Never before had Europe's statesmen restricted the right of a Great Power to maintain a fleet in its territorial waters.[11]

To offset this humiliation, the Russians claimed a moral victory. In a manifesto published in St Petersburg on 31 March, Tsar Alexander II announced that an act of Providence had fulfilled 'the original and principal aims of the war': 'From now on, the future destiny and the rights of all Christians in the Orient are assured. The Sultan solemnly recognized them . . . Russians! Your efforts and your sacrifices were not in vain. The great work is accomplished.'[12] To some extent this manifesto was an ingenious attempt to keep faith with the historic claims of the Russian Church to assert a protective right over Christian believers within the Sultan's empire.

There was, however, behind the Tsar's pronouncement a more serious purpose than this somewhat specious attempt at saving face. On 18 February, a week before the opening of the Congress of Paris, Abdul Medjid had issued in Constantinople a Firman – a decree written for proclamation – which promised an improved status in the law and government of the Ottoman Empire for his non-Turkish and Christian subjects. This major reform, the Hatt-i-Humayun, was forced on Abdul Medjid by the insistence of Stratford de Redcliffe and the French and Austrian ambassadors. Tsar Alexander, however, instructed Orlov to urge the Congress to have the reforming edict written into the peace treaty, so as to guarantee the improved status of the Sultan's Christians in perpetuity. Although Napoleon III showed some sympathy with the Russians over this question, all references to the Hatt-i-Humayun in the final settlement were toned down, largely at the insistence of the Austrians and the British: Article IX of the Peace Treaty did, indeed, recognize the 'high value' of the decree, but it denied the right of any foreign Power to interfere in the Sultan's relations with his subjects or in the internal administration of his Empire. In St Petersburg – and even more in Holy Moscow – it was assumed that, with so vague a commitment to reform, the Turkish authorities would soon cease to observe the rights promised by the Hatt-i-Humayun. The Tsar's manifesto therefore sought to give the Sultan's 'act of justice' international recognition, in order to emphasize the enormity of any future backsliding by the Turkish authorities. The manifesto did not, however, in any way restore Russian influence within the Sultan's Empire and it was as silent about 'Holy Places' as was the Hatt-i-Humayun and the Peace Treaty itself, so swiftly are the quarrels of yesterday forgotten. Yet even before the end of the decade there was rioting in Jerusalem and Christian communities were being put to the sword in Syria, Lebanon and the Arabian peninsula. Ironically, on this occasion it was Napoleon III who intervened, taking the opportunity to assert French primacy at Constantinople.[13]

The Congress of Paris was, outwardly, a triumph for the Emperor of the French. But it did not, as he had hoped, give a neo-Bonapartist cut to a refashioned map of Europe. Nothing was done for Poland: Orlov asked that the Polish Question should not be raised at the conference table as discussion of so sensitive a problem might hamper his sovereign's plans to bestow concessions on his Polish subjects after his coronation at Moscow later that summer; and this plea was accepted by the French and the British.[14] Little was done for the Roumanians: Wallachia and Moldavia, enlarged by the three districts from southern Bessarabia, were nominally confirmed under the suzerainty of the Sultan although they were promised 'independent national administrations' which, within six years, brought a Roumanian national state into being under French patronage. More surprisingly, despite Napoleon's assurances to Cavour while La Marmora's men were fighting in front of Sebastopol, no tangible reward for services rendered went to Sardinia-Piedmont, not least because the Emperor was anxious not to offend the French clerical party by supporting an Italian state in conflict with the Church.

In the absence of French support it was left to the British to champion the Italian cause. Palmerston, with engaging eccentricity in the first days of the Congress, suggested to Clarendon that Cavour might be invited to abandon claims to Austrian-held Lombardy and Venetia in return for the cession of the Crimea, to be developed as the first colony of an Italian state; and in March he was still proposing extraordinary changes of territory, although by now less distant from Piedmont.[15] Clarendon, more temperate than his Prime Minister but sincerely believing that 'the state of Italy . . . was a scandal to Europe', contented himself with a speech on 8 April in which he denounced the repressive measures of the King of Naples, Papal misrule and the presence in the Romagna of Austrian troops. Clarendon told Palmerston that he had spoken 'in rather stifled terms and whether my speech was good or bad it completely satisfied Cavour and angered Buol'; and Cavour later told Parliament in Turin that Clarendon had 'laid the cause of Italy before the bar of public opinion'. Yet, at the time, Cavour did not hide his disappointment with the Congress. He recognized that after Clarendon's speech Italian unification under the House of Savoy seemed to the British public, not simply a 'respectable' cause, but the natural consequence of a wartime partnership. He convinced himself, wrongly, that Clarendon would be prepared to perpetuate this comradeship, with British troops soon fighting alongside 'the Sardines' in a war against Austria 'for the aggrandisement of

Piedmont'. A campaign of this character would have been the oddest of all consequences from the Crimean alliance.[16]

Although the Treaty of Paris was signed on 30 March, news that the war was officially over did not reach the Crimea until 2 April, peace being welcomed by the shattering reverberation of a 101–gun salute. On the following day, as though to mock the general mood of relief, the spring weather turned sour: 'As nasty a snowstorm, with heavy squalls, as I have seen this winter', commented General Codrington in a letter next day.[17] Soon the opposing armies were fraternizing, with official approval. At the end of January, General Gorchakov had given up the command of Russia's southern armies to become commander-in-chief in Poland; he was succeeded by General Luders, who in July 1854 had been the first of the Tsar's senior officers to see British troops in the field, when Cardigan's ill-fated reconnaissance patrol reached the banks of the Danube. Now it was Luders who, on 13 April, invited Pélissier and Codrington to take the salute at a review of the Tsar's troops on the Mackenzie Heights, subsequently entertaining the allied generals at a belated breakfast under the canvas of an ornately decorated double marquee. 'Nothing could be more nicely done, with the ornamental show of arms, colours, drums, guns etc.,' Codrington reported. 'We sat down about 50 or 60 in it; every luxury – caviare, bottled porter, roast beef, any number of dishes in succession, and last of all two large sturgeon.' Two days later the compliment was returned, Marshal Pélissier being host to the Russians, while the French army organized horse races and a carrousel of the Chasseurs d'Afrique. On 17 April allied and Russian top brass were together again. Luders stood beside Pélissier as 88 battalions of French infantry, 5 regiments of cavalry, siege artillerymen, sappers and 198 guns trailed past. After a luncheon provided by Codrington, 49 battalions of the British army, with 86 guns, went by at the salute. The victors, however, could not provide such luxuries as the Russians.[18]

A generous issue of passes allowed the troops of the various nations to mix freely as well. The ex-enemy soldiers, it was observed a trifle primly, had no head for liquor. Soon hundreds of Russians were coming into Balaclava to purchase sugar, salt and tea, while the enterprising Mrs Seacole made various excursions into the interior, visiting both Bakchisarai and Simferopol. On the other hand, a horse fair held on the Mackenzie Heights was a dismal failure: the Russians would not pay the prices asked by the British officers; and the whole notion of selling trusted allied steeds to 'our recent enemies' was soon scotched by indignant protests from the Queen herself. But to the men in the Crimea the enemy now was, not the Russians, but sheer boredom. Horse races, athletic competitions and cricket were tried as diversions; and the British followed the example of the French in encouraging amateur dramatics on the improvised stage of a camp theatre. At one of these entertainments, the Light Division raised £70 'for the humbler class of sufferers' left destitute when the Theatre Royal, Covent Garden, went up in flames early in March.[19]

'We have no wish to loiter in the Crimea', Palmerston had remarked to Clarendon in a letter congratulating him on the completion of the Treaty of Paris.[20] The Russians did not object to the use of Sebastopol harbour for embarkation, and by the last week of April the transports were moving down through the Straits and out into the Mediterranean. 'I think the Sardinians ought to go first, so as to relieve them from expense as they have been so true and so quiet in their assistance, and are so little gainers by the result', Codrington told Panmure.[21] La Marmora's men duly sailed for Genoa and a triumphant reception in Turin. They were followed by French transports bound for Marseilles. But soon it became clear that many of the British troops would not be seeing home shores that year at all. The regular army was needed to relieve militia regiments who were garrisoning Malta, Corfu and Gibraltar. And unexpectedly, within a week of the signing of peace, Codrington was ordered to send five regiments as soon as possible to Canada. It is one of the minor ironies of the Crimean War that while the fighting continued no precautions whatsoever were taken along the only frontier common to the British and Russian Empires, the remote border between the Yukon and the Russo-American Company's Alaskan territories, but with the return of peace Palmerston became worried by complaints from President Pierce's administration that the British had been enticing US citizens to enlist in their projected Foreign Legion. Palmerston had been Secretary-at-War in 1812, when the Americans mounted an invasion of Canada during the struggle with Napoleon, and he mistrusted Pierce. Not a day should be 'lost . . . in properly reinforcing the garrison of our North American colonies', he declared.[22]

The last regiment for North America sailed from Sebastopol at the end of the first week in May, but on 1 June Codrington still had more than 41,000 men under canvas awaiting ships. The General was irritated by the refusal of the Royal Navy to use warships as transports and seriously alarmed that a new wave of typhus or cholera would spread as rapidly as the diseases at Varna two summers before. The blunt personal intervention of Queen Victoria after reading Codrington's despatches swept aside the Admiralty's reluctance to bring 'her noble and gallant troops' home 'by ships of the Navy'; and embarkation went ahead speedily throughout June. Marshal Pélissier and the last French contingent left Sebastopol on 5 July. A week later, with HMS *Algiers* standing by to evacuate Codrington and his personal staff, a British bugler sounded reveille for the 666th, and last, time in the Crimea.[23]

In the first week of May the Secretary of State for War gave the earliest detailed casualty figures to the House of Lords. From the day of disembarkation in the Crimea until the occupation of the city of Sebastopol was completed at the end of September 1855, the British lost 158 officers and 1,775 men killed in action, with 51 officers and 1,548 men dying from their wounds, Panmure said. Deaths from cholera up to the end of 1855 were 35 officers and 4,244 men, while deaths from other diseases were 26 officers and 11,451 men. Another 322 men had died from wounds or disease in the first three months of 1856. Panmure therefore informed Parliament that, over eighteen months, there had been in all 19,584 deaths, of which fewer than one in ten had happened in action.[24] Since more than 111,000 British officers and men saw service in the Crimea, the casualty rate, as reported by Panmure, was not as high as in earlier or later wars on the Continent. His figures were, however, deceptively low; not only did they exclude deaths in other theatres of war (notably the Baltic) but they also omitted losses from disease at Varna, where the cholera claimed its first victims. Nevertheless, the proportion between those killed on the battlefield and those who perished from disease was probably accurate. French losses were certainly higher – 10,240 killed in action, with about another 70,000 dying from wounds or disease, says the most conservative estimate[25] – but the French sent out almost three times as many men as the British. No one attempted to count the number of Turks killed or wounded, let alone sick; nor did they then know the extent of Russian casualties, although the newspapers spoke of the Tsar's army having suffered 'enormous losses'. These reports seem to have been true, for the most careful modern analysis of Tsarist and Soviet sources suggests 'that the number of members of the Russian armed services who lost their lives during the Crimean war was probably somewhat over 450,000'.[26] At all events it was clear, even in the spring of 1856, that despite the misery exposed by the war correspondents and by Roebuck's Committee, Britain's sailors and soldiers had not suffered so grievously as their sovereign and her statesmen had feared.

A few diehards in London thought that peace had been made too soon and on disgraceful terms, for to them it seemed monstrous that the Tsar lost so little territory.[27] But, in general, people were thankful for the ending of a war which, contrary to Tennyson's prediction, rarely shone 'in the sudden making of spendid names'. There was no single victory parade, although the Brigade of Guards marched triumphantly through London in the second week of July. Queen Victoria, however, asked her ministers to keep her informed of troop movements so that she could welcome home every regiment returning to English shores. The royal calendar that summer accommodated a succession of reviews at Portsmouth, Aldershot and Woolwich, and the Queen and her consort were punctilious in visiting hospitals and entertaining the walking wounded at Windsor.

An incident at the earliest disembarkation parade throws a sharp light on the Queen's prejudices. The cavalry from Ismit – the 8th Hussars and the 17th Lancers – were needed for service in Ireland and landed at Portsmouth as early as 12 May. They disembarked in the morning and, despite a fortnight spent below decks, they were ready for inspection by the Queen, Prince Albert and their three eldest children in the late afternoon. Among the officers' wives around the parade ground that Monday was Fanny Duberly, whose *Journal during the Russian War* had been published shortly before Christmas. Fanny's brother-in-law, Francis Marx, had prepared the journal for the press and toned down some of the incidents, but, although this bowdlerized version lacks the sparkle of her letters home, some implied criticism of Raglan and Cardigan slipped through, as also did an account of how Fanny had defied the Commander-in-Chief so as to accompany Henry from Varna to the Crimea. Fanny had suffered one disappointment, the Queen having declined permission for the *Journal* to be dedicated to her, but the book was a success with the reading public; and Fanny, having spent longer in the Crimea than any other officer's wife, might reasonably regard herself as a heroine. As such she had been petted by the officers of the Chasseurs d'Afrique, and it was in the light blue riding habit of a Chasseur that she waited, not too inconspicuously, for the royal visitors to cross from Osborne that afternoon. But it was not the sunniest of occasions for the Duberlys. Fanny's brief note to her sister that evening is eloquent in its omissions: 'My dear Selina,' she began, 'The Queen has just inspected us. She and Prince Albert made me low bows and the Princess Royal said, "Oh – there's Mrs Duberly" '. Majesty, however, passed on without a word.[28]

There was one great ceremony which had to wait until the following summer. Since Christmas in 1855, the Queen had shown constant interest in some way of recognizing supreme acts of valour in the face of the enemy. It was Prince Albert who proposed and designed the first military and naval decoration open to men of all ranks, the Victoria Cross. An announcement was made on 5 February 1856 that, six days previously, the Queen had approved the creation of 'The Victorian Order of Merit' (as it was originally called), but the earliest awards were not gazetted for another twelve months, and it was midsummer in 1857 before the Queen personally distributed the first sixty-two VCs, at a great review in Hyde Park.

More than 100,000 people crowded into the park on 26 June, hoping to see the ceremony from a distance. They burst into wild cheering when the Earl of Cardigan, mounted once more on Ronald, led the 11th Hussars past the Queen; and four survivors of the 'gallant six hundred' had the Cross pinned on their chests by their sovereign that afternoon.[29] So, too, did heroes from the Alma and Inkerman, including Major Henry Clifford. But it was emphasized that, although the new decoration was said to be made of captured gun-metal from Sebastopol, the award was not specifically a Crimean campaign medal. Indeed, chronologically, the first VC went to a naval officer in Napier's Baltic Fleet, Lieutenant Charles Lucas, who, as the mate of HMS *Hecla*, threw overboard that live shell during the bombardment of Bomarsund on 21 June 1854.[30] It was fitting that, at this final parade of heroes, a place should be found for the deed that inspired the war's earliest popular action prints.

CHAPTER EIGHTEEN

Into History

To the British public the Hyde Park review brought down the curtain on the war with Russia. Already, in that last week of June 1857, there were alarming tales of mutiny spreading across the Ganges plain from Meerut; and soon the attention of newspapers and weeklies focused on Cawnpore rather than on the Crimea. To some Londoners the two emergencies in the East became closely associated with each other; and the red granite column which still catches the eye to the west of Westminster Abbey is a memorial to scholars of Westminster School who died both in the Crimean War and in the Indian Mutiny. Tributes in stone to the dead of the 'Russian War' are few. Only the 2,162 officers and men of the Brigade of Guards who perished in the Crimea or at Varna are commemorated by a special monument in London, its sides honouring by name Alma, Inkerman and Sebastopol; and, as if to spite the French ally, the site found for this memorial lies in the middle of Waterloo Place. Not a street-name in central London recalls the conflict with the Tsar's Empire. By contrast, Napoleon III's Paris could boast a Boulevard de Sébastopol, a Pont d'Alma, and a suburb named after Fort Malakoff. When Victor Emmanuel II became king of Italy even Rome acquired a Via Cernaia.

In Russia the defenders of Sebastopol were treated as heroes when they passed through Moscow on their way northwards to St Petersburg. Within six months of the allied departure, plans were completed for rebuilding the ravaged city, although the Russians found that they had to employ an American engineer, Colonel John C. Gowen, to salvage the sunken vessels blocking the harbour, a six-year task. Work began on a restored Cathedral of St Vladimir, not completed until 1888 but designed to offer spiritual inviolability to the souls of a hundred thousand Orthodox believers who had died in the year-long battle for the city. Across the harbour, on the north shore, was the great Russian cemetery, where a new church shaped like a pyramid listed the losses of each regiment in the campaign. In this cemetery the remains of commanders who survived the war were later interred – notably, in 1861, General Gorchakov and, in 1884, Totleben.

Diplomatic relations between Russia and her former enemies were soon restored. Queen Victoria welcomed Brunnow back to London as early as 3 May 1856, giving a dinner for him at Buckingham Palace three days later at which Aberdeen and Clarendon were among the guests;[1] he stayed on as ambassador for another eighteen years. British diplomats arrived by sea at St Petersburg at the end of the first week in August. 'We all felt rather humbled at being brought up in a Russian ship through the forts which had successfully defied the splendid Baltic fleet', wrote the Foreign Secretary's nephew, Thomas Lister; although Colonel Maude, a Balaclava artilleryman attached to the mission, declared that 'from what he saw' the forts 'might have been attacked with success'. A week of embassy parties and receptions left Lister with the impression that Austria's alleged treachery to her Russian partner rankled in St Petersburg more than any action by the belligerents themselves: 'The hatred between the Austrians and Russians knows no bounds', he noted in his journal on 14 August.[2]

A speedy reconciliation drew Russia and her old adversaries in France and Sardinia-Piedmont closer together.[3] Alexander II, Napoleon III and their foreign ministers met at Stuttgart in September 1857 in an attempt to alarm the German states by showing that a Franco-Russian entente really did exist. Ten years later the Tsar came to Paris in great state; but, despite careful re-routing of carriage processions to avoid the Boulevard de Sébastopol, the visit was not a success, Alexander narrowly escaping assassination from a young Polish patriot. At heart the Tsar continued to resent bitterly the humiliating restraints on Russian activity in the Black Sea: in 1863, at a meeting of ministers, he banged his fist on the table upon which he had signed the final ratified version of the Treaty of Paris, wretchedly reproaching himself for that 'act of cowardice' seven years before; and when in September 1870 he was told that Napoleon III and his army had surrendered to the Prussians at Sedan, he made the sign of the cross and exclaimed, 'Thank God, Sebastopol is now avenged.'[4]

The defeat of France and the preoccupation of the European Powers with the German Question gave Russia the chance to cast off the shackles of the Paris Settlement. Early in November 1870 the Tsar sent a circular note to his embassies abroad instructing them to let it be known that Russia no longer considered herself bound by the Black Sea clauses of the Treaty of Paris. This unilateral abrogation of solemn commitments provoked protests in London and Vienna, with new outbursts against the Russian menace in the British press and with peppery speeches in Parliament. The Tsar agreed to suspend action on the circular and send delegates to a conference in London which would consider revising the Treaty of Paris. In March 1871 the Great Powers concluded the London Convention: full sovereign rights in the Black Sea were restored to the Russians, although Turkey was authorized to open the Dardanelles and Bosphorus to foreign warships, even in time of peace, should the Sultan's Government consider the remaining clauses of the Treaty of Paris at risk.

The Tsar and Alexander Gorchakov, who had succeeded Nesselrode at the Foreign Ministry in April 1856, regarded the London Convention as a diplomatic triumph. But since Russia was too impoverished to refortify Sebastopol or build up a Black Sea fleet until well into the eighteen-eighties, it was a less effective victory than they claimed. However, the recovery of full sovereignty mattered greatly to Alexander II's imperial conscience. From St Petersburg the British ambassador reported that the Tsar 'prayed with signs of deep emotion' at his father's grave, telling his attendants as he emerged from the cathedral in the fortress of St Peter and St Paul that 'the shade of the Emperor Nicholas would now be appeased'.[5]

By the winter of 1873-4 the Crimean War lay twenty years into history, far enough away for Queen Victoria to welcome the first direct marriage joining the British and Russian royal families. Alfred, Duke of Edinburgh – the baby whom Victoria was expecting during Nicholas I's visit in 1844 – married Grand Duchess Marie, Nicholas's granddaughter, at St Petersburg in January 1874; and four months later Tsar Alexander II himself came to London on a state visit. But the close dynastic contacts of the next half-century owed more to British and Russian links with the Danish and Greek Royal House and to the family of Victoria's second daughter, Princess Alice, Grand Duchess of Hesse. It was through these Greco-Danish and Hessian connections that, a century after the Crimean War, the heir to the British throne (Prince Charles) came to be a great-great-great-grandson not only of Victoria but of her enemy, Nicholas I, as well.

After 1856 the British and Russian Empires, between them encompassing one-third of the land surface of the globe, were never again at war with each other. On several occasions peace seemed at risk – most notably in 1878 when, in another war with Turkey, Alexander II's army reached the outskirts of Constantinople and a wave of British

'Jingoism' matched in folly the self-confident warmongering of a quarter of a century before. But statesmen at home and abroad had learned from the errors of their recent past; and in the Congress of Berlin a peaceful settlement was reached which ensured that Eastern Europe was free from any major conflict for over a third of a century.[6]

Russia's war with Turkey in 1877–8 enabled one famous soldier to add fresh distinction to his career: Totleben secured the surrender of the fortress of Plevna after two other generals had failed. Apart from Totleben, only three senior officers from the Crimean War later enhanced their military reputations: Sir Hugh Rose and Sir Colin Campbell in India; and Adolphe Niel who, during the two years before his premature death in 1869, proved to be France's ablest minister of war for over half a century. MacMahon, although victorious at Magenta in Napoleon III's brief Italian campaign of 1859, was defeated at Worth in 1870 and discredited as a crypto-royalist President of the Third French Republic. La Marmora, Italy's Prime Minister from 1864 to 1866, suffered a bad military defeat against the Austrians at Custozza. Two junior officers of Raglan's army are remembered as Victorian heroes: Garnet Wolseley, who as a company commander took part in the two assaults on the Redan, was an archetypal 'Soldier Who Made The Empire', renowned for expeditions against King Kofi of the Ashanti, King Cetewayo of the Zulus, and the Egyptian nationalist colonel, Arabi Pasha; and Charles Gordon, who travelled out to Balaclava in January 1855 as a sapper subaltern, was to become 'Chinese Gordon' eight years later and to win posthumous fame in 1885 as 'Gordon of Khartoum'.[7]

The most famous woman veteran from the Crimean War was, of course, Florence Nightingale. She came back to England broken in health, but was long able to continue her fight for an efficient nursing service. In 1907, three years before her death, she became the first woman recipient of the Order of Merit. Sister Sarah Anne Terrot, who lived until 1902, also suffered poor health after her return from Scutari; she was able to nurse in St Thomas's Hospital at Lambeth and in Victoria's Diamond Jubilee year she travelled to Balmoral to receive the Royal Red Cross from the Queen.[8] Poor Mrs Seacole did not survive so long. She appeared in the London Bankruptcy Court in November, 1856, but her cause was taken up by *The Times* and *Punch* and has a happy ending. In recognition of her 'disinterested services' to 'the Army, Navy and British Nation' a 'Seacole Fund' was established, with the Queen's 'approbation' and under the patronage of the Prince of Wales and two royal dukes; she was encouraged to write her *Wonderful Adventures* and was able to visit Jamaica and live in London in reasonable comfort until 1881; but Mary Seacole's achievements were then largely forgotten until the centenary of her death.[9] Fanny Duberly, on the other hand, has enjoyed a good press. She was with the 8th Hussars in India from 1857 until 1864: her *Campaigning Experiences in Central India and Rajputana during the Suppression of the Mutiny* was published in London in 1859, but is less vivid than her Crimean recollections. Her husband – stolid, dull and reliable Henry – retired as a lieutenant-colonel and settled (predictably) in Cheltenham, where he died in 1891. Fanny outlived the Queen who had snubbed her at Portsmouth by almost exactly two years.[10]

Survivors of the war lingered on well into the twentieth century. As late as June 1918 the pink and white Crimean War ribbon could be seen alongside the blue of a naval VC on the chest of a serving officer at the Admiralty, Sir Arthur Wilson, once an outstanding fleet commander and in his later years a consultant on almost every naval enterprise of the First World War. Yet another Crimean midshipman was still alive when the Second World War began: Colonel Rookes Crompton, founder of an electrical engineering company at Chelmsford, brought to the committee responsible for developing 'land ships' (tanks) in 1914–15 an experience of trench warfare which went back sixty years to the days when, as a cadet aboard HMS *Dragon*, he had gone ashore to visit his soldier brother before the assault on the Redan. He could recall the sound of the 'whistling Dicks' (the shells fired from the Lancaster rifle guns) and of the 'Carcasses' (flare shells) lighting the battlefield at night, and how after the end of the fighting what appeared to be 'a bluish sort of gravel' in front of the trenches was 'the remains of countless lead bullets'.[11] Colonel Crompton died in February 1940, less than three and a half years after the last surviving officer who had fought throughout the war against Russia, Sir Fitzroy Maclean. On the eve of Inkerman Maclean became aide-de-camp to Sir George Brown, but he had already seen service with the Light Dragoons at Varna and during the battle of the Alma. He was well into his hundred and second year when he died, late in November 1936.

Eighty-four years after the Treaty of Paris was signed, the pride of the Crimean troopships at last became a casualty of war: the screw-propelled *Himalaya*, which had transported thousands of soldiers during the years when she was the largest vessel in the world, was sunk by German bombers while serving as a storeship moored in Portland

Harbour.[12] Within a few months of the old troopship's sinking, the German thrust into Soviet Russia brought familiar place-names back into the headlines, as war returned to the Crimea. For 248 days – from 30 October 1941 until 4 July 1942 – Sebastopol endured a far tighter siege than during the 349 days of battle in the Crimean War. Anti-tank ditches, stretching from Balaclava to the mouth of the Belbec, kept out Hitler's Roumanian allies as they advanced southwards from Simferopol as well as German armoured divisions thrusting westwards from Yalta along the Chernaya towards Inkerman. In the end, the city was beaten into surrender by dive bombing and shelling far more terrible than anything envisaged by Totleben. In February 1945, nine months after the Red Army liberated Sebastopol, a British prime minister walked for the first time in the streets of Balaclava, scrutinizing with interest the Russians whom he met. 'There is pride in their looks,' Churchill remarked to his personal doctor, adding, on reflection, 'They have a right to feel proud.'[13]

During the 1920s and 1930s the Crimean War seemed as remote and irrelevant as Minden or Dettingen. A reading public filled with revulsion at the slaughter of the Ypres salient, Verdun, the Somme and Gallipoli found little of interest – or surprise – in the record of a mismanaged expedition on the outer fringe of Europe. They did not look for the first warning signs of the future warfare, with its poisonous gas, tanks, submarines and minefields. Even for military specialists, the Crimea appeared an unrewarding study: the allied victories owed nothing to good generalship; they were tributes to a resilient soldiery engaged in a succession of close combats, like the battle scenes of a Shakespeare history. In Britain only two enduring legends – the Charge of the Light Brigade and 'The Lady with the Lamp' – differentiated this campaign from a dozen others over the last century and a half. The political and social significance of the war was largely ignored by the historians. G. M. Young's highly perceptive *Victorian England: Portrait of an Age*, for example, mentioned the Crimea only in passing. It was, Young wrote in 1936, an 'event abroad' which, like 'the Australian gold discoveries and India', gave 'the nation an aggressive, imperial self-consciousness'. A few years later Philip Guedalla, outlining Bazaine's military career, aptly described Raglan's troops as 'Wellington's army without Wellington', but he could not resist the irreverent temptation to dismiss the Crimean War itself as 'one of the bad jokes of history'.[14]

The second siege of Sebastopol in 1942, and the westward advance of the Red Army two and a half years later, rekindled interest in the Crimean War. For, with the collapse of Hitler's 'New Order', what had seemed during the years of German primacy a succession of senseless battles fell into new historical perspective. It became clear that, even if much of the Treaty of Paris was torn up in 1870, the Crimean War formed the true watershed of nineteenth-century diplomacy. Before 1854 conservative statesmen – survivors like Nesselrode, Aberdeen and, for most of the period, Metternich – were convinced that a great European conflict would unleash 'Jacobinism' and violent social change; they therefore avoided war by upholding an ideal of collective responsibility, the so-called 'Concert of Europe'. The Forty Years Peace ended in 1853–4 because the Great Powers, shaken by the revolutions of 1848, sought to affirm their international prestige by resort to a peremptory diplomacy. Without conscious intent – for they had in mind only limited expeditions to attain particular objectives – they abandoned embryonic concepts of a public law between the nations and reverted to older practices which assumed that armies and navies were the natural instruments of external policy. Hence the contrast between the period before 1853 and that after 1856, when there were in fifteen years four separate conflicts on European soil, each involving at least two of the Great Powers.

The chief beneficiary from what John Morley called 'this vast subversion of the whole system of European States' was not, however, one of the participants in the Crimean War; it was neutral Prussia, given new political purpose by that one-time ambassador in St Petersburg and Paris, Otto von Bismarck. Britain's interests during these years of 'subversion' lay in more distant continents; defeated Russia was, as Alexander Gorchakov enigmatically remarked, 'communing with herself'; Buol's diplomatic pirouettes (and a threat of bankruptcy) left Francis Joseph's Austria militarily weak and politically isolated; and the grandiose schemes of Napoleon III were wrecked on the Emperor's poor health and the ruthless ability of Prussia's chief minister to explode his fantasies. Berlin, rather than Paris or Vienna, thus emerged as Europe's central capital; and it was only with the division of Germany in 1945 that the post-Crimean era came to an end.[15]

The creation of a Prussian-dominated Germany had, of course, entered into none of the allied statesmen's calculations during the Crimean War. Their war aim was basically a simple one: they hoped that their fleets and armies could destroy Russia's capacity for aggression. Yet, even while the Congress of Paris was in session, they recognized the need to be content with lesser gains. With Russian troops encamped along the shores of the Sea of Marmora in Alexander II's second war against Turkey, less than a quarter of a century later, it seemed as if all the sacrifice and suffering of the allied soldiers and sailors had been in vain. But with the passage of the years the victory in the Crimea acquired a new significance. After the Bolshevik Revolution destroyed the old Russian State, certain dates from the Tsarist past began to stand out as milestones beside the road to disaster. For forty years after 1814, when Tsar Alexander I had led the triumphant Russian and Prussian armies into Paris, the empire of the Tsars was respected as the strongest power on the European mainland. That reputation was lost in September 1855 when the Russian troops fell back across the bridge of boats from the devastated fortress beside the Black Sea. For another sixty years Imperial Russia continued to cast the shadow of a colossus over the Balkans, central Asia and the Far East. But never again did the ruler in St Petersburg seek to dominate the continent of Europe, from the Seine to the Urals, as had that 'crowned gendarme', Nicholas I, in the eighteen-thirties and eighteen-forties. The legend of an all-powerful Tsardom was dissolved in the battle-smoke of Sebastopol.

Reference Notes

Abbreviations used in the Notes

Add. MSS. : Additional Manuscripts in the British Library.
Airlie: Airlie, Mabel, Countess of, (ed), *With the Guards We Shall Go* (Letters of Colonel Strange Jocelyn).
Bod.Lib.: Papers deposited in the Bodleian Library, Oxford.
Cal. Lett.: S. J. Gough Calthorpe, *Letters from Headquarters.*
Clar. MSS.: Clarendon Papers, Bodleian Library, Oxford.
Cliff. Lett.: *Henry Clifford V.C., his letters and sketches from the Crimea.*
EHR: *English Historical Review* (London).
FO: Foreign Office papers, Public Record Office, Kew.
Gr. Pap.: Microfilm of Graham Papers, Bodleian Library, Oxford.
Hansard: Hansard's Parliamentary Debates, Third Series.
HJ: *Historical Journal* (Cambridge).
ILN: *Illustrated London News.*
Ist.Vk. : *Istoricheski Vestnik* (St Petersburg).
JRUSI : *Journal of the Royal United Services Institution* (London).
JSAHR: *Journal of the Society of Army Historical Research* (London).
KA: *Krasnyi Arkhiv* (Moscow).
Pan. Pap.: G. Douglas and G. D. Ramsay (eds), *The Panmure Papers.*
PRO: *Public Record Office, Kew*
QVL: A. C. Benson and Viscount Esher, *Letters of Queen Victoria,* first series.
RS: *Russkaia Starina.*
S-A: *Lettres du Maréchal Saint-Arnaud,* Vol. 2.
SEER: *Slavonic and East European Review* (London).
Tarlé : E. Tarlé, *Krymskaia Voina.*
Temp.: H. Temperley, *Britain and the Near East: The Crimea.*
TG: Temple Godman letters in P. Warner (ed.), *The Fields of War.*
Zai.: Zaionchkovskii, A. A., *Vostochnaia voina v sviazi s sovremennoi i politicheskoi obstanovki.*

Chapter One

1 Tatischev article, Ist. Vk., XXIII, no. 3, p. 603

2 Bloomfield to Aberdeen, 18 May 1844, and Brunnow to Aberdeen, 27 May 1844, Add. MSS. 43144; Aberdeen to Queen Victoria 27 May 1844, and Queen Victoria to Aberdeen, 29 May 1844, Add. MSS. 43044.

3 For disembarkation and the encounter in the Mall, see *The Times,* 3 June 1844. For Nicholas at Ashburnham House, see Tatischev, loc. cit., and Brunnow to Aberdeen,

2 June 1844, Add. MSS. 43144
4 A. Palmer, *The Chancelleries of Europe*, pp.72–3.
5 Queen Victoria to King Leopold, 4 and 11 June 1844, QVL, II, pp. 12-15.
6 C. Stockmar, *Memoirs*, II, p. 110
7 *The Times*, 7 June 1844
8 Bloomfield to Aberdeen, 10 July 1844, Add. MSS. 43144.
9 Aberdeen to Brunnow, 3 August 1844, Add. MSS. 43144.
10 Nesselrode's visit and the subsequent exchanges are well documented: see Temp., pp. 254–6 and M. Chamberlain, *Lord Aberdeen*, p. 380. The Brunnow–Aberdeen correspondence, Nesselrode's letter to Aberdeen of 28 December 1844 and Aberdeen's reply of 21 January 1845 may be found in Add. MSS. 43144, together with a revised copy of Nesselrode's memorandum on the Tsar's impression of his June conversations. See also Zai., I, pp. 129–31.
11 ILN 8 June 1844, Vol. IV, no. 166, p. 369.

Chapter Two

1 Nicholas I to Queen Victoria (in French), 3 April 1848, QVL, II, p. 166. For Nicholas's reactions to the 1848 revolutions, see W. Bruce Lincoln's biography, *Nicholas I*, pp. 278–90
2 A. Palmer, *The Chancelleries of Europe*, pp. 88–9.
3 See Temp., pp. 261–5 and J. Ridley, *Palmerston*, pp. 378–9.
4 Asa Briggs, *Victorian People*, pp. 46–52. For a retrospective attack on Crystal Palace 'pacifism' see the powerful passage in A. W. Kinglake, *The Invasion of the Crimea*, I, pp. 79–81. On Kossuth's visit, see Anon., *Authentic Life of Louis Kossuth*, with Copenhagen Fields speech, p. 80.
5 Temp., pp. 292–5. There is an interesting statement of the Russian

position on the Holy Places in a contemporary memorandum (in French), Zai., I, pp. 333–4.
6 A. J. P. Taylor, *The Struggle for Mastery in Europe*, p. 47.
7 Temp., pp. 292–5; Zai., I, p. 337.
8 Aberdeen to Palmerston, 10 January 1853, Add. MSS. 43049; M. Chamberlain, *Lord Aberdeen*, pp. 472–85.
9 Zai., I, pp. 356–7.
10 Seymour to Malmesbury, 4 December 1852, quoted in Schiemann, *Geschichte Russlands*, IV, p. 423; cf. Bruce Lincoln, op. cit., p. 332.
11 Seymour Journal, 9 January 1853, Add. MSS. 60306; Seymour to Russell, 11 January 1853, FO 65/424, no. 16
12 Seymour Journal, 14 January 1853, Add. MSS. 60306; Alexandra Feodorovna to Anna Pavlovna, 19 January 1853, S. Jackman, *Romanov Relations*, p. 336.
13 Seymour Journal, 26 January, 28 February, Add. MSS. 60306; Seymour to Russell, 21 and 22 February 1853, FO 65/424, nos 87 and 88.
14 The most comprehensive treatment of these talks is in G. H. Bolsover, 'Nicholas I and the Partition of Turkey', SEER, XXVII (1948–9), pp. 139–43; but it now needs to be supplemented by Seymour's journal entries. For remarks on Candia, see Seymour to Russell, 22 February 1853, FO 65/424, no. 88.
15 Aberdeen to Queen Victoria, 8 February, 1853, QVL, II, p. 437.
16 Russell to Seymour, 9 February 1853, FO 65/429, no. 38. A version of this despatch, with the Tsar's marginal comments, is printed in Zai., I, pp. 359–62; extracts Temp., pp. 274–5.
17 Bruce Lincoln, op. cit., p. 336.
18 Temp., pp. 306–8; full text, Zai., I, pp. 371–7.
19 Bruce Lincoln, op. cit., p. 336, citing Tarlé.
20 Rose to Dundas, 5 March 1853,

Add. MSS. 42801; Rose to
Clarendon, 6 March, FO 78/930,
no. 73; Temp., pp. 311–12;
Aberdeen to Queen Victoria, 20
March 1853, Add. MSS. 43047.

21 J. Curtiss, *Russia's Crimean War*, p.
95.

22 Graham to Clarendon, 1 April
1853, Clar. MSS. Dep. C4.

23 Aberdeen to Russell, 15 February
1853, Clar. MSS. Dep. C4.

24 Clarendon to Rose, 23 March 1853,
Curtiss, op. cit., p. 95.

25 Stratford to Clarendon, 11 April
1853, FO 78/931, no. 12.

26 Clarendon to Stratford, 18 April
1853, FO. 352/36.

27 Bosphorus landing project, Zai., I,
p. 599; for 'show of strength' see
the Tsar's comments on Menshikov
to Nesselrode, 10 April 1853, Ibid,
I, p. 401.

28 Curtiss, op. cit., pp. 118–40;
Palmer, op. cit., p. 100.

29 '*Shilly-shally*', Stratford to Lady
Stratford, 29 May 1853, S. Lane-
Poole, *Life of Stratford Canning*, II,
p. 274; 28 May cabinet and its
consequences, Aberdeen to Queen
Victoria, 29 May 1853, Add. MSS.
43047; Aberdeen to Clarendon 30
May and 1 June, Clar. MSS. Dep.
C4; Brunnow to Aberdeen, 29
May, Add. MSS. 43044; Russell to
Clarendon, 29 May and 31 May,
Clar. MSS. Dep. C4; Clarendon to
Aberdeen, 29 May 1853, Add. MSS.
43188. See also Chamberlain, op.
cit., pp. 480–1.

30 Aberdeen to Clarendon, 7 June
1853, Maxwell, *Life . . . Clarendon*,
II, p. 15.

31 Aberdeen to Palmerston, 4 July
1853, Add. MSS. 43049.

32 *The Press*, 28 May 1853, cited by
Kingsley Martin, *The Triumph of
Lord Palmerston*, p. 116.

33 Robert Blake, *Disraeli*, pp. 353–43.

34 Aberdeen to Graham, 31 May
1853, Add. MSS. 43191.

35 Aberdeen to Queen Victoria, 6
August 1853, Add. MSS. 43047;

Chamberlain, op. cit., pp. 483–4.

36 Lady Clarendon to Lady Theresa
Lewis, 18 August 1853, Bod. Lib.
MSS. Eng. hist. C 1034.

37 Aberdeen to Queen Victoria, 4
September 1853, Add. MSS. 43047.

38 Temp., pp. 349–50, 354 and 475; J.
L. Herkless, 'Stratford, the Cabinet
and the Outbreak of the Crimean
War', HJ, XVIII, 3 (1975), pp.
497–8 and 515–16; Aberdeen to
Queen Victoria, 4 September 1853,
Add. MSS. 43047.

39 Clarendon to G. Cornewall Lewis,
9 October 1853, Maxwell, op. cit.,
II, p. 26.

40 Nicholas 1 to Anna Pavlovna, 19
October 1853, Jackman, op. cit.,
pp. 339–40.

41 The same to the same, 15 February
1854, Ibid, p. 341. See also A.
Seaton, *The Crimean War*, p. 41.

Chapter Three

1 Clarendon to Lady Clarendon, 3
October 1853, Maxwell, *Life . . .
Clarendon*, II, p. 30.

2 Aberdeen to Prince Albert, 24
October 1853, Add. MSS. 43049,
enclosing a copy of Russell to
Clarendon of 4 October, of which
the original is in Clar. MSS. Dep.
C3.

3 Palmerston to Aberdeen, 2 October
1853 and Aberdeen to Palmerston,
5 October, Add. MSS. 43049.

4 Morley, *Gladstone* I, pp. 481–2; S.
Herbert to Clarendon, 6 October
1853, Clar. MSS. Dep. C3.

5 Aberdeen to Graham (at
Balmoral), 8 October 1853,
submitted to Queen Victoria, and
printed as a footnote in QVL, II, p.
454.

6 Graham to Aberdeen, 9 October
1853, Add. MSS. 43191.

7 C. Alison to Lady Stratford, 25
November 1853, S. Lane-Poole, *Life
of Stratford Canning*, II, pp. 316–17.

8 Nesselrode to Meyendorff, 17
October 1853, quoted from the
Vienna archives by J. Curtiss,

Russia's Crimean War, p. 197.

9 A. J. P. Taylor, *The Struggle for Mastery in Europe*, p. 58. The Foreign Secretary reported that when Sir John Burgoyne arrived in Paris in January 1854 he was surprised to find so little enthusiasm for war with Russia; Clarendon to Graham, 30 January 1854, Gr. Pap.

10 Curtiss, op. cit. pp. 186–8.

11 For the life and career of Prince Paskevich see the biography by A. P. Scherbatov, of which all except the last of the eight volumes were published in a French translation.

12 Albert Seaton, *The Crimean War*, pp. 29–33.

13 Paskevich Memorandum of September 1853, Zai., III, pp. 102–4.

14 Adolphus Slade, *Turkey and the Crimean War*, pp. 148–55: E. V. Bogdanovich, *Sinop, 18 Noiabria 1853 Goda*.

15 *The Times*, 13 December 1853: *Morning Chronicle*, 20 December 1853.

16 Palmerston to Clarendon, 13 December 1853, Clar. MSS. Dep. C3.

17 Rothschild incident, Graham to Clarendon, 22 November 1853, Clar. MSS. Dep. C4; *Aurora* and Russian spies, Graham to Clarendon, 30 November 1853, Clar. MSS. Dep. C4; *The Times*, 6, 7 December 1853; Brunnow to Aberdeen, 7 December 1853, Add. MSS. 43144; Graham to Queen Victoria and Graham to Clarendon, 8 December 1853, Gr. Pap.

18 Aberdeen to Graham, 10 December 1853. Gr. Pap.

19 'Let him go', Queen Victoria to Aberdeen, 7 December 1853, Add. MSS. 43048; *The Times* 15, 16 December; *Morning Post* 15, 16, 17 December 1853.

20 Lord Derby, House of Lords, 31 January 1854, Hansard, Vol. 130,

p. 102; A. Palmer, *Crowned Cousins*, pp. 116–17; J. Ridley, *Lord Palmerston*, pp. 422–4.

21 Stratford to Clarendon, 18 December 1853, FO 78/941, no. 393.

22 J. B. Conacher, *The Aberdeen Coalition*, pp. 240–2; Morley, op. cit., I, pp. 490–1; Aberdeen to Graham, 19 December 1853, Gr. Pap.; Aberdeen to Queen Victoria, 20 December 1853, Add. MSS. 43048; Russell to Clarendon, 18 December 1853, Clar. MSS. Dep. C3; Temp., pp. 375–8.

Chapter Four

1 Aberdeen to Clarendon, 27 September 1853, Clar. MSS. Dep. C4.

2 Graham to Clarendon, 15 January 1854, Gr. Pap.

3 G. P. Evelyn, *A Diary of the Crimea*, pp. 31–2; J. B. Conacher, *The Aberdeen Coalition*, p. 246.

4 C. S. Parker, *Life . . . Graham*, II, p. 226.

5 Granville to Clarendon, 25 December 1853, Clar. MSS. Dep. C4.

6 Queen Victoria to Aberdeen, 24 February 1854, QVL, III, p. 12; Aberdeen to Queen Victoria, 24 February 1854, Add. MSS. 43048.

7 Conacher, op. cit., p. 251.

8 Graham to Newcastle, 11 January 1854, Gr. Pap.

9 G. Wrottesley, *The Military Opinions of General Sir John Fox Burgoyne*, pp. 165–80; F. A. Wellesley, *The Paris Embassy*, pp. 40–1; B. D. Gooch, *The New Bonapartist Generals*, pp. 67–8.

10 J. Ridley, *Napoleon III and Eugénie*, pp. 363–4.

11 Nicholas I to Napoleon III, 8 February 1854, Zai., II, pp. 189–91. The Tsar's reply was printed in *The Times* on 6 March 1854.

12 Graham circulated Burgoyne's first memorandum, together with an assessment by a colonel of the

Royal Artillery, to his principal
cabinet colleagues, 19 January
1854, Gr. Pap. The second
memorandum is preserved in the
Graham Papers in the form of a
letter to Graham from Burgoyne,
20 January 1854. These documents
have been summarized by
Conacher, op. cit., pp. 252 and 254.
See also Hew Strachan, 'Soldiers,
Strategy and Sebastopol', HJ, 21,
pp. 311–12.

13 Palmerston to Graham, 19 January
1854, Gr. Pap.
14 Russell to Graham, 19 January,
and Newcastle to Graham, 20
January, 1854, Gr. Pap.
15 Graham Memorandum, 22 January
1854, Gr. Pap.
16 Graham to Clarendon, 28 February
1854, Gr. Pap.
17 Aberdeen to Queen Victoria, 8
February 1854, Add. MSS. 43048;
Aberdeen to Brunnow, 2 February
1854, Add. MSS. 43144; F. F.
Martens *Recueil des traités*, XII, pp.
338–41.
18 G. Dodd, *Pictorial History of the
Russian War*, p. 76.
19 ILN, 11 February 1854, p. 118. For
a historical assessment of the ILN
at this time, see the excellent study
by Mathew Paul Lalumia, *Realism
and Politics in Victorian Art of the
Crimean War*, especially p. 65.
Lalumia prints (p. 42) a longer
extract from the editorial of 11
February, but incorrectly dates it
as 1855.
20 Conacher, op. cit., pp. 294–311; J
Prest, *Lord John Russell*, pp. 364–5.
21 *The Times*, 15 February 1854.
22 *The Times*, 17 February 1854.
23 Dodd, op. cit., p. 79; N. Bentley
(ed.), *Russell's Despatches from the
Crimea*, p. 24.
24 Griselda Fox Mason, *Sleigh Ride to
Russia* pp. 3–15. This book, written
by a kinswoman of all three of the
Quakers who went to St
Petersburg, includes more family
letters than earlier works on the

Mission; but see also Richenda C.
Scott's *Quakers in Russia*.
25 Henry Pease to Edward Pease Jnr.
11 February 1854, Fox Mason, op.
cit., p. 79.
26 Ibid, pp. 81–90.
27 *The Times*, 23 February, 28
February and 19 March 1854.
28 Clarendon to Nesselrode, 27
February 1854, Zai., II, pp. 221–2.
29 Conacher, op. cit., pp. 249–50; P.
Schroeder, *Austria, Great Britain and
the Crimean War*, pp. 130–42.
30 Queen Victoria to King Leopold,
28 February 1854, QVL, III, p. 14.
31 Queen's comment on 13 February,
E. Longford, *Victoria RI*, p. 301.
32 The famous last stanzas of *Maud*
were apparently written earlier
than the main body of the poem,
traditionally 'when the cannon was
heard, booming from the
battleships in the Solent before the
Crimean War'. Presumably this
was the royal salute fired on 11
March 1854. For Tennyson and the
Crimean War see the biography by
Sir Charles Tennyson, pp. 280–8.
33 K. Robbins, *John Bright*, p. 103; J.
A. Froude, *Carlyle in London*, II, p.
151.

Chapter Five

1 J. S. Curtiss, *Russia's Crimean War*,
p. 254.
2 Clarendon, H. of Lords, 31 March
1854, Hansard, 132, pp. 142–50; A.
Palmer, *The Chancelleries of Europe*,
p. 104.
3 Schroeder, *Austria . . . Crimean War*,
pp. 160–85.
4 Palmerston to Aberdeen and
Aberdeen to Palmerston, 10
January 1853, Add. MSS. 43049.
5 Wellesley, *The Paris Embassy*, p. 43.
6 B. Gooch, *The New Bonapartist
Generals*, pp. 20–6 and 42–4.
7 M. Quatrelles l'Epine, *Le Maréchal
de Saint-Arnaud*, II, pp. 297–9.
8 S-A (23 April 1845) p. 418.
9 Evelyn, *Diary of the Crimea*, p. 61.
10 S-A (2 May 1845), p. 418.

11 N. Bentley (ed.), *Russell's Despatches from the Crimea*, p. 28.
12 *The Times*, 4 and 8 May 1854; Dodd, *Pictorial History of the Russian War*, p. 86.
13 Evelyn, op. cit, p. 51.
14 Dodd, op. cit, pp. 91–2.
15 Curtiss, op. cit., pp. 245–6.
16 Anon., 'Voina Rossii s Turtsiei', RS, XVI, no. 9, p. 89; Zai., II, pp. 402–3.
17 Cal. Lett. I, p. 35; S-A (30 May 1854), p. 427.
18 Ibid.
19 Alex. Gordon to Aberdeen, 10 and 30 May 1854, Add. MSS. 43225.
20 C. Hibbert, *The Destruction of Lord Raglan*, pp. 45–7.
21 *The Times*, 28 April 1854; Dodd, op. cit., pp. 95–6; Rose Journal (earliest entry), 14 June 1854, Add. MSS. 28509; Bosquet, *Lettres . . . à sa Mère*, IV, pp. 162–73.
22 M. I. Bogdanovich, *Vostochnaia Voina*, II, 90–2; Zai., II, pp. 413–14.
23 Curtiss, op. cit., pp. 264–5; Zai. II, 409–12.
24 L. Tolstoy to T. A. Yergolskaya, 5 July 1854 (in French), V. Cherthoff (ed.), *Tolstoy, Polnoe sobranie sochineniy*, LIX, pp. 269–73; English version in R. F. Christian, *Tolstoy's Letters*, I, pp. 39–42.
25 Tarlé, II, pp. 10–11; Curtiss, op. cit., pp. 264–5.
26 Ibid; Bruce Lincoln, *Nicholas I*, p. 348.
27 Cardigan's Mansion House speech, 6 February 1855, from Dodd, op. cit., p. 97; cf. a slightly different version in D. Thomas, *Charge! Hurrah! Hurrah!*, p. 193; F. Duberly to S. Marx, Add. MSS. 47218A; Duberly, *Journal*, pp. 34 and 39; A. Mitchell, *Recollections*, p. 24.
28 Dundas to Admiralty, 29 June, 1854, Bonner-Smith and Dewar, *Russian War, 1854*, p. 280.
29 S-A (28 June 1854), pp. 441–4.
30 *The Times*, 15 June 1854; J. N. Conacher, *The Aberdeen Coalition*, pp. 452–3; Kinglake, *The Invasion of the Crimea*, II, pp. 248–50.

31 Graham to Clarendon, 1 March 1854, Gr. Pap. See Huw Strachan, 'Soldiers, Strategy and Sebastopol', HJ, Vol. 21, pp. 312–15.
32 Erickson, *Graham*, p. 339, citing Admiralty Papers
33 S. Eardley-Wilmot, *Life of . . . Lyons*, pp. 144–8 and 160.
34 C. S. Parker, *Graham*, II, pp. 243–4; Graham to Clarendon, 6 April 1854, Clar. MSS. Dep. C.14; Graham to Lyons, 8 May and 13 June 1854, Gr. Pap.
35 Gladstone Memorandum, 22 June 1854, Add. MSS. 44744; Aberdeen Memorandum, late June, Add. MSS. 43253.
36 E. Longford, *Wellington, The Years of the Sword*, p. 109 (quoting despatch of 11 May 1809).
37 Kinglake, op. cit., II, p. 271.
38 S-A (letters of 13 July 1854, pp. 446–9).
39 Rose's Journal, 16 and 18 July 1854, Add. MSS. 42837.
40 S-A (19 July 1854), p. 450.
41 J. Martineau, *Life . . . Newcastle*, pp. 149–50.

Chapter Six

1 'Nelson touch', Graham to Clarendon, 6 October 1853, Clar. MSS. Dep. C.14; ILN, 8 October 1853, Vol. XXIII, no. 652, p. 333.
2 W. Napier (ed.), *The Navy, its Past and Present Strength*, p. 73, quoted *Dictionary of National Biography* entry on Sir C. Napier.
3 Graham to Clarendon, 8 December 1853, Clar. MSS. Dep. C14.
4 Graham to Queen Victoria, 9 February 1854, Gr. Pap., printed in part QVL, III, pp. 9–10.
5 Graham to Napier, 6 March 1854, Add. MSS. 40024.
6 ILN, 4 March 1854, Vol. XXIV, no. 672, p. 207.
7 *The Times*, 8 March 1854; Fitzstephen French, H. of Commons, 13 March 1854, Hansard, 131, pp. 674–5; J. Ridley, *Palmerston*, p. 426.

8 Ibid, p. 427; G. M. Trevelyan, *John Bright*, pp. 223–4; C. S. Dessain, *Life and Letters . . . Newman*, XVI, p. 82.

9 Extract from *Chambers Journal* of 15 April 1854, printed in K. Chesney, *Crimean War Reader*, pp. 32–7.

10 Paget's Journal, Bonner-Smith and Dewar, *Russian War, 1854*, p. 5.

11 Memorandum by Sir Byam Martin, 5 March 1854, Add. MSS. 41370.

12 Graham to Clarendon, 31 March and 3 April 1854, Clar. MSS. Dep. C14.

13 Russell to Clarendon, 16 April, and Palmerston to Clarendon 27 April 1854, Clar. MSS. Dep. C15.

14 Aberdeen to Clarendon, 16 August 1854, Clar. MSS. Dep. C14.

15 Admiralty to Napier, 5 June 1854, Bonner-Smith and Dewar, op. cit., p. 59; Erickson, *Graham*, pp. 347–8; Tsarevich Alexander to Queen Anna Pavlovna, 11 May 1854, Jackman, *Romanov Relations*, p. 344; A. F. Tiutcheva, *Vospominaniia . . .* I, p. 135.

16 Graham to Clarendon, 30 April 1854, Clar. MSS. Dep. C14.

17 Napier to Admiralty, 30 May 1854, Bonner-Smith and Dewar, p. 59.

18 G. F. Mason, *Sleigh Ride to Russia*, p. 93; Graham, H. of Commons, 29 June 1854, Hansard, 134, pp. 913–21.

19 O. Anderson, *A Liberal State at War*, p. 180; K. Robbins, *John Bright*, p. 103. For the closest examination of Bright's wartime speeches, see A. J. P. Taylor, 'John Bright and the Crimean War', *Bull. of J. Rylands Lib.*, Vol. 36, no. 2, pp. 502–22.

20 *The Times*, 27 April 1854; Tsarevich Alexander to Queen Anna Pavlovna, 15 February 1854, Jackman, op. cit., p. 341.

21 *Punch*, 24 June 1854; J. Conacher, *Aberdeen Coalition*, pp. 404–11.

22 Napier to Admiralty, 20 June 1854, Bonner-Smith and Dewar, op. cit., p. 80; Napier to Graham, same

date, ibid, pp. 7–9.

23 Tsarevich Alexander to Queen Anna Pavlovna, 14 July 1854, Jackman, op. cit., p. 345; Bonner-Smith and Dewar, op. cit., pp. 80–7.

24 Admiralty to Napier, 11 July 1854, ibid, pp. 87–8.

25 The Dundonald project fills more than 60 folio sheets in the Martin Papers at the British Library, Add. MSS. 41370. The basic outline by Lord Dundonald was dated 22 July 1854.

26 M. Faraday to Sir Byam Martin, 7 August 1854, Add. MSS. 41370. For the later history of the Dundonald project, see Pan. Pap., I, pp. 308 and 340.

27 For the Bomarsund landings compare the documents in Bonner-Smith and Dewar, op. cit., pp. 90–103 with Napier's version in Butler Earp, *Baltic Campaign*, pp. 362–80.

28 ILN, 26 August 1854, Vol. XXV, No. 699, p. 173; *The Times*, 4 September 1854.

29 Admiralty to Napier, 4 and 9 September 1854, Bonner-Smith and Dewar, op. cit., pp. 114–15 and 118–19; Aberdeen to Graham, September 1854, Gr. Pap.

30 Napier to Admiralty, 18 September 1854, Bonner-Smith and Dewar, op. cit., pp. 121–3; Erickson, op. cit., pp. 349–50.

31 ILN, 16 September 1854, Vol. XXV, no. 702, p. 247 and 21 October 1854, no. 708, p. 387.

32 Palmerston to Clarendon, 10 August 1854, Clar. MSS. Dep. C15; M. Chamberlain, *Aberdeen*, pp. 505–6.

33 Dodd, op. cit., pp. 188–94. See also the interesting article by Edmond de Hailly, 'Une campagne dans l'Océan Pacifique. L'éxpedition de Petropavlovsk', *Revue des deux Mondes* (1857), XVI, pp. 687–709.

34 A. J. P. Taylor, *The Struggle for Mastery in Europe*, p. 65; Schroeder, *Austria, Great Britain and the Crimean*

War, pp. 190–8.
35 Ibid, p. 200; Zai., II, p. 368; Curtiss, *Russia's Crimean War*, pp. 289–90.
36 Palmerston to Clarendon ('marshes of Wallachia'), 10 August 1854, Clar. MSS. Dep. C15; Russell to Clarendon, 5 and 11 September 1854, Clar. MSS. Dep. C15.
37 Palmerston to Clarendon, 5 September 1854, Clar. MSS. Dep. C15.

Chapter Seven

1 Clarendon to Russell, 22 and 29 August 1854, PRO 30/22/11/D; Palmerston to Clarendon, 25 August 1854, Clar. MSS. Dep. C15; Newcastle to Clarendon, 30 August 1854, Clar. MSS. Dep. C15.
2 C. G. Bapst, *Le Maréchal Canrobert*, II, pp. 148–52; S-A (29 July 1854), pp. 451–2; Cal. Lett., I, p. 99.
3 S-A, pp. 448–56, is a succession of letters from 19 July to 9 August from which the incidence of disease may be traced; B. D. Gooch, *The New Bonapartist Generals*, pp. 101–3.
4 Alexander Gordon to Aberdeen, 10 August 1854, Add. MSS. 43225.
5 *The Times*, 18 and 23 August 1854.
6 F. Duberly, *Journal*, pp. 54–62; C. Hibbert, *Destruction . . . Raglan*, pp. 53–5; D. Thomas, *Charge! Hurrah! Hurrah!*, p. 201; F. Robinson, *Diary*, pp. 128–32.
7 Cal. Lett, I, p. 106; Bentley, *Russell's Despatches*, p. 55.
8 Ibid, p. 54; G. Paget, *Letters and Journal*, p. 8; S-A (11 August 1854), pp. 459–61.
9 *The Times*, 28 August 1854; *History of The Times*, II, p. 174.
10 Proclamation, Dodd, *Pictorial Hist.*, pp. 105–6; S-A (2 and 5 September 1854), pp. 474–8.
11 Undated letters from F. Duberly to S. Marx: 'wonderful rides', early August; 'passion of tears', first week September; Add. MSS.

47218A. For additional background material, see E. Tisdall, *Mrs Duberly's Campaigns*, pp. 58–62.
12 TG, p. 55; Dodd, op. cit., p. 106.
13 Krylov, 'Kniaz A.S. Menshikov', RS, VII (1873), p. 853; Seaton, *Crimean War*, p. 55.
14 Alex. Gordon to Aberdeen, 4 September 1854, Add. MSS. 43225.
15 Rose to Clarendon, 25 August 1854, Add. MSS. 42802; Lyons to Graham, 13 September 1854, Eardley-Wilmot, *Lyons*, pp. 203–5; Bazancourt, *L'Expédition de Crimée*, III, p. 162; Hew Strachan, 'Soldiers, Strategy and Sebastopol', HJ, 25, pp. 320–3.
16 Rose's Journal, 10 September 1854, Add. MSS. 42837; Raglan to Stratford, 12 September 1854, FO 352/38/5; Cal. Lett., I, p. 131; Lyons to Dundas, 11 September 1854, Bonner-Smith and Dewar, *Russian War 1854*, pp. 307–8.
17 S-A (16 September 1854) p. 487; Gooch, op. cit., p. 117; Bapst, op. cit., II, pp. 235–6.
18 Seaton, *Crimean War*, pp. 57–8, using contemporary Russian sources.
19 Ibid.
20 A. Mitchell, *Recollections*, pp. 40–1.
21 S-A (18 September 1854), p. 492; Cal. Lett., I, pp. 140–1; landing reports from Dundas, Bonner-Smith and Dewar, op. cit., pp. 309–10.
22 Thomas, op. cit., p. 206; Airlie, p. 67.
23 Ibid, pp. 68–9; Hibbert, op. cit., pp. 70–1; Paget, op.cit., p. 16.

Chapter Eight

1 A. Seaton, *The Crimean War*, pp. 104–8.
2 Ibid, p. 55; Schilder, 'Priezd E.I. Totlebena . . .', RS, XVIII (1877), pp. 508–9.
3 N. I. Schilder, *Graf . . . Totleben*, I, pp. 43–4.
4 S-A (11 September 1854), pp. 481–2; Seaton, op. cit., p. 60.

5 Ibid, 73–4.
6 C. Woodham-Smith, *The Reason Why*, pp. 182–4; Thomas, *Charge! Hurrah! Hurrah!*, p. 209.
7 Cal., Lett., I, p. 151; Seaton, op. cit., p. 75.
8 Hodasevich, *Voice . . . Sebastopol*, p. 35.
9 Cal. Lett., I, p. 156; Bapst, *Maréchal Canrobert*, II, p. 242–3.
10 Cal. Lett., I, pp. 159–60.
11 Tyrell, *Hist . . . War with Russia*, II, p. 227; Seaton, op. cit., p. 101.
12 Ibid, p. 95, quoting from Kornilov's diary.
13 Kinglake (an eye-witness), *Invasion of Crimea*, III, pp. 82–3; Cal. Lett., I, pp. 169–70.
14 Russian officer, cited by Seaton, op. cit., p. 83; Lysons, *Crimean War from First to Last*, p. 97; letter from Major J. Adye, 22 September 1854, JSAHR, 17 (1938), p. 224.
15 Paget, *Light Cavalry*, p. 26; F. Robinson, *Diary*, pp. 154–9. For the fullest modern accounts of the battle by British military historians see the works by A. J. Barker, P. Gibbs and W. Baring Pemberton listed in the bibliography. Although Quatrelles l'Epine's biography of Saint-Arnaud is nearly sixty years old, it contains a judicious assessment of the Alma, II, pp. 416–25.
16 ILN, 11 November 1854, Vol. XXV, no. 711, p. 481. For Bosquet's own version of events, see his *Lettres . . . à sa Mère*, IV, pp. 189–90.
17 Seaton, op. cit., p. 78.
18 *The Times*, October 1854.
19 Cal. Lett., I, pp. 171–3.
20 Seaton, op. cit., pp. 90–4, a critical assessment of Kvetsinsky's account.
21 Cal. Lett., I, p. 192.
22 Hodasevich, op. cit., p. 86.
23 S-A (21 September 1854), p. 493.
24 Russell, *The Great War*, p. 116. For a modern assessment of Nolan as a military theorist see Hew Strachan, *From Waterloo to Balaclava*, pp. 63–7.

25 Bentley, *Russell's Despatches*, p. 89.
26 All casualty figures are questionable and those for the Alma especially so, because of difficulty in separating those killed in action from those dying from disease. See Dodd, op. cit., p. 218; Barker, pp. 113–14; Pemberton, p. 65; Seaton, op. cit., pp. 101–2. For Russian misery on battlefield, see J. Keep, *Soldiers of the Tsar*, p. 340. For Calthorpe comments, Cal. Lett., I, pp. 189–203. Absence of ambulances, Woodham-Smith, *Nightingale*, p. 96.
27 C. Hibbert, *Destruction . . . Raglan*, p. 119; S-A (21 September), p. 494; and later letters while awaiting resumption of the march, pp. 496–505; Gooch, *New Bonapartist Generals*, p. 128.
28 Cal. Lett., I, p. 200.
29 Ibid, pp. 202-12; Gooch, op. cit., pp. 129–30; Hibbert, op. cit., pp.124-6.
30 Duberly, *Journal*, pp. 84–5.
31 Seaton, op. cit., p. 102.
32 Ibid, pp. 102–3.
33 Graham to Aberdeen, 30 September 1854, Add. MSS. 43191.
34 *The Times*, 3 October, 1854; Ridley, *Napoleon III*, p. 371.
35 *The Times*, 2 and 3 October 1854; *History of The Times*, II, p. 175.
36 Graham to Clarendon, 17 and 29 September, 1 October 1854, Clar. MSS. Dep. C14; Palmerston to Clarendon, 1 October 1854, Clar. MSS. Dep. C15.
37 Aberdeen to Clarendon, 1 and 3 October 1854, Clar. MSS. Dep. C14.
38 ILN, 7 October 1854,. Vol. XXV, no. 706, p. 334; *The Times*, 6 and 7 October 1854.
39 Seaton, op. cit., pp. 110–14; Hodasevich, op. cit., pp. 89–91.

Chapter Nine

1 Cal. Lett., I, pp. 204–7.
2 H. to C. Clifford, 28 September 1854, Cliff. Lett., pp. 51–2; Bentley,

Russell's Despatches, p. 101.

3   A. C. Macintosh Memorandum, 5
November 1853, FO 352/38/5. For
Burgoyne and Macintosh's book,
see Strachan, 'Soldiers, Strategy
and Sebastopol', HJ, 21, pp. 319–
20. See also Gooch, *New Bonapartist
Generals*, p. 135, and Bapst,
Canrobert, II, pp. 358–60.

4   Memorandum by Raglan, 26
September 1854, Add. MSS. 42805.

5   S-A, pp. 502–5; Quatrelles l'Epine,
Le Maréchal de St Arnaud, II, pp.
437–44; ILN, 28 October 1854,
Vol. XXV, no. 709, pp. 423–4.

6   Cal. Lett., I, pp. 207–8.

7   Bapst, op. cit., II, pp. 339–40;
Bazancourt, op. cit., III, pp. 299–
300; Wrottesley, *Burgoyne*, p. 241.

8   Seaton, *Crimean War*, pp. 111–22;
Schilder, *Graf Totleben*, I, pp. 313–
16.

9   Dubrovin, *Vostochnaia Voina*, pp.
191–3; Seaton, op. cit., pp. 123–4.

10 Cal. Lett., I, p. 267.

11 The fullest naval account may be
gathered from Dundas's letter to
the Admiralty of 18 October 1854,
printed (with six enclosures) in
Bonner-Smith and Dewar, *Russian
War, 1854*, pp. 339–45.

12 Ibid, pp. 225 and 342; Duberly,
Journal, p. 106.

13 Rose's Journal, 17 October 1854,
Add. MSS. 42837; Cal. Lett., I, p.
275; Alexander Gordon to
Aberdeen, 18 October 1854, Add.
MSS. 43225.

14 Cal. Lett., I, pp. 275–6; Rose to
Raglan, 17 October 1854, Add.
MSS. 42805.

15 Godman to his sister, 17 October
1854, TG, pp. 66–8.

16 Cal. Lett. I, p. 289.

17 Rose's Journal 17 and 18 October
1854, Add. MSS. 42837; Alexander
Gordon to Aberdeen, 18 October,
Add. MSS. 43225.

18 Dundas to Admiralty, 18 and 23
October 1854, Bonner-Smith and
Dewar, op. cit., pp. 339–47.

19 Seaton, op. cit., p. 127, using
Russian contemporary accounts;
Curtiss, *Russia's Crimean War*, pp.
319–20.

20 Alexander Gordon to Aberdeen, 18
October, Add. MSS. 43225.

21 Cal. Lett., I, p. 295; TG, pp. 69–70.

22 Seaton, op. cit., p. 139.

23 Dubrovin, op. cit., pp. 252–62;
Tarlé, II, pp. 73–4.

24 Hibbert, *Destruction . . . Raglan*, pp.
172–3.

25 C. Woodham-Smith, *The Reason
Why*, pp. 207–13.

26 Paget, *Light Cavalry Brigade*, p. 163.

Chapter Ten

1   F. Duberly to S. Marx, 27 October
1854, Add. MSS. 47218A. Duberly,
Journal, p. 116; Cal. Lett., I, p. 300;
Rose Journal, 25 October 1854,
Add. MSS. 42837.

2   Ibid; Cal. Lett., I, p. 302.

3   A. Mitchell, *Recollections*, p. 80; F.
Duberly letter to S. Marx, cited
above; Bentley, *Russell's Despatches*,
p. 121.

4   Kinglake, *Invasion . . . Crimea*, V, p.
81; *The Times*, 15 November 1854.

5   Seaton, *The Crimean War*, p. 145,
quoting Liprandi's report.

6   I. I. Ryzhov, 'O Sprazhenie pri
Balaklavoi', *Russkii Vestnik*, Vol. 86
(1870), p. 467.

7   Mitchell, op. cit., p. 82; Hibbert,
Destruction . . . Raglan, p. 173.

8   Seaton, op. cit., p. 149.

9   Rose's Journal, 25 October 1854,
Add. MSS. 42837.

10 Photograph pencilled order,
Woodham-Smith, *The Reason Why*,
p. 235.

11 *The Times*, 14 November 1854; Cal.
Lett., I, pp. 312–13; Kinglake, op.
cit., V, pp. 211–16; Rose's Journal
cited above.

12 A. Mitchell, *Recollections*, p. 83.

13 *The Times*, 14 November 1854; F.
Duberly to S. Marx, 27 October
1854, Add. MSS. 47218A.

14 Woodham-Smith, op. cit., pp.
246–7; Cliff. Lett., p. 73. There is a
fine narrative account of the

Charge in Pemberton, *Battles of the Crimean War*, pp. 96–106.

15 Seaton, op. cit., pp. 148–54, based on little-known Russian sources; Ryzhov article, loc. cit., p. 468.
16 Duberly letter cited above.
17 Cal. Lett., I, pp. 319–20; Pemberton, op. cit., p. 108.
18 *The Times*, 14 November 1854; Mitchell, *Recollections*, p. 89; Woodham-Smith, op. cit., p. 264.
19 Mitchell, op. cit., pp. 89–90; Thomas, *Charge! Hurrah! Hurrah!*, pp. 316 and 326.
20 Gooch, *New Bonapartist Generals*, p. 142.
21 Burgoyne to Raglan, 31 October 1854, Add. MSS. 42805.

Chapter Eleven

1 R. G. Richardson, *Nurse Sarah Anne*, pp. 65–8 and 80.
2 E. Cook, *Short Life . . . Nightingale*, pp. 68–85; *The Examiner*, 28 October 1854.
3 C. Woodham-Smith, *Nightingale*, p. 98.
4 *The Times*, 12 October 1854; *History of The Times*, II, pp. 176–7.
5 Cook, op. cit, pp. 69–75; Woodham-Smith, op. cit., pp. 99–107.
6 'Receipts for Miss Nightingale', 21 October 1854, Add. MSS. 43401.
7 Clarendon to Stratford de Redcliffe, 19 October 1854, FO 352/40; *History of The Times*, II, pp. 177–8.
8 Graham to Dundas, 25 October 1854, Bonner-Smith and Dewar, *Russian War, 1854*, pp. 417–18.
9 Woodham-Smith, op. cit., p. 169; J. D. Conacher, *The Aberdeen Coalition*, pp. 480–1.
10 T. W. Reid, *Life . . . Monckton Milnes*, I, p. 500.
11 *Daily News*, 16 January 1855; *Morning Post*, 12 March 1856; *History of The Times*, II, pp. 185–215; M. P. Lalumia, *Realism and Politics*, pp. 48–56.

12 ILN, 18 November 1854, Vol. XXV, no. 713, pp. 502 and 518–19.
13 ILN, 21 October 1854, Vol. XXV, no. 708, pp. 381–2.
14 ILN, 4 November 1854, Vol. XXV, no. 710, pp. 447–8.
15 Richardson, op. cit., p. 82.
16 Nightingale to Dr Brown, 14 November 1854, Cook, *Short Life*, p. 89.
17 Ibid, p. 96.
18 Letters to Florence Nightingale from Lady Stratford (3 November) and Lord Stratford de Redcliffe (9 November 1854), Add. MSS. 43401; Woodham-Smith, op. cit., pp. 136, 138, 146.
19 Richardson, op. cit., pp. 81 and 83.
20 Woodham-Smith, op. cit., pp. 129–46.
21 *The Times*, 4 November 1854; Cantlie, *Hist . . . Army Med. Dept.*, I, pp. 158–60.
22 Cook, *Short Life*, p. 96.
23 Richardson, op. cit., pp. 48–9.
24 For the most detailed study in English see J. S. Curtiss, 'Russian Sisters of Mercy in the Crimea', *Slavic Review*, no. 25 (1966), pp. 84–100.
25 Krupskaya, *Vospominaniia*, pp. 8–13.
26 Pirogov, *Sevastopolskie Pisma*, pp. 5, 17–18, 31.
27 Letters from Pirogov of 16, 17 and 19 November 1854, ibid, pp. 106–7.
28 *The Times*, 14 November 1854; cf. Bentley, *Russell's Despatches*, pp. 114 and 123.
29 Cook, *Short Life*, p. 140.
30 F. Nightingale to S. Herbert, March 1855, Woodham-Smith, op. cit., p. 168.

Chapter Twelve

1 Cal. Lett., I, pp. 333–43.
2 Ibid, p. 342; Bapst, *Canrobert*, II, pp. 331–3.
3 Kinglake, *Invasion . . . Crimea*, VI, p. 5; Bogdanovich, *Vostochnaia Voina*, III, pp. 131–3; Pemberton, *Battles*, p. 126.

4 Dubrovin, *Vostochnaia Voina*, pp. 270–4; Seaton, *Crimean War*, pp. 161–4.
5 Ibid, pp. 165–6.
6 Bentley, *Russell's Despatches*, p. 130; Cal. Lett., I, p. 344; Rose to Clarendon, 6 November 1854, Add. MSS. 42802.
7 Cliff. Lett., p. 88. This is an extract from a very long letter from Henry Clifford to his 'dear relations and friends', dated 6 and 7 November; it describes the episode for which he was subsequently awarded the VC.
8 Pemberton, op. cit., p. 162; Vulliamy, *Crimea*, p. 171; Bosquet's letters after Inkerman make interesting reading – see his *Lettres à sa Mère*, IV, pp. 198–9, 204–5, 211–13.
9 Seaton, op. cit., pp. 170–1.
10 Hodasevich, *Voice from Within*, pp. 191–8.
11 Pemberton, op. cit. pp. 141–3.
12 Ibid, pp. 143–61; Cal. Lett., I, p. 359; Rose to Clarendon, 6 November 1854, Add. MSS. 42802.
13 Kinglake, op. cit., VI, pp. 430–5.
14 Airlie, p. 114.
15 ILN, 25 November 1854, Vol. XXV, no. 714, pp. 526–7 and 530.
16 Duberly, *Journal*, p. 128: F. Duberly to S. Marx, November 1854, Add. MSS. 47218A.
17 Seaton, op. cit., pp. 173–4.
18 Alexander III, *Souvenirs de Sébastopol*, p. 252.
19 Pirogov, *Sevastopolskie pisma*, pp. 145–8; Seaton, op. cit., pp. 180–3.
20 Tiutcheva Diary; see Lincoln, *Nicholas I*, p. 349.
21 L. Tolstoy to S. N. Tolstoy, 20 November 1854, R. F. Christian, *Tolstoy's Letters*, I, pp. 43–6.
22 TG, p. 82; for discontent, see Hibbert, op. cit., p. 236.
23 Rose's Journal, 6 and 7 November 1854, Add. MSS. 42837; Bosquet to Rose, 7 November 1854, Add. MSS. 42804; Cal. Lett., I, pp. 392–7.

24 Alexander Gordon to Aberdeen, 8 November 1854, Add. MSS. 43225.
25 Alex. Gordon to Aberdeen, 13 November 1854, Add. MSS. 43225.
26 Edward of Saxe-Weimar to Queen Victoria, 28 November 1854, QVL, III, pp. 54–6.
27 Queen Victoria to Newcastle, 20 November 1854, QVL, III, pp. 56–7.
28 For Nicklin, see H. and A. Gernsheim, *Roger Fenton*, pp. 11–12.
29 ILN, 9 December 1854, Vol. XXV, no. 717, p. 578.
30 Sterling, *Letters from the Army in the Crimea*, p. 151; TG, p. 88; Raglan to Stratford, 14 November 1854, FO 352/36/42A.
31 Airlie, p. 120; Campbell, *Letters from Camp*, pp. 23–4.
32 See the letter of L. Tolstoy, already cited, with footnote on p. 44.
33 *Punch*, Vol. XXVIII, p. 64.

Chapter Thirteen

1 ILN, 16 December 1854, Vol. XXV, no. 718, pp. 613–14.
2 Argyll (17 November) and Palmerston (22 November 1854) to Russell, PRO 30/22/11F; Conacher, *Aberdeen Coalition*, pp. 507–9.
3 Ibid, pp. 504–8; C. E. Bayley, *Mercenaries for the Crimea*, pp. 44–8.
4 Prince Albert to Aberdeen, 11 November 1854, Stanmore, *Aberdeen Corr. 1854–5*, pp. 272–4.
5 Cobden, 22 December 1854, H. of Commons, Hansard, 136, pp. 667–8.
6 Bayley, op. cit., p. 109.
7 Bright, 22 December 1854, H. of Commons, Hansard, 136, pp. 883–93.
8 The most powerful attack came from Cobden. A section of the speech is cited above. The main parts are included, as the only example of Cobden's oratory, in the anonymously edited Everyman's Library anthology, *British Orations*, pp. 258–72.

9 Disraeli, 15 December 1854, H. of Commons, Hansard, 136, pp. 197–215.
10 Layard, 15 December 1854, ibid, pp. 466–8.
11 D. Mack Smith, *Cavour*, pp. 76–8; Aberdeen to Clarendon, 29 November 1854, Stanmore, *Aberdeen Corr.* p. 254.
12 Newcastle to Clarendon, 6 November 1854, Clar. MSS. Dep. C15.
13 Palmerston to Clarendon, 22 August and 7 September 1854, Clar. MSS. Dep. C15.
14 Layard, 12 December 1854, H. of Commons, Hansard, 126, p. 160.
15 *The Times*, 12 December 1854; Thackeray to Lady Stanley, 4 December 1854, Ray, *Thackeray Letters*, Vol. II, p. 403.
16 *The Times*, 23 December 1854.
17 Dickens reference, Cliff. Lett. (16 December), p. 124. For these paragraphs see also: ibid, p. 139; TG, pp. 110–16; Tisdall, *Mrs Duberly's Campaigns*, p. 118; A. H. Taylor, 'Letters from the Crimea', JRUSI, CII (1957), p. 237.
18 Thomas, *Charge! Hurrah! Hurrah!*, p. 259 and 263–4: Hibbert, *Destruction ... Raglan*, p. 236.
19 H. Duberly to F. Marx, 12 December 1854, Add. MSS. 47218A; Airlie, p. 147–8; Alex. Gordon to Aberdeen, 7 March 1855, Add. MSS. 43225.
20 Airlie, p. 154: Alex. Gordon to Aberdeen, 11 January 1855, Add. MSS. 43225; H. Duberly to F. Marx, 17 January 1855, Add. MSS. 47218A.
21 Arthur Gordon's Journal, 7 November 1854, Add. MSS. 49269.
22 Alex. Gordon to Aberdeen, 17 November 1854, Add. MSS. 43225.
23 Same to the same, 3 and 13 December 1854 and 11 January 1855, Add. MSS. 43225.
24 Same to the same, 26 December 1854, 25 January and 2 February 1855, Add. MSS. 43225.
25 F. Duberly to S. Marx, 28 December 1854, Add. MSS. 47218A.
26 Arthur Gordon's Journal, 8 January 1855, Add. MSS. 49269
27 Privately printed version of Arthur Gordon's Journal, 22 January 1855, Appendix to Stanmore, *Aberdeen Corr.*, 1854–5, pp. 378–9. Much of it is quoted by Conacher, op. cit., pp. 531–3.
28 On Roebuck and the background to his motion, see Asa Briggs, *Victorian People*, pp. 72–5.
29 Conacher, pp. 533–47, gives a detailed report of the debate. It may now be supplemented by Gladstone's memoranda of 24, 25 and 26 January, printed in Brock and Sorensen, *W.E. Gladstone*, III, *Autobiographical Memoranda*, pp. 153–5.
30 L. Iremonger, *Lord Aberdeen*, pp. 302 and 305–6.
31 Palmerston's diary, 23 January to 6 February 1855, printed as Appendix 6 to Brock and Sorensen, op. cit., pp. 274–7; Gladstone memoranda, 31 January to 6 February 1855, ibid, pp. 156–75.
32 *United Service Gazette*, 10 February 1855; Thomas, op. cit., pp. 264–5.
33 Text of Napier's speech, Bonner-Smith and Dewar, *Russian War, 1854*, pp. 24–8. Graham's reply, February 1855, H. of Commons, Hansard, 136, pp. 1469–72.
34 Ridley, *Palmerston*, p. 441; Gladstone memoranda of 7–9 February 1855, Brock and Sorensen, op. cit., pp. 175–7.
35 Ibid, pp. 177–87; Briggs, op. cit., p. 79.
36 Palmerston to Raglan, 22 February 1855, Add. MSS. 48579; O. Anderson, *Liberal State at War*, pp. 180–1. For General Channon, see Palmerston's diary, 7 February 1855, Brock and Sorensen, op. cit., p. 277.
37 Palmerston to Sir Huw Ross, 24 and 17 April, to Panmure 5 and 8 May and to Sir Charles Fox 22 and

24 June 1855, Add. MSS. 48579.
Liddell Hart, *The Tanks*, I, p. 13.

38 F. Duberly to S. Marx, 17 February
1855, Add. MSS. 47218A; J.
Swetman, 'Military Transport in
the Crimean War', EHR, Vol. 88
(January 1973), pp 84–7.

39 Richardson, *Sister Sarah Anne*, p.
159; *Annual Register*, 1855, p. 40;
Woodham-Smith, *Nightingale*, p.
152; Cal. Lett., II, p. 95.

40 Seacole, *The Wonderful Adventures of
Mrs Seacole in many lands* (ed.
Alexander and Dewjee) p. 55.

41 Ibid, pp. 137–84.

42 Dewar, *Russian War, 1855: Black Sea*,
pp. 82–6.

43 Rose Journal, 29 January 1855,
Add. MSS. 42837; Gooch, *New
Bonapartist Generals*, p. 174.

44 Text of telegram, Cal. Lett., II, p.
139. Russell's reports of Tsar's
death, from Berlin, are in Pack 2 of
PRO 30/122/18.

45 H. to C. Clifford, 11 March 1855,
Cliff. Lett., p. 181.

46 Rose Journal, 22 March 1855, Add.
MSS. 42837.

Chapter Fourteen

1 Seaton, *Crimean War*, pp. 184–5.

2 Nicholas I to Anna Pavlovna, 12
February 1855, Jackman, *Romanov
Relations*, p. 350.

3 Bruce Lincoln, *Nicholas I*, pp. 349–
50, makes use of the earliest
Russian contemporary accounts.
These may now be supplemented
by the valuable 13,000-word
reminiscences of Countess
Solohuba in *Oxford Slavonic Papers*,
XVI (1983), pp. 164–81.

4 Mosse, *Rise and Fall of the Crimean
System*, p. 12.

5 T. Lister's Journal, 10 March 1855,
Bod. Lib., MSS. Eng. hist. d 483.
For Russell in Vienna see Packs 3
to 7 of PRO 30/122/18.
Background in Palmer, *Chancelleries
of Europe*, p. 106 and in Rich, *Why
the Crimean War?*, pp. 149–56.

6 Lister's Journal, 22 March 1855,
Bod. Lib., MSS. Eng. hist. d 483.

7 Gooch, *New Bonapartist Generals*, pp.
181–4.

8 Ibid; Ridley, *Napoleon III and
Eugénie*, pp. 374–6; Wellesley, *Paris
Embassy*, pp. 67–9.

9 Pan. Pap., I, pp. 90–1, 101, 156–7;
Queen Victoria, *Leaves from a
Journal*, pp. 23–70; Ridley, op. cit.,
pp. 376–80.

10 Gooch, op. cit., pp. 176–7.

11 Pan. Pap., I, pp. 154 and 157; Cal.
Lett., II, p. 152.

12 Simpson to Panmure, 16 April
1855, Pan. Pap., I, pp. 152–3.

13 Panmure to Raglan, 27 April 1855,
ibid, p 169.

14 Gooch, op. cit., 189–91; Rose
Journal, 23 March and 2 April
1855, Add. MSS. 42837.

15 Ibid (8 April); Cal. Lett., II, pp.
178–9.

16 Ibid, p. 187; Rose Journal, 9 April
1855, Add. MSS. 42837.

17 L. Tolstoy to T. A. Yergolskaya, 7
May 1855 (in French), V.
Cherthoff (ed.), *Polnoe sobranie
sochineniy*, LIX, pp. 312–14; English
version, Christian, *Tolstoy's Letters*,
I, p. 50.

18 Gooch, op. cit., pp. 184–6.

19 *The Times*, 3 April 1855. See also
Bonner-Smith, *Russian War 1855:
Baltic*, pp. 3–9.

20 Schroeder, *Austria, Great Britain and
the Crimean War*, p. 273.

21 Rich, op. cit, pp. 152–4.

22 Rose Journal, 26, 29 and 30 April,
1 May, Add. MSS. 42837;
Derrecagaix, *Pélissier*, pp. 346–7;
Bapst, *Canrobert*, II, pp. 438–40;
Dewar, *Russian War, 1855: Black Sea*,
pp. 145–7.

23 Raglan to Panmure, 8 May, Pan.
Pap., I, p. 189; Rose Journal, 13,
14, 16, 20 and 21 May 1855, Add.
MSS. 42837; Rose to Clarendon, 2
June 1855, Add. MSS. 42802;
Derrecagaix, op. cit, pp. 348–56;
Bapst, op. cit., II, pp. 458–67.

24 Derrecagaix, op. cit., p. 388.

25 Gernsheim, *Roger Fenton*, pp. 77–86;

Bentley, *Russell's Despatches*, pp. 195–203; Dewar, op. cit., pp. 164–86; Biddulph, 'Expedition to Kertch', JSAHR, 21 (1942), pp. 128–35.
26 Panmure to Raglan, no date (? mid-May 1855), Pan. Pap., I, p. 197.
27 A. Soyer, *Soyer's Culinary Campaign*, p. 171.
28 Lane-Poole, *Stratford Canning*, II, pp. 402–6.
29 Cook, *Short Life . . . Nightingale*, pp. 143–8 and 151–5.
30 Paget, *Light Cavalry*, p. 95; Lane-Poole, op. cit., II, pp. 404–5.
31 Soyer, op. cit., pp. 310 and 524–33.
32 TG (15 June 1855), p. 163.
33 Fenton to his wife, 29 April 1844, Gernsheim, op. cit., p. 71; H. to C. Clifford, 29–30 April, Cliff, Lett., p. 206; G. Coombs (Royal Dragoons) to his sister, 26 April 1855, Add. MSS. 45680.

Chapter Fifteen

1 Gernsheim, *Roger Fenton*, pp. 8–9.
2 F. Duberly to S. Marx, 'Friday night' (?8 June 1855), Add. MSS. 47218A (cf. the inferior edited version in Duberly, *Journal*, pp. 221–3); Cliff. Lett., p. 221.
3 Pemberton, *Battles*, p. 190.
4 Cal. Lett., II, pp. 305–7.
5 Mosse, *Rise and Fall of the Crimean System*, pp. 13–14.
6 Bonner-Smith, *Russian War, 1855: Baltic*, pp. 52–4, 78 and 155.
7 Macartney, *Habsburg Empire*, p. 483; Redlich, *Emperor Francis Joseph*, p. 259.
8 Curtiss, *Russia's Crimean War*, pp. 438–40.
9 Rose to Clarendon, 15 June 1854, Add. MSS. 42802; Cal. Lett., II, pp. 314–16.
10 Gernsheim, op. cit., p. 101.
11 Lushington to Admiral Lyons, 10 June 1855, Dewar, *Russian War, 1855: Black Sea*, p. 202.
12 Ibid, pp. 199–200; Pan. Pap., I, pp. 258–9.

13 Derrecagaix, *Pélissier*, pp. 430–48; Hibbert, *Destruction . . . Raglan*, pp. 330–2.
14 Biddulph, 'Assault on the Redan', JSAHR, 21 (1942), pp. 128–5; Cliff. Lett., pp. 222–6; Cal. Lett., II, pp. 326–41; Rose Journal, 18 June 1855, Add. MSS. 42838, TG, pp. 164–5.
15 Raglan to Panmure, 19 June 1855, Pan. Pap., I, pp. 244–6; Rose to Clarendon, 23 June 1855, Add. MSS. 42802; Rose Journal, 20 and 25 June 1855, Add. MSS. 42838.
16 Gooch, *New Bonapartist Generals*, p. 223.
17 Palmerston to Panmure, 21 June 1855, Pan. Pap., I, p. 247.
18 Kinglake, *Invasion . . . Crimea*, XI, p. 266.
19 Simpson to Panmure, 30 June 1855, Pan. Pap., I, pp. 256–8.
20 Ibid, pp. 304–6.
21 Alexander III, *Souvenirs*, pp. 263 and 273–5; Seaton, *Crimean War*, pp. 191–3.
22 L. to S. Tolstoy, 20 November 1854, Christian, *Tolstoy Letters*, I, p. 45.
23 Tarlé, II, pp. 401 and 429; Schilder, *Graf Totleben*, I, pp. 445–9; Seaton, op. cit., p. 198.
24 Gooch, op. cit., p. 241; Pan. Pap., I, p. 350.
25 Barker, *Vainglorious War*, pp. 310–12; Tarlé, II, pp. 430–8; Seaton, op. cit., pp. 201–8. See also Biddulph's contemporary account, JSAHR, 1 (1939), pp. 133–4.
26 Krupskaya, *Vospominaniia*, pp. 32–4.
27 Mosse, op. cit., p. 14.
28 Astley, *Fifty Years of My Life*, I, pp. 268–9.
29 Tarlé II, pp. 401 and 429; Schilder, op. cit., I, pp. 439–41.
30 Palmerston to Panmure, 7 August 1855, Pan. Pap., I, pp. 340–2.
31 Queen Victoria, *Leaves from a Journal*, p. 96.
32 Bonner-Smith, op. cit., pp. 184–97.
33 Guedalla, *The Two Marshals*, p. 72.
34 Gooch, op. cit., p. 245.
35 Rose Journal 5 September 1855, Add. MSS. 42838.

36 Lyons to Admiralty, 10 September 1855, Dewar, op. cit., pp. 291–2.
37 Rose to Clarendon, 9 September 1855, Add. MSS. 42803 (a long report of the battle); Rose Journal, 8 September 1855, Add. MSS. 42838; Biddulph, 'The Fall of Sebastopol', JSAHR (1940), pp. 197–9.
38 Ranken, Six Months at Sebastopol, pp. 49–50.
39 Cliff. Lett. (9 September 1855), pp. 255–61.
40 Seaton, op. cit., p. 217.
41 Curtiss, op. cit., p. 458, quoting Major R. Delafield.
42 Lyons to Wood, telegram, 9 September, and Lyons to Admiralty, 10 September 1855, Dewar, op. cit., pp. 290–1.
43 Queen Victoria to King Leopold I, 11 September 1855, QVL, III, p. 142.
44 F. Duberly to S. Marx, a long and undated letter (?10 September 1855), Add. MSS. 47218B.
45 Seacole, The Wonderful Adventures of Mrs Seacole in many lands (ed. Alexander and Dewjee) p. 210.
46 Duberly, Journal, pp. 281–93.

Chapter Sixteen

1 L.M. Case, French Opinion on War and Diplomacy (especially pp. 38-43).
2 D. Mack Smith, Cavour, pp. 84–5; E. di Nolfo, Europa e Italia, pp. 110–11.
3 Gooch, New Bonapartist Generals, pp. 232–5
4 C. Tennyson, Tennyson, pp. 284–9.
5 Briggs, Victorian People, p. 98; Ray, Thackeray: The Age of Wisdom, pp. 250–3; O. Anderson, 'Janus Face . . .', Victorian Studies (1965), VIII, pp. 231–42; Anderson, Liberal State at War,, pp. 104–8, 114–15, 120–2.
6 O. Anderson, 'Cabinet Government and the Crimean War', EHR LXXIX, (1964) pp. 548–51.

7 Palmerston to Archbishop Sumner, 16 September 1855, Add. MSS. 48579.
8 Panmure to Simpson, 17 September 1855, Pan. Pap., I, pp. 389–90.
9 See correspondence, ibid, I, pp. 406–18.
10 Simpson to Panmure, 10 November 1855, Pan. Pap., I, p. 482.
11 Gooch, op. cit., p. 253, based on Derrecagaix's biography of Martimprey.
12 Guedalla, The Two Marshals, p. 73; Dewar, Russian War, 1855: Black Sea, pp. 346–59.
13 On the French and Odessa, see ibid, no. 210, p. 354.
14 Mosse, Rise and Fall of Crimean System, pp. 15–16.
15 Codrington to Panmure, 13 November 1855, Pan. Pap., I, pp. 486–7.
16 See the extract from a despatch of Karnicki, the Austrian chargé d'affaires, printed in Mosse, op. cit., p. 15.
17 Karnicki to Buol, 22 September 1855, ibid, p. 16.
18 On Nesselrode in Napoleonic Wars see Palmer, Alexander I, pp. 190, 198, 207, 219–20. For Lieven in Crimean War, see Baumgart, Peace of Paris, p. 59.
19 Ibid, pp. 60–5.
20 Curtiss, Russia's Crimean War, p. 482.
21 For Muraviev and Kars, see Barker, op. cit., pp. 274–9.
22 Mosse, op. cit., p. 22.
23 Queen Victoria, Leaves from a Journal, p. 82.
24 Palmerston Memorandum, 26 September 1855, Add. MSS. 48579; see also Mosse, op. cit., p. 1.
25 Curtiss, op. cit., pp. 478–80 uses Swedish sources.
26 The Times, 8 December 1855; Bapst, Canrobert, III, 52–3.
27 Mosse, op. cit., p.21.
28 Schroeder, Austria, Great Britain, pp. 321–36.
29 Alexander II to M. Gorchakov, 23 December 1855, Tatischev,

Aleksandr II, p. 179.

30 Panmure to Codrington, 3 December 1855, Pan. Pap., II, p. 10.

31 Ibid, II, p. 17; Rose Journal, 11 December 1855, Add. MSS. 42838.

32 Codrington to Panmure, 8 December 1855 and 29 January 1856, Pan. Pap., II, pp. 13 and 82.

33 F. Duberly to S. Marx, November, 1855, Add. MSS. 47218B; *The Times*, 31 December 1855.

34 For the Council, see: Mosse, op. cit. pp. 24–5; Tatischev, op. cit., pp. 181–4; Curtiss, op. cit., pp. 495–6.

35 Mosse, op. cit., p. 26.

36 Napoleon III to Queen Victoria, 14 January 1856, QVL, III, pp. 162–3.

37 On the council of war: Pan. Pap., II, pp. 20, 22, 42, 44, 47, 53, 58, 60, 65, 67, 70, 73, 78–9, 93; Cambridge to Queen Victoria, 20 January 1856, QVL, III, p. 167; Bapst, op. cit., III, pp. 78–9.

38 Queen Victoria to Clarendon, 28 January 1856, QVL, III, p. 168.

39 Curtiss, op. cit., pp. 499–500; Mosse, op. cit., pp. 27–30; Tatischev, op. cit., pp. 186–7.

40 *History of The Times*, II, p. 191.

41 Panmure to Codrington, 28 January and 8 February 1856, Pan. Pap., II, pp. 81 and 99.

42 Rich, *Why the Crimean War?*, pp. 180–1.

43 Cal. Lett., II, pp. 434–5.

44 Bentley, *Russell's Despatches*, pp. 275–6.

Chapter Seventeen

1 Baumgart, *Peace of Paris*, pp. 134–7.

2 Queen Victoria to Clarendon, 7 February 1856, QVL, III, p. 170; TG, p.158.

3 Persigny to Walewski, 12 February 1856, Di Nolfo, *Europa e Italia*, p. 482; Palmerston to Clarendon, I, February 1856, Clar. MSS. Dep. C49.

4 Lady Clarendon to Lady T. Lewis,

18 February 1856, Bod. Lib. MSS. Eng. hist. C 1034.

5 Palmerston to Clarendon, 26 September 1855, Add. MSS. 48579, and 25 February 1856, Add. MSS. 48580.

6 Nesselrode to Orlov, 11 February 1856, Bessmernaja, 'K Istorii Pariskogo Mira 1856g', KA, 75 (1936), p. 16.

7 Clarendon to Stratford de Redcliffe, 25 April 1856, Lane-Poole, *Stratford Canning*, II, p. 436.

8 Same to the same, 22 March 1856, ibid, p. 435; Rich, *Why the Crimean War?* pp. 172 and 186.

9 Palmerston to Clarendon, 28 February 1856, Add. MSS. 48580; Clarendon to Palmerston, 29 February 1856, Maxwell, *Clarendon*, II, p. 116.

10 Orlov to Nesselrode, 2 March 1856, Bessmernaja article already cited, KA, 75, pp. 27–30.

11 Baumgart, op. cit., pp. 113–16.

12 Ibid, p. 130.

13 M. S. Anderson, *The Eastern Question*, pp. 156–7.

14 Baumgart, op. cit., p. 140; Palmerston to Clarendon, 7 March 1856, Add. MSS. 48580.

15 Palmerston to Clarendon, 25 and 27 February and 7, 8, 9 and 11 March 1856, Add. MSS. 48580.

16 Clarendon to Palmerston, 8 April 1856, Di Nolfo, *Europa e Italia*, p. 508; Mack Smith, *Cavour*, pp. 88–92.

17 Codrington to Panmure, 5 April 1856, Pan. Pap., II, p. 191; Rose Journal, 2 and 5 April 1856, Add. MSS. 42838.

18 Codrington to Panmure, 15 April 1856, Pan. Pap., II, p. 92; Cliff. Lett., pp. 277–82.

19 Dodd, *Pictorial Hist.*, p. 510.

20 Palmerston to Clarendon, 30 March 1856, Clar. MSS. Dep. C49.

21 Codrington to Panmure, 1 April 1856, Pan. Pap., II, p. 178.

22 Palmerston to Panmure, 30 March 1856, ibid, p. 172.

272

23 Correspondence, Ibid, pp. 226, 234, 269.
24 Panmure, H. of Lords, 8 May 1856, Hansard, 142, p. 187.
25 De la Gorce, *Histoire . . . Second Empire*, I, pp. 413–14 and 472.
26 Curtiss, *Russia's Crimean War*, p. 471.
27 Mosse, *The Rise and Fall of the Crimean System*, pp. 2–5.
28 F. Duberly to S. Marx, 12 May 1856, Add. MSS. 47218B; Tisdall, *Mrs Duberly's Campaigns*, pp. 164–8.
29 *The Times*, 26, 27 and 29 June 1857; correspondence, Pan. Pap., II, pp. 37, 46, 50, 66, 81, 217, 274–5, 354, 390–1; Thomas, *Charge! Hurrah! Hurrah!*, p. 283.
30 See the incidents mentioned above pp. 72 (Lucas) and 153 (Clifford).

Chapter Eighteen

1 Queen Victoria to King Leopold, 6 May 1856, QVL, III, pp. 189–90.
2 Lister Journal, 8 and 14 August 1856, Bod. Lib. MSS. Eng. hist. d 483.
3 For much of this paragraph see Mosse, *Rise and Fall of Crimean System*, especially pp. 33 and 105–26.

4 A. Buchanan to Lord Granville, 16 November 1870, FO 65/805/466.
5 H. Rumbold to Lord Granville; 19 March 1871, FO 65/820/28; Mosse, op. cit., pp. 160–82.
6 Sumner, *Russia and the Balkans*, p. 238; Palmer, *Chancelleries of Europe*, pp. 153–8.
7 See Wolseley, Lord, *A Soldier's Life*, Vol. 1, which includes interesting first impressions and an account of the struggles for the Redan.
8 Richardson, *Nurse Sarah Anne*, pp. 165–9.
9 Seacole, *The Wonderful Adventures of Mrs Seacole in many lands* (ed. Alexander and Dewjee), pp. 31–40.
10 Tisdall, *Mrs Duberly's Campaigns*, pp. 171–215.
11 R. E. B. Crompton, *Reminiscences*, pp. 11–12.
12 TG, p. 11; J. Colledge *Ships of the Royal Navy*, I, p. 267.
13 Moran, *Winston Churchill: The Struggle for Survival*, p. 234.
14 Young, *Victorian England, Portrait of an Age*, p. 80; Guedalla, *The Two Marshals*, p. 67.
15 These points are developed in more detail in Palmer, op. cit., pp. 111–42. See also Morley, *Life of Gladstone*, I, pp. 550–1.

SELECT BIBLIOGRAPHY

Manuscript Sources

Aberdeen Papers (including Alexander Gordon and Arthur Gordon letters and journals), British Library.
Clarendon Papers, Bodleian Library, Oxford.
Coombs Letters (Trooper G. Coombs; Add. MSS. 45680), British Library.
Duberly Letters (Captain Henry and Mrs Frances Duberly), British Library.
Foreign Office Papers, Public Record Office.
Gladstone Papers, British Library.
Graham Papers, Microfilm deposited in Bodleian Library, Oxford.
Lister Papers, Bodleian Library, Oxford.
Martin (Sir Henry Byam Martin) Papers, British Library.
Napier Papers, British Library.
Nightingale Letters (Add. MSS. 43401), British Library.
Palmerston Letterbooks, British Library.
Russell Papers, Public Record Office; and Russell Correspondence (Add. MSS. 38080), British Library.
Seymour Papers (Journals of Sir Hamilton Seymour), British Library.
Stanmore Papers, British Library.
Strathnairn Papers (Letters and Journals of Sir Hugh Rose), British Library.

Privately Printed

Mitchell, A., *Recollections of One of the Light Brigade*, printed at Canterbury in 1885, copies in Bodleian and British Libraries.
Stanmore, *Aberdeen Correspondence*, British Library.

Contemporary Newspapers, Official Publications and Periodicals

Daily News
Gentleman's Magazine
The Illustrated London News
Morning Chronicle
Morning Post
Punch
Select Committee on the Army before Sebastopol ('Roebuck Committee'), Three Reports (L. 1855)
The Times

274

Published Books

(L. indicates published London. For other abbreviations, see p. 255)

Anon, *Authentic Life of Louis Kossuth* (L., 1851).
   Louis Kossuth, His Speeches in England (L., 1851).
   History of The Times, Vol. 2 (L., 1939).
Airlie, Mabell, Countess of, *With the Guards We Shall Go* (letters of Strange Jocelyn) (L., 1933).
Alexander III, *Souvenirs de Sébastopol* (Paris, 1894).
Anderson, M. S., *The Eastern Question* (L., 1966)
Anderson, Olive, *A Liberal State at War* (L., 1968).
Argyll, G. D. C., Duke of, *Autobiography and Memoirs*, Vol. 1 (L., 1906).
Astley, Sir John D., *Fifty Years of My Life*, Vol. 1 (L., 1894).
Bapst, C. G., *Le Maréchal Canrobert*, six vols (Paris, 1898–1912).
Barker, A. J., *The Vainglorious War* (L., 1970).
Baumgart, W., *The Peace of Paris, 1856* (Santa Barbara and Oxford, 1981).
Bayley, C. C., *Mercenaries for the Crimea* (Montreal, 1977).
Bazancourt, C. L. de, *L'Expédition de Crimée jusqu'à la Prise de Sébastopol*, two vols. (Paris, 1856).
Benson, A. C. and Esher, Viscount (eds), *Letters of Queen Victoria*, first series, three vols (L., 1907).
Bentley, N. (ed.), *Russell's Despatches from the Crimea* (L., 1966).
Blake, R., *Disraeli* (L., 1966).
Bogdanovich, E.V., *Sinop, 18 Noiabria 1853 Goda* (St Petersburg, 1868).
Bogdanovich, M. I., *Vostochnaia voina 1853–1854 gg.*, four vols in two (St Petersburg, 1876).
Bonner-Smith, D., *Russian War, 1855: Baltic* (L. 1944).
Bonner-Smith, D., and Dewar, A. C. (eds), *Russian War 1854* (L., 1943).
Bosquet, P. F. J., *Lettres du Maréchal Bosquet à sa Mère*, IV (Pau, 1879).
   Lettres du Maréchal Bosquet (Paris, 1894).
Briggs, Asa, *Victorian People* (L., 1954; Chicago, 1955).
Brock, J., and Sorensen, M., *Prime Ministers' Papers Series; W. E. Gladstone, III: Autobiographical Memoranda* (L., 1978).
Calthorpe, S. J. G., *Letters from Headquarters* (L., 1856).
Campbell, Colin, *Letters from camp to his relatives during the siege of Sebastopol* (L. 1894).
Cantlie, C., *History of the Army Medical Department*, Vol. 1 (Edinburgh, 1975)
Case, L. M., *French Opinion on War and Diplomacy during the Second Empire* (Philadelphia, 1954).
Chamberlain, M. E., *Lord Aberdeen* (L. and New York, 1983).
Cherthoff, V. (ed.), *Tolstoy, Polnoe sobranie sochineniy*, Vol. LIX (Moscow, 1938).
Chesney, K., *Crimean War Reader* (L., 1960).
Christian, R. F., *Tolstoy's Letters*, Vol. 1 (L., 1978).
Clifford, H., *Henry Clifford v.c.; his letters and sketches from the Crimea* (ed. C. Fitzherbert) (L., 1956)
Colledge, J. J., *Ships of the Royal Navy*, Vol. 1 (Newton Abbot, 1969).
Compton, P., *Colonel's Lady and Camp-Follower* (L., 1970).
Conacher, J. B., *The Aberdeen Coalition, 1852–1855* (L., 1968).
Cook, E., *Short Life of Florence Nightingale* (ed. R. Nash) (L., 1925).
Cowley, *see* Wellesley.
Crompton, R. E., *Reminiscences* (L., 1924).
Curtiss, J. S., *The Russian Army under Nicholas I* (Durham, NC, 1965).
   Russia's Crimean War (Durham, NC, 1979).

275

Derrecagaix, V. B., *Le Maréchal Pélissier* (Paris, 1911).
Dessain, C. S., *Life and Letters of Cardinal John Henry Newman*, Vol. XI (L., 1965).
Dewar, A. C., *Russian War, 1855: Black Sea* (L., 1945).
Di Nolfo, Ennio, *Europa e Italia nel 1855–1856* (Rome, 1967).
Dodd, C., *Pictorial History of the Russian War 1854–1856* (L., 1856).
Douglas, G., and Ramsay, G. D. (eds), *The Panmure Papers* (L., 1928).
Duberly, Mrs Henry, *Journal Kept during the Russian War* (L., 1855).
Dubrovin, N. F., *Vostochnaia Voina 1853–1856 godov* (St Petersburg, 1878).
Eardley-Wilmot, S., *Life of Vice-Admiral Edmund, Lord Lyons* (L., 1898).
Earp, G. Butler, *The History of the Baltic Campaign of 1854* (L., 1857).
Erickson, A. B., *The Public Career of Sir James Graham* (Oxford, 1952).
Ernst II, Duke of Saxe-Coburg-Gothà, *Memoirs* (L., 1888).
Evelyn, George P., *Diary of the Crimea* (ed. C. Falls) (L., 1954).
Froude, J. A., *Carlyle in London*, Vol. II (L., 1884).
Gernsheim, H. and A., *Roger Fenton, Photographer of the Crimean War* (L., 1954).
Gibbs, P. B., *The Battle of the Alma* (L., 1963).
Gleason J. H., *The Genesis of Russophobia in Great Britain* (Cambridge, Mass., 1950).
Godman, R. Temple, *The Fields of War* (ed. P. Warner) (L., 1977).
Gooch, Brison D., *The New Bonapartist Generals in the Crimean War* (The Hague, 1959).
Gowing, T., *Voice from within the Ranks* (ed. K. Fenwick) (L., 1954).
Guedalla, P., *The Two Marshals* (L., 1943).
Hamley, E. B., *The War in the Crimea* (L., 1891).
Henderson, G. B., *Crimean War Diplomacy* (Glasgow, 1947).
Hibbert, C., *The Destruction of Lord Raglan* (L., 1961; edition cited: Penguin, 1963).
Hodasevich, R., *A Voice from within the Walls of Sebastopol* (L., 1856).
Hubner, J. A., *Neuf ans de souvenirs d' un ambassadeur d' Autriche à Paris sous le Second Empire, 1851–1859*, two vols. (Paris, 1904).
Iremonger, Lucille, *Lord Aberdeen* (L., 1978).
Jackman, S. W. (ed.), *Romanov Relations* (correspondence between Russian Court and Queen Anna Pavlovna of the Netherlands) (L., 1969).
Keep, John, *Soldiers of the Tsar* (Oxford, 1985).
Kinglake, A. W., *The Invasion of the Crimea*, nine vols (Edinburg, 1877–8).
Krupskaya, Aleksandra, *Vospominaniia Krymskoi voiny sestry krestovozdvizhenskoi obschciny* (St Petersburg, 1861).
La Gorce, P. de, *Histoire du Second Empire*, Vol. 1 (Paris, 1894).
Lalumia, M. P., *Realism and Politics in Victorian Art of the Crimean War* (Ann Arbor, Michigan, 1984).
Lane-Poole, S., *The Life of Stratford Canning*, two vols (L., 1888).
Liddell Hart, B. H., *The Tanks*, Vol. 1 (L., 1959).
Lincoln, W. Bruce, *Nicholas I* (L., 1978)
Longford, E., *Victoria RI* (L., 1964).
   Wellington, The Years of the Sword (L., 1969).
Lysons, D., *The Crimean War from First to Last: Letters* (L., 1895).
Macartney, C. A., *The Habsburg Empire, 1760–1918* (L., 1968).
Mack Smith, D., *Cavour* (L., 1985).
MacMunn, G. F., *The Crimea in Perspective* (L., 1935).
Martens, F., *Recueil des traités et conventions conclus par la Russie avec les puissances étrangères*, Vol. XII (St Petersburg, 1895).
Martin, Kingsley, *The Triumph of Lord Palmerston; A Study of Public Opinion in England before the Crimean War* (L., 1924).
Martineau, J., *Life of Henry Pelham, fifth Duke of Newcastle* (L., 1908).
Mason, Griselda Fox, *Sleigh Ride to Russia* (York, 1985).

276

Maxwell, Sir H., *Life and Letters of . . . Fourth Earl of Clarendon*, two vols (L., 1913).
Moran, Lord, *Winston Churchill: The Struggle for Survival* (L., 1966).
Morley, J., *Life of Gladstone*, Vol. 1 (L., 1903).
Mosse, W. E., *The Rise and Fall of the Crimean System, 1855–1871* (L. 1963).
Paget, G. A. F., *The Light Cavalry Brigade in the Crimea, Letters and Journals of Lord George Paget* (L., 1881).
Palmer, A., *Alexander I* (L., 1974).
    The Chancelleries of Europe (L., 1983).
    Crowned Cousins, The Anglo-German Royal Connection (L., 1985).
Parker, C S., *Life and Letters of Sir James Graham* (L., 1907).
Pemberton, W. Baring, *Battles of the Crimean War* (L., 1962).
Pirogov, N. I., *Sevastopolskie pisma i vospominaniia* (Moscow, 1950).
Prest, John, *Lord John Russell* (L., 1972).
Quatrelles l'Epine, Maurice, *Le Maréchal de Saint Arnaud 1798–1854, d'après sa correspondance et des documents inédits*, two vols (Paris, 1928–9.
Ranken, G., *Six Months at Sebastopol* (L., 1857).
Ray, Gordon, *Letters and Private Papers of W. M. Thackeray*, Vol. II (L., 1946).
Ray, Gordon, *Thackeray: The Age of Wisdom* (L., 1958).
Redlich, J., *Emperor Francis Joseph* (L., 1929).
Reid, T. Wemyss, *Life, Letters and Friendships of Richard Monckton Milnes*, Vol. 1 (L., 1920).
Rich, N., *Why the Crimean War? A Cautionary Tale* (Hanover. NH, 1985).
Richardson, R. G., *Nurse Sarah Anne* (edited edition of Sarah Anne Terrot's diary) (L., 1977).
Ridley, J., *Lord Palmerston* (L., 1970).
    Napoleon III and Eugénie (L., 1979).
Robbins, K., *John Bright* (L., 1979).
Robinson, F., *Diary of the Crimean War* (L., 1856).
Russell, W. H., *The Great War with Russia* (L., 1895).
Saint-Arnaud, L., *Lettres du Maréchal Saint-Arnaud*, II (Paris, 1858).
Schiemann, T., *Geschichte Russlands unter Kaiser Nikolaus I*, four vols (Berlin, 1904–19).
Schilder, N. K., *Graf Eduard Ivanovich Totleben*, two vols (St Petersburg, 1885–6).
Schroeder, P. W., *Austria, Great Britain and the Crimean War* (Ithaca, NY, 1972).
Scott, Richenda C., *Quakers in Russia* (L., 1964).
Seacole, Mary (eds. Z. Alexander and A. Dewjee), *The Wonderful Adventures of Mrs Seacole in many lands* (Bristol, 1984).
Seaton, Albert, *The Crimean War, A Russian Chronicle* (L., 1977).
Shcherbatov, A. P., *General-feldmarsal Kniaz Paskevich* (French edition, St Petersburg, 1904).
Slade, Adolphus, *Turkey and the Crimean War* (L., 1858).
Soyer, A., *Soyer's Culinary Campaign* (L., 1956).
Sterling, A., *The Highland Brigade in the Crimea* (L., 1895).
Sterling, A., *Letters from the Army in the Crimea* (L., 1857).
Stockmar, E. von, *Memoirs of Baron Stockmar* Vol. II (L., 1882).
Strachan, Hew, *From Waterloo to Balaclava* (L., 1985).
Sumner, B. H., *Russia and the Balkans, 1870–1880* (Oxford, 1937).
Tarle, E. V., *Krimskaya Voina*, two vols (Moscow, 1943).
Tatischev, S. S.: *Imperator Aleksandr II*, two vols (St Petersburg, 1903).
Taylor, A. J. P., *The Struggle for Mastery in Europe* (L., 1954).
    The Troublemakers (L., 1957).
Temperley, H. W. V., *Britain and the Near East, The Crimea* (L., 1936).
Tennyson, Sir Charles, *Tennyson* (L., 1949).

Thomas, Donald, *Charge! Hurrah! Hurrah! A Life of Cardigan of Balaclava* (L., 1974).
Tisdall, E. E. P., *Mrs Duberly's Campaigns* (L., 1963).
Tiutcheva, A. F., *Pri dvore dvukh imperatorov: Vospominaniia, Dnevnik*, I (Moscow, 1928).
Trevelyan, G. M., *Life of John Bright* (L., 1913).
Tyrell, H., *History of the War with Russia*, three vols (L., 1855–8).
Victoria, Queen, *Leaves from a Journal, 1855* (L., 1961).
Vulliamy, C. E., *Crimea* (L., 1939).
Wellesley, F. A., *The Paris Embassy during the Second Empire* (L., 1928).
Windham, C. A., *The Crimean Diary and Letters of Lieutenant-General Sir Charles Windham* (ed. H. W. Pearse) (L., 1897).
Wolseley, Lord, *A Soldier's Life*, I (L., 1903).
Wood, H. Evelyn, *The Crimea in 1854 and 1894* (L., 1895).
Woodham-Smith, C., *Florence Nightingale* (rev. edn, L., 1952).
  The Reason Why (L., 1953).
  Queen Victoria, Life and Times, 1819–1861 (L., 1972).
Wrottesley, G. (ed.), *Military Opinions of General Sir John Fox Burgoyne* (L., 1859).
Young, G. M., *Victorian England; Portrait of an Age* (Oxford, 1936).
Zaionchkovskii, A. A., *Vostochnaia voina v sviazi s sovremennoi i politicheskoi obstanovki* (St Petersburg, 1908–13).

Articles Cited in Text from Periodicals

Adye, John M., 'The Battle of the Alma, a contemporary account', ed. W. Y. Baldry, JSAHR; 17 (1938), pp. 223–6.
Anderson, Olive, 'Cabinet Government and the Crimean War', EHR, LXXXIX (July 1964), pp. 548–81.
  'The Janus Face of mid-nineteenth century English radicalism: The Administrative Reform Association of 1855', *Victorian Studies*, VIII (1965), pp. 231–42.
Bessmertnaja, M. J. 'Istorii: K Parizskogo mira 1856 g', KA, 75 (Moscow, 1936), pp. 10–61.
Biddulph, Robert, 'The Battle of the Chernaya'; 'The Fall of Sebastopol'; 'The Assault on the Redan'; 'The Expedition to Kertch'; all ed. H. Biddulph, JSAHR, 18 (1939), pp. 133–4; 19 (1940), pp. 197–9; 21 (1942), pp. 52–4 and 128–35.
Bolsover, G. H., 'Nicholas I and the Partition of Turkey', SEER, XXVII (1948–9), pp. 115–45.
Curtiss, J. S., 'Russian Sisters of Mercy in the Crimea, 1854–1855', *Slavic Review* (Columbus, Ohio, 1966), pp. 84–100.
Hailly, E. de, 'Une campagne dans l'Océan Pacifique. L'expédition de Petropavlovsk', *Révue des Deux Mondes* (2e Série), XVI (Paris, 1858), pp. 687–709.
Hall, John, 'The diaries of John Hall' (ed. R. E. Barnsley), JSAHR, 41 (1963), pp. 3–18.
Herkless, J. L., 'Stratford, the Cabinet and the Crimean War', HJ, XVIII, 3 (1975), pp. 497–523.
Jarnac, Comte de, 'Lord Aberdeen, Souvenirs et Papiers Diplomatiques', *Révue des Deux Mondes* (2e Série), XXIV (Paris, 1861), pp. 429–71.
Ryzhov, I. I., 'O Sprazhenie pri Balaklavoi', *Russkii Vestnik*, Vol. 86 (Moscow, 1870), pp. 465–9.

278

Schilder, N. K., 'Priezd E. I. Totlebena v Sebastopol avguste 1854 g', RS, XVIII (St Petersburg, 1877), pp. 508–9.
Solohuba, Countess, 'Death of Nicholas I', Oxford Slavonic Papers, XVI (1983), pp. 164–81.
Strachan, Hew, 'Soldiers, Strategy and Sebastopol', HJ, 21 (1978), pp. 303–25.
Sweetman, John, 'Military Transport in the Crimean War', EHR, Vol. 88 (1973), pp. 81–91.
Tatischev, S. S., 'Imperator Nikolai I v Londone v 1844 godu', Ist Vk., XXIII (St Petersburg, 1886), no. 2, pp. 343–59 and no. 3, pp. 602–21.
Taylor, A. H., 'Letters home from the Crimea', JRUSI, Vol. 102 (1957), pp. 79–85, 232–8, 399–405, 564–70.
Taylor, A. J. P., 'John Bright and the Crimean War', Bulletin of the John Rylands Library, Vol. 36, no. 2 (Manchester, March 1854), pp. 501–22.

Index

282

Daily News: 140, 174
D'Allonville, General, French officer: at Balaclava 132
Dannenberg, General, Russian officer: Menshikov's deputy at Inkerman 151–2, 154–5, 157
Danube: 3; Russo-Turkish war on 24; Russians retreat from 59; Austria controls 78; and Russia 231; Paris Congress and 238
Danubian Principalities: 15; Russia occupies 9, (1853) 21; Austro-Prussian interest in 49–50, 59; Russia leaves 60; Austria occupies 78; Russia and 231; Paris Congress and 237, 238–9, 241
Dardanelles, 4, 39; British and French ships at 9, 12, 23, 52–3; Paris Congress and 239; London Convention and 249
Delafield, Major, American officer: at Sebastopol 218
Delane, John, *Times* editor: in Turkey 84, 96; and army medical services 136, 139
Delane's Fund, for casualties: 136–7, 140–1, 142, 144
Denmark: 228
Derby, Lord, British statesman: 12, 33, 178
Deschenes, Admiral: French commander in Baltic, 72, 75
Devna: British camp at 59, 82
Dickens, Charles: *Hard Times*, 172
Disraeli, Benjamin, British MP: 10, 20–21; attacks government 169, 180
Dnieper estuary: allied raid on 225
Dobrudja: French in 80–81
Don Pacifico crisis: 9–10
Drouyn de Lhuys, Edouard: French Foreign Minister 187; and Vienna Conference 192–3; resigns 193
Drummond, Captain, British naval officer: and Sebastopol 37, 61
Duberly, Fanny: at Varna 60; and Cardigan, 82–3, 85; in Crimea 85, 117, 172; at Balaclava 125, 130, 131–2; and Inkerman 160; and peace rumours 176; and Mamelon assault 199–200; and fall of Sebastopol 219; leaves Crimea 230; publishes journal, snubbed by Queen 245–6; in India 251
Duberly, Henry, British captain, husband of above: at Balaclava 124, 131; and Raglan's staff 173–4; and fall of Sebastopol 219; leaves Crimea 230; after war 251
Dundas, James, British Admiral: commander in Mediterranean 18, 20; in Black Sea 36–7; and French 51; and Crimea invasion 61, 63–4, 88; and Sebastopol bombardment 117, 119; leaves Crimea 188
Dundas, Richard, British Admiral:

commander in Baltic 192, 214, 228–9; and War Council 232
Dundonald, Lord, British Admiral: 67; career 73; poison gas plan 73–4, 214

Eastern Question: 3–4, 13
Egypt: 3, 5, 15
Electric telegraph: 48; links Crimea to rest of Europe 189; Napoleon III instructs generals by 193–4, 195, 224; intelligence report by 209–10; reports peace 234
Elena Pavlovna, Grand Duchess: and Seymour conversations 13–14; and nursing order 145–6; and Menshikov 161
England, Sir Richard, British General: at Inkerman 155
Erzerum: Russian assault on 202, 222
Estcourt, General, British officer: 207
Esterhazy, Count, Austrian ambassador in St Petersburg: and peace terms 229, 230
Eugénie, Empress; 39, 108; visits Britain 187
Eupatoria: allies at 88–9, 91, 116; gale off 164; Russians attack 182, 184
Eupatoria Road: 93–4, 105
Evans, Sir George de Lacy, British general: 150; and Sebastopol 162, 175; goes home 172
Evelyn, George, British militia colonel: 53

Farady, Professor Michael: 74
Fenton, Roger, war photographer: 195–6, 197; at final assault on Sebastopol 199–200, 203
Filder, James, British Commissary-General: 53, 56
Finland: Gulf of, 29, 37, 70, 72, proposed campaign in 228–9, Paris Congress and 239; Sweden, Russia and 69–70, 228
Flahault, Comte de: 187
Fortescue, Sir John, British military historian: on Chernaya 210
'Four Points': basis for peace 78, 176, 185–6, 192–3; 'Fifth Point' added 231
France: in 1848 revolution 8; influences Turkey 11–12; Press in 147; tired of war, 221, 227, 230; and peace terms 229; and Paris Congress 237–8; and Russia after war 248
Francis Joseph, Habsburg Emperor: 9, 23, 49–50, Nicholas I and 59, 78; promises neutrality 78, and Poles 169, demobilizes 202, Alexander II and 233
Frederick William IV, King of Prussia, 49; warns Tsar 227–8, 232–3
French army: in 1854 38; in Turkey 52–3; compared to British 53, 85, 90, 137, 166; in Baltic expedition 72–3; cholera in 81; in Crimea invasion 85–6, 90–1; at Alma 97;